LAOIS COUNTY
LIBRARY SERVICE

www.laois.ie
library@laoiscoco.ie

CLASS NO.

641.5

Date of Return	Date of Return	Date of Return

Tearma iasachta 21 la.
Athnuaigh leabhair le
ghuthan no ar line.

Loan term 21 days.
Renew book by phone
or online.

D0272872

21st COOK

C 21st

COOK

THE BIBLE OF INGREDIENTS
TERMS, TOOLS & TECHNIQUES

Angela Nilsen and Jeni Wright

CASSELL
ILLUSTRATED

First published in Great Britain in 2006
by Cassell Illustrated
a division of Octopus Publishing Group Limited
2–4 Heron Quays, London E14 4JP

Text copyright © 2006 Angela Nilsen and
Jeni Wright
Design copyright © Cassell Illustrated
Illustrations by Matt Windsor and Abby Franklin
(pages 1–326, 395b and c, 397, 431 and 465) and
Richard Burgess (pages 327–437 with the exception
of those listed above).

The moral rights of Angela Nilsen and Jeni Wright
 to be identified as the authors of this work have been
asserted in accordance with the Copyright, Designs
and Patents act of 1988.

Managing Editor: Anna Cheifetz
Editor: Robin Douglas-Withers
Art Director: Auberon Hedgecoe
Designer: Austin Taylor

A CIP record for this book is available from the
British Library.

ISBN-13: 978-1-844033-69-0
ISBN-10: 1-84403-369-4

10 9 8 7 6 5 4 3 2 1

Printed in China

CONTENTS

HOW TO USE THIS BOOK

Have you ever wanted to know the best way to roast a chicken, how to prepare the fluffiest couscous, or which potatoes make the smoothest mash?

You'll find the answers to these questions and much more in *21st Century Cook* – the perfect guide to keep on the kitchen shelf or take with you when you go shopping.

Chapter 1 helps you to understand recipe instructions quickly and easily using an A–Z list of terms and techniques, then gives you advice on the best kitchen equipment to buy, and how to choose and use it.

The ingredients chapters tell you everything you need to know about selecting, storing, preparing and cooking all types of food – from basil, star anise, apples and squash to steak, salmon and eggs.

You'll also find basic food preparation and cooking skills, such as how to chop an onion, boil pasta and peel a prawn, the latest techniques used by chefs, and heaps of handy hints and tips.

With all this, plus some quick and easy recipe ideas, *21st Century Cook* is all you need to become a modern maestro in the kitchen.

Terms, Techniques and Kitchen Kit

TERMS AND TECHNIQUES

KEEP THIS A–Z BY YOU WHEN YOU COOK. IT GIVES DEFINITIONS OF
ALL THE MAIN COOKING TERMS AND TECHNIQUES YOU ARE LIKELY
TO COME ACROSS IN RECIPES, BOTH FOR SIMPLE AND STRAIGHT-
FORWARD EVERYDAY MEALS AND ALSO FOR MORE ELABORATE
SPECIAL-OCCASION DISHES. THE MOST FREQUENTLY USED FRENCH
TERMS ARE INCLUDED TOO, AND SOME CHEFS' TECHNIQUES THAT
YOU MAY BE LESS FAMILIAR WITH.

Acidulated

Describes a liquid to which acid
(usually lemon juice in water) has been
added, to prevent the flesh of fruits
and vegetables from discolouring.

■ To make acidulated water, fill a dish
with cold water, squeeze in the juice of
a lemon, then drop the lemon in too.

■ Apples, pears and celeriac quickly
go brown after peeling and/or cutting,
so drop them immediately into
acidulated water.

■ Cooking cauliflower in acidulated
water will help keep it white.

Aerate

A term used in cake, pastry and batter
recipes to describe the technique of
incorporating air to give a light result.
It is mostly used with flour, although
icing sugar can also be aerated.

■ The best way to aerate is by sifting.
Even if a flour is labelled 'pre-sifted', it
can become compacted in its packet, so
sift it before use in baking. Hold the
sieve high over the bowl and tap gently
so the flour cascades slowly down.

■ Flour can also be aerated in cake
and pastry recipes when the fat is
added – see Rub in (page 40).

Aged

Describes food that has been allowed
to mature under controlled conditions.

■ Meat that has been aged is darker
and more tender than younger meat –
see page 328.

■ *Aceto balsamico tradizionale di
Modena* is balsamic vinegar aged in
wooden barrels for at least 10 years.

■ Ageing affects cheeses differently –
Parmesan becomes stronger in taste,
while aged Stilton is mellow and creamy.

Al dente

Italians use this expression when testing boiled pasta to see if it is done 'to the bite'. This means it should be tender, but with a slight resistance or nuttiness when bitten into. When the drained pasta is mixed with a hot sauce, it will then cook a little more, so boiling to the *al dente* stage makes sure it won't be overcooked when served.

AERATE

Bain marie

The term *au bain marie* means to heat or cook in a pan or bowl placed over, or in, a pan of water.

■ A *bain marie* is used when slow cooking or gentle heating is required, such as when setting a custard made with eggs or melting chocolate.

■ The water in the *bain marie* may be either cold or hot at the beginning of cooking, depending on the degree of gentleness required.

BAIN MARIE

Bake

To cook in the oven. The term is used in two ways: for the cooking of bread, cakes, pastries and pies, and for cooking in an open baking dish or other ovenproof container. See also Papillote, page 34.

TERMS AND TECHNIQUES

Bake blind

To bake a pastry case partially or fully before adding the filling. Line your tin or dish with pastry, prick the bottom all over with a fork (this helps the steam escape and keeps the pastry flat), then line the pastry with a sheet of foil so that it is covered by the foil and comes about 2.5 cm (1 in) above the rim of the tin. Spread a thick, level layer of baking beans (see page 69) over the foil and then 'bake blind' according to the recipe instructions.

■ Most pastry cases are baked blind at 190°C/375°F/Gas Mark 5 (170°C/340°F in fan ovens) on a preheated baking sheet for 10–15 minutes, then the foil and beans are removed and the pastry is baked empty for another 15–20 minutes until it is crisp and golden. This will give you a fully baked pastry case, to be used when the filling needs no cooking.

■ When a recipe calls for a partially baked case, bake the pastry blind for 10–15 minutes, then remove the foil and beans. Add the filling and carry on baking until both the filling and pastry are fully cooked. Partial baking is good when you are cooking runny fillings that would make the pastry soggy if they were poured over raw pastry before cooking.

Barbecue

To cook on a barbecue of charcoal or gas-fired coals, with or without a lid. Barbecuing is a quick, dry cooking method and the heat is intense, so the food benefits from being marinated, basted and/or glazed to help make it moist and succulent.

Baste

To spoon liquid or fat over food during cooking, to make it moist and glossy and help prevent it drying out.

■ Meat and poultry are usually basted with hot fat during roasting, but if you want crisp crackling on a joint of pork, leave well alone (see page 347).

Beat

To mix or stir one or several ingredients in a bowl, using a vigorous action and a circular motion, to make smooth and/or incorporate air. It is a similar technique to whipping (see page 50) and whisking (see page 50).

■ For beating by hand, a wooden spoon or a fork is used; a quick, fast alternative is to use a hand-held or tabletop electric mixer (see page 60).

■ Eggs are often beaten by hand, especially for scrambling or omelettes.

■ Butter or margarine and sugar are usually beaten by machine to make the batter for cakes and biscuits (see Cream, page 17).

Beurre manié

This is a mixture made of softened butter and flour that is used for thickening liquids, especially soups, sauces and stews, at the end of cooking. It is also called a liaison.

■ Quantities vary, but usually consist of an equal measure of butter and flour. Work them together to a paste on a plate using a palette knife, then add to the hot liquid a little at a time and simmer until the liquid has thickened, whisking hard.

Blacken/ Blackened

A technique of pan-frying meat, chicken or fish over a very high heat so the outside is charred, or blackened.

■ Blackening produces a lot of smoke, and is more common in restaurants than at home, but you can use the Cajun technique of rubbing food with 'blackened spices', a mix of ground peppers, herbs, garlic and salt (see page 163). As the spices fry, they develop a blackened crust.

BAKE BLIND

1 *Prick the pastry all over with a fork.*

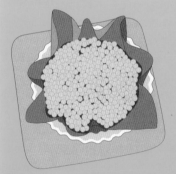

2 *Line with foil and fill with a thick, level layer of baking beans.*

Blanch

From the French word *blanchir*, meaning to whiten or purify.

■ Bacon, ham and other cured or salted meats are blanched to remove excess salt, while onions, garlic and offal are blanched to remove strong flavours and/or blood. For this type of blanching, immerse the ingredient in cold water, bring to the boil and then drain.

■ Blanching is also used to keep vegetables a bright colour, especially if they are green. Plunge the vegetables into a pan of rapidly boiling water and boil for the time stated in the recipe (rarely more than seconds or a minute or two). As soon as the time is up, drain and rinse under cold running water to stop further cooking. This is a useful technique for getting ahead, as the vegetables need only reheating or short cooking before serving. Fruits and vegetables are often blanched in this way before freezing, to help preserve their quality during storage time in the freezer.

■ To loosen tough skins from fruits and vegetables so they can be peeled easily, they are blanched by being plunged into boiling water, then into cold. This technique is often used for apricots, peaches and tomatoes.

Blood heat

This term is most often used for water and/or milk in breadmaking. The liquid should be at blood temperature, about 37°C (100°F), which means it will feel lukewarm or tepid when you dip a finger into it.

■ For quick 'blood heat', mix one-third boiling water and two-thirds cold water.

Boil

When bubbles break across the entire surface of a liquid, it is boiling. Water boils at 100°C (212°F).

■ With a rolling boil, the bubbles get larger and break at a rapid pace so they keep bubbling even when stirred.

■ When a recipe gives a boiling time, this should be calculated from the moment the water returns to the boil after the food has been added.

Braise

To cook gently in liquid for a long time in a covered saucepan or casserole dish, on the hob or in the oven.

■ The ingredients for a braise, usually meat, poultry or game with vegetables, are cut into large pieces and often browned in fat at the start of cooking, or simply braised from raw.

- The liquid in a braised dish is usually quite shallow, distinguishing it from a stew, which has more liquid.
- When joints of meat or whole birds are braised, they are called pot roasts.

Brochette

The term *en brochette* describes food that is threaded on skewers and grilled or barbecued.

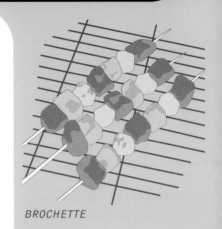

BROCHETTE

Broil

The US term for cooking under the grill. Broiler is the word for the grill itself.

Brûlée

Sugar that has been caramelized to give food a shiny glaze, in the oven or under the grill, or with a blowtorch.

- Fruits are often brûléed, so are the tops of tarts, especially *tarte au citron*.
- *Crème brûlée* is one of France's most famous desserts.

Butterfly

To cut through food partially so that it can be opened out flat with butterfly 'wings' on either side.

- The foods most commonly butterflied are lamb (see page 342), prawns (see page 429) and sardines (see page 413).

TERMS AND TECHNIQUES

■ A spatchcocked bird is sometimes described as butterflied. See Spatchcocked, page 46.

Cappuccino

see FOAM, *page 25*

Caramelize

There are several ways to caramelize:

■ Boil sugar to the caramel stage, when it becomes liquid and turns colour from golden to deep brown. Water can be added to the sugar. The degree of caramelization varies according to the heat used and the boiling time, but it shouldn't exceed 180°C (350°F) or it may burn. This kind of caramel is used in desserts like *crème caramel*, and in sauces.

■ Sprinkle sugar over food and put it under the grill, or use a blowtorch, until it is melted and golden brown.

■ To cook ingredients like onions and shallots over a high heat until they are tinged brown and sticky. Oil and butter are good cooking fats for this, and sometimes sugar is added to help the process. This technique gives intense colour and flavour, and is often used at the start of meat dishes, especially stews, braises and casseroles. See also Deglaze (page 20) and Sear (page 42).

Cartouche

A disc of greaseproof paper cut exactly to the diameter of a pan. It is used to tightly cover the surface of ingredients in the pan, to prevent evaporation.

■ A cartouche can be used on its own or with the pan lid on top, for sweating vegetables and fruits, and for long-cooking stews and casseroles.

Ceviche

A Latin American dish of raw fish marinated in citrus juice (usually lime) until the flesh turns opaque. You may also see it spelled *seviche*. See also Marinade/marinate, page 32.

Chargrill

To cook on the hob on a ridged chargrill pan (see page 54) so that lightly charred lines are imprinted on the food – the indoor equivalent of barbecuing. Also known as griddling; the pan can be called a griddle pan.

■ Chargrilling is a healthy cooking method for meat, poultry, fish and vegetables. The food sits across the ridges of the pan, above any fat.

■ To prevent sticking, the chargrill pan must be hot before the food is added.

■ Always oil the food not the pan, or the pan will smoke.

■ Allow time for the food to char underneath before moving or turning it. If you try to move it too soon, it will stick.

■ For a cross-hatch effect, give the food a quarter turn once there are lines on the underside.

Châteaubriand

A small, prime joint for roasting, enough to serve 2 people. It is cut from the centre of a fillet of beef.

Chiffonade

Thin strips or shreds of soft, leafy vegetables, herb or salad leaves. To make a *chiffonade* of herb leaves, see page 129.

Chill

When this word is used in a recipe, it means to refrigerate.

■ Recipes for cold desserts made with ingredients like cream, eggs, chocolate and gelatine often say 'chill until set'. In most cases this will take at least 4 hours. Desserts set with gelatine shouldn't be chilled for longer than 24 hours or they will begin to go rubbery.

■ Very rich pastry dough needs to be chilled before shaping, or it will be too soft and sticky to handle. If rolling out is difficult, even after chilling, simply press the pastry into the tin with your fingertips.

■ It is a good idea to chill pastry for about 30 minutes after shaping and before baking. This firms up the fat so that it doesn't melt as soon as the pastry goes in the oven, and it helps prevent the pastry shrinking.

■ Chill containers and food before putting them in the freezer. This speeds up the freezing process, helping preserve the quality of the food.

Chine

To remove the backbone (spine) from meat, most usually from a rack of lamb or rib of beef, for easy carving.

■ Unless you are proficient with a meat cleaver, chining is best left to the butcher, so check that it has been done when you buy the meat.

Chinois

A conical sieve with a very fine mesh, mostly used by chefs to purée sauces and make ultra-smooth coulis.

Clarify

This term has two meanings, depending on the food in question.

■ Using egg whites and/or egg shells to make a cloudy liquid clear, as in the making of consommé. Impurities in the stock cling to the egg, which is then removed.

■ Butter is clarified to remove the milk solids (see page 455). Older recipes may refer to this as drawn butter. Ghee is a type of clarified butter used in Indian cooking.

Cocotte

see RAMEKINS, *page 59*

Compôte

Fresh and/or dried fruits, poached with sugar, or in a sugar syrup.

■ Wine or liqueur can be used to add flavour, as well as sweet spices such as cinnamon, cloves and star anise.

■ Compôtes are cooked gently, so the fruits retain their shape.

Confit

Preserved duck or goose (see page 374).

Coulis

A sauce that has been sieved to make a smooth purée.

■ Sweet, red fruits are the most popular, but any soft fruit can be used.

■ Tomatoes can be made into a coulis.

Court bouillon

Poaching liquid for fish that is simmered for 30 minutes at the most.

■ A typical court bouillon is water
delicately flavoured with onion, celery, carrot and bouquet garni, often
with lemon juice or vinegar to keep
the fish white and firm up the flesh.

CHINOIS

Couverture

Chocolate with a high cocoa butter
content used by professional pâtissiers
for tempering (see page 48), to get a
silky finish and high gloss for hand-
made chocolates and decorations.

Cream

A term used in cake and biscuit
recipes meaning to beat fat (usually
butter or margarine) and sugar with a
wooden spoon or electric mixer so
that they form a creamy mass that is
light, fluffy and pale in colour.

■ The purpose of creaming is to incorporate air – the more you cream, the
lighter your results will be.

■ You will find creaming easier if the
fat is at room temperature to start
with, not taken straight from the fridge.

■ Creaming can take up to 5 minutes
by hand (with a few rests in between);
a machine will cut this time in half.

Crème pâtissière

Pastry cream or confectioner's custard that is made very thick with eggs and flour. Most often used as a filling for pastries, tarts and buns.

Crêpe

The French for pancake. French *crêpes* are generally thinner and lacier than British or American pancakes, and they can be sweet or savoury.

Cross-hatch

To score lines in the surface of food, in one direction then in the other, to make a diamond or square pattern.
- The rind or fat on meat and the skin on poultry (especially duck) are cross-hatched to release fat and allow heat to penetrate. Cross-hatching fish skin makes fish cook faster and stay flat.
- Mango flesh is cross-hatched so it is easy to cut into cubes (see page 227).
- To get a cross-hatch effect by char-grilling, see page 15.

Crudités

Raw vegetables cut into sticks or florets, often served for dunking in dips.

Crush

Ingredients are described as crushed when they are very finely chopped or smashed with a knife, pounded with a pestle and mortar, or whizzed in a blender or food processor.
- The term is also used to describe boiled root vegetables that are crushed with a fork or potato masher (see page 317).

Crystallize

When fruits, flowers and leaves are preserved with a sugar syrup or egg white and sugar they are described as 'crystallized'. The term also describes what can happen to sugar syrup when boiling – the sugar may become grainy and 'crystallized'. To avoid this, do as follows:
- Make sure every grain of sugar is completely dissolved over a low heat before bringing to the boil.
- Don't stir the syrup.
- Watch that crystals don't form up the side of the pan. If they do, brush them down with a pastry brush.

Curdle

When custards and sauces made with egg become too hot too fast they curdle or 'split' and look grainy or bitty.

crème–debeard

■ As a precaution against cooking over too high a heat, use a *bain marie* (see page 9).

■ Don't substitute skimmed milk or low-fat cream for whole or full-fat unless a recipe says so. They tend to curdle, especially when mixed with an acid ingredient like citrus juice or raw onions.

■ When making a custard with eggs, cheat a little by mixing 1–2 tsp corn-flour with the cold ingredients at the beginning. Cornflour is a stabilizer that helps prevent curdling. It can't be detected in the finished custard.

■ To rescue a curdled custard, see right.

Dariole

see TIMBALE, *page 49*

Darne

The French word for a cut from a whole round fish, such as salmon or tuna, recognizable by its central bone.

Debeard

To remove the beards from live mussels in their shells. The beards are the wispy, hair-like threads protruding from the shell hinges. See page 433.

CROSS-HATCH

TIPS & TRICKS: CURDLING

An effective rescue remedy for an overheated curdled mixture is to remove it immediately from the heat and cool it down quickly in an ice bath (see page 29), whisking vigorously until it becomes smooth again.

Deep-fry

To immerse food briefly in hot deep
fat until cooked crisp and golden on
the outside, moist and tender inside.
■ For safety and best results, use an
electric deep-fat fryer with an inbuilt
thermometer, and don't put the food
in the oil until the oil has reached the
required temperature.

Defrost

A term used interchangeably with
'thaw', meaning to bring frozen food
to room or refrigerator temperature
so that no ice crystals remain.
■ Meat, poultry, fish and dairy
produce should be defrosted in the
fridge, especially in warm weather
when bacteria grow rapidly. A sudden
change in temperature can also spoil
the texture of set desserts.
■ The microwave is good at rapid
defrosting. Follow the manufacturer's
instructions for best results and cook/
reheat immediately after defrosting.

Deglaze

When meat and poultry cook (especially
during roasting), juices, sediment and
fat collect underneath, often caramelizing and sticking to the pan. Deglazing
is the technique of dislodging them.

■ Remove the meat from the pan,
pour or spoon off any excess fat, then
put the pan on the hob over a high
heat and pour in a few spoonfuls of
liquid – stock, wine or water. Boil the
liquid until it has reduced and the
bottom of the pan is clean, stirring
vigorously to dislodge all the bits
stuck to the bottom. Serve poured
over the meat, or use in gravies
and sauces.

Dégorger

To remove impurities.
■ When meat, offal, poultry or fish
are soaked in cold water, sometimes
with vinegar or salt added, it is called
dégorgéing. The technique is used to
remove blood from meat and the
muddy taste from freshwater fish.
■ The same word is used to describe
sprinkling salt over vegetables such as
aubergines, courgettes and cucumber,
to draw out the juices.

Degrease

To remove fat from the surface of
liquids, especially gravies, stocks,
sauces, soups and stews.
There are four effective methods:
■ Slowly draw a metal spoon or ladle
across the surface of the liquid to
skim off the fat, tilting the pan when

you get to the edge (see illustration, right). Repeat as many times as it takes until the liquid is grease-free.

■ Blot the surface with a wad of absorbent kitchen paper. Discard and repeat until all the grease has gone.

■ Drop an ice cube into the hot liquid – the fat will cling to it – then quickly scoop it out.

■ If the recipe allows for cooling and reheating, chill the liquid until the fat rises to the surface and sets in a solid layer (this is best done overnight), then lift or scrape off.

DEGREASE

Demi-glace

A classic brown sauce, most often used as a base for other sauces. Enriched and reduced with Madeira, sherry or red wine, it has a shiny glaze and an intense flavour.

Deseed

see SEED, *page 42*

Devein

Prawns and lobsters have a black vein running the length of their backs. Although perfectly safe to eat, the vein looks unsightly and is best removed. The technique for deveining prawns is shown on page 431.

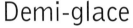

Dice

To cut food into equal-sized cubes. Dicing is a more precise technique than simple chopping.

■ The size of the cubes may or may not be given in a recipe but, as a general rule, the longer the cooking time, the larger the dice. Small dice are about 5 mm (¼ in) square, and the largest dice are 5 cm (2 in).

■ The French term *mirepoix* (see page 34) refers to a mixture of diced vegetables.

Discoloration

The process by which the flesh of certain fruits and vegetables turns brown or black on exposure to air – the technical term is oxidization.

■ Avocados and globe artichokes discolour when they are cut, and the best way to prevent this is to rub or coat the cut surfaces with lemon juice immediately after cutting.

■ Acidulated water (see page 8) can also be used when preparing fruits and vegetables that discolour.

Drain

Not to be confused with strain (see page 48). When food is drained, excess liquid or fat is poured off, usually using a sieve, strainer, colander or slotted spoon. In most cases, the drained food is used and the liquid or fat discarded.

Dredge

To coat liberally with flour or sugar.

■ Food that is to be fried is often dredged with flour, to form a protective layer around it. Use a flour sifter or a sieve to dredge straight on to the food, or spread the flour out on a flat plate and dip and turn the food in it until evenly coated on all sides (see illustration, opposite). In both cases, shake off the excess flour before cooking.

■ Icing sugar is often dredged through a sieve over cakes, pastries and biscuits before or after baking, and over desserts before serving for a pretty presentation. When it is dredged before baking, it melts and makes the topping shiny.

Dressed

A term with four culinary meanings.

■ A salad is described as dressed when it has been tossed in a dressing, often a vinaigrette.

■ Dressed poultry and game have been hung and prepared for cooking. In other words, they are oven-ready.

■ A dressed crab has had the white and

dice–dry-fry

dark meat removed from the shell, the inedible parts discarded, then the meat returned to the cleaned shell.
■ Blanched tripe (see page 360) is described as dressed.

Dropping consistency

In cake, biscuit and dessert recipes, beating a batter or creamed mixture to a 'dropping consistency' means that the mixture will drop off the spoon or whisk when you shake it.
■ A 'soft dropping consistency' has a higher ratio of liquid or eggs to dry ingredients than a dropping consistency, and is therefore slightly slacker. It will drop when you lift the mixture out of the bowl, without shaking.

DREDGE

Dry-fry/ dry-roast

To heat food without fat or liquid, on the hob or in the oven. Also called 'toasting'. Used for nuts, which are tossed in a pan until golden brown, and for spices (see page 162). Also used for cooking duck breasts, and for cooking or heating up flat breads and tortillas. For best results, use a non-stick or heavy cast-iron frying pan.

Dry marinade

see RUB, *page 40*

Duxelles

Very finely chopped mushrooms cooked with shallots and butter until quite dry. The mixture is used to flavour savoury dishes, or as a stuffing or garnish.

Egg wash

Used for glazing pastry and bread and applied with a brush, this can be a whole beaten egg or just the yolk or white, often diluted with a little milk or water. Brush on before or during baking, depending on the recipe.

■ The more concentrated the egg yolk, the darker the colour of the glaze.

■ For a high gloss finish, add the egg wash in layers during baking, as you would apply a lacquer.

Emulsify

To combine ingredients that don't usually mix well, to form an emulsion. Two of the best-known are mayonnaise (egg and oil) and hollandaise (egg, butter and lemon juice). There are three secrets to success:

■ Have all the ingredients at a similar temperature.

■ Add one ingredient to another a little at a time, allowing them to combine before adding more.

■ Beat or mix vigorously, to help disperse the ingredients so they come together readily as a smooth whole.

Entrecôte

A beef steak from between the ribs. See also page 337.

Escalope

A thinly cut slice of tender, prime-quality meat, poultry or fish without bones. Pork, veal and chicken escalopes are tenderized by pounding before being cooked (see page 369).

Flake

A term often used with fish, to describe two different techniques.

■ In fish recipes you will often see 'the fish is done when it flakes with a fork'. Tease a small section of the flesh apart – if it separates into flakes without any resistance it is done.

■ If you need small pieces of fish for a dish such as a pie, flake a whole cooked fish or a large piece of fish with a fork (see opposite), or simply press gently on the flesh with your fingers.

Flame

There are two ways of flaming food:

■ Setting light to food with alcohol, usually a spirit or liqueur, is called flaming or flambéing. The alcohol is warmed, ignited and poured over the food. As the flames burn, the alcohol burns off. Flambéing gives depth of flavour to a dish, but take care when doing it. Stand back from the pan and don't have the alcohol too hot – it will ignite when just warm.

■ When cooking on a gas hob, chefs often have the heat so fierce that flames lick up the sides of the pan. When liquid is added and the pan tilted, the fat in the pan catches light. This type of flaming intensifies flavours, and works especially well with stir-frying in a wok. It cooks the food in seconds rather than minutes, so natural colours and nutrients are retained, but it isn't a technique for the novice cook.

FLAKE

Foam

Food served topped with a 'foam' produced by frothing or syphoning was made popular by Catalan chef Ferran Adrià at his restaurant El Bulli. Some foam dishes, especially soups, are described as 'cappuccino', for obvious reasons.

TERMS AND TECHNIQUES

Fold

To combine two mixtures together, one of which is usually lighter, or less dense. A gentle action, used with mixtures where you need to retain volume and air. For technique, see page 450.

- Whipped cream and/or whisked egg whites are folded into a fruit purée or melted chocolate to make a mousse or soufflé.
- Whisked egg whites are folded into a cake batter to make it lighter.
- To make meringues, sugar is folded into whisked egg whites.

Fondant

A term with two meanings.

- A paste made from sugar syrup used by pâtissiers for decorating and filling confectionery and chocolates. Diluted, it is used to ice cakes and pastries.
- Chocolate fondant is a steamed or baked chocolate pudding with a liquid chocolate centre.

Fondue

This French word for melted is used for two dishes: the pot of melted cheese and wine served with cubes of bread for dipping and the meat version (known as *fondue bourguignonne)* in which cubes of steak are dunked into hot oil.

- The modern, healthier version of *fondue bourguignonne* uses stock instead of oil, and chicken and vegetables for dipping.
- Chocolate fondue consists of melted chocolate and cream, with fruits and cubes of cake as dippers.
- Tabletop fondue sets with skewers for spearing the food are suitable for all kinds of fondue.

Freezer burn

When food in the freezer is insufficiently wrapped and/or air isn't excluded from the packaging before freezing, it turns white and looks dry – a condition known as freezer burn. Food with freezer burn is safe to eat, but you may want to cut the burn off to make the food look more appetizing.

Fry

To cook in a frying pan in hot, shallow fat over a moderate or high heat. Also called pan-frying, and most often used for ingredients that cook quickly.

- For healthy frying, use a small amount of oil to cover the bottom of the pan. Be sure it is hot before adding food – hold your hand over to feel the heat rise. If not hot from the start, fat can seep into the food and make it greasy, and the food may stick.

Fumet

An intensely flavoured fish stock, although the term is sometimes used to describe a game stock.

Galette

A flat cake or tart made from flaky pastry, sometimes raised with yeast.

Gaufre

The French for waffle. A *gaufrette* is the fan-shaped wafer often served with ice cream.

Gigot

Gigot d'agneau is a leg of lamb, but it is often shortened to *gigot*.

Glaze

A shiny coating that covers food, to protect and moisten it, and make it look appetizing.

■ Egg wash (see page 24) is used to glaze both sweet and savoury foods.

■ Aspic and jellied stock are for glazing savoury dishes only, which can also be glazed with melted butter, oil, sauces, melted jellies or dressings.

■ Melted fruit jellies, sieved jam and chocolate are three good sweet glazes.

■ For a very smooth finish, always spoon a glaze on slowly and wait until completely set before serving. Brush strokes will show and will spoil the glossy effect.

Gluten

A mixture of proteins that gives dough its stretch and spring. When bread dough is kneaded, the gluten strengthens and becomes elastic, helping the dough rise and expand.

■ The stronger the gluten, the lighter and more spongy the texture of the bread, which is why you should use a high-gluten flour milled from hard wheat in breadmaking – described as 'strong' or 'bread' flour on the bag. Flour labelled 'very strong' is even richer in gluten – good for breads such as sourdough that need a long fermentation time.

■ Ordinary plain flour made from soft wheat is low in gluten. It is suitable for making cakes, biscuits and pastries, not bread. See also Flour (page 86) and Knead (page 30).

Gratin

Food cooked under the grill or in the oven until it has a golden crust is described as a gratin, or cooked *au gratin*. Often grated cheese or bread-crumbs are sprinkled on top before cooking. See also Tian (page 49).

Griddle

This term has evolved over the years.

■ The traditional griddle is a flat, rimless pan made of a heavy metal such as cast iron. It is used for cooking griddle scones and flat breads.

■ A modern griddle is a ridged, heavy frying pan that is either made of cast iron or is non-stick. It is sometimes called a chargrill pan. This is used to cook meat, poultry, fish and vegetables and to give charred lines on the food characteristic of barbecuing. See also Chargrill (page 14), and Chargrill pan (page 54).

■ When food on restaurant menus is described as 'griddled' or cooked 'on the griddle', this invariably means that it has been cooked on a very hot metal plate on the cooker, or on a grid or rack over charcoal as on a barbecue.

Grill
(US: broil)

To cook or brown food under the grill, which may be in the oven or on top of the stove. Little or no fat is needed and grilling times are usually short, making it a healthy cooking method.

■ Preheat the grill before the food goes under, and move the pan or tray up or down to regulate temperature rather than adjusting the heat.

■ If steaks and chops are thick, you will need to turn them at least once during grilling to help them cook evenly and look appetizing on both sides.

HULL

Grind

To cut, chop or pound food into small pieces, sometimes as fine as powder.

■ Grind meat by fine chopping with a blade, either with a very sharp knife or in a mechanical mincer or electric food processor.

■ Nuts and spices can be ground with a pestle and mortar (see page 65), or you can use a special electric grinder or the mini bowl in a food processor (see page 60).

Hull

To remove the leafy green calyx and stalk of soft fruit, especially strawberries. See illustration (right) and page 208.

Ice bath

This is a bowl of ice cubes and water. Half fill a wide bowl with ice cubes and pour in cold water until it is about three-quarters full.

■ When you need to cool a hot mixture quickly, sit it in its bowl or pan in the ice bath. This technique is invaluable for speeding up the preparation of custard, cream and gelatine-based mousses, and for rescuing a curdled custard.

■ After draining blanched, boiled or parboiled vegetables, plunge them into an ice bath to stop cooking from continuing. This is called Refreshing (see page 37).

Infuse

To soak aromatics in a warm or hot liquid to extract flavour from them. Infused liquids are usually strained of their flavourings before use.

■ To infuse milk with vanilla for a custard, split a vanilla pod lengthways in half, scrape the seeds into the pan of milk and drop in the pod halves. Scald the milk (see page 444), cover and leave to stand until cool.

■ For flavoured milk for white or bread sauce, stud a small peeled onion with cloves and place in a pan of milk with 1–2 bay leaves. Bring to the boil, cover and leave to cool.

■ To make a perfumed sugar syrup for a fruit salad, add a few pieces of pared citrus zest and a few whole spices such as star anise, cinnamon and cloves to the syrup.

Jerk

A Jamaican term meaning to rub food (especially pork and chicken) with jerk seasoning, then cook over charcoal so it forms a charred spicy crust.

■ You can buy jerk seasoning (see page 164), or make it at home. Traditional recipes usually include Jamaican allspice, hot chillies and thyme, plus bay, nutmeg, cinnamon and cloves.

Julienne

Very thin sticks of vegetables with squared-off edges, cut with precision. Carrots, celery, celeriac and peppers are often cut into *julienne*, to use in cooked dishes and salads, or to make a neat and stylish garnish.

Jus

The juices that collect in the bottom of the pan when roasting meat. If a dish is described as *au jus*, it means it is served with these juices poured over, or that the juices have been diluted and reduced with stock or wine.

Knead

There are two ways of kneading. In pastry making, it describes the way dough is gathered lightly and gently to bring it together as a smooth ball. In breadmaking, it is the working of the dough so that the gluten in the flour stretches and becomes elastic, and helps the dough rise. It also distributes the air in the dough so that it will rise evenly. Kneading bread dough can be done by hand or machine, and instructions and times vary from one recipe to another, but the basic technique is as follows:

KNEAD
On a floured surface, hold the dough in one hand and push it away from you with the heel of other hand.

■ To knead by hand, lightly flour the work surface, then hold the dough in one hand and push it away from you with the heel of the other hand (see right). Fold the dough back on itself and give it a quarter turn. Repeat for 8–10 minutes (with rests in between) until the dough is smooth and springy.

■ In an electric mixer fitted with a dough hook, kneading should take about 5 minutes to get the dough to the smooth, springy stage. Take care not to overwork the dough or it will collapse and you will have to start again with fresh ingredients.

■ To test if you have kneaded a dough enough, press a finger into it – the dough should spring back straightaway when the finger is withdrawn.

Knock back
see PUNCH DOWN, page 36

Liaison

Mixture of two ingredients, used to thicken hot liquids like soups or stews.
■ Common liaisons are *beurre manié*, (butter and flour, see page 11), egg yolks and cream (see page 467), and cornflour or arrowroot mixed to a paste with water.

Lukewarm

see BLOOD HEAT, *page 12*

Macédoine

Mixed diced fruits or vegetables used as a decoration or garnish. Fruit is often soaked in sugar syrup or liqueur; vegetables are coated with butter and herbs, sometimes cream.

Macerate

To soak food in liquid so it softens and takes on the flavour of the liquid. It often refers to fruit in alcohol, such as prunes in armagnac or peaches in brandy.

Marinade/ marinate

To marinate is to soak, or steep, food in a marinade. Recipes for marinades

vary, but are usually a blend of oil and lemon juice or wine vinegar, sometimes combined with natural yogurt, plus a mixture of herbs, spices, onion and garlic to give added flavour.
■ The purpose of marinating is to flavour, moisten and tenderize, and it is most often used before cooking by dry heat, such as grilling, barbecuing or roasting.
■ Meat, poultry and game are the most common foods to be marinated, followed by fish and vegetables.
■ Food that is marinated is usually raw, although occasionally it can be seared beforehand.
■ For a marinade to be effective at softening tough fibres in meat, an acid ingredient such as lemon juice or vinegar is essential. Natural yogurt is also used for this reason. Fresh pineapple and papaya contain enzymes that tenderize, so you may see these in marinades for tough meat (see also page 242).
■ The longer food is left in a marinade, the more successful the result will be. Overnight in the fridge is generally recommended, although some meat and game recipes may suggest up to 3–4 days. The exception to this is fish, which shouldn't be left for more than 4 hours or the acid will start to 'cook' the delicate flesh, as in Ceviche (see page 14).

Mash

To crush cooked root vegetables until they have been broken down into a lump-free 'mash'.

■ You can use a fork or a potato masher, but a ricer will produce a smoother result. See page 71 for information on these. When the mash is pushed through a sieve or a food mill, it becomes a purée (see page 36).

Médaillon

A medallion-shaped piece of meat that may be round or oval.

■ Traditionally it was cut from a fillet of beef (and also called *filet mignon* or *tournedos*), but now most prime cuts of meat and poultry are used, and you will also see *médaillons* of fish and lobster on restaurant menus.

■ To moisten the lean meat during cooking, fat is sometimes wrapped around the edges and tied with string.

Mille-feuille

Layers (French for a thousand leaves) of puff pastry traditionally sandwiched with jam and cream or *crème pâtissière* (see page 18), but now used to describe any layered puff pastry shape with either a sweet or savoury filling.

TIPS & TRICKS:
MARINADES
As marinades usually contain acid, always use non-metallic containers for marinating.

Mirepoix

Diced vegetables, usually onion, celery and carrot, sweated in butter and/or oil and used as a base for stocks, sauces, soups, braised dishes and stews. Size varies according to length of cooking – see Dice, page 22.

Noisette

This French word literally translates as 'hazelnut', but in cookery it has two other meanings:

■ It describes the round nugget or 'eye' of prime-quality meat – fillet (tenderloin) of beef, veal and pork, and the fillet from the loin of lamb. Fat is often tied around the sides of these to help moisten the lean meat as it cooks.

■ *Beurre noisette* is butter that has been heated to a nut-brown colour. It is used for drizzling over fish.

Oxidization

Describes the deterioration that occurs when a cut or peeled ingredient is exposed to air. See Acidulated (page 8) and Discoloration (page 22).

Pan-fry

see FRY, *page 26*

Papillote

Meat, poultry, fish or vegetables baked or steamed in a parcel of greaseproof paper, baking parchment or foil are described as *en papillote* (see illustration, opposite). Vine and banana leaves can also be used as wrappers.

■ Cooking *en papillote* is healthy – little or no fat is required.

■ Flavourings packed inside the parcel make the food moist and tasty.

Parboil

To partially cook food in boiling water. Most often used to soften vegetables, especially potatoes before roasting (see page 309).

■ Parboiling times vary and should be given in individual recipes, but they are generally quite short and never more than half the full cooking time. This distinguishes parboiling from Blanching (see page 12), when food is boiled for a much shorter time.

Pare

This means to peel fruits and vegetables very thinly, for which you will find a paring knife (see page 72) most helpful. The zest of citrus fruits is described as pared when the thin outer coloured part is removed (see page 51).

Pass

see SIEVE, *page 44*

Poach

Strictly speaking, poaching is to cook in liquid at a slightly lower temperature than simmering, but it is difficult to gauge the difference between the two.

■ Poaching can be done on the hob or in the oven. The liquid should barely simmer – the surface should murmur and break with the occasional bubble.

■ It is a gentle method, best suited to delicate foods like fish and soft fruits that would fall apart if simmered or boiled, and for tough cuts of meat and mature birds that need long and low cooking to make them tender. To poach eggs, see pages 54 and 466.

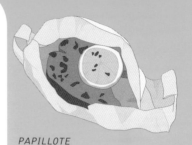

PAPILLOTE

Pod

see SHELL, *page 44*

Pot roast

see BRAISE, *page 12*

Preheat

■ When a recipe calls for a specific oven temperature, you should allow time for the oven to heat up to this temperature before cooking or you won't get a reliable result, especially when baking.

■ The usual time for preheating is 15–20 minutes, but ovens vary in the time they take to reach temperature, so consult your oven handbook. Some fan ovens don't need preheating.

■ When cooking pastry, bread and pizza on a flat baking sheet or stone, you will get the best results if it is hot when the dough is placed on it, so you should preheat it at the same time as you preheat the oven.

■ Preheating is essential before grilling, so the food starts to cook immediately it is put under the grill.

■ To prevent food sticking, woks and cast-iron chargrill (griddle) pans should be preheated until hot before any ingredients are added.

Proving

A term used in breadmaking for the second, or last, rising of the dough before baking. The purpose of proving is to lighten the dough, but it isn't always necessary and you should only prove the dough if the recipe says so. If a dough is made with easy-blend yeast, it won't need proving.

■ To prove, shape the dough in its tin or straight on to a baking sheet, then leave in a warm place, usually for

half the time of the first rise. It won't double in size as it does with the first rise; it will just increase to the size it will be when baked.

■ To prevent dough from drying out, most recipes say to cover with oiled cling film or a tea towel during proving, but instructions do vary.

■ To test if the dough is ready to put in the oven, press a finger into it – the dough should spring back when the finger is withdrawn.

Punch down

To knock the air out of bread dough after the first rise, also called 'knocking back'. This prevents the baked loaf from having large holes in the crumb. (Open-textured breads like ciabatta aren't punched down – one of the reasons why they have so many holes.) The technique of punching down is the same as kneading, but for a much shorter time: half a minute at most.

Purée

A smooth mixture that is made by whizzing, or puréeing, ingredients in a machine (a blender or food processor), or by pushing through a sieve or using a food mill. If a machine is used and you want the purée to be completely smooth, it will need to be sieved afterwards.

Quenelle

A small, soft, oval dumpling of puréed
or minced meat, poultry or fish bound
together with eggs and/or a sauce then
poached in stock. This is the traditional quenelle from the Lyon region in
eastern France, but now the term is
used to describe oval shapes of many
different foods, such as mashed potato, vegetable purées and ice cream.

Reduce

To boil a liquid in an uncovered pan
so that it evaporates and reduces in
volume, to become a reduction. Wine,
stock and cream are often reduced in
sauce making so they become thicker
and more concentrated in flavour.

■ For the quickest results, use a wide,
shallow pan rather than a tall,
narrow pan, as this will speed up
evaporation.

■ Reducing intensifies the saltiness of
stock, so wait until after reduction
before tasting and adding seasoning.

Refresh

Vegetables are refreshed after blanching, boiling or parboiling to stop cooking from continuing and to keep their
colours bright. There are two ways to
refresh, both equally effective:

■ Drain the vegetables in a sieve or colander and hold under the cold tap until they cool down.

■ Drain and plunge into an ice bath (see page 29).

Rehydrate

Dried fruits such as prunes and apricots, and dried vegetables such as mushrooms and sun-dried tomatoes, are full of concentrated flavour, but often too chewy or hard to be eaten or cooked as they are. Before you use them, you need to rehydrate them so that they plump up and become juicy and tender.

■ Hot water is a quick and effective way of rehydrating, although sometimes tea, alcohol or fruit juice may be used to add flavour.

■ Soaking times vary and should be specified on the packet or in the recipe. For general guidelines, see page 96 for dried mushrooms, and pages 118–19 for sun-dried tomatoes.

Relax

This is when food is allowed to rest, either before or after cooking.

■ Pastry should be relaxed in the fridge after shaping to help prevent it from shrinking in the oven. Joints of meat should be left to relax after

roasting, to make carving easier (see pages 333 and 368).

Rémoulade

When mayonnaise is mixed with mustard, capers and gherkins it becomes a *rémoulade*. This is a piquant cold sauce that goes well as an accompaniment to meat, poultry and fish, and with raw vegetable julienne, especially celeriac. Recipes vary, and often include chopped parsley and/or anchovies.

Render

When the fat in meat melts and becomes liquid, this is called rendering.

■ The fat from ducks and geese renders naturally during roasting. Both have a distinctive flavour, and are excellent for roasting potatoes (see pages 309 and 378).

■ To render the fat from a piece of meat or bacon, put the meat or bacon in a pan over a very low heat and let the fat melt out slowly. Strain the rendered fat to remove any sediment or crispy bits, leave until cool, then keep in a covered container in the fridge. It can be used in cooking like any other fat.

Rest

see RELAX, *left*

Ribbon trail

A term used in dessert and cake making. It describes the stage when eggs and sugar are whisked to such a thick consistency that they leave a trail on top of the mixture when the whisk is lifted across it (see right). Instructions are usually 'whisk until the mixture leaves (or holds) a ribbon trail' or 'whisk to the ribbon stage'. With an electric mixer this takes about 10 minutes, depending on the amount of mixture and the machine's speed; with a hand beater or balloon whisk it can take up to 20 minutes. If you stand the bowl over a pan of hot water, this will speed up the thickening process.

RIBBON TRAIL

Roast

To cook food uncovered in the oven, usually with some extra fat, until it is brown on the outside and tender within.
■ Prime cuts of meat and young birds are best for roasting, as are fish and certain vegetables.
■ To prevent food stewing in its own fat or juices, place it on a rack in the roasting tin, or on a bed of vegetables or herbs.

- Always preheat the oven before starting to roast, so that cooking times can be calculated accurately.
- Basting during roasting helps prevent food drying out, but there are exceptions – see Baste, page 10.
- When roasting meat, a thermometer (see page 58) will help get good results. For internal temperatures, see page 333.

Roux

A mixture of butter and flour cooked together to a paste, used as a thickening base for sauces, soups and stews before the liquid is added.

- The amount of flour and butter varies according to individual recipes, but is usually equal volumes.
- A *roux* can be cooked to different colours, from white to blond and russet brown, and this will give the colour of the finished sauce.

Rub

Dried herbs or spices that are rubbed over food before cooking are called 'rubs' or 'dry marinades'.

- Using a rub is a quick way to inject flavour and/or give a flavoured crust to meat, poultry and fish. The longer it is left, the more effective it will be.
- You can buy ready-mixed spices to use as rubs (see page 163) or you can make your own, but don't add salt until just before cooking or it will draw out the juices from the food and make it dry.

Rub in

In cake, biscuit and pastry recipes, you may see the instruction 'rub the fat into the flour until the mixture resembles fine breadcrumbs'. This technique distributes the fat in tiny pieces in the flour so that it melts evenly during baking.

- Make sure the fat (usually butter or margarine) and your hands are cold, or the fat will stick to your fingers and/or clog in the flour. Take the fat out of the fridge and let it come to room temperature. Hold your hands under the cold tap and dry them.
- Cut the fat into small cubes and drop them over the surface of the flour. With your fingertips, gently and lightly work the cubes into the flour, lifting the flour up above the top of the bowl, to incorporate air (see illustration, opposite).

Sauté

From the French verb *sauter* meaning to jump, this means to fry food quickly in hot, shallow fat (usually butter and/ or oil), turning and tossing it frequently so that it 'jumps' about, as in stir-frying.

■ For best results, use a sauté pan or frying pan with deep, sloping sides that allow room for the food to move without jumping out of the pan.

■ Don't add too much food at once as this lowers the temperature in the pan and the food will stew rather than fry.

RUB IN

Scald

To bring a liquid (usually milk) to just below boiling point, when bubbles start to appear around the edge. Watch carefully and catch it just at this point or the liquid may boil over and scorch.

■ Milk is scalded when it is infused with aromatics – see Infuse, page 30.

Score

SCORE

When shallow cuts or slashes are scored in the surface of food with a sharp knife, often in parallel lines or as a diamond or square pattern (see Cross-hatch, page 18, and illustration, right). Scoring makes food look attractive, but the main purpose of this technique is to help with the cooking process in the following ways:

■ Scoring or slashing opens up food so that it cooks more quickly.

■ Liquids such as marinades, dressings and sauces penetrate the slashes to make the food moist and inject flavour. They can also help tenderize (see Marinade/marinate, page 32).

■ Herbs and garlic are often pushed into the slashes in meat and fish to flavour the flesh. Asian flavourings can be used in this way too.

■ Scored lines in the skin of pork help make crackling crisp (see page 347). In the skin of duck, they help release the fat underneath. When the skin of fish is scored, this helps keep the fish flat during cooking.

■ In the oven, steam escapes from a pastry lid that is slashed before baking, preventing it from becoming soggy.

■ Bread that is scored on the top before baking will rise evenly without bursting open.

Sear

To pan-fry or roast food for a short time over a high heat, or in a very hot oven, so it becomes dark brown on the outside. Foods most often seared are meat and poultry, and fish with its skin on.

■ Searing doesn't seal in juices. It releases juices on to the surface of the food where they caramelize. This makes the food look appetizing, and gives depth of flavour from the start.

■ A heavy cast-iron frying pan or chargrill pan is ideal for searing as it retains heat well. Get the pan hot over a high heat before food is added.

■ Make sure the food is thoroughly dry before searing by patting it with kitchen paper, then brush with oil. Always oil the food, not the pan – if you oil the pan it will smoke.

■ Don't overcrowd the pan, as it will lower the temperature. It is better to sear in several small batches than in one large one.

■ Don't move, stir or turn the food until it is browned underneath. Once one side is seared, turn and sear the others (including the edges).

■ After searing, deglaze the pan (see page 20) so the caramelized juices aren't wasted. If the food stays brown when liquid is added, you have seared it successfully – if the colour washes off, you haven't.

■ After searing, cooking is usually finished at a lower temperature, often with liquid added – see Braise (page 12) and Stew (page 47).

Seed

To remove and discard the seeds, stones or pips from fruits and vegetables, sometimes called deseeding.

Seize/seized

A term used to describe melted chocolate that has solidified or 'seized' into a lump with an unpleasant grainy texture. Seizing occurs for two reasons – when the chocolate is melted too quickly over too high a heat, and/or if moisture (even steam) gets into the chocolate while it is melting. There are a few ways to prevent seizing:

■ Break chocolate into small pieces and melt in a bowl over a *bain marie* (see page 9) of hot, not boiling, water.

■ Don't let the bottom of the bowl touch the water and don't let the water get too hot – it is better to melt slowly than in a rush.

■ If the bowl seems to be getting too hot and/or if you see steam rising around it, remove the bowl from the *bain marie* and let it cool down, stirring gently from time to time. The chocolate will melt gradually, even off the heat.

■ Don't cover the bowl at any time as this will cause droplets of moisture to fall into the chocolate.

■ To rescue seized chocolate, try beating in 1–2 tsp vegetable oil, off the heat. Or start again and melt more chocolate, then beat this into the seized lump.

Separate

This term has three culinary meanings:

■ If a recipe calls for an egg to be separated, it means that the shell should be cracked in half and the white separated from the yolk (see page 465).

TIPS & TRICKS: SEED
A word of caution: contrary to what you may think, grapes labelled 'seeded' have their seeds in them. Grapes without seeds are described as 'seedless'.

■ Custards and egg-based sauces are often described as having separated or 'split' when they have curdled. See Curdle, page 18.

■ When you are making mayonnaise, it may separate if the ingredients aren't at the right temperature and/or if the oil is added too quickly to the egg. For a foolproof mayonnaise recipe, see page 467.

Seviche

see CEVICHE, *page 14*

Shell

To remove the outer covering of fruits, vegetables, nuts, eggs and shellfish – see individual names of these for specific techniques. Removing peas and beans from their shells is called podding (see page 261).

Shred

Food that is cut into thin strips is described as shredded.

■ Use a very sharp chef's knife. Leaves can be stacked on top of each other and shredded together, either kept flat or rolled into a cigar shape if they are soft enough (see page 129). *Chiffonade* (see page 14) is the French term for leaves that have been finely shredded in this way.

■ The large holes of a grater, or a food processor with a shredding disc, make light work of shredding hard foods like carrots and white cabbage.

■ For very fine shredding, a mandolin is used (see page 70).

Shuck

Removing shellfish from their shells is called shucking. The term is most often used for oysters, but it can also be used for shelling mussels, clams and scallops. Oysters and scallops are raw when they are shucked, which is difficult to do at home, so let the fishmonger do the job, or see page 435 for instructions. Mussels and clams are usually shelled after cooking, which is easier though still fiddly – the technique is described on page 432.

Sieve

To sieve is to press food through a sieve (see page 66) to make a smooth purée. The contents of the sieve are pushed through the mesh by pressing and rotating a metal spoon or ladle (or a pestle) against the inside; solids such as skins and pips are left behind in the sieve. Chefs often use a special chinois sieve (see page 16) for this technique, which they refer to as 'passing'.

Sift

To shake food through a sieve or
strainer, or a special sifter that may
have large holes or a fine wire mesh.
The term is most often used for dry
ingredients such as flour and sugar.

■ Sifting incorporates air (see Aerate,
page 8) and, in recipes with ingredients such as flour, cocoa powder and
salt, it mixes them together.

■ Tap firmly on the rim of the sieve
while shaking to help food go through.

■ To remove lumps, press down hard
with the back of a metal spoon and
they will disperse.

Simmer

To cook food in liquid just below boiling point (85–95°C/185–200°F for
water). A few small bubbles should
break on the surface of the liquid, so
that food is cooked more gently, and
often for a longer time, than by boiling.

Skim

To remove fat, froth or scum from the
surface of a liquid. Special spoons
called skimmers can be used, but you
can just as easily use an ordinary
metal spoon which isn't perforated.

■ When stock or jam is boiling, or
when clarifying butter (see page 455),

TERMS AND TECHNIQUES

a frothy scum often rises to the surface. Scoop it off gently without disturbing the liquid underneath.

■ To skim fat off gravies, stocks and stews, see Degrease (page 20).

■ For information on skimmed milk, see page 442.

Smoke point

This describes the stage at which fat starts to smoke when it is heated. Never heat fat beyond this point or it may reach 'flash point' and burst into flames.

■ Butter has a low smoke point, but it is raised slightly when the butter is clarified (see page 455).

■ If you like to use butter because of its flavour, combine it with oil. This will help prevent smoking.

■ Grapeseed and groundnut (peanut) oils have very high smoke points, so are good for deep-frying.

■ Extra virgin olive oil has a low smoke point, but then is too good for frying. Use for dressings and for sprinkling over food before serving.

■ Don't re-use any oil that you have used for frying. Throw it away.

Spatchcocked

A term applied to birds, usually chickens and poussins, which have had their spines removed and are opened out flat (see illustration opposite).

■ Spatchcocked birds are excellent for barbecuing and grilling because they cook faster than a whole bird.

■ It is very easy to spatchcock a bird (see pages 369 and 387), but they are often available ready spatchcocked at supermarkets, especially in the barbecue season.

■ For ease of handling and to help keep the bird flat, insert skewers through its wings and legs before cooking (see page 387).

Split

see SEPARATE, *page 43*

Steam

To cook in the vapour produced by boiling water. Place the food in a perforated container above the water, then cover with a lid so that the steam will surround the food and cook it gently. For information on steamers, see page 54.

■ Steaming is a healthy method of cooking as no fat is used, and vitamins and minerals don't leach out into the water as they do in boiling, simmering and poaching.

Steep

To soak an ingredient in liquid so it plumps up, softens and/or takes on the flavour of the liquid. See Marinate (page 32) and Rehydrate (page 38).

A SPATCHCOCKED BIRD

Stew

Stewing is similar to braising in that food is cooked gently in liquid in a covered pan (often a casserole dish) for a long time, either on the hob or in the oven, but the ingredients are usually cut into smaller pieces and more liquid is used. Stewing is an especially good way of cooking tough cuts of meat.

■ When all the raw ingredients and liquid are put in the pan together at the start, this is called a white stew.

■ To make a brown stew, the main ingredients are browned in fat before the liquid is added.

■ Stews and casseroles are the same thing – a casserole is a stew that has taken its name from the dish it is cooked in.

Stir-fry

To cook food fast in a wok or other deep-sided pan by stirring and tossing over a fierce heat.

■ Originally an Asian technique,

stir-frying is healthy and nutritious. It uses a small amount of oil and the food is cut thinly so that it cooks in a very short time and retains maximum nutrients.

■ For successful stir-frying, get the wok and oil hot before adding the ingredients, and allow the food to sizzle and colour on the bottom of the pan in between stirring.

Strain

To let a liquid pass through a sieve (see page 66) or strainer to separate it from any solids such as skin, seeds or bones. In most cases the liquid is used and the solids are discarded (the opposite of draining, see page 22), although sometimes both liquid and solids may be kept and used, depending on the recipe.

Sweat

An unfortunate term for a frequently used technique, this means to cook food slowly and gently so that it softens without colouring. Sweating also concentrates the flavour of the food.

■ Onions, celery, garlic and carrots are often sweated and used as a flavouring base for soups, sauces and stews.

■ Butter is a favourite fat for sweat-

ing because it gives a good flavour and colour. To stop it burning, add a spoonful of vegetable or olive oil.

■ Duck and goose fats are excellent for sweating because they give a good flavour, but don't burn like butter.

■ For the ingredients to cook as gently as possible, use a heavy-based pan over a low heat. You can also use a heat-diffusing mat under the pan as an extra precaution.

■ To stop evaporation and help concentrate juices, press a circle of greaseproof paper over the vegetables (see Cartouche, page 14).

Tempering

This is the technique of melting, cooling and re-warming chocolate so that it becomes malleable and sets hard with a gloss. It can be done at home, but it is more often used by pastry chefs working with a special kind of chocolate called *couverture* (see page 17).

Tenderize

To break down tough connective tissue in meat and poultry before cooking so that it will be more tender to eat. There are two methods – you can use either, or both together:

■ Cover the meat with cling film and pound with a meat mallet or rolling pin. If you don't have either of these, use the base of a saucepan.

■ Soak in a marinade (see page 331).

Tepid
see BLOOD HEAT, *page 12*

Thaw
see DEFROST, *page 20*

Tian
A *tian* is both the French name for a baking dish and the food that is cooked in it, usually a creamy vegetable gratin topped with cheese. Traditional *tian* dishes are square or rectangular, and are made from earthenware.

Timbale
A small, round, metal mould used for baking or steaming both sweet and savoury mixtures. The mould lends its name to the food cooked in it, which is always served turned out.

■ Timbales have straight tapering sides, while a dariole mould, which is used in much the same way as a timbale, has rounded sides and looks like a mini pudding basin. See also page 57.

TERMS AND TECHNIQUES

Toast
see DRY-FRY, *page 23*

Tournedos
see MÉDAILLON, *page 33*

Tranche
The French word for a slice. Most often used to describe a rectangle of puff pastry, or a piece of boneless fish.

Truss
To keep poultry and game birds in shape by tying them with string or securing them with skewers. Birds are often sold ready trussed, which looks neat and tidy, but they will cook better if the strings or skewers are removed before roasting (see page 366).

Turn/turned
To pare vegetables, especially potatoes, carrots and turnips, into torpedo shapes. A classic chef's technique that is rarely used at home.

Whip
To beat vigorously in a wide and sweeping circular motion, to incorporate air into an ingredient or mixture so it increases in volume. The term is most often used with cream or creamy mixtures, and the whipping may be done by hand with a fork or a balloon whisk (see page 68), or by machine with a 'wand' blender or an electric mixer (see page 60).
- Always use a large, deep bowl for whipping. This will allow for maximum volume without splattering.
- Contrary to what you may think, you will get more volume by hand with a balloon whisk than with an electric machine, and the mixture will hold its shape better – and longer.

Whisk
Using a whisk (see page 68) to beat an ingredient, or a mixture of ingredients, incorporating varying amounts of air.
- A coiled whisk is used for dressings and sauces so the ingredients come together and emulsify.
- A balloon whisk is used for whisking egg whites to incorporate as much air as possible (see pages 68, and 465).

Wilt
To cook vegetable leaves very briefly so they lose their springiness and become soft. Cabbage and spinach are

toast–zest

often wilted (see page 312), and the same technique is used with leaves like rocket and radicchio in warm salads.

Zest

This is the outer coloured part of the rind or skin of citrus fruit, not including the bitter white pith underneath. It contains aromatic oils that have an intense flavour, especially when heated (see Infuse, page 30).

ZEST

■ If you know you are going to use the zest, buy unwaxed fruit. Scrub in hot water, then dry well.

■ The zest can be removed in strips with a vegetable peeler or paring knife and then cut into thin strips, or you can use a zester (see right and page 72).

■ In recipes calling for 'grated zest', rub the fruit against the fine holes of a grater, moving it round frequently so that you don't grate too deep and include any of the pith. Use a brush to remove the zest stuck to the grater's teeth, both inside and out.

KITCHEN KIT

ALWAYS BUY GOOD-QUALITY EQUIPMENT. IT WILL BE A PLEASURE TO USE, AND HELP YOU PREPARE FOOD EFFICIENTLY AND WELL, WHICH WILL GO A LONG WAY TO MAKING YOU A GOOD COOK. START WITH A FEW BASIC ESSENTIALS AND COLLECT EXTRA PIECES AS AND WHEN YOU NEED THEM. THIS WILL SPREAD THE COST, AND MAKE SURE THAT YOU DON'T BUY THINGS YOU WILL NEVER USE – CLUTTERED SURFACES AND CUPBOARDS WILL HINDER YOUR WORK AND SLOW YOU DOWN, SO TOO WILL CHEAP EQUIPMENT, WHICH WON'T LAST.

ON THE HOB

Before buying any equipment to use on top of the stove, check to see what types of hob it is suitable for. Induction hobs require special pots and pans.

MUST HAVE

Saucepans

Essential for all cooking that involves liquid, especially boiling vegetables, rice and pasta, and making sauces and soups.

■ A starter set of three sizes should cover most of your needs: one small 16 cm (6½ in) pan will hold 1.5 litres (2½ pints), one medium 18 cm (7 in) pan will hold 2 litres (3½ pints) and pan will hold 2 litres (3½ pints) and one large 20 cm (8 in) pan will hold 2.8 litres (5 pints).

■ Stainless steel is the most durable metal and an excellent conductor of heat. It also washes up well. Look for heavy gauge, described as 18/10, and a 5 mm (¼ in) base.

■ Lids are a must, but not always included in the price of the pan.

■ Long handles are good as they stay cooler than short ones, but pans with two stubby ovenproof handles (sometimes called stockpots) are more versatile as they can double as casseroles in the oven. Check if the lids are ovenproof – if not, use foil instead.

■ When buying a large pan, consider choosing a pasta pot with an inset drainer. Apart from safely boiling and draining pasta, it can be used as a stockpot and steamer, and for cooking bulky or large quantities of vegetables (especially potatoes and spinach).

Wok/ Stir-fry pan

Woks are extremely versatile, as they are shallower and wider than saucepans, with curved or rounded sides. Their open shape cooks food quickly and easily, such as pasta sauces, risotto, curries, pan-fried or sautéed chicken, meat or fish in a sauce – and stir-fries, of course. An oriental-style wok with a long handle will fit the bill, but it may have an unstable round bottom and no lid. A wok with two short handles, a flat bottom and an ovenproof lid is safer and more useful. Sometimes called a 'stir-fry pan' rather than a wok, it can double as a flameproof casserole so you can start cooking on the hob then transfer to the oven. A 28 cm (11 in) pan is ideal.

STIR-FRY PAN

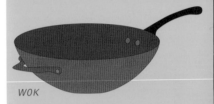

WOK

Frying pan

A great complement to a wok or stir-fry pan, a shallow frying pan is essential for frying food that needs to be crisp and/or flat. Cast iron is a popular metal for frying pans as it is heavy duty and won't buckle over high heat, but non-stick is lighter and easier to use. Titanium is the best, and it can be used with metal utensils, which is a real bonus. A useful size (it takes 4 fried eggs) is 25–30 cm (10–12 in).

GOOD
TO HAVE

Chargrill pan

Also called a griddle pan, this is a
heavy pan with ridges on the bottom
that imprint charred lines on the food.
Food is raised above any fat so this is
a healthy way to cook – see Chargrill
(page 14) for more information.
■ Cast iron is the traditional material
for these pans, but it can be very
heavy, so you may prefer non-stick.
■ A pan with a rim is useful. It will
allow you to add liquid at the end of
cooking, to make a sauce or gravy.

Small
frying pan

An 18–20 cm (6–8 in) pan is good for
one person, and the best size for a
2- or 3-egg omelette.
■ Choose a pan with shallow curving
sides so that you can slide omelettes
out easily. This will also come in useful for pancakes.
■ Non-stick is the most practical,
with a thick base. For tossing and
flipping, it shouldn't be too heavy.

Steamer

If you do a lot of steaming, buy a
tiered steamer so you can cook several
different things at once. For occasional steaming, a collapsible basket is a
cheaper alternative – it will fit inside
a saucepan of any size and fold flat
for compact storage when not in use.
■ Tiered or stacking steamers in
stainless steel are hygienic and easy
to clean. Bamboo steamers are less
expensive. They look good and can be
used over a wok, but food tends to
stick in them (unless they are lined
with leaves) and they tend to retain
smells and flavours, so they aren't the
most practical choice.

Egg poacher

Poaching eggs isn't the easiest of
techniques, so if you like poached eggs
a lot, invest in one of these. The best
kind has non-stick cups that fit into an
insert. When the insert is lifted out,
the pan doubles as a deep frying pan
or sauté pan. To poach eggs with or
without using a poacher, see page 467.

IN THE OVEN

MUST HAVE

Roasting tin

Heavy duty is essential, so the tin stays rigid and doesn't buckle or warp in a very hot oven, or when making gravy on the hob.

■ Tins with ridges in the bottom prevent food sitting in its own fat, and a corner spout is handy for draining off fat and pouring out gravy.

■ Buy the largest tin your oven will take, about 35 x 28 cm (14 x 11 in), and perhaps a medium-sized one for smaller amounts. These should cover you for most occasions.

■ Choice of material is up to you – stainless steel or a non-stick hard anodized metal will serve you well.

Roasting rack

Many roasting tins come complete with their own rack. If not, an adjustable or hinged V-shaped rack is a good buy. It acts as a cradle for meat and poultry, holding it securely in position throughout roasting and stopping it sitting in fat.

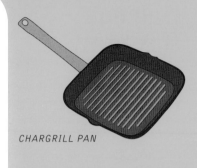

CHARGRILL PAN

COLLAPSIBLE STEAMER

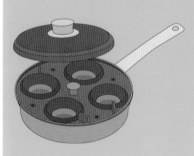

EGG POACHER

KITCHEN KIT:IN THE OVEN

Baking sheet/tray

Strictly speaking, a baking sheet is completely flat, so it is easy to slide things off, and it usually has one shallow raised edge for easy handling, while a baking tray has raised edges on all sides. Makers are generally unaware of this distinction, so choose by looks and buy one as large as your oven will take. The best material is non-stick hard anodized metal, as it is very sturdy, conducts heat evenly, and doesn't buckle in extreme heat.

Cooling rack

Allows air to circulate under food, making cooling quicker and preventing food getting soggy. Most cakes, biscuits and pastries benefit from being cooled on a rack (if left in their tins they can stick). It is also useful if you are sifting them with sugar – excess falls through the rack and gives the food a clean edge.

Flameproof casserole dish

If you don't have a stubby-handled saucepan or stir-fry pan that will go in the oven (see pages 52–53), you will need a casserole dish. Ensure it is flameproof, i.e. it can be used on top of the stove and in the oven (if the label says heatproof or ovenproof, it can't be used on the hob). For a casserole to serve 4–6 a diameter of 28–30 cm (11–12 in) with a capacity of 3.6–4.2 litres (6–7 pints) is a good size.
■ A casserole should heat up quickly on the stove and not stick, then retain its heat during cooking in the oven. Cast iron fits the bill, is durable and looks good to serve, saving on washing up.

Baking dish

Oven-to-table ceramic baking dishes are invaluable as they are so versatile. Use to make dishes like pasta bakes, fish and shepherd's pies, gratins and puddings, for roasting, reheating and serving. Most baking dishes are strong enough to resist the fierce heat of a grill (useful for gratins and browning things before serving), but aren't usually flameproof and can't go on the hob. A good size is 25 x 20 cm (10 x 8 in) – 5 cm (2 in) deep.

Oven gloves

These protect hands and wrists from hot oven racks and pan handles. Try them on in the shop, to be sure they are comfortable and not too thick to make handling difficult. Gauntlets that cover your forearms are best.

■ Look for the word 'insulated' on the label. The type made of flexible silicone can withstand temperatures up to 300°C (570°F).

BAKING SHEET

GOOD TO HAVE

Cake tins

Sturdy, non-stick, springform, loose-bottomed tins are best for easy removal of delicate cakes, cheesecakes, and cakes and desserts that are set in the fridge or freezer.

BAKING TRAY

■ Most recipes for 4–6 people specify either a 20 cm (8 in) or a 23 cm (9 in) tin, so it is unlikely you will need more than these two sizes. A depth of 7.5 cm (3 in) is good for most purposes. Always use the tin size that is specified in the recipe. Using the wrong-sized tin is one of the main reasons for failure with cake recipes.

SPRINGFORM CAKE TIN

Dariole moulds

Also called mini pudding basins, these are made of metal for good heat conduction. Use for baked or steamed sponge puddings, custards and *crème caramel* that are served turned out. Usual capacity is 175 ml (6 fl oz).

KITCHEN KIT:IN THE OVEN

Flan tin

For cooking flans, tarts and quiches, with fluted sides and a lift-out base. Look for silver anodized metal with a satin finish – this conducts heat well and evenly and won't warp, so gives a crisp, professional finish to pastry.

■ Deep tins are the most versatile, especially for savoury flans and quiches. Shallow tins make continental-style dessert tarts look stylish.

■ The most useful size is 23 cm (9 in), which will serve 4–6 people.

■ Individual 12 cm (4½ in) tins are perfect for starter-size portions.

■ A ceramic flan dish looks good for taking from oven to table, but ceramic isn't as good a conductor of heat as metal, so pastry bases may be soggy, and the first slice is difficult to get out without breaking. Removal is easier with a loose-based metal tin, and you can always serve the tart from the metal base.

Loaf tin

For breads, cakes, pâtés and terrines.

■ Heavy-gauge non-stick is best. The sturdiest ones are made of hard anodized metal.

■ They come in two sizes – a small one is 450 g (1 lb), and a large one is 900 g (2 lb).

Meat thermometer

For cooks who worry whether meat is properly cooked, especially when roasting, this is an essential confidence booster. Meat thermometers measure internal temperature, which is the best guide to doneness – cooking times can never be accurate as ovens vary so much. Dial thermometers are pushed into the meat at the beginning of cooking and left there until they reach the correct temperature; instant-read digital thermometers can be inserted at any time. For an accurate reading with either type, insert the probe into the thickest part of the meat, away from any bones.

Muffin mould

Not just for muffins; also for cup cakes, buns, deep fruit tarts, mince pies, Yorkshire puddings and individual deep-dish quiches. Depths vary, as do sizes of moulds – the choice is usually between 6, 12 and 24 cups. Deep, flexible, silicone-rubber ones are completely non-stick and easy-release, and won't rust. Metal muffin tins with non-stick coatings are also good, but are best lined with paper cases to ensure they don't stick.

Ramekins

These little ceramic baking dishes, also called cocottes, are used for individual portions of soufflé, custard, baked eggs, mousses and dauphinois potatoes. They come in handy as serving bowls too; in fact you will find yourself using them again and again for all sorts of things. Sizes vary enormously, so it is a good idea to buy more than you need to allow for breakages – you may not be able to get the same size again. The most useful size is 150 ml (¼ pint).

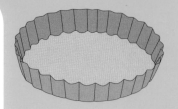

FLAN TIN

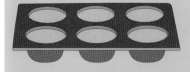

MUFFIN MOULD

Traybake tin

A tray-cum-tin useful for baking, roasting and heating things up, a traybake tin is more versatile than a Swiss roll tin because it is deeper, usually about 4 cm (1½ in) deep. The best ones are made of hard anodized metal, which is non-stick, and a useful size is 30 x 23 cm (12 x 9 in) or 33 x 20 cm (13 x 8 in).

ELECTRICS

There is a huge range of electrical equipment to choose from, most of which you will never need and will only clutter your kitchen. Electric machines are expensive, so buy with caution and think about the type and amount of cooking you do. Many of the machines duplicate each other's functions.

MUST HAVE

Blender

Choose between two types:
■ A hand-held 'wand' works directly in your saucepan or bowl, without the need to decant the mixture into a machine. Apart from speed and convenience, this saves on washing up. Good-quality wands come with many attachments, and will beat, blend, purée, chop, grind, whip and whisk – and make smoothies and crush ice.
■ A more expensive option is a free-standing blender or liquidizer. This performs the same functions as the wand, but has a stronger motor, making it easier to blend or purée large quantities quickly. More cumbersome to store than a wand, this type of blender isn't good for small quantities that don't cover the blade.

GOOD TO HAVE

Food processor

For the serious cook, this expensive machine will soon pay for itself – it is a real multi-tasking workhorse. One with a powerful motor will make light work of chopping, slicing, grinding and grating large quantities, and it will also make pastry and knead dough for bread as well as purée, whisk and extract juice. Buy one with a separate mini bowl for chopping small quantities of herbs and grinding spices or nuts.

Mixer

If you have a wand blender with attachments and/or a food processor, you may not need an electric mixer. There are two types, hand-held and tabletop, both of which whisk and whip air into egg whites and cream, and cake and biscuit mixtures.
■ The hand-held mixer does little more than a good-quality wand blender, so you won't need both, but a heavy-duty freestanding mixer is more efficient at beating air into cake mixtures, and is better for large quantities. It will also make pastry, bread and pasta dough and, if you buy the right attachments, will mince, slice, peel and shred.

PREP TOOLS

MUST HAVE

HAND-HELD 'WAND' BLENDER

TABLETOP MIXER

SOFT PASTRY BRUSH

Brushes

There are many different types.
These two are the most useful:

■ A soft pastry brush is indispensable for glazing, sealing pastry edges and greasing tins and moulds. A small, flat paint brush with natural bristles is just as effective as a pastry brush bought from a kitchenware shop – and less likely to have wayward bristles.

■ For scrubbing vegetables such as potatoes and artichokes clean, and removing the zest from the teeth of graters, you need a brush with hard bristles. A sturdy nail brush will do the job, but don't use it for cleaning delicate vegetables such as mushrooms as it will damage their fragile gills.

Can opener

Not all cans have ring pulls, so you are bound to need a can opener at some time or other. Choose a practical one that has a good grip and is easy to use, not a gimmicky gadget.

Chopping boards

Food scientists say wooden chopping boards are more hygienic than plastic, as long as they are scrubbed in hot water and dried thoroughly after using.

■ You really need three boards – one for raw meat and poultry, one for strong ingredients like onions and garlic, and a third for everything else. Colour-coded sets are practical, or buy a selection of wood and plastic.

■ Boards with a dip in, for use with a mezzaluna (a half-moon-shaped blade with a handle at either end), are good for chopping herbs.

■ To prevent your board slipping during use, put a special mat or a folded tea towel underneath.

Corkscrew

The simplest but most efficient is the screw-pull. It screws into the cork, then, as you keep screwing, the cork pulls out. Keep one in the kitchen, so you know where it is when you need it.

Fish slice

Flat and wide, made from stainless steel, a fish slice is used to lift and turn delicate foods like fish fillets and eggs, and for draining fat and/or liquid through the perforations or slots. It is also a good tool for pressing food flat when cooking – chargrilling chicken breasts and steaks, for example.

Grater

Apart from the mandolin (see page 70), there are two basic types:

■ A traditional box grater is inexpensive to buy and has different cutters on each surface. Choose one with a comfortable handle and a wide, stable base. Some have special grippers on the bottom to keep them in place.

■ Expensive, flat, stainless steel graters with double-edged, super-sharp blades are excellent for very fine grating, especially hard ingredients like citrus zest, Parmesan cheese, fresh ginger and chocolate. There are coarse versions for softer ingredients, and there is also a type with a single blade for shredding and shaving. These graters should have long handles, non-slip 'feet' and a guard to protect your fingers.

Knives
see KNIFE BOX, *page 72*

Ladle

Indispensable for decanting liquids from one container to another, especially hot liquids that can be messy and/or dangerous. One small and one large ladle are the most you will need. Some have pouring spouts, which are useful but not essential.

FISH SLICE

BOX GRATER

Lemon squeezer

You can squeeze juice out of halved citrus fruit by inserting a fork and twisting and squeezing, but a lemon squeezer will make the job easier and less messy. There are many to choose from – try not to be tempted by looks alone. The traditional reamer is most efficient at squeezing out lots of juice, but the kind that has a strainer to catch the pips and a container under-neath to hold the juice is more practi-cal. Stainless steel is both hygienic and sturdy.

Measuring cups

If you use American recipes, you will notice that both solids and liquids are measured in cups, which are always levelled off in the cup measure. Sets of US cups can be bought in the UK, and there are usually 4 of them – 1 cup, ½ cup, ⅓ cup and ¼ cup. A US cup holds 250 ml (8 fl oz), so you can always use your usual measuring jug, provided you make sure that the ingredient is exactly level with the marked line on the jug. Note that a British pint is 568 ml (20 fl oz), whereas a US pint is 480 ml (16 fl oz). See pages 470–1 for more information on converting British and US measurements.

Measuring jugs

You will find two sizes of measuring jug useful – one for measuring up to 500–600 ml (18–20 fl oz/1 pint) and the other up to 1.2 litres (40 fl oz/2 pints).

■ Toughened or tempered glass is both heat-resistant for boiling liquids and microwave-proof.

■ Plastic angled jugs allow you to read the measurements simply by looking into the jug from above, which makes measuring easier and more accurate than with a conventional jug.

Measuring spoons

For successful results, especially in baking recipes, always use proper measuring spoons.

■ Nesting sets usually contain four spoons – 15 ml (1 tbsp), 5 ml (1 tsp), 2.5 ml (½ tsp) and 1.25 ml (¼ tsp).

■ Stainless steel is the most practical material, and slim-line spoons are good for fitting into the narrow necks of small herb and spice jars.

■ When spoon measures are specified in recipes, the ingredient should be levelled off with a knife. Occasionally you will read 'heaped' or 'rounded', which means what it says – it isn't intended to be an exact measure. The term 'scant' is also sometimes used, meaning slightly less than level.

Mixing bowls

A nest of different sizes is the most practical choice, as it will take up the least amount of storage space. A set of four bowls should be enough for most cooks.

■ Heatproof glass and stainless steel are more versatile and robust than plastic, and some come with lids that make them airtight for storage.

■ If you use the microwave a lot, look for tempered glass bowls suitable for microwave use.

Palette knives

These should be flexible and thin with a rounded end. Useful for all spreading jobs and for turning and lifting delicate foods, as well as helping to release cakes and desserts from tins and moulds. Two sizes (large and small) are sufficient; stainless steel will last longest.

Peeler

There are two basic types of peeler for you to choose from. To decide which you prefer, check whether it feels comfortable in your hand and that you can get a good grip. Stainless steel blades are best as they won't rust.

- A fixed-blade vegetable peeler is good for peeling most fruits and vegetables. If it has a sharp, pointed end it will double as a corer, and can also be used for removing stems and hulls from soft fruits and digging out the 'eyes' in potatoes.

- Swivel-bladed peelers are quick and easy to use once you get the hang of them. They are good at sliding over curved or knobbly vegetables to remove the skin.

Pestle and mortar

The heavier, larger and deeper the mortar is, the better, so you can use force without spillage when crushing and grinding. A pouring spout is useful for homemade mayonnaise, pesto and other sauces. Pestles and mortars

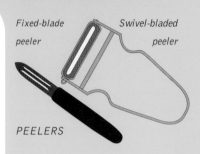

Fixed-blade peeler   Swivel-bladed peeler

PEELERS

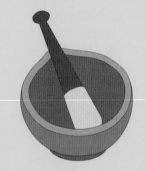

PESTLE AND MORTAR

can be made from:

Granite: The heaviest and best. Rock solid, it won't slip on the work surface, and an unpolished bowl is perfect for getting a good grip.

Frosted glass: This is tough and heavy, surprisingly good for the job.

Unglazed ceramic or porcelain: This is less heavy than granite or glass, but it is the classic choice with its comfy wooden handle, and it does the job well. Some have angled or elliptical mortars, others are conical, but there is nothing to beat the traditional round bowl – 20 cm (8 in) diameter is a good size.

Salt and pepper mills

So often chosen by looks, but other features are more important.

■ Ceramic mechanisms last longer than metal because they don't rust or corrode when they get wet (if you grind salt or pepper into hot food the steam can damage the mechanism just as easily as water).

■ Electronic mills are excellent, although they can be noisy.

■ An adjustable grind, from fine to coarse, is a must.

■ To prolong the life of your mills, don't screw them too tightly at the top.

Scales

For precision when weighing small amounts electronic, digital scales are best, and they take up the least amount of storage space too. Buy the ones which convert from metric to imperial at the touch of a button, and that you can return to zero when weighing more than one ingredient in the bowl at the same time.

Scissors

Keep a pair for kitchen use only, so you know where they are when you need them. Apart from using them for opening packets, you can also use them for snipping herbs, shredding leafy vegetables, topping and tailing beans and mangetouts, and chopping bacon and pancetta into lardons.

Sieve/colander

Stainless steel is the most practical material for sieves and colanders, and is easy to clean. Choose a large sieve that has one or two hooks opposite the handle, so it will stay in position when you are using it over a bowl or pan. Colanders are freestanding with larger holes than sieves, and are useful for rinsing and draining vegetables and pasta, especially when you are cooking

pestle–**s**patulas

large quantities. If storage space is tight in your kitchen, a large sieve may be more versatile. A small sieve is handy for sifting small amounts of dry ingredients like icing sugar or cocoa powder, and for straining tea.

■ For rinsing, draining and straining, a round bowl with a medium mesh is best, and can also be used for purée-ing if you don't have a blender or food processor.

■ A conical sieve (called a chinois, see page 16) with a fine mesh is good for straining or puréeing sauces into jugs.

■ A fine mesh is best for sifting dry ingredients.

COLANDER

SIEVE

Spatulas

They can be wooden, plastic or rubber.

■ A wooden spatula does almost the same job as a wooden spoon, but is more effective at scraping round the bottom of bowls and pans. As they are flat, spatulas can also be used to lift and turn food.

■ Plastic and rubber ones are flexible, good for folding in whipped cream and whisked egg whites, also indispensable for scraping pans and bowls clean. Rubber is more bendy than plastic, but there is little to choose between them.

Spoons

Apart from measuring spoons (see page 64), there are three types of spoon that you will need again and again.

■ Wooden spoons are essential for stirring, mixing, beating and creaming. For use on the stove, a long-handled spoon will protect hands from heat, while short-handled ones are best for beating and creaming. A useful wooden spoon is one with an angled edge, for scraping round the bottom of bowls and pans.

■ Wash and dry wooden spoons well, especially after using strong ingredients like onions and garlic, as wood retains smells and flavours.

■ A slotted spoon, sometimes called a perforated or draining spoon, is a metal spoon with holes in – for lifting and draining food from liquid and fat, and for skimming. A wide, round, fairly flat one is best to lift large and/or heavy food from deep liquid. A curved, oval one with a pointed tip will lift and serve food out of fat or liquid.

■ A large, stainless steel spoon with a slightly curved bowl and pointed tip is perfect to scoop, skim and serve.

Timer

Get into the habit of using a timer, no matter what you are cooking for how short a time. Digital timers can be set for the longest number of hours and minutes, and they are the most accurate. The type you can hang round your neck or clip on to your clothes is the most practical, and the longer and louder the ring, the better.

Tongs

These are the best implement for lifting and turning food without piercing so no juices escape, and are especially useful when frying or grilling. The simpler the design, the better – don't bother with gimmicky extras like spring-action hinges as these are likely to break. Stainless steel is the most practical material.

Whisk

Although you can whisk with a fork, it takes ages and is very hard work, so it pays to buy at least one or two whisks as they are inexpensive. You will find both of the following useful:

■ A stainless steel balloon whisk with large, springy coils makes light work of whisking air into egg whites and cream, and is indispensable for beating lumps out of sauces and batters.

■ For making dressings and gravy and whisking small quantities, buy a flat coil whisk.

GOOD TO HAVE

Baking beans

For baking pastry blind (see page 10). Re-usable and heavy in weight, they do a good job of keeping pastry bases flat. Dried peas or beans can be used instead, as can rice. Alternatively, line the pastry with foil and insert a smaller tin inside the tin you are baking in – it will hold the pastry in shape.

Blowtorch

Gas-powered and simple to refill with gas lighter fluid, a blowtorch is far better than the grill for bruléeing the tops of custards and getting gratins a good golden brown – it gives a quick, even colour without scorching and melting, and you can direct the flame to a specific area with great accuracy. Buy from a reputable source.

Carving board

You can use a chopping board for carving meat and poultry, but if you like to carve roasts at the table, a carving board with prongs to steady the meat will give greater stability, and the channel running round the edge will catch the juices as they flow.

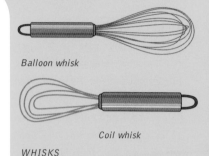

Balloon whisk

Coil whisk

WHISKS

Cutters

Even if you don't make biscuits very often, a set of round, stainless steel cutters will come in useful for other jobs when you want a professional finish. Use them to get a sharp edge on discs of pastry, potato and bread, and to serve neat individual portions of vegetables and rice. The ones that are double-sided (plain and fluted) are the most useful.

Garlic crusher/press

For speed, and to avoid garlicky fingers, a well-designed garlic press is a good gadget to have. Make sure it has a detachable grill for easy cleaning. Another gadget that works well is a garlic peeler – a simple rubber tube in which you roll garlic cloves until the skins slip off. It makes light work of this fiddly job.

Ice-cream scoop

Serving hard ice cream can be difficult unless you have a good scoop, which can be used to dollop mash and vegetable purées as well. A stainless steel one with an angled or sculpted blade is a good choice as it will glide easily through the ice cream. A short rubber handle will let you get a good grip. If you dip the scoop in warm water between each portion, it will work better.

Mandolin

For very fine slicing and shredding, nothing beats the ultra-sharp blades of a mandolin. Traditionally used only by professional chefs, especially the Japanese, mandolins are now widely available in kitchenware shops and aren't expensive. Choose from wood, stainless steel or plastic frames – they all have very sharp blades that adjust for fine or coarse shredding (some even have rippled blades for fancy cutting). A mandolin with a 'carriage' is a good buy. It will steady the food while you slice, and protect your fingertips at the same time.

Meat mallet

Made of either metal or wood, a meat mallet is useful for pounding poultry and meat to tenderize and flatten – so that it cooks quicker and more evenly. Always protect food by covering it with cling film or dampened grease-proof paper before pounding, or the food may tear. If you don't have a meat mallet, pounding with a rolling pin or the base of a saucepan makes a good substitute.

MEAT MALLET

Potato masher

Of course you can mash potatoes and other root vegetables with a fork, but a potato masher makes the job easier.

■ The classic design with round perforations, a sturdy handle and a good rubber grip is best, though newfangled mashers look more stylish, and most perform well.

■ An alternative is a potato ricer, a perforated metal drum with a metal disc attached that forces the potato through (the same principle as a garlic press only larger). Although more expensive than conventional mashers, potato ricers are exceptionally effective and will give you light and fluffy, lump-free mash every time.

Rolling pin

For rolling out pastry, and pounding poultry and meat. Choose a straight wooden pin that is smooth and heavy, without handles.

■ A large empty jam or pickle jar can be used as a substitute.

KITCHEN KIT:PREP TOOLS

Salad spinner

After washing salad leaves, the best way to shake off the water is in a salad spinner. When you turn the handle on the lid, the basket of leaves spins inside the drum so they dry without bruising. Choose a sturdy one (they are all made of plastic) with a well-fitting lid.

Skewers

Use these not only for kebabs and brochettes, but also for piercing food to see if it is cooked.

■ Flat metal skewers are best used for cooking meat and vegetables. They are good conductors of heat, and the food won't swivel when you turn the skewers round.

■ Bamboo skewers look good and can also be used for cooking meat and vegetables, but you need to soak them in water for at least 30 minutes before use or they will char.

Zester

A nifty cutting tool with a row of tiny holes, for removing the zest (the outer coloured part of the rind) from citrus fruit in long, thin strips. A canelle knife does the same job, but its V-shaped blade removes the zest in one wide strip. See also page 51.

KNIFE BOX

Knives are a major investment, so choose carefully and build up your collection according to your needs. Good-quality knives will last for years if you look after them properly. Keep them on a magnetic strip or in a block, and wash them by hand rather than in the dishwasher. Using a steel is the professional choice for sharpening, but it isn't the easiest of techniques, so you may prefer to use a sharpener. Good makes of knives generally have a sharpener in their range.

Apart from a serrated bread knife and a carving knife for roasts, a good basic 'starter set' of three knives will be adequate for most jobs.

■ *A large chef's knife with an 18–20 cm (7–8 in) blade is a good all-rounder for chopping and slicing, and it can also double as a carving knife.*

■ *For peeling fruits and vegetables a small paring knife with a 7.5–10 cm (3–4 in) blade is best.*

■ *A small serrated knife is useful for all sorts of jobs, like cutting squidgy tomatoes and slicing cheese.*

Kitchen Cupboard

KITCHEN CUPBOARD

AS YOU BUILD UP THE CONTENTS OF YOUR KITCHEN CUPBOARD IT WILL BECOME A SOURCE OF TASTY QUICK SUPPERS, EXCITING FLAVOUR BOOSTERS, RELIABLE STAPLES AND HEALTHY SNACKS. BUY IN BULK ONLY IF YOU HAVE ROOM AND KNOW YOU WILL USE THE ITEM. BUYING IN SMALLER AMOUNTS WILL ENSURE THAT NOTHING WILL BE WASTED. KEEP SMALLER, MORE FREQUENTLY USED ITEMS AT THE FRONT OF THE CUPBOARD SO YOU DON'T FORGET WHAT YOU HAVE IN THERE.

Anchovy

Slim little fillets of fish which can be chopped, mashed or left whole to add a sophisticated burst of flavour to your food. They will keep for ages in your kitchen cupboard.

CHOOSE Available packed in oil in cans or jars, or packed in salt which gives a great flavour. Anchovies in jars are very tightly packed – use a bit of gentle persuasion to lure them out carefully so they don't get broken. The most foolproof way is to tip them straight into a sieve, then, if you want to wash the salt off, you can rinse them straight under the tap.

COOK Anchovies don't need cooking – they are ready to eat straight from the jar or can. You might need to use only a couple of anchovies to give the salty bite you require, so after opening tip the rest into a plastic container. They will keep for up to a week in the fridge.

USE FOR

- Jazzing up a take-away pizza.
- Snipping a few with scissors and scattering over a salad (especially one with crisp green leaves and Parmesan cheese, such as Caesar), or stirring into a pasta sauce (they break down and flavour the sauce as they cook).
- Mash one or two with some butter and let it melt over grilled or pan-fried lamb or fish.
- Creating a no-cook starter – arrange in a casual cluster on a platter, drizzle with oil, scatter with chopped parsley and surround with grilled vegetables and olives from the deli.

Beans

Collectively known as 'pulses', beans are a great and cheap way to bump up your protein, especially if you are a vegetarian. There are many types with both subtle and striking differences in looks, texture and taste, but basically they all add a certain 'meaty' texture to a dish. Dried beans will keep for up to a year in an airtight container, although once they get too hard they won't cook as well.

CHOOSE AND USE Canned beans are easy and convenient, while dried ones give you more choice and tend to have more taste and texture. It really depends how organized you are, as dried need soaking before they can be cooked. As there are so many types to choose from, it's good to experiment to find your favourites.

Butter bean: This flat, creamy-coloured bean is softer in texture than most, so purées easily, but can break down if overcooked.

■ Purée in soups, or add to stews and salads.

Borlotti: Recognizable by their attractive, pinky-red freckles.

■ Mix with rice and pasta or use in stews and soups.

Cannellini: Pale cream in colour, oval in shape.

■ Use in similar ways to haricot.

Chick pea: A little, knobbly, round bean with a chunky texture; looks a bit like a skinned hazelnut.

■ Adds a sturdy crunch to salads, or toss with oil, lemon juice, parsley and finely chopped garlic as a simple side salad. Blend to a purée for hummus or as a great alternative to mashed potato

KITCHEN CUPBOARD STARTER KIT

Ten top ingredients you'll find it hard to do without:

■ Bouillon
■ Flour
■ Mustard
■ Olive oil
■ Pasta
■ Rice
■ Soy sauce
■ Sugar or honey
■ Tomatoes (canned)
■ Vinegar

by mixing with a little oil and garlic to serve with fish or chicken. Chick peas are used a lot in Moroccan dishes and are a great meat substitute in Indian vegetarian curries.

Flageolet: Looks like a slimmed-down, pale green version of the red kidney bean. Keeps its shape well while cooking.

■ A pretty addition to salads (canned are handy for this), flageolets are also good with lamb and in stews. They can be used instead of haricot beans.

Haricot: In its naked form this is a white bean, and is the one used for canned baked beans.

■ Good in slow-cooked stews, soups and casseroles such as cassoulet or Boston baked beans, as it is quite sturdy and keeps its shape well.

Red kidney bean: The brightest-coloured bean, kidney-shaped.

■ Integral to chilli con carne, kidney beans are used a lot in Mexican cook-ing where they are mashed to a paste for refried beans. They also add a splash of colour and texture to salads, especially when combined with rice, sweetcorn or paler-coloured beans.

COOK

Canned: Drain and rinse them first. For salads they are then ready to eat, or heat them up in the dish you are cooking so they take on the flavour.

Dried: Soak the beans first in plenty of cold water for at least 5 hours, or overnight if that's more convenient. Alternatively use the quick-soak method (see opposite). Beans expand a lot: make sure the bowl is big enough so they have room to grow by at least double. Before cooking, it's worth noting that there are a couple of things that can toughen the skins of dried beans – prolonged boiling, or adding too much salt early on (that includes salty ingredients like soy sauce and bouillon as well as any acidic ingredients such as tomatoes, lemon juice, vinegar). To cook, drain and rinse the soaked beans, then tip them into a large pan. Cover with about 5 cm (2 in) of cold water, bring to the boil, scoop off any foam, then boil hard for 10 minutes. Skim off any more foam and add a pinch of salt. Half cover with the pan lid, turn the heat down and simmer gently for the suggested time, skimming and adding more water if needed. Cooking times for dried beans vary, so check the packet instructions – it's usually about 1–1½ hours. Drain when done.

Bouillon

This is stock in an easily accessible, concentrated form that has a long shelf life.

beans–bovril

CHOOSE Comes in either powder form, paste or as a compact cube. Bouillon powder has a subtle herby taste. The rule of thumb is always to get the best quality you can, such as organic, as a good stock should be something you can drink on its own if it's going to do its job properly.

COOK Dissolve in the required amount of boiling water, then use as your recipe suggests.

USE FOR
■ Giving an instant flavour base for soups, risottos, stews, gravies.
■ Sprinkling or crumbling into mince dishes like bolognese or shepherd's pie to bump up the taste.

Bovril

Originally made from beef extract, but the recipe has been changed and is now made with yeast extract and flavourings, so is fine for vegetarians.

USE FOR
■ Stirring a spoonful into robust soups, stews and gravies and bolognese sauce to give a rich, meaty taste.

USE INSTEAD Marmite or Vegemite.

KITCHEN CUPBOARD VEGGIE SNACK
Serves 2–3; ready in 10 minutes

For a quick hummus, tip a rinsed and drained 410 g (14 oz) can chick peas into a food processor or blender, add ½ tsp crushed garlic (from a jar or fresh), a few pinches of ground cumin, 2–3 tsp lemon juice (fresh or bottled), 2 tbsp olive oil and whizz all together. Whizz in enough water (a few tbsp) to make it as soft as you like it, and season with salt. Serve with a drizzle of oil and a sprinkling of ground cumin or paprika, pita bread and raw vegetables for dipping into the hummus.

■ Optional extras: Add 1 tbsp tahini (or to taste), or a handful of finely chopped parsley.

QUICK-SOAK BEANS
If short of time when soaking dried beans you can speed things up by tipping them into a large bowl, pouring in boiling water to cover by 5 cm (2 in), then covering and leaving until they have doubled in size, about 1½ hours. Drain and rinse, then continue to cook as opposite.

Caper

If you like the sharp taste of things pickled in vinegar, these little green flower buds are a culinary treasure.

CHOOSE You can buy really petite capers called *nonpareille* that are about the size of a peppercorn. More commonly available are the slightly larger ones. You'll find capers come in jars, either pickled in vinegar or snugly preserved in salt. The salted ones need rinsing first. If they are still too salty for your taste, rinse again and soak in water for a bit. For real caper flamboyance, try caperberries. They are the seed pods of the caper plant and are much bigger and bolder than the bud. They are very handsome, have an elegant stem, and are milder and slightly sweeter in taste.

USE FOR

■ Scattering over meat and fish dishes – they go well with tuna and anchovy. They also look pretty, so can double up as a garnish as well as a flavour hit.
■ Adding to sauces or vegetables to give a lively tang.
■ Italian and Spanish dishes, such as *spaghetti puttanesca*, made with capers, anchovies, tomatoes and olives.

USE INSTEAD Gherkins.

Chick pea

see BEANS, *page 75.*

Chilli (dried)

see SPICES, *page 169.*

Chocolate

Made from cocoa beans found in the big pods that hang from the cacao tree. The beans are roasted, then ground to extract the chocolate liquor. This liquor contains cocoa butter, and the more of this a chocolate has, the more expensive and better it will be.

CHOOSE Check out the wrapping to find the information you need. Cooking chocolate shouldn't have too much sugar added, as it is the taste you are after, not sweetness. But the most important thing to look for is the amount of cocoa solids. You could say the more, the merrier, as cocoa solids are what give the chocolate its delicious flavour and richness, but if you go very high, over 70%, you may find the taste too bitter; 50% is middle of the road, whereas 60–70% is a good-quality all-rounder. Taste it and see which percentage suits you – if you like the way it tastes out of its wrapper, you'll like the way it tastes

caper–chocolate

when cooked. Chocolate keeps well as long as it's dry, so a cool cupboard is better than the fridge. Moisture can give it a white, frosty-looking film on its surface. If the chocolate feels gritty when you taste it, it's past its best.

Dark: Great for cooking. It will give the most chocolaty flavour, as it has more cocoa solids and less sugar.

Milk: Sweeter than dark, with less cocoa solids (about 30–40%) and some milk, so is lighter both in flavour and colour. It isn't so good to cook with as it doesn't withstand high temperatures as well as dark.

White: Not technically chocolate at all as it has no cocoa solids, but is made up of cocoa butter, milk solids, vanilla and a lot of sugar, so it tastes less chocolaty than dark chocolate. A good-quality white chocolate has lots of cocoa butter and a good vanilla taste. White is trickier to melt as it can easily seize (see FIX IT, right).

TO MELT

On the cooker: Pour 2.5–5 cm (1–2 in) water into a small pan. Rest a heatproof bowl over the pan, one that will sit above the water rather than in it. (Chocolate doesn't get along well with water if it comes in direct contact.) Break the chocolate into pieces and put into the bowl, turn the heat to

FIX IT: CHOCOLATE

Overheating or letting any moisture get into the chocolate can cause it to 'seize' – which means it tightens and thickens. To rescue it, try stirring in a teaspoon or two of vegetable cooking oil – if that works the chocolate can be used in a sauce. If it's too far gone or if it gets really overheated and burns, the best thing is to throw it away and start again.

medium so the water just simmers gently and let it sit and melt in the warmth from the water. When the chocolate feels soft, give it a stir and take off the heat when melted. **In the microwave:** Break the chocolate into a non-metallic bowl. Microwave, uncovered, in spurts of 30 seconds on defrost, stirring between each – timing depends on how much chocolate you are melting. Chocolate melted in the microwave keeps its shape, so you need to stir to check if it's done or not.

USE FOR (apart from in desserts and baking)

- Dropping a cube or two into Mexican meat recipes such as chillies and stews. You don't actually taste the chocolate, but it adds an exotic richness.
- A mug of hot real chocolate for a cosy bedtime drink: melt grated dark chocolate, then whisk in hot milk and sugar to taste.
- Making a quick fondue for dipping fruit in – melt a 200 g (7 oz) bar of dark or milk chocolate, take off the heat and stir in about 6 tbsp milk.

Chutney

A spicy Indian relish with a sweet-savoury kick, its name comes from the Indian word *chatni*. Because it is made with a base of sugar and vinegar, both of which are preservatives, chutney has a long shelf life, lasting up to 2 years in the cupboard, or, once opened, several months in the fridge. Chutney comes in many flavours, such as mango, apple or tomato.

USE FOR

It's handy to have a jar to accompany your Indian take-away or make a cheese snack, but it has other uses.

- An instant creamy dressing for a cold chicken salad: stir a little tropical fruit chutney into mayonnaise with a dash of curry powder, then thin with milk until it's the thickness you like.
- Adding a spoonful to flavour a sauce for pan-fried chicken and pork: deglaze the pan with some stock or water (or wine if you have a bottle open), then stir in some double cream and a spoonful of chutney. Or omit the cream and flavour with tomato chutney for fish, chops and steaks.

Coconut milk/ cream/creamed

Indispensible for Thai or Indian food. Coconut milk is not the thin liquid found in a fresh coconut, but the liquid pressed from the snowy white coconut flesh. By soaking grated coconut flesh

chocolate–coconut

in boiling water, then squeezing out the liquid, a thick milk is produced from the first squeezing, a thinner one from the second, and the cream is what rises to the top of the milk when it is cold. So having it on tap in a can saves an awful lot of work.

CHOOSE Coconut milk is available in cans, thicker cream in small cartons, and solid creamed coconut in blocks. There is also a low-fat version of the milk. The cream keeps for up to a year and milk for 2 years. When open, both will keep in the fridge for up to 1–2 days. If you don't use a whole block of creamed coconut in one go, wrap it well so it won't dry out and keep in an airtight container in the fridge.

COOK Coconut milk and cream are ready to use straight from their containers. Give milk a good stir before using. Grate, chop, crumble or dilute the block of creamed coconut first, depending on how it is to be used.

USE FOR
- As well as for enriching and flavouring Indian and Thai curries and soups (lovely with fish), it can be used instead of milk and cream for homemade ice cream.
- Giving custard a change of flavour by using coconut milk instead of milk.

KITCHEN CUPBOARD THAI SUPPER

The only fresh thing you need to buy is chicken; everything else can come from your kitchen cupboard.

Serves 2 generously; ready in 20–25 minutes

Heat 1 tbsp vegetable oil in a wok or large pan. Drop in 1 rounded tbsp Thai chilli paste (red or green), 3 freeze-dried lime leaves and a pinch of crushed dried chillies and fry for 1 minute. Tip in a 400 ml (14 fl oz) can coconut milk, ⅓ can water (measured in the coconut milk can), 1 tbsp Thai fish sauce and 1 tsp sugar and bring to a simmer. Add 300–375 g (10–12 oz) skinless, boneless chicken breasts (cut into bite-size chunks) and a 225 g (8 oz) can bamboo shoots, drained. Simmer for 10 minutes until the chicken is cooked. Serve with Thai rice or noodles.

- *Optional extras: Add a handful of frozen peas just before the chicken is cooked, or some torn coriander at the end.*

- Pouring coconut cream over a tropical fruit salad.
- Mixing coconut milk, yogurt and chopped fresh mango to make a mango smoothie.

USE INSTEAD Double cream will give you the creaminess, but not the unique flavour.

Cornflour

This is a fine, white, powdery starch made from maize. Unlike flour made from wheat it contains no gluten (protein). Rub it between your fingers and see how silky and fine it feels – this is the smooth texture it will give to your cooking, and it is less likely to create lumps as flour can when used to thicken certain sauces.

COOK Cornflour needs to be mixed to a paste with a liquid first. When using it to thicken a sauce, gravy or stew that is too runny, mix 1 tsp cornflour with 1 tsp water, stir it in to the sauce gradually, off the heat, then put it back on the heat and keep stirring until the sauce thickens. Keep doing this until you get the thickness you want. Once the sauce has thickened take it off the heat quite quickly – if you cook cornflour for too long it can break down and go thin again.

USE FOR
- Thickening sauces, both sweet and savoury, such as custards and gravies; also stir-fries, soups and stews.
- Baking: when mixed with flour it gives an extra-light texture to biscuits such as shortbread.
- Whisking into a meringue mixture for a gooey inside: use ½ tsp cornflour to each egg white.

USE INSTEAD Plain flour, but cornflour blends in more easily and turns clearer when cooked, so is better for sweet sauces, such as the one used as a base for lemon meringue pie. For a crystal-clear sauce, use arrowroot.

Cornmeal
see POLENTA, *page 108*

Couscous

This tiny yellow grain is actually a type of pasta usually made from semolina and used in Moroccan and North African dishes. It becomes miraculously light and fluffy after a quick soak and, since it has hardly any flavour of its own, loves being mixed with other tasty ingredients.

CHOOSE Either the plain couscous you can add your own flavourings to,

coconut–curry

or the more expensive packets of pre-flavoured couscous.

COOK Couscous traditionally had to be slowly steamed; now it is available precooked and, after soaking, is ready to eat in minutes. Tip the couscous into a large bowl and pour over boiling water or stock (see right for the amounts). Stir, cover with cling film and leave for 5 minutes. Once all the liquid is absorbed, use a fork to break and lighten up the couscous. Enrich and moisten with a drizzle of olive oil or a knob of butter if you want.

USE FOR
■ Bulking out salads.
■ Tossing with different flavourings such as toasted pine nuts, raisins, lemon zest, olives and parsley and serving with lamb, chicken or fish.
■ A base for stuffing instead of rice or bread.
■ An accompaniment in place of rice, pasta or mashed potatoes.

USE INSTEAD Rice or a small shaped pasta.

Curry paste

When you find a good one you are happy with, whether it is based on Indian or Thai spices, these ready

FIX IT: CORNFLOUR
If you end up with a lumpy sauce, give it a vigorous whisk with a wire whisk until you've got it back to a smooth texture. If that doesn't work, push the sauce through a fine sieve.

KITCHEN CUPBOARD
MOROCCAN SALAD
Serves 4; ready in 10 minutes

Soak 250 g (9 oz) couscous (see left). Tip in a rinsed and drained 410 g (14 oz) can chick peas, a couple of handfuls each of toasted whole almonds, raisins and chopped apricots, and a handful of pistachio nuts (or toasted pine nuts). Mix 2 rounded tsp harissa (see page 89) with 4–5 tbsp olive oil, a pinch of dried mint and seasoning to taste and toss everything together. Pile into bowls and drizzle with extra olive oil. Serve as is, or with barbecued or roast chicken breasts.

HOW MUCH COUSCOUS?
FOR 2: 125 g (4 oz) couscous to 150 ml (¼ pint) liquid
FOR 4: 250 g (9 oz) couscous to 300 ml (½ pint) liquid
FOR 6: 375 g (12 oz) couscous to 500 ml (16 fl oz) liquid

mixed pastes really cut corners when it comes to adding authentic flavour to a speedily made curry. They save you having to stock up on lots of different herbs and spices too.

CHOOSE There are so many to choose from that experimentation is the best way to find ones that suit your taste buds.

Indian:

On the heat scale, these include:
- MILD: biriyani, jalfrezi, korma, tikka masala.
- MEDIUM: balti, rogan josh, dhansak.
- HOT: madras, vindaloo.

Thai: Green and red curry paste – both are a blend of chillies, herbs and spices such as coriander, lemon grass, lime leaves, garlic, galangal, cumin and coriander, the difference being that green is made with a pounded base of green chillies, red with red chillies. Use both interchangeably.

COOK AND USE Curry pastes are usually fried off first when making curries to bring out all their intricate flavours. When not cooking with them (if adding a spoonful to flavour a dressing or mayonnaise, for example) you still need to heat Indian curry pastes through briefly rather than using them straight from the jar.

Dried fruit

As a group these are a healthy alternative to many other snacks since they contain no fat or cholesterol and are very low in sodium (salt) – and a handful can be counted as one of the 'five a day fruit and veg' (see page 326). If well wrapped, they will keep for up to a year.

CHOOSE Go for the plumpest-looking ones that have a good, even colour.

Apricot: the plump and moist 'ready-to-eat' soft dried apricots can be used straight away. They go well with chicken, beef and lamb dishes.

Cherries and berries: A summery mix of tart and sweet blueberries, cranberries, cherries and raisins. Or buy individually. Check on the packaging that they aren't coated in sugar.

Currant: Not a dried currant at all, but a particularly tiny type of grape.

Date: Medjool dates are a prize variety – deliciously sweet, sticky and succulent. Hand them round at the end of a meal with cups of espresso.

Fig: Dried figs are a lot sweeter than fresh. Some get quite flattened after drying, so if you are after plumpness and shapeliness look for the ready-to-eat soft ones.

curry–dried fruit

Prune: A dried plum, containing fibre, iron and potassium. *Mi-cuit* prunes are semi-dried, so have a lovely soft, creamy texture, Agen prunes are also very succulent.

Raisin: This is a dried, usually seedless grape.

Sultana: These are golden or dark in colour, depending on the variety of grape they are dried from.

Tropical fruits: Often available in bags of mixed fruits such as mango, papaya, pineapple and melon. Mango is a good source of vitamin E and carotene.

COOK All dried fruits can be used straight away, but to add flavour and extra juiciness to recipes like fruit cakes and tea breads, you can plump the fruit up first by soaking in tea, wine, fruit juice, rum or brandy, depending on the recipe.

USE FOR

- Nibbling on.
- Mixing into baking recipes.
- Adding a natural sweetness to savoury stews, or salads.
- Apricots, dates, figs and prunes are good with Moroccan spicings and help bulk out and thicken stews.
- A quick starter (see right).
- Chopping prunes into couscous with toasted pine nuts and mint.

DRIED FRUIT STARTER
Figs and prosciutto make good partners. Slit ready-to-eat dried figs and stuff with a thin slice of goat's cheese, wrap the prosciutto around and serve on a bed of salad leaves drizzled with a herb dressing.

- Soaking in rum to liven up a winter fruit salad. Figs also go well in fruit compôtes.
- Mixing into stuffings or rice salads – cranberries, apricots and raisins are especially good mixed with pine nuts.
- Slit Medjool dates and stuff with a soft cream cheese for a party snack.

USE INSTEAD If you can't find the fruit you are looking for, follow this list of substitutes:
APRICOT: peach
CRANBERRY: raisin, cherry
CURRANT: snipped raisin
DATE: fig or raisin
FIG: prune, apricot, date or raisin
MANGO: papaya

Fish sauce

Used throughout South-East Asia as we might use salt, particularly in Thailand (where it is known as *nam pla*) and Vietnam (where it is known as *nuoc cham*). It is made from salted, fermented dried fish (usually shrimp or anchovy). Once you have acquired a taste for it, you'll want to spoon it into all sorts of things.

CHOOSE A little goes a long way, so as you need only a splash to have an effect, the small bottles are very handy. The lighter-coloured sauce usually indicates a finer, more refreshing, salty flavour than the darker one. If you notice the colour dramatically darkening once the bottle has been opened it means it's getting a bit old, so best to discard.

USE FOR
- Capitalize on its very fishy, salty taste to perk up stir-fries, noodle dishes and salad dressings.
- A dipping sauce with a few chopped chillies scattered in and a little sugar to give a sweet/sour taste – goes with fish cakes or cold chicken or beef.
- Leave the bottle on the table and use sparingly as a seasoning.

USE INSTEAD No substitute.

Flour

Wheat flours are made from two types of wheat, 'hard' and 'soft'. Hard wheat contains a lot of gluten (a mixture of proteins, see page 28) which becomes elastic, so the flour produced from this makes good bread and pasta, as it creates a dough that will stretch and rise. Flour from soft wheat has less gluten, so is better for making cakes, biscuits and sauces. The three basic types of flour are brown, white and wholemeal (see Basic Flour Types, opposite). White flour keeps for up to 9 months,

dried fruit–flour

wholemeal or brown for about 3 months. Don't mix old flour with new – it will just go off more quickly.

CHOOSE AND USE (see also Basic Flour Types, right). Flour shouldn't need sifting before use.

Plain: A mix of hard and soft flours with no raising agent added. Has only a small amount of gluten, so no good for breadmaking.
- Use in pastry, sauces and gravies, biscuits, or as a coating.

Self-raising: Plain flour with a raising agent added.
- Use in cakes, scones, teabreads, sponge puddings.
USE INSTEAD Plain flour with baking powder added – use 2 tsp baking powder to 225 g (8 oz) flour.

Spelt: Made from a very nutritious wheat variety that has more protein, fat and fibre than wheat. Nothing else is added to make spelt flour.
- Good for pizza crusts, cakes and bread.

Strong: Available in white, brown and wholemeal, this flour is made from hard wheat. Wholemeal used on its own gives quite a heavy texure, but it can be easily lightened by mixing it half and half with strong white flour.
- Suitable for bread (use in bread-making machines), Yorkshire pud-dings, pizza dough, puff pastry.

BASIC FLOUR TYPES

BROWN: Some of the bran and wheatgerm have been removed, about 85% of the original grain is left. It is a bit lighter than whole-meal flour.
WHITE: About 75% of the wheat-germ is left.
WHOLEMEAL: 100% of the wheat grain is used to make this flour – nothing is added, nothing taken away.

LABELS ON FLOUR: WHAT THEY MEAN

GRANARY: A malted wheat grain flour with wheat grains added.
ORGANIC: Flour that has been milled by registered growers and millers, from grain grown to organic standards.
STONEGROUND: Wholemeal flour that has been traditionally ground between two stones.
WHEATGERM: White or brown flour, with about 10% wheatgerm added.

GLUTEN-FREE

For a gluten-free flour, use buckwheat, gram or rice flour.

'00' and '0': Italian flour. '00' is most common, '0' is more likely to be found in an Italian deli. '00' is milled finer than '0' and has less bran in it.
■ Use for pasta, pastry, Italian cakes, pizza dough and other breads.

Ginger (in syrup)

Tender round nuggets of fresh root ginger that have been simmered in syrup. The syrup takes on the gingery flavour, the ginger takes on the sweetness from the syrup, so everything in the jar can be used. Lasts for ages.

USE FOR

Ginger: Chopping into biscuit and cake mixes, or chopping and scattering over cake icings as a flavourful decoration (goes well with lemon, orange and chocolate).

Syrup: Soaking a sponge with to flavour and moisten, then serving with fresh fruit and cream. Stir a spoonful or two into a crushed biscuit base for creamy desserts like cheesecake.

Both: Spooning over ice cream and adding to fresh fruit salads, especially tropical ones. Cooking with poached rhubarb or pears.

USE INSTEAD Crystallized ginger (no syrup, though).

Ginger (pickled)

A Japanese accompaniment of wafer-thin slivers of fresh root ginger which have been pickled in vinegar, sugar and salt.

CHOOSE Available in a delicate shade of pink (dyed with food colouring) or in a natural pale golden colour.

USE FOR

■ Accompanying sushi or anything else you care to try it with.
■ Serving with grilled or pan-fried fish (especially salmon and tuna) or chicken.
■ Chopping into salads with bean sprouts and cold beef or cooked prawns.
■ Tossing into noodle stir-fries, or piling on top as a garnish.
■ Scattering between slices of smoked salmon on a bed of rocket as a starter.

Golden syrup

It's the cheapest syrup to buy and keeps for ages – up to a year.

COOK The best thing about golden syrup is that it doesn't go grainy (crystallize) when heated. The hardest thing is to measure it. Because it is so sticky, the easiest way is to brush your measuring spoon with a little oil first and the syrup will just glide off.

USE FOR

- Making cakes and biscuits – it helps make flapjacks and gingerbread sticky.
- Pouring over waffles, pancakes or porridge.
- Giving a shiny gloss to a simple homemade chocolate sauce by stirring in a spoonful as the chocolate melts.

USE INSTEAD Maple syrup, though it's more expensive, thinner and has a more distinctive flavour.

Harissa

A fiery red paste with a flavour to match. Its hot base is due to chillies which have been pounded to a paste, then enlivened even further with ingredients such as coriander, caraway, cayenne, garlic, cumin and salt, plus beetroot and carrot. It is spicy, fragrant and hot – if you have a jar of this, your food will never taste dull again. It crops up a lot in North African, Moroccan, and Tunisian recipes.

CHOOSE Comes in jars, cans and in tubes as a paste (you might also find it as a powder which just needs oil and garlic adding). Once opened, it will keep in the fridge for 5–6 weeks.

USE FOR There's no end to the possibilities, but don't go mad with it

RICH SHORTCRUST PASTRY

Makes about 400 g (14 oz, enough to line a 23–25 cm (9–10 in) flan tin; takes 10–15 minutes

BY HAND

Tip 200 g (7 oz) plain flour into a large bowl and stir in 1 tsp salt. Rub in 100 g (3½ oz) cold, diced butter (see page 40), until the mixture is evenly coloured and resembles fine breadcrumbs. Lightly beat 1 medium-sized egg, make a well in the centre of the flour mixture and pour in the egg. Add about 2 tsp water, 1 tsp at a time, as necessary, mixing with a round-bladed knife until the dough begins to hold together. Gather the dough into a smooth ball with your hands. Do not overwork or you will toughen it, and use according to your recipe.

IN THE FOOD PROCESSOR

Put the flour, salt, butter, egg and 1 tsp of water into the processor. Process just until the mixture comes together, adding a little more water if necessary. Gather into a smooth ball as above.

KITCHEN CUPBOARD

unless you know how hot you like it.
■ Stirring a teaspoonful into a
tomato-based pasta sauce, or livening
up a soup, stir-fry or couscous.
■ Diluting with olive oil and drizzling
over summer veg, new potatoes,
chicken or fish before roasting.
■ Spreading neat on to chicken or fish
before barbecuing or roasting, or
adding to a marinade before cooking.
■ Putting a small dollop on the side of
your plate as an ultra-spicy version of
tomato ketchup.
■ Brightening up a dip – just swirl a
little into mayonnaise, crème fraîche,
yogurt or soured cream and serve with
potato wedges or raw veggies.

USE INSTEAD Chilli paste, though
flavourings and spices vary.

Herbs
see pages 127–161

Hoisin sauce
Some find this reddish-brown sauce
rather overpowering, while others
couldn't eat Peking duck without it.
Made from soya beans, spices, vinegar, sugar and garlic, it can't be beat-
en if you want to add an authentic
sweet and spicy Chinese flavour.

CHOOSE Available in bottles, it is
cheaper to buy from Chinese supermarkets. Keep in the fridge once open.

USE FOR
■ A dipping sauce straight from the
bottle with Chinese food, in particular
Peking duck and spring rolls.
■ Spooning into marinades, stir-fries,
vegetable dishes (especially good with
broccoli).
■ The perfect oriental barbecue sauce.

Honey
Honey is a natural sweetener and
when used in cooking can give a
unique flavour to both sweet and
savoury dishes.

CHOOSE You can buy it pourable
and runny, so thick you have scrape it
out the jar, or as a honeycomb which
you have to work at a bit to retrieve
the delicious sweet liquid. There are
also many different flavours. Taste
and colour are determined by which
flowers the bees have visited when
collecting the nectar to make it with.
If the honey is pale in colour, the
chances are that it will be more
delicate in flavour, like acacia honey.
For a more robust taste, go for a
darker honey such as Greek or
Scottish heather. Other flavours to

try include eucalyptus from Australia and orange blossom from Spain and Mexico.

USE FOR

- Drizzling over a bowl of thick yogurt for a super-quick dessert (the Greek way), or over scoops of ice cream.
- Mixing into marinades.
- Adding sweetness and flavour to salad dressings, desserts and bakes.
- Spooning into Moroccan savoury dishes, especially tagines.
- Squirting into your favourite fruit smoothie.
- A quick lunch or starter – toast slices of French bread, top with slices of goat's cheese and a drizzle of honey. Grill until melting and caramelized and serve on dressed salad leaves.

USE INSTEAD Sugar, depending on the recipe. Honey is sweeter and also stronger, so, if you are experimenting, try replacing half the amount of sugar with honey.

Kidney bean
see BEAN, *page 76*

FIX IT: HONEY

Clear honey can go cloudy after a while. To restore its clarity, stand the jar in a bowl of very hot water.

Lentils

Like beans, lentils are an excellent vegetarian food and a good substitute for meat as they contain lots of protein and fibre.

CHOOSE You can get green lentils in cans; the rest are mostly sold dried. If you want a lentil that will break down more as it cooks, or to purée, choose red lentils. If you want the lentil to keep its shape and bite, go for the little speckled French Puy lentil – check the packet for the authentic Puy lentil which is grown in the Puy region of France. Lentils keep for a good year, and are less likely to deteriorate after opening if you transfer them to an airtight container.

COOK Unlike beans, lentils don't need soaking before cooking. Simmer red lentils for about 20 minutes; after that they can turn quite mushy. Simmer Puy lentils for about 25 minutes, green ones for about 40–45 minutes.

USE FOR
Green: Adding to soups and stews as they keep their shape quite well; to salads and vegetarian versions of lasagne and moussaka instead of meat.
Puy: Serving as a vegetable in their own right, flavoured with a little onion, carrot and herbs (good with fish). When simmered with red wine they go really well with any meat, especially game. Also good in salads.
Red: Thickening wintery soups and stews; in Indian cooking, especially vegetarian dishes (used to make dhal).

Maple syrup

A classic Canadian sweetener with a distinctive taste, made by collecting sap from the maple tree which is then boiled and reduced down. It is thinner than golden syrup, so pours easily. Keep in the fridge after opening.

CHOOSE The real thing is the most expensive and will say 'pure' maple syrup on the label. 'Flavoured' maple syrup is a cheaper imitation.

USE FOR
■ Pouring over pancakes or waffles.
■ Sweetening North American cake mixtures such as muffins and tray bakes, also pumpkin pie.
■ Adding a lovely flavour and shine when glazing vegetables (good with carrots and squash) and for pork, especially spareribs.
■ Deglazing a pan, particularly when cooking pork. Pour in 1 tbsp each maple syrup and balsamic vinegar with some stock for a sticky, rich gravy.

■ Pouring over American hot cakes and bacon, for breakfast, or over porridge with a handful of blueberries scattered on top.

■ Marinades (see right).

USE INSTEAD Runny honey, though the flavour is quite different.

Marmite
USE FOR

People love it or hate it, but this yeast extract with a meaty taste can intensify the colour and flavour of a stew or shepherd's pie, or be diluted with water and used instead of stock. Add in moderation so the balance is just right. A teaspoonful should do it as too much can kill the dish's flavour.

USE INSTEAD Bovril.

Mayonnaise

CHOOSE Available in a jar or a handy squeezable container. Apart from the classic plain mayonnaise, you can get a variety of flavours, such as mustard, lemon and garlic, as well as a reduced-calorie (light) version. Mayonnaise will keep fresh for a year unopened. Once it's opened you need to put it in the fridge, then use within a couple of months. See also page 467.

KITCHEN CUPBOARD
MAPLE SYRUP
MARINADE FOR CHICKEN
Serves 2; ready in 45 minutes

Mix 2 tbsp maple syrup, 1 tbsp soy sauce and 2 tsp sesame oil, 2 crushed garlic cloves, ½ tsp ground ginger and a generous grinding of black pepper in a shallow baking dish. Add 2 chicken breasts, turn to coat in the marinade and leave for 5–10 minutes. Roast at 190ºC/ 375ºF/Gas Mark 5 (170ºC/340ºF in fan ovens), for about 30 minutes or until the chicken is cooked, basting half way through. Serve with rice and the juices poured over.

KITCHEN CUPBOARD

USE FOR

■ Serving as a sauce on its own with salads or fish (for an instant tartare sauce, chop up and stir in a few capers and gherkins, or add some crushed garlic for the French dip aïoli).

■ A dressing for tossing into boiled new potatoes – flavour with a little horseradish sauce and some snipped chives and thin with milk.

■ Making a dip by stirring in one of your favourite flavourings, such as pesto, mustard or harissa, to serve with raw veg or tortilla chips.

Mirin

Not to be confused with the Chinese ingredient rice wine, mirin is a sweet, spirit-based rice liquid used in Japanese cooking, never for drinking.

USE FOR

■ Bringing a sweet taste to Japanese marinades such as teriyaki. Its high sugar content gives food a lovely shine.

■ Adding to dressings and stir-fries.

USE INSTEAD Sweet sherry is best (though not really the same). If you have only dry sherry, throw in a little sugar for the required sweetness.

Miso soup

A Japanese product made from soya-bean paste.

CHOOSE AND USE Just mix the mustardy-coloured paste sold in sachets with boiling water.

■ Making soup – mix with boiling water, then combine with pre-soaked rice noodles, cubed tofu, shredded spinach, watercress or bok choi, cooked chicken and a splash of soy sauce.

■ Dilute and use instead of stock.

■ As a glaze for spreading over grilled chicken or fish – mix 2 sachets miso with 1 tbsp sugar and mirin.

Molasses syrup

A concentrated, dark, sticky syrup, because of its intense flavour best used in small amounts.

USE FOR

■ Giving colour and flavour to gingerbread, sticky sponge puddings.

■ Making Boston baked beans.

■ Spooning into Christmas cake and pudding mixtures for a dark colour and rich taste.

■ Drizzling over a bowl of porridge.

USE INSTEAD Black treacle – it's cheaper, but not as rich-tasting.

Moroccan lemons

Whole juicy lemons preserved and pickled in salt. They have a zesty, almost sweet-and-sour taste.

CHOOSE Whole lemons are packed snugly into big jars. No need to refrigerate, even after opening, as the salt preserves them for about a year.

USE FOR Use whole, in wedges, diced, sliced or zest only.

- Flavouring Moroccan tagines (good with fish and chicken) and soups, or Mediterranean dishes.
- A salad – chop the zest only into little pieces and scatter over torn strips of roasted red pepper, crumbled feta cheese and a generous drizzle of olive oil.
- Adding to stuffings for fish.
- Stirring into couscous with lots of chopped fresh parsley, mint and spring onions.
- Tucking a whole lemon into the cavity of a chicken ready for roasting so it flavours as it roasts.
- Cutting into wedges and roasting with a mix of Mediterranean vegetables and bay leaves for a refreshing fragrance.
- Serving as part of an antipasto – mix strips of lemon with green olives,

chopped coriander and olive oil.

■ A colourful, zingy salsa – chop and mix with chopped tomatoes and coriander and a drizzle of olive oil and serve with fish.

USE INSTEAD Fresh lemons, but the flavour isn't quite the same.

Mushrooms
(dried)

for FRESH, see pages 292–95
Some look so shrivelled you may be forgiven for thinking they are past their best. But it's the drying that preserves them and really concentrates the flavour. Their meaty texture makes them popular with vegetarians.

CHOOSE Amongst the varieties you will find are ceps, shiitake, porcini (the strongest tasting) and morels. All taste a bit different, but all add a rich and wonderful mushroom flavour to a dish. They are expensive to buy, but you need add only a few pieces to get your money's worth of flavour. If you don't use the whole packet up at once, keep it tightly sealed, or their amazing aroma may take over your kitchen cupboard.

COOK Soaking them for 20–30 minutes in water or stock (use hot if you want to speed things up a bit) or wine will quickly bring them back to life. Their soaking liquid becomes like a concentrated stock, so you can use that too. If it tastes a bit strong, thin it down with water or stock.

USE FOR
■ Livening up scrambled eggs and omelettes (chop and fry in butter first) as well as stuffings (chop a few into the stuffing for the Christmas turkey).
■ Adding to casseroles and stews, especially ones with gutsy flavours made with game or beef.
■ Tucking slices into potato gratins.
■ Stirring them fried into risottos.
■ Tossing with freshly cooked pasta (fry first with olive oil, garlic and some thyme or parsley).
■ Mixing with fresh mushrooms to intensify their flavour (see page 293). Ideal for a fresh mushroom soup.

USE INSTEAD Fresh mushrooms, but the flavour isn't nearly as intense so you will need more.

Mustard

Made by grinding mustard seeds to a paste, the taste and colour varying from strong to mild according to the type of seeds used and the other flavourings added.

moroccan–mustard

COOK Mustard, especially Dijon, can taste bitter if it cooks too long, so best to add towards the end.

CHOOSE AND USE It's useful to have more than one type of mustard in your cupboard as each has something different to offer.

American: This is a brash yellow colour with a sweeter, milder taste than English mustard, so can be used more liberally.

English: The hottest of mustards, buy as a powder or ready-made. Livens up simple English dishes, giving a real bite to ham, roast beef, sausages and anything with cheese. To make up the powder (which is more potent than ready-made), mix with an equal amount of cold water, then let it sit for about 15 minutes so the flavour can develop. Best to mix up small amounts as needed – you don't need much to get the effect, and freshly made tastes so much better.

French: The most famous is Dijon which is blended with white wine and is used in sauces (especially cheese sauces), salad dressings and for serving with steaks. It has a sharp, fresh taste, and is milder than English mustard. There is also Bordeaux (smooth and mild) and Moutarde de Meaux (grainy).

German: Not quite as hot as English mustard, but still very bold in taste.

Try in traditional German style – with sausages.

Wholegrain: The mustard seeds are not completely crushed, so the grains give an interesting look and texture, making it a good mustard for stirring into salad dressings, sauces or creamy mashed potato.

USE INSTEAD Despite their differences in strength of flavour, mustards can be used interchangeably. If you are unsure of the strength of the one you are substituting, the best thing is to add cautiously to begin with and keep tasting.

Noodles

Noodles are the oriental version of pasta. They should last 1–2 years in the cupboard.

CHOOSE AND COOK Chinese and Japanese noodles can be made from several different types of flour – rice, buckwheat or wheat – and can also be found in a variety of sizes. All that the noodles need before using is a quick soak in boiling water. If they are going to be tossed into a salad, tip them into a colander after soaking and then run them under the cold tap. This will cool them and stop them from sticking together.

Bean thread noodles: Also called cellophane noodles, these are very thin and almost see-through, so all they need is a quick soak before using. Put in a large pan, cover with boiling water and leave for 3 minutes. Add to things like soups and stir-fries rather than serving as an accompaniment.

Chinese egg noodles: Made from wheat flour and eggs, they come in various widths – fine, medium and broad. Cook the fine in boiling water for 3 minutes, medium for 4 minutes and broad for 7 minutes.

Rice noodles: Soak in boiling water for 4 minutes before using.

Rice vermicelli: A very fine delicate noodle, soak in boiling water for 4 minutes before using.

Soba noodles: Also Japanese, they look a bit like wholewheat spaghetti and are made from buckwheat and whole wheat flours. Boil them for 5–7 minutes.

Stir-fry rice noodles: A thin noodle, often packaged in separate bundles. Soak in boiling water for 4 minutes, then drain.

Udon noodles: Fat, white Japanese noodles. Those sold fresh in vacuum packs are ready in 1 minute.

USE ALL FOR

■ Adding to soups, stir-fries and salads with Asian flavours.

■ As an accompaniment instead of rice, tossed with a little sesame oil.

USE INSTEAD Pasta noodles of a similar size.

Nuts

Nuts are bursting with protein and, though high in calories, give you lots of energy. Once opened, they are best kept in the fridge or freezer. They will go off more quickly if left in the cupboard because of all the fat that they contain.

CHOOSE Buy them in well-sealed containers so they stay fresh for the longest possible time. Nuts in their shells are fun to have around, but go stale more quickly.

COOK To really bring out the flavour of nuts, toast them first. Tip into a heavy pan (no need to add oil as nuts give off their own when heated, so they won't stick). Keep the pan moving the whole time so the nuts colour evenly without burning. To keep their crunchy texture in savoury dishes, scatter them on to whatever you are making at the end of cooking, particularly if there is a sauce involved, or they will go a bit soft.

KITCHEN CUPBOARD
NOODLE SOUP
Serves 3–4; ready in 10 minutes

Soak 125 g (4 oz) stir-fry, rice or medium egg noodles in boiling water for 4 minutes. Break up with a fork, then drain and tip into a saucepan. Pour in about 1 litre (1¾ pints) hot chicken or vegetable stock, a 330 g (11 oz) can sweetcorn, drained, a 200 g (7 oz) can crabmeat, drained and flaked, a few splashes of soy sauce and a few pieces of pickled ginger and warm through. Serve sprinkled with a little sesame oil.

■ Optional extras: Add sliced bok choi or spinach leaves when warming through, and roughly torn coriander or parsley at the end.

USE FOR

- Snacking on while you prepare supper (any type).
- Tossing into a pan of stir-fried veg (cashew and almond).
- Giving a crunch to pasta dishes (pine nut, walnut and almond).
- Adding extra protein to vegetarian dishes (any type).
- Scattering over salads and cooked vegetables (almond, pine nut, walnut, hazelnut).
- Slicing and sprinkling over fruit desserts (pistachio, hazelnut, pecan, almond).
- Baking – for special-occasion biscuits and cakes try the luxurious Australian macadamia nut (creamy flavour, crunchy texture) or pistachio (for its lovely green colour).

Oats

Oats are the most nutritious of grains, rich in soluble fibre, vitamins and minerals, so starting the day with a bowl of porridge helps keep your energy levels up.

CHOOSE Rolled porridge oats are ultra-quick to cook, so you can have a bowlful of porridge ready in approximately 10 minutes. Bigger oat flakes are called 'jumbo' oats, and oats that have been ground are called oatmeal,

which is available in varying degrees of coarseness.

USE FOR

- Adding to crumble toppings.
- Stirring into cakes and biscuit mixtures for added texture.
- Mixing into stuffings.
- A crunchy coating for fish.

Oil

A kitchen cupboard is the perfect place to store oil, especially if it's cool, as a bottle of oil deteriorates if it gets too hot sitting on the kitchen counter, or stands bathing in bright sunlight. Once opened, it should be used as soon as possible.

CHOOSE AND USE

Argan oil: A nutritious oil (high in vitamin E), made from nuts of the Moroccan argan tree. It has a nutty flavour, and is milder than other nut oils such as walnut. Not for cooking.

- Drizzle over salads or mix with lemon juice to make a dressing.
- Flavour Moroccan tagines and vegetable soups such as pumpkin at the end of cooking, or drizzle over couscous to moisten and enrich.
- Make a spread for toast by mixing the oil with crushed almonds and honey – a bit like peanut butter.

nuts–oil

Avocado oil: This is an extra virgin oil extracted from avocados and has a smooth, rich taste and colour.
- Use as a dipping oil with crusty bread, or for marinades.
- Great for stir-frying as it can be used at high temperatures.
- Adds a lovely green splash of colour to your plate when drizzled over salads, grilled fish and chicken.

Corn oil: Sometimes called maize oil, it is a good all-round cooking oil.
- Especially good for deep-frying.
USE INSTEAD Groundnut oil.

Flavoured oils: Oils that have been infused with flavourings such as chilli, basil, garlic and lemon. Truffle oil is a more expensive treat, and a few drops will elevate risottos, pastas dishes, potato salad or mashed potatoes.
- As a lively addition to salad dressings and marinades. Lemon oil is good marinated with cubes of feta cheese, rosemary and crushed dried chillies.
- For drizzling over pasta and risottos, as well as simply cooked grilled or barbecued meats, fish (prawns and lemon or chilli oil make great partners) and steamed or grilled vegetables – try lemon oil with asparagus, basil oil with peppers.
- Stir garlic oil and some snipped chives into crushed new potatoes.

THE FOUR MOST USEFUL NUTS
- *ALMOND*
- *CASHEW*
- *PECAN (and/or walnut)*
- *PINE (not technically a nut, but used like one, so fine to use if you have a nut allergy) – toast for best flavour.*

COOKING WITH OIL
First, check the oil you are using is suitable to cook with (see the individual oils). Some, like sesame, are splashed on at the end of cooking as a flavouring since they can burn if over-heated.

When frying, heat the oil before adding any food – you want to hear that instant sizzle as the food goes in. If the ingredients go into cold oil the fat gets absorbed rather than creating a golden outer colour and crust which gives so much flavour.

FIX IT: NUT OILS
Nut oils have a lot of flavour, so if you find it too strong, tone it down for a salad dressing by diluting with a little olive, sunflower or groundnut oil – about 1 part nut oil to 2 parts other oil.

Grapeseed oil: Very mild in flavour, almost bland, and best used for cooking.

■ Its lack of flavour makes it perfect for frying mild-flavoured foods like fish, as it doesn't overpower.

■ Good for deep-frying.

USE INSTEAD Groundnut oil.

Groundnut oil: Also known as peanut oil, this is a good, light, all-purpose oil, very mild in flavour.

■ Can be heated to a high temperature, so good for Chinese stir-fries – in fact for any frying, shallow or deep. To flavour it for stir-frying, fry a few pieces of sliced ginger, garlic or spring onion in the oil before using.

■ Mixes well with olive oil for dressings to give a light taste.

USE INSTEAD Sunflower oil, corn oil, grapeseed oil.

Nut oils: The most popular ones are walnut (rich and nutty) and hazelnut (a bit lighter). They don't last as long as other oils (about 6 months), after which time they can go rancid.

■ Great served in a little dish as a dipper for bread.

■ In salad dressings and for leafy-based salads – walnut oil goes especially well with cheese and chicory, hazelnut with pears and rocket or watercress.

Olive oil: Choosing olive oil is a bit like choosing wine – the choice is wide and the different types vary in taste, smell and colour, so it all boils down to what flavour you like. The styles are judged on fruitiness, bitterness and pepperiness. 'Extra virgin' olive oil tends to be more expensive. This is the fresh fruit of the olive with the water taken away – very pure. If an olive oil is not good enough to be extra virgin, it goes to the refinery to be cleaned up, and because it is tasteless some extra virgin oil is added for flavour. This is called simply 'olive oil'. You can use extra virgin olive oil for everything except cooking at a very high temperature, and olive and olive pomace oil (see right) can be used for everything, including high-temperature cooking.

Olive oil is produced in several countries, mainly Greece, Spain and Italy. The typical characteristics of their oils are:

■ Greek: Fruity and herby in flavour. Great for salads, not good for making mayonnaise. A good all-purpose oil.

■ Italian: Italy produces the biggest range of flavours. Oil that comes from the north is more gentle and nutty in flavour and goes well with fish. Oil from central Italy is more aggressive in taste, with lots of grassy flavour, so tastes good drizzled over things like

oil

steak on a rocket or watercress salad. Southern Italy (especially Sicily) produces oil that has more 'tomato-on-the-vine' type flavours, and complements all sorts of vegetable salads.

■ Spanish: Fruity and sweet, with very little bitterness – tastes more of melon, passion fruit and nuts. A good all-rounder. Not so good as a dipping oil but goes especially well with salads that include fruit.

■ Olive pomace oil: When the olives have been pressed and the juice is extracted, a paste is left called pomace. The oil that is extracted from the pomace is called pomace oil. It is the cheapest of all the olive oils and is a healthy choice for deep-fat frying.

Palm oil: Used in African cooking. High in saturated fat.

■ Gives a rich red colour to fish and meat stews.

USE INSTEAD Vegetable oil, but you won't get the authentic colour.

Sesame oil: This has an intense, concentrated sesame flavour, especially the darker 'toasted' version, so a few drops are often all that's needed to give a superb exotic taste. Not good for cooking with as it can burn easily, but ideal for adding a teaspoonful or two at the end of cooking to give flavour.

SALAD DRESSINGS IN SECONDS

Tip 2 tbsp white wine or cider vinegar into a little bowl with a pinch each of salt and pepper. Slowly whisk in 6 tbsp olive oil (or use half olive and sunflower oil for a lighter taste), so everything mixes in together.

You can tart this up in one of the following ways:

■ *NUTTY: As above, substituting half the olive oil for walnut oil. Scatter a couple of tbsp of finely chopped toasted walnuts on top just before serving. Goes well with cheese salads.*

■ *MUSTARD AND HONEY: Mix 1 tbsp cider vinegar with 1 tsp runny honey and 1 tsp wholegrain mustard. Whisk in 5 tbsp extra virgin olive oil as above. Goes well with chicken.*

■ *DELICIOUSLY DARK: Mix 2 tsp balsamic vinegar with 1 small finely chopped garlic clove and a pinch of salt and pepper. Slowly whisk in 4 tbsp olive oil. Goes well with tomatoes.*

■ *CHEESY: Mix 4 tbsp sunflower oil with 1 tbsp wine vinegar, salt and pepper. Mash 90 g (3 oz) blue cheese with a fork, then slowly add the dressing until everything is creamy. Goes with mixed salad leaves and nuts, or on crisp leaves to serve with burgers.*

- Toss with cooked noodles and rice – nice in salads too.
- Splash sparingly over stir-fries.
- Add to marinades.
- Drizzle over steamed fish with a few slices of fried garlic and ginger.
USE INSTEAD Olive oil – it adds the richness but not the flavour.

Stir-fry oil: A blend of oils mixed specially for stir-frying, plus flavourings such as ginger, pepper and garlic.
USE INSTEAD Groundnut oil flavoured (see page 102), and a splash of sesame oil at the end.

Sunflower oil: A light, thin oil, extracted from sunflower seeds.
- An excellent cooking oil, better for shallow- rather than deep-frying.
- Good for mixing with olive oil for salad dressings.
USE INSTEAD Groundnut oil.

Vegetable oil: Often a blend of oils, usually including rapeseed.
- A good, cheap frying oil.

Olives

Olives come in green and black and many shades in between. Their colour reflects their age when they were picked: green ones are the youngest and first off the tree, purple are picked half ripe, while wrinkly, brownish-black ones have been left longer to ripen. Because they aren't fully ripe when picked, green olives are actually too bitter to eat, so have to be soaked, washed and cured. Canned or bottled olives keep for up to a year. After opening transfer to the fridge in a plastic container, and use quickly.

CHOOSE You will find olives from many Mediterranean countries, mostly Italy, Spain, Greece, and also France. When deciding which ones to buy, it depends on what colour, size and strength of flavour you are after (see below). Olives with their stones in are juicier and fresher than pitted olives.
Black: These have had longer on the tree to ripen, so contain more oil, making them softer and milder in flavour. Look for glossiness in a black olive, the good ones are small and wrinkled. The almost ink-black (usually pitted) olives are actually green olives that have been dyed.
Green: The younger green olives tend to be plumper and firmer and often have a sharper taste. Varieties include the Spanish Manzanilla and the plump Italian Cerignola.
Kalamata: This is the large Greek olive with a wonderful tinge of purple and a fruity flavour which makes it ideal for a classic Greek salad.

Stuffed: Being firmer in texture and sharper in taste, it is usually green olives that get stuffed. It can be with all sorts of things, including anchovies, capers, pimientos and nuts – more for handing round as a party nibble than for use in cooking.

USE FOR
- Tossing into rice and pasta dishes.
- Making your own tapenade.
- Scattering over pizzas and into salads.
- Adding to rich stews, especially chicken and beef.
- Chopping and adding to a tomato salsa for topping pan-fried fish.

Oyster sauce

You would think this thick, brown Chinese sauce would taste of the oysters of which it's made, yet its taste is quite different – salty like soy sauce, but richer and tangier. It's not so strong, however, that it overpowers other foods.

CHOOSE Sold in bottles. After opening, keep in the fridge.

COOK You can cook with it, but more often it's added at the end of cooking as a last-minute flavouring, a bit like any thick bottled sauce.

USE FOR

- Flavouring chicken and other meat dishes.
- Thinning down with a little oil and serving drizzled over stir-fried or steamed vegetables such as broccoli or bok choi, or over an omelette.

Passata

This is purely and simply tomatoes that have been puréed and sieved to get rid of all the bitty seeds and skin.

CHOOSE Available in bottles and cartons, it will keep for a year in the cupboard, and in the fridge for 4–5 days after opening.

USE FOR

- Giving a creamy smoothness to soups, casseroles and Italian-based sauces.
- Curries where you want the tomato taste without the tomato texture.
- Spreading over pizza bases – add more flavour by stirring in some herbs and garlic.

USE INSTEAD If you don't have passata, you can simply whizz a can of tomatoes in a blender or food processor then sieve them. It's a more time-consuming way of doing it, but gives the same effect.

Pasta (dried)

Most pasta is made with flour and water, and a simple sauce is all it needs for serving. Pasta that has been made with eggs is richer both in taste and colour, so is better suited to richer, creamier sauces. Once the packet of pasta has been opened, use within a month or two as dried pasta can get quite brittle.

CHOOSE

Cannelloni: Longish, wide tubes of egg pasta for spooning a filling, such as spinach and ricotta, into. For a more casual tube, use cooked lasagne sheets and fold them around the filling.

Conchiglie: Shell-shapes, either small or big enough to be stuffed. Orechiette can be used instead.

Farfalle: Little bows that look pretty in salads. Often sold in packs that contain a mix of green, red and white pasta.

Fusilli: Available as short spirals, or long ones called *fusilli lunghi* which are a bit like a curly spaghetti and can be used instead of it.

Lasagne: Broad, flat sheets of (usually egg) pasta, used in pasta bakes. For convenience buy the type that doesn't need cooking first.

Linguine: A flat version of spaghetti, which can be used instead of it.

oyster sauce–pasta

Macaroni: This is the small version of cannelloni, the holes in macaroni being tiny.

Orecchiette: These look like mini ears. You could use small conchiglie instead.

Orzo: Look like fat grains of rice, and the texture ends up quite creamy, rather like risotto. Goes well in salads. You can use small pasta shapes instead (the type used for soup).

Pappardelle: Very wide ribbons of pasta that sometimes have frilly edges. Similar to, but slimmer than, tagliatelle.

Penne: Small tubes of pasta, sliced off diagonally at each end. Similar to rigatoni and fusilli.

Rigatoni: A plumper, ridged, slightly curvaceous version of penne.

Spaghetti: Long strands of pasta, also sold in shorter lengths. If your pan isn't big enough to take the very long strands, just snap in half – easier to eat this way too. Similar to linguine.

Tagliatelle: Can be bought in tight bundles shaped like nests which makes it easy to add them to the pan. Also available in straight lengths. Similar to pappardelle, only thinner.

Tortellini: These look like tightly pinched little bonnets, and because they have a filling, usually of spinach or cheese, will keep for only about 3 months in the cupboard. Store in the fridge after opening.

WHICH SAUCE FOR WHICH SHAPE?

■ *LONG AND THIN, such as spaghetti or linguine: Use a medium-thick sauce or an oil-based one like pesto that will cling to the strands rather than a chunky one that slides off.*

SHORT AND RIBBED, such as fusilli: The sauce catches in the little ribs of the pasta, so you need a bit more sauce for these shapes, one that is not too chunky.

■ *HOLLOW TUBES, such as macaroni, penne and rigatoni: The sauce sneaks into the holes, so choose one that won't plug them up too much, such as tomato and creamy cheese.*

■ *RIBBONS, such as tagliatelle or pappardelle: Thinner sauces are better – creamy ones that will stick to their broad lengths.*

■ *FANCY SHAPES, such as farfalle, orecchiette, conchiglie: These can take thicker, chunkier meat sauces or creamy ones that get trapped in their shapes.*

COOK Use a big saucepan and plenty of water (fill the pan until it is at least half full) so that the pasta has enough room to move around and cook evenly. Bring the water to the boil, add salt, then drop the pasta in and give it a stir to stop it clinging together. Keep the water boiling so the pasta keeps moving. Check the packet for timings – the pasta should be *al dente* (that is, have a bit of bite in the centre), so test a piece by eating it before draining off the water. Drain well if adding to a runny sauce otherwise, if just serving with something like pesto or cheese, keep back half a mug of the cooking water so you can moisten the sauce up if you need to. Mix the pasta and its sauce together while both are still hot – if the pasta sits on its own getting cold, it will stick to itself. To use the pasta for a salad, cool it quickly in a colander or sieve under running cold water and toss with olive oil.

Pesto

This wonderfully fragrant Italian sauce, made from the magical combination of fresh basil, Parmesan or pecorino cheese, pine nuts, a little garlic and olive oil, transforms the flavour of whatever it comes into contact with.

CHOOSE All pesto adds a bonus flavour to your cooking. Basil-based pesto is the most versatile, but you can also buy it made with rocket, red pepper and aubergine. After opening, transfer pesto to the fridge where it will keep for a couple of weeks. If it starts to dry out in that time, just top it up with a bit more olive oil.

USE FOR

- Tossing with pasta – splash in a little of the pasta cooking water as well to give an extra sauciness.
- Spreading on chicken breasts before roasting or grilling them.
- Mixing with olive oil and a squirt of lemon juice to make a speedy dressing for drizzling over new potatoes, salads, fish or grilled tomatoes on toast.
- Spreading generously over a ready-made pizza base before piling on your choice of fillings.
- Stirring into mayonnaise for a dip, or spreading on bread instead of butter, especially on Italian bread for a mozzarella and tomato sandwich.
- Livening up your mashed potatoes.

Polenta

Made from cornmeal which is coarsely or finely ground from dried maize. It has a slightly sweet taste. In Italian kitchens it is as common as plain flour

pasta–polenta

is in British ones. Polenta can be creamy and sloppy, or so firm you can slice and fry it. The words cornmeal and polenta can be used interchangeably.

CHOOSE The quickest way to make polenta is with the instant polenta flour (precooked cornmeal) which can be made up in under 10 minutes. Regular cornmeal takes about 30 minutes to cook. Polenta can also be bought ready-made in a solid block or tube shape – all you have to do to this is slice and heat it.

COOK Follow the instructions on the packet for the type of polenta you are using. To give it more flavour, replace half the water with stock or milk. At the end of cooking stir in a big knob of butter to give it a shine, then season to taste.

USE FOR
■ An accompaniment instead of potatoes, rice or pasta. Try flavouring it with cheese, such as grated Parmesan or cubes of dolcelatte.
■ Spread the cooked polenta on a baking sheet and let it set, then cut into squares, grill or fry and use as a base for fried mushrooms, roasted peppers and cheese.
■ A colourful coating for protecting chicken or fish when frying.

HOW MUCH PASTA?

FOR 1: 85–100 g (2¾–3½ oz)
FOR 2: 150–200 g (5–7 oz)
FOR 4: 300–400 g (10–14 oz)
FOR 6: 500–600 g (1 lb–1 lb 5 oz)

FIX IT: PASTA
If pasta has stuck after cooking, tip it into a colander, pour boiling water through it to loosen, let it drain, then toss with a little olive oil.

Pulses

see BEANS, *page 74*

Redcurrant jelly

CHOOSE You can also get redcurrant and cranberry jelly, which has more of a sweet-tart taste.

USE FOR

■ Stirring into sauces and gravies to give them a slight sweetness and glossiness, especially good with lamb.

■ Livening up pan-fried sausages and onions – just bubble in some stock and 1 tbsp redcurrant jelly at the end of frying.

■ Making a snack – spread on toasted French bread, top with slices of goat's cheese and melt under the grill.

Rice

Rice falls into three camps: long (basmati and American long-grain), medium (Thai and risotto) and short (pudding and sushi rice). Each of the many varieties available has its own characteristics. A lot are interchangeable, but if you are cooking a speciality, such as an Italian risotto, Spanish paella or Indian biriyani, it's best to stick to the right rice. All rice will keep for about a year in the cupboard.

CHOOSE, COOK AND USE Rice can be cooked easily by boiling in a pan two-thirds full of lightly salted boiling water which is drained afterwards in a sieve. Another, more exact method is where the water is carefully measured and it all gets absorbed into the rice (the absorption method). As a generalization, this usually requires 1 part rice to 2 parts water – to measure this ratio, tip the weighed rice into a measuring jug and measure double that volume of water, then tip both into a pan. Bring to the boil, stir, then cover and cook on a low heat until the water is absorbed. Don't lift the lid to peek, or stir while cooking. Take the rice off the heat, and if you let it stand covered for 3–5 minutes, it's less likely to be soggy. A quick fluff up with a fork and it's ready to serve. Alternatively you can use the microwave: there's less mess, but it's no speedier (see page 113).

American long-grain: A good

quality one has a slightly sweet aroma, almost like popcorn.

■ Very good for salads, stuffings or on its own. It is the rice to serve with chilli con carne and other Mexican food. COOK Boiling: 12 minutes. Absorption: 1 part rice to 2 parts water, 15 minutes.

pulses–rice

Basmati: An elegant long-grained rice from India, this has a fluffy texture and an aromatic fragrance when cooked that perfectly complements the spiciness of Indian food.

■ Apart from using for Indian dishes, try it instead of long-grain rice in spicy salads, or whenever you want to serve rice with a distinctive flavour.

COOK It helps to rinse basmati rice before cooking, not to clean it, but to get it going and give a fluffier, lighter texture.

Boiling: 10–12 minutes.

Absorption: 1 part rice to 1½ parts water, 12–15 minutes.

Flavour it: Drop in a few cardamom pods, cinnamon sticks, star anise or strips of lemon or lime zest as it cooks. Or for Thai and Indian food, cook in half water, half coconut milk.

Colour it: With turmeric, sprinkle and stir ½ tsp into the water after you've added enough rice for four servings. If you add too much the rice can taste bitter and the colour be too vivid.

Brown: Tastes nuttier than white long-grain rice and takes longer to cook.

■ With its chewier texture, it's a good base for vegetarian dishes and salads.

COOK Boiling: 30–35 minutes.

Absorption: 100 g (3½ oz) rice to 250 ml (8 fl oz) water, 25 minutes.

HOW MUCH RICE?
FOR 1: 60–90 g (2–3 oz)
FOR 2: 125–150 g (4–5 oz)
FOR 4: 250 g (9 oz)
FOR 6: 300–375 g (10–12 oz)
FOR 8–10: 500 g (1 lb)

WHEN IS RICE DONE?
To check, lift a grain of rice from the pan with a fork, let it cool, then take a bite. It should be tender with a bit of firmness to it still. If it's crunchy and the centre looks hard and uncooked, it's not quite done.

REHEATING LEFTOVER RICE
Rice must be cooled quickly after cooking, then it is perfectly safe to use. If it sits around keeping warm, it can cause mild food poisoning. Tip the hot leftover rice into a sieve, put it under the cold tap and run the water through it. Drain and put it in a covered container in the fridge and it will keep for up to 2 days. To use, steam, microwave or fry until piping hot – but reheat only once.

Camargue red: This is wine red in colour when cooked and tastes nutty.
■ Makes a stunning-looking salad, or serve as an accompaniment to gutsy meat dishes.
COOK Boiling: 30 minutes. Take off the heat and let stand for 15 minutes. Absorption: 100 g (3½ oz) rice to 300 ml (½ pint) water, 20 minutes.

Easy-cook: This rice, whatever the type, has been very briefly steamed which makes it indestructible and easier to cook, so you are always assured of a non-stick grain. The disadvantages are that it takes longer to cook and as it loses some of its natural flavour in the steaming process, the taste is not as good as pure rice.
COOK Follow the packet instructions.

Paella: This rice is to Spain what risotto rice is to Italy. It has a slightly chewy texture when cooked.
COOK Follow the packet instructions or your recipe. Paella rice should be shaken, not stirred, so when you want to move it around, just shake the pan – no need to use a spoon.
USE INSTEAD Arborio rice.

Pudding: These plump grains absorb a lot of liquid as they cook and give a soft, slightly sticky texture. A lot of good pudding rice comes from Italy.

■ Classically used for rice pudding.
COOK Follow the recipe or packet instructions.

Risotto: This plump Italian rice absorbs a lot of liquid when cooking, which gives it its characteristic creamy texture. Italy has many varieties of risotto rice, all of which are interchangeable for making risotto. The most popular are:
Arborio: A softer grain, and the easiest to overcook.
Carnaroli: The most forgiving when cooking, so good for beginners.
Vialone nano: A smaller, slightly harder grain, often favoured for seafood risottos.
COOK Follow the recipe or packet instructions as the amount of liquid needed can vary.

Sushi: A short-grained white Japanese rice with a slightly sweet flavour.
■ Making sushi. It turns sticky and malleable when cooked, so can be shaped around the sushi filling easily to make an edible wrapper.
COOK Check the packet, but soaking for 30 minutes is often recommended before cooking for a lighter grain.
Boiling: 10–12 minutes.
Absorption: 1 part rice to 2 parts water, 10 minutes. Drain but don't rinse.

rice

Thai fragrant: Another aromatic rice like basmati. It goes very slightly sticky when cooked, so it's easy to pick up with chopsticks. Also known as 'jasmine' rice.

■ Use as for basmati, or as an accompaniment with Thai, Indonesian and Chinese dishes.

COOK Boiling: 10 minutes.
Absorption: 1 part rice to 1½ parts water, 12 minutes.

Wild: Very nutty in taste and chewy in texture, and smells a bit like a freshly mown lawn as it cooks – which is not surprising as this slender, black grain is not really a rice but a North American semi-aquatic grass that grows in shallow water. This makes harvesting difficult, so true wild rice (which has a longer, bigger grain than the cultivated one) is expensive. To lighten it up and give colour contrast, it is often sold mixed with white rice and this mix cooks more quickly.

■ Excellent with salmon. Also good in stuffings with lots of herbs, nuts and dried cranberries, blueberries or raisins (try it with the Christmas turkey), in salads (it goes well with Chinese flavours), and with gutsy stews and casseroles.

COOK Unlike most rice that keeps its shape when cooked, wild rice will start to burst open when tender. If the

MICROWAVING RICE

It's no quicker to cook rice this way, but there is less mess. Use the right water amount and timing (given below) for your type of rice. There is no need to stir during cooking.

1 Tip half a 500 g (1 lb) packet of rice into a deep (to avoid spills) microwaveable bowl.

2 Stir in the right amount of boiling water (see below), ½ tsp salt and a knob of butter if you like.

3 Cover with cling film, leaving a little vent on one side.

4 Cook on full power (750W) for 6 minutes.

5 Continue to cook on medium (350W) for the time given below.

6 Let the rice stand for 5 minutes, then uncover and fluff up.

AMOUNT OF WATER AND TIMINGS (from step 5 on 350W)

■ *AMERICAN LONG GRAIN: 600 ml (1 pint) water, for 10 minutes.*

■ *BASMATI: 500 ml (16 fl oz) water, for 10 minutes.*

■ *EASY COOK LONG GRAIN AMERICAN: 600 ml (1 pint) water, for 14 minutes.*

■ *THAI: 500 ml (16 fl oz) water, for 10 minutes.*

■ *WILD: 750 ml (1¼ pints) water, for 35 minutes.*

grains begin to curl it means they are overcooked, but it doesn't go soggy so is still edible. If you soak wild rice for 1 hour first, you can then reduce the cooking time to 30 minutes.

Boiling: 45–50 minutes.

Absorption: 1 part rice to 3 parts water, 40 minutes (stir after 30 minutes).

OTHER GRAINS TO TRY

Buckwheat: A staple in Russian cooking, often sold toasted, used to make the Russian porridge-type dish *kasha*. Buckwheat is also sometimes referred to as *kasha*. Like rice it can be served on its own or added to salads or stuffings

Bulgur wheat: Wheat grains that have been cooked, dried and cracked. Used a lot in Middle Eastern cooking, it is the main ingredient for tabbouleh salad. Treat it like couscous: simply tip it into a bowl, pour boiling water or stock over to cover, leave for 15 minutes, then drain and dry on kitchen paper. Use instead of rice in salads.

Quinoa: A tiny South American gluten-free grain with a very mild taste. Quinoa is high in protein, so is great for vegetarians. Cook like rice and use in a similar way to rice and couscous.

Rice wine

A Chinese wine which you can both drink and cook with, made from rice, yeast and water. Not to be confused with sake, the Japanese version of rice wine which you drink, or mirin which you cook with.

CHOOSE Many consider Shaoxing rice wine to be the best. Store as you would any other wine, making sure the cork is tightly in.

USE FOR

■ Flavouring Chinese marinades, sauces and stir-fries.

USE INSTEAD A pale dry sherry, though the taste is harsher.

Salt
CHOOSE AND USE

Rock salt: Large crystals of salt for putting in a salt mill for grinding.

Sea salt: Available as coarse, mild or in flaky crystals, as in sea salt from Maldon, Essex. These pure flakes of salt are strong in taste, so you don't need to use much. Looks pretty if sprinkled over food.

Table salt: A finely ground salt, this contains anti-caking agents to stop it from clogging up.

rice–salt

COOK If you are cooking foods that are already salty, such as bacon, ready-made stocks and cheese, taste before adding extra salt. When cooking a dish with lots of flavours and spices, add salt lightly and gradually: the flavours will develop as they cook, affecting how much salt you need.

Salt before: Salting fish before cooking helps firm up the flesh. When cooking pasta, salt the water before adding the pasta – it makes the water boil more furiously and the pasta move around more quickly so it is less likely to stick. If you are cooking with onions, add a pinch of salt as they fry and they are less likely to burn. When frying meat, salt just before cooking – if done too early, the salt will draw out the moisture and the meat will stew rather than fry.

Salt after: Salt roast potatoes at the end of roasting – if added too early, the salt will draw out their moisture so they won't go crispy. Salt dishes that have dried beans and fresh broad beans (unless you are going to skin these) at the end of cooking, as too much too soon can toughen their skins.

USE FOR
- Flavouring.
- Preserving food, such as Moroccan lemons.
- Helping bread rise.

FLAVOURED SALT
By mixing salt with a few other ingredients from your kitchen cupboard, you can create imaginative flavour combinations:
- *RED HOT: Mix in some dried crushed chillies – use with beef, chicken, minced meat dishes and roast veggies, or for tossing through a simple pasta dish.*
- *NICE AND SPICY: Stir in equal amounts of toasted cumin and coriander seeds – sprinkle over roast squash or lamb.*
- *NUTTY: Grind with sesame seeds and use to season rice, or use as a crunchy nutty coating for chicken and fish before pan-frying.*
- *FRAGRANT: Grind with a dried lime leaf and use for sprinkling on fish.*
- *PEPPERY: Mix with ground black pepper and dried thyme and sprinkle over new potatoes as they roast.*

FIX IT: SALT
If you have over-salted a casserole, curry or stew, adding a few raw chopped potatoes will help dilute the salty taste.

USE INSTEAD If you want to use less salt in cooking, flavour dishes with extra herbs, lemon juice, vinegar and spices.

Soy sauce

Comes from fermenting soya beans, wheat and water with salt, then leaving the mix to age for a few months.

CHOOSE Between dark and light. Dark soy is that way because it is left to age for longer, it is also thicker and a bit sweeter. Light soy is paler in colour, thinner in consistency and saltier in taste. Dark gives more depth of colour to slowly cooked meat dishes, or if you prefer a darker-looking marinade, stir-fry or dipping sauce. Both keep well for about a year.

COOK Because soy sauce contains so much salt, it's best to taste before adding extra seasoning.

USE FOR
■ Sprinkling over Chinese rice dishes, rather as you would use Worcestershire sauce.
■ Splashing over steamed vegetables to flavour, as well as into heartier meat and chicken dishes to give both colour and flavour.

Spices
see pages 162–198

Stock cubes
see BOUILLON, *page 76*

Sugar

The choice of sugars ranges from pure white and powdery (refined icing) to dark and sticky molasses. Most sugar is extracted from sugar cane. The range of flavours, colours and textures depends on how much molasses the sugar has and how much it has been refined. The more molasses there is, the darker, stickier and more flavoursome the sugar will be. After opening, sugar will keep longer if put into an airtight container.

CHOOSE AND USE
Caster: Available as golden caster (unrefined) or caster (refined). Golden caster sugar has good flavour and a pale butterscotch colour. Refined caster sugar is pure white, so is popular for making meringues.
■ Its fine texture makes it especially suited to baking. Use as a quick-dissolving sweetener for fruits and puddings – if you sprinkle some over a bowl of strawberries, it dissolves

salt–sugar

and draws out the natural fruit juices to create an instant syrup.

Dark muscovado (unrefined): A moist sugar full of natural molasses, hence its colour. The refined version is milder in taste and called dark soft brown sugar.

■ Brings a rich taste to baking, sauces and marinades.

Demerara: This has a crunchy texture and the small amount of molasses it contains imparts a delicate flavour.

■ Adds a crunchiness to toppings for fruit crumbles and pies, and in a coating for roast hams. Its flavour makes it ideal for sweetening coffee.

Granulated: Available as golden granulated (unrefined) or granulated (refined). Granulated is coarser than caster, finer than demerara.

■ Good for making caramel and in crunchy dessert toppings.

Icing: Available as golden icing (unrefined) and icing (refined).

■ To sift over cakes and desserts as a decoration. When using for cake icings, refined icing sugar gives a sparkling white icing for wedding or Christmas cakes, whereas golden icing sugar gives a mild butterscotch flavour and colour.

Light muscovado (unrefined): This has a well-balanced taste and is milder than dark muscovado. The refined version is called light soft brown sugar and is milder.

KITCHEN CUPBOARD EASY STIR-FRY SAUCE

Make an instant sauce for stir-fries by splashing some soy sauce and a little stock or water into your wok at the end of stir-frying meat or vegetables. This works well, especially if you have started with a little fry of garlic, onion and ginger which are great cooking partners to soy.

WHAT THE LABEL MEANS: SUGAR

Sugar is labelled either 'refined' or 'unrefined' on the packet. All sugar cane goes through some refining process to extract the sugar; unrefined just goes through less. Because of this, unrefined sugars lock in rather than refine out the molasses of the sugar cane during production, which gives them a natural colour and flavour.

Refined soft brown sugar is white refined sugar sprayed with molasses and sometimes caramel colouring, so it is brown on the outside only.

■ Gives a mild fudgy flavour to cakes, biscuits, sweet sauces (such as toffee), or use in marinades and savoury sauces. Use also as for dark muscovado.

Molasses: The darkest of all sugars with the most flavour, due to the high amount of molasses it contains, so it is usually used in smaller amounts.

■ Adds richness to marinades and sauces (especially barbecue), fruit cakes, chocolate cakes and chutneys.

Palm: Known as jaggery in South-East Asia, this brown sugar has a distinctive caramel flavour and is often sold in a solid block. It is produced from the syrup of palm trees, often coconut.

■ To sweeten savoury and sweet Thai and other South-East Asian dishes.

Pectin: This is sugar with pectin added. Pectin helps preserves to set, and so reduces the boiling time.

■ Jams and other preserves.

Preserving: Its large sugar crystals dissolve quicker than granulated as they don't stick together when mixed with liquid.

■ Jams, marmalades, jellies.

Rock: Big yellow chunks of Chinese sugar, a bit like small rocks, that you need to break into smaller pieces with a rolling pin or meat mallet (see Kitchen Kit, pages 70–1) before using.

■ Gives a shiny glaze to slow-cooked Chinese dishes and sauces.

Vanilla: Finely ground caster sugar made fragrant and speckled in colour with vanilla seeds.

■ Cakes, biscuits, sprinkling over pies and fresh summer fruits, making vanilla ice cream.

USE INSTEAD Use the following sugars interchangeably:

Caster: granulated (though not as suitable for cake making).

Light muscovado: dark muscovado.

Palm: light or dark muscovado.

Preserving: granulated.

Rock: granulated or amber-coloured coffee crystals.

Sundried tomatoes

CHOOSE Dried ones sold in packets might look a bit wrinkly, but are chewy and full of sweet flavour. Or you can get them in jars preserved in oil. Both keep for about a year; put the ones in oil in the fridge after opening. *Mi-cuit* sundried tomatoes in packets are semi-dried, plump and soft.

COOK The ones in oil are softer, so can be snipped into dishes straight from the jar. You can cook with the oil they are in too. The dry and wrinkly

ones in packets (not *mi-cuit*) are best softened before cooking by soaking in warm water for about 15 minutes.

USE FOR
- Snipping two or three into a tomato sauce or soup while it cooks, or into a pasta dish at the end of cooking.
- Eating as a snack instead of sweets.
- Brightening up roast chicken breasts or fish fillets – lay a few on top towards the end of cooking and drizzle with a little oil from the jar.
- Adding to a tomato and mozzarella salad scattered with basil.

Sweetcorn

see also VEG, *page 318*
Available in cans as kernels of corn, or creamed corn which adds a creaminess as well as texture to soups. Mix with other vegetables and rice in salads and use in Mexican cooking. Use the kernels to make corn fritters or serve on its own as a veg.

Tabasco

Just a few drops of this hot fiery sauce, made from Tabasco chilli peppers, vinegar and salt, will liven up whatever you care to add it to, whether it is vodka for a Bloody Mary or your breakfast scrambled eggs.

FIX IT: SUGAR
Sugar has a habit of going solid. If it dries out, to soften it put the block in a mixing bowl, lay a slice of bread on top, anoint it with a little water, cover and microwave for 30–40 seconds on high. Leave to stand for 5 minutes, then throw away the bread and put your now-loosened sugar in an airtight container. (This doesn't work for icing sugar.)

Alternatively, put the sugar in a basin, cover with a clean damp cloth and leave overnight. Store as above.

SHORT CUT:
VANILLA SUGAR
To buy vanilla sugar is expensive. You can make your own cheaply at home by tucking a vanilla pod into a jar of caster sugar. In a couple of days it will have soaked up the vanilla scent, and will then keep for ages.

USE FOR

■ Livening up pasta sauces, especially tomato-based ones.

■ Adding both heat and chilli flavour to burgers and fish cakes.

■ Salad dressings – add a drop or two to dressings to serve with chicken, prawns, eggs, vegetables or rice.

■ Splashing on to plain grilled or pan- fried fish, chicken or pork, or even onto poached eggs.

USE INSTEAD Chilli sauce.

Tapenade

An olive-based paste which is further flavoured with other ingredients, including anchovies and vinegar.

USE FOR

■ Serving as it is as a dip with raw vegetables, or stretch it and dilute the taste by mixing with mayonnaise first.

■ As an appetizer. Spread on French bread that has been drizzled with olive oil, then bake the bread in the oven until crisp.

■ Putting a dollop straight from the jar on top of barbecued or griddled prawns or scallops just before serving.

■ Spreading over a pizza base instead of tomato sauce.

■ Mixing with a little olive oil, then brush over salmon or other fish fillets

just before grilling or roasting.

■ Spreading over a joint of lamb before roasting.

■ Spreading a thin layer under the skin of a whole chicken before roasting.

■ Stirring a teaspoonful into gravies or sauces for meat or fish.

■ Mixing a few spoonfuls into a bean salad with herbs, olive oil and finely chopped red onion.

Tomatoes

Canned tomatoes are one of the most useful and versatile ingredients to have in your kitchen cupboard. No peeling is required – just open the can and tip them out. They keep at least a year. If you don't use the whole can in one go, tip the rest into a plastic container and keep in the fridge for up to 4 days.

CHOOSE AND USE The different types can all be used in similar ways, but these are their strengths:

Chopped: A convenient short-cut for making a sauce, but more expensive and the quality may not be as good as that of whole tomatoes.

Crushed: More like a chunky sauce, canned crushed tomatoes are mixed with tomato purée. They are a bit chunkier than passata (see page 106) and perfect for pizza toppings, soups and pasta sauces.

Whole cherry: Toss them into simple pasta dishes when fresh ones are not at their peak, or into sauces.
Whole plum: Give a rich taste and texture to sauces, casseroles, stews, curries.

Tomato sauce/ purées
CHOOSE AND USE

Tomato ketchup: A very sweet mix of tomatoes, vinegar, sugar and spices. Once opened, store it in the fridge and use within 2 months.
Tomato purée: Adds concentrated tomato flavour to your cooking. Available in a can, tube or jar. The can is great if you are going to use it all at once, but if you need only a small amount, a tube or jar is more practical, as it can be resealed and used at a later date. Tomato purée thickens and adds colour to curries, chilli and Bolognese sauce, or whenever you want extra tomato flavour. Once opened, keep in the fridge; the tube and jar will last for longer than the can, up to 1 month.
Sundried tomato purée: Gives a richer taste and colour than tomato purée, so use sparingly. Useful for Italian sauces, soups and marinades.

*KITCHEN CUPBOARD
EASY TOMATO SAUCE*
For tossing with pasta, spreading on pizza, or as a sauce for fish or chicken.

Finely chop a small onion and a plump garlic clove. Heat 2 tbsp olive oil in a pan, add the onion and garlic with a pinch of salt and stir-fry until softened and golden. Tip in a 400 g (14 oz) can whole plum tomatoes, some pepper and a pinch of sugar. Bring to the boil, then stir, turn the heat down and let it gently bubble away for about 5–10 minutes (depending how thick you want it), stirring every now and then, until the tomatoes break down to a rich sauce. To bump up the flavour sprinkle in any or all of the following: a pinch of dried oregano, a good squirt of tomato purée, a handful of torn fresh basil.

*TIPS & TRICKS:
CANNED TOMATOES*
Add a pinch of sugar to a dish made with canned tomatoes to help bring out their natural sweet flavour.

Tuna (canned)

The canning process gives this a different taste from fresh tuna, but it is very handy as a ready-to-use cooked protein. For fresh tuna, see page 416.

COOK Simply drain before using.

CHOOSE AND USE Available in cans packed in oil, brine or water or in meatier chunks packed in jars. If you don't use the whole can at once, tip the rest into a non-metal container and keep in the fridge for up to a day.
■ Flake into cooked pasta with finely grated lemon zest, fried garlic, a few crushed chilli flakes, some rocket and a good drizzling of olive oil.
■ Mix with mayonnaise and chives or spring onions and serve on top of jacket potatoes, or flake on top of pizza with tomato sauce, cheese and olives.
■ Mix with a jar of tomato-based pasta sauce and toss with pasta.
■ For making quick fish cakes instead of using fresh fish.

Vinegar

Most vinegars are made from wine, cider or other alcohol. Though this gives them different characteristics, they can be used interchangeably.

Vinegars flavour, preserve and tenderize your food and it is fun to build up an interesting selection. Light and heat can spoil the flavour of vinegar, so store it in a cool kitchen cupboard.

CHOOSE AND USE
Balsamic (dark): Made from grape juice, this deliciously rich, sweet and syrupy vinegar varies in colour, taste and consistency. The genuine article comes from Modena in Italy and if it has 'tradizionale' on the label, this is real top-of-the-range stuff, and the most expensive. Usually the more expensive balsamic is, the longer it has been aged and the sweeter and more syrupy it will be. Balsamic needs to be flavoured by ageing (you won't find its age on the label, but cost is a good clue). So whatever your price range when choosing, check that additives such as caramel haven't been included to give it flavour instead. Cheaper balsamics are fine for using in cooking, but it's worth spending a bit more for one you want to use for drizzling on things like salads.
■ Brush over chicken or duck breasts as they roast for a crisp, slightly sweet-tasting skin.
■ Toss a spoonful with pasta and roasted vegetables, or stir into a tomato sauce for pasta.
■ Drizzle over salads that have been

tossed with oil, especially tomato ones.

■ Use the thick syrupy type as a decoration – trickle a few flavourful droplets round plates of salad.

■ Add a few drops to a bowl of summer strawberries.

Balsamic (white): This has a sweet but delicate taste.

■ Because of its pale colour, it can be added to marinades, sauces (when deglazing pans, see page 20) and dressings where you don't want the colour to affect the food, as with fish, seafood and chicken or simple steamed vegetables.

Cider: This has a golden colour and delicate flavour and is less overpowering than some other vinegars. Use in a similar way to white wine vinegar.

■ In salad dressings it complements fruit – try with rocket and pear.

■ Use in marinades – it's especially good with pork.

■ For making fruit chutneys.

Fruit: Summer berries, sometimes plums, are used to flavour red or white wine vinegar. These vinegars should be flavoured with fresh fruits, so check this on the label.

■ Dressings – the flavours of fruit vinegars and nut oils combine really well together.

■ Deglazing pans for gravies and sauces to add fruitiness to a dish.

Herb: Made from white wine vinegar

and herbs. Tarragon vinegar goes well with chicken and fish.

- Dressings.
- Marinades.

Malt: The cheapest vinegar you can get, also the crudest, strongest-tasting.

- Splashing on your chips.
- For making rich, dark chutneys.

Rice: A clear, slightly sweet, mild-flavoured vinegar distilled from rice.

- Chinese and Japanese cooking for making dipping sauces, salad dressings and sweet-and-sour dishes.

Sherry: Has a deliciously rich, sweet taste, and can be sprinkled on to food in the same way as balsamic vinegar.

- Deglazing pans for making a sauce.
- Sprinkling on to salads.

Wine: Red and white wine vinegars can be used interchangeably, but each has its own strengths. Aged red wine vinegar from speciality shops is wonderfully fruity and less sharp-tasting.

- Red tastes stronger, so is good for deglazing pans for meat sauces, or in rich-flavoured dressings and marinades.
- White is particularly popular for the classic oil and vinegar dressing.

Wasabi

Made from Japanese horseradish, this has a spicy hot taste, quite different from the British version. Wasabi is a green paste that can be too hot if you take too much, but lifts the taste of many mild-flavoured Japanese dishes if you get the balance right.

CHOOSE Comes in a tube and keeps for at least a year.

USE FOR

- Dabbing on your sushi.
- Using sparingly to flavour salad dressings and Japanese noodle dishes.
- Adding a couple of teaspoons to a soy sauce-based marinade for fish.
- Serving with salmon or tuna – it is especially good if the fish has been pan-fried in a coating of sesame seeds.

Worcestershire sauce

The actual recipe for this is a secret, but its ingredients include tamarind, soy, vinegar, anchovies, molasses, spices, sugar and garlic.

USE FOR

- Splashing a few drops over fish.
- Adding to a dressing to serve with meat, or in a Caesar salad.
- Bringing depth of flavour to a meat stew, soup or gravy.
- Adding a teaspoon or two to cheese dishes, such as cauliflower cheese.
- Mixing with soy sauce in a stir-fry.

- Livening up stroganoff, Bolognese, beef burgers or shepherd's pie.
- Serving with a juicy steak sandwich.

Yeast (dried)

Fresh yeast is not always easy to buy, so dried is handy to have. Though inactive until introduced to warmth and liquid, yeast is a living thing, and once stale it will not make bread rise.

CHOOSE Available in packets or tins in dried granular form (dissolve with warm water and sugar first, and leave to go frothy), or powdered dried easy-blend yeast (mix straight into the flour). Both do the same job – easy-blend is quicker and easier to use.

STORE Check the tin or packet for the best before date. If not used by then, it may not raise the dough. You can tell when granular dried yeast is stale as it doesn't froth up when mixed with sugar and warm water.

COOK Just as gentle warmth allows yeast to grow, the intense heat needed to bake it kills it off, so make sure your bread has risen sufficiently before it goes in the oven.

USE FOR Raising sweet and savoury breads.

TIPS & TRICKS: YEAST
- *2 tsp of dried yeast is sufficient to raise 500 g (1 lb) flour.*

KITCHEN CUPBOARD BOOZE BOX

With a few bottles tucked away, you'll always have something punchy to slip into your cooking.

■ **Di Saronno (Amaretto)** If you love flavoured coffees or cooking with chocolate, one of the Italian nut liqueurs is ideal and great for sipping too. It goes beautifully in chocolate cheesecake. Or make a five minute dessert – sandwich soft Italian amaretti biscuits together with scoops of coffee ice cream and serve drizzled with amaretto.

■ **Angostura bitters** Never forget the little bottle from Trinidad. A few drops will refresh a fruit salad, spice up a tonic, or perk up a Bolognese sauce perfectly.

■ **Baileys** This creamy liqueur is brilliant for drizzling over ice cream and lovely in homemade chocolate truffles.

■ **Crème de cassis** This is the essence of blackcurrants. Put a dash at the bottom of a glass, then top up with sparkling wine. Drizzle over or through ice cream or add a dash to boost summer fruit salad or fruits for summer pudding.

■ **Limoncello** You get the flavour of Italian lemons in a bottle, tart and sweet all at the same time. Serve in small chilled glasses as an after-dinner liqueur. Or drizzle lightly over shop-bought lemon tarts to smarten them up.

■ **Ruby port** Not as old-fashioned as you might think. It's a fantastic drink loaded with fruity taste. Top it up with cranberry juice, ice and a dash of lemon for a cooling summer drink. You could also poach pears and plums in it, then serve with crème fraîche or put them in a crumble, or add a dash to boost the richness of gravy.

■ **Vodka** The great thing about vodka is that, except for the flavoured ones, it has no taste, so you can add an alcoholic oomph to anything where you don't want to change the flavour base, as in a beetroot soup, or a pepper jelly served in a little glass as a starter. As part of the base liquid for fruit jellies, citrus vodka is great.

3

Herbs and Spices

HERBS

KNOWING HOW TO RECOGNISE AND USE FRESH HERBS, AND HOW TO PREPARE AND STORE THEM, WILL HELP YOU ENJOY THEM TO THEIR FULL. MANY HERBS CAN BE BOUGHT IN THE SUPERMARKET, OTHERS CAN BE FOUND IN GARDEN CENTRES, WHILE SOME YOU MAY WANT TO GROW YOURSELF. THE CREATIVE WAYS GIVEN FOR USING HERBS AND SUGGESTIONS FOR WHAT EACH ONES GOES WELL WITH WILL MAKE IT EASY TO BRING INSTANT FLAVOUR TO YOUR FOOD.

STORING FRESH HERBS

CHILL OUT IN THE FRIDGE

Delicate herbs, such as coriander, dill, chervil, tarragon and chives, will keep fresh and perky in the fridge for several days, depending on the individual herb. Give them a quick rinse only if they need it and pat dry with a teatowel (or use a salad spinner). Lay the herbs on a bed of dampened kitchen paper, then tuck them into a ziplock bag so they have plenty of room, and keep in the vegetable drawer of the fridge.

KEEP FRESH IN THE FREEZER

If you end up with a glut of herbs, some can be frozen in individual blocks of ice. Chop or shred the leaves, pack into ice-cube trays to fill loosely, then top up with cold water. Once the cubes have frozen, put them into freezer bags. They will remain fragrant for up to 3 months – very handy for dropping into all sorts of things such as sauces, soups and stews. Parsley freezes best if frozen in sprigs on a tray first, then it's easy to crumble into a freezer bag for storing.

PREPARING FRESH HERBS

Herbs are used whole, in sprigs, or chopped in various ways depending on the type and how it is to be used.

CHOP When you want the flavour to mingle completely with that of other ingredients, or for scattering over at the end of cooking as a fresh garnish. Chopping immediately releases the herbs' flavour; whether it's done finely or coarsely is up to you and the dish you are making.

store–prepare

■ Strip the leaves from their stems on to a board. Hold a sharp knife in one hand (a blunt blade bruises rather than chops) and lay the fingers of your other hand on the pointed end. Keeping the pointed end in one place, move the knife backwards and forwards over the herbs in a continuous rocking motion. Keep scooping them back into a pile and chopping until done (see illustration, right).

POUND To make a paste or sauce, such as Thai curry paste or pesto.
■ Use a pestle and mortar (see page 65), or mini food processor to crush to the desired consistency.

SHRED If you want to add texture to a dish, or to use as a garnish (Chiffonade, see page 15). Used for bigger leaves such as basil or mint.
■ Lay several leaves on top of each other and roll them up like a cigar. Cut thinly across the width with a sharp knife and the slices will fall into fine shreds (see illustration, right).

SNIP Some herbs, especially chives, cut better with scissors than with a knife.
■ Snip chives with scissors in small pieces for flavouring, or into long strands for use as a garnish. This method is handy for cutting small

CHOPPING HERBS

SHREDDING HERBS

BOUQUET GARNI

This is a little bundle of herbs, traditionally a few sprigs of parsley and thyme and a bay leaf, wrapped in muslin or a fresh bay leaf and tied up with string. It is used to flavour slow-cooked dishes such as stews and soups and is thrown away at the end of cooking. The herbs used can be added to or varied, depending on the dish in which the bouquet garni is being used. For example, rosemary goes well with lamb dishes or sage with pork dishes.

amounts of parsley too – drop parsley sprigs into a cup or small bowl and snip them finely with scissors. Or snip other herbs such as coriander, mint or parsley straight over a dish to get the full flavour effect.

COOKING WITH HERBS

When cooking with herbs, taste before serving, remembering that packets of fresh herbs from supermarkets often have a milder flavour than home-grown.

DRIED HERBS are mostly added at the beginning of cooking, both to soften them and release their flavour.

FRESH HERBS with sturdy stems, such as thyme and rosemary, are added early on for flavour, later to give colour. Soft, leafy herbs, such as coriander, chervil, basil and dill, have more flavour when raw so are better scattered on at the end of cooking to keep their vibrancy.

FRYING HERBS

Some herbs, such as parsley, basil and sage, make wonderful garnishes when they are briefly fried until crisp. Make sure the leaves are really dry first, then heat about 2.5 cm (1 in) vegetable or groundnut oil in a small pan. To test if it's ready, drop a leaf in and it should immediately sizzle. When the oil is hot enough, drop just a few leaves in at a time to give them room (parsley can be done in sprigs), and after a few seconds, when they are crisp and just turning colour, lift them out with a slotted spoon and drain on kitchen paper. Delicious scattered on risottos and pasta.

DRIED HERBS

Nothing matches the flavour that fresh herbs give to a dish, but dried are handy to be able to use at a moment's notice and especially good in slow-cooked dishes. Robust herbs keep their flavour best when dried. The top five to have in your kitchen cupboard are:

- Bay
- Oregano
- Rosemary
- Sage
- Thyme

SUBSTITUTING FRESH FOR DRIED:
1 tbsp fresh = 1 tsp dried.

basil

HERBS A–Z

BASIL

Basil

Think of basil and you invariably think of Italy. But this herb has a lot more going for it than pesto. You'll find it in many Thai, Malaysian, Indonesian and other South-East Asian recipes.

CHOOSE Available fresh (for the varieties you are most likely to find, see below). Also freeze-dried, dried or in sunflower oil.

TASTE The different fresh varieties have similar taste characteristics to the most common sweet basil. Generally Mediterranean basils are milder and sweeter, Asian ones more pungent.

Mediterranean:

- Sweet basil: Its large, bright green leaves are a must for making traditional pesto. The taste is peppery with a hint of cloves, mint and anise.
- Greek basil: Its small leaves are perfect for nipping off the stem and tossing into salads. Peppery in taste.
- Purple basil: A dark, rich colour makes it look good in salads. Similar in taste to sweet basil, just a bit milder.

Asian:

- Lemon basil: Looks a little like oregano. Its fresh, citrusy taste and

MAKE YOUR OWN PESTO

There are many ways to make pesto. This is an easy one with loads of flavour that includes parsley as well as basil.

Strip the leaves from a 20 g (¾ oz) bag of basil and a 20 g (¾ oz) bag of flat-leaf parsley. Drop them into a food processor with 60 g (2 oz) pine nuts, 30 g (1 oz) Parmesan cheese (cut into small cubes) and 1 roughly chopped garlic clove. Whizz until mixed, then gradually pour in 125 ml (4 fl oz) olive oil, keeping the machine running until you have a moist paste.

The pesto will keep in the fridge for up to a week – if it starts to dry out, just pour a little more oil on top to keep it well covered.

fragrance make it a good partner for fish and seafood.

■ Thai basil: This has all the flavours of sweet basil, but more so.

■ Holy basil: More intense, aromatic, and spicy and, unlike sweet basil, its flavour is better when cooked than raw. Used a lot in Thai cooking.

STORE Keeps only briefly in the fridge as the leaves soon wilt and darken. Lasts longest when bought in a pot. Put in a sunny but sheltered spot, water and use it, and new leaves should grow to keep you supplied for several months (see Storing Fresh Herbs, page 128).

PREPARE Keep the leaves whole and strew over dishes just before serving. For a rougher look, tear them up with your fingers. Thin shreds of basil leaves (see page 129) look pretty scattered on soups or rice dishes such as risotto.

COOK Basil is a tender herb and loses its flavour and colour if added too soon, so best to sprinkle over a dish after cooking.

USE FOR

■ Making pesto (see page 131).

■ Scattering over salads and pizzas, into pasta and noodle dishes, sauces and stir-fries, over fish before steaming.

■ Tucking a few leaves under chicken skin before roasting.

■ Frying whole leaves to use as a garnish (see Frying Herbs, page 130).

■ Flavouring cream for using in custards or savoury sauces – chop the basil, then heat it in the cream and leave it to take on the flavour for about an hour. Strain and use.

■ Making flavoured butter (see opposite).

■ Adding to summer fruit, especially raspberries and strawberries.

GOES WITH Tomatoes and garlic, mozzarella cheese, courgettes, aubergines, new potatoes, fish, chicken, raspberries and strawberries.

USE INSTEAD All the basils can be used interchangeably. Use dried basil instead of fresh only if you have to, as the flavour is nowhere near as vibrant. Substitute with fresh mint if using in Thai recipes, oregano if using for tomato recipes, parsley or coriander for a different-flavoured pesto.

Bay

The shiny, elegant-looking leaf from an evergreen tree is one of the hardiest of herbs. It is used a lot in Mediterranean cooking and many other cuisines too.

basil–bay

CHOOSE Fresh (available all year round), freeze-dried or dried.

TASTE When picked straight from the tree, bay leaves have a slightly bitter after-taste, but this quickly fades as the leaf wilts, so better to use them dried or semi-dried. It is not a herb for eating, so when it has given its flavour to a dish, throw it away. Adds a complex, slightly sweet, spicy, almost astringent flavour, dried bay being more intense.

STORE Fresh leaves will keep that way for up to 4–5 days. To dry your own, just lay them flat, away from direct light, and leave for a few days until brittle and a dull green colour. Dried bay will keep in an airtight container for about 9 months. Once the leaves turn brown, the flavour is lost.

PREPARE The leaves are usually used whole, although tearing them into a couple of pieces helps to release the flavour more quickly.

COOK Bay is the opposite of basil – cook it long and slow in a dish and it loves it. You usually don't need to add more than a couple of dried leaves to a gutsy stew, but if using fresh, one or two more won't go amiss.

HERB BUTTERS

These are great to have for melting over fish, into mashed or crushed potatoes, over steaks and chicken, spreading on toast to go with scrambled eggs, or to make herby garlic bread. Beat the herbs with softened butter, tip on to a piece of cling film and shape into a log. Wrap tightly with another piece of cling film. The butter will keep in the fridge for up to 5 days, or in the freezer for up to 2 months.

WITH 125 G (4 OZ) SOFT BUTTER YOU CAN MAKE:

■ *SUMMER HERB BUTTER Beat in 3–4 tbsp chopped mixed herbs such as parsley, basil and marjoram.*

■ *CHIVE AND GARLIC BUTTER Beat in 2–3 tbsp snipped chives and 1 crushed plump garlic clove (or use just garlic chives, omitting the fresh garlic).*

■ *HOT TARRAGON BUTTER Mix in 1 tsp chopped tarragon and 1 tbsp wholegrain mustard, or ½ tsp crushed dried chilli flakes.*

■ *LEMON GRASS BUTTER Mix in 1 finely sliced stalk of lemon grass, 2 tsp finely grated lime zest and a handful of chopped coriander. Goes well with chicken or fish.*

USE FOR

■ Flavouring stews (especially beef or fish), soups, stocks, tagines, sauces (lovely with tomato), marinades, infusing savoury white sauces, even in a sweet custard.

■ Scattering amongst potatoes, fish or chicken fillets while they roast, or inside the cavity of a whole chicken or fish for fragrance.

■ Threading on to skewers between chunks of fish, meat, chicken or vegetables to flavour kebabs.

■ Dropping into the cooking water of rice (for taste), cabbage or cauliflower (to help eliminate the smell).

■ A garnish with melted butter on top of meat or fish pâtés.

GOES WITH Beef, chicken, lamb, pulse and rice dishes, fish, shellfish, lemons, tomatoes.

USE INSTEAD Juniper berries (see page 180), for slow-cooked meat dishes, or sprigs of thyme (see page 159) – these have a different flavour.

Borage

The best thing about borage is its perky little star-shaped vibrant-blue flowers, though the leaves can be used too. Used in European dishes.

CHOOSE You can only ever get borage fresh.

TASTE Quite mild, often likened to cucumber. Use the leaves sparingly.

STORE Use flowers soon after picking. The leaves don't last much longer – up to a day or two in the fridge (see Storing Fresh Herbs, page 128). Whole flowers can be frozen in ice cubes for dropping into drinks (see Storing Fresh Herbs, page 128).

PREPARE The leaves are best used when tender and young, and, as they are rather prickly and hairy, need to be finely chopped.

COOK Not a cooking herb – salads are its thing.

USE FOR

■ **Flowers**: Floating in tall glasses of Pimms or other summer drinks, scattering over fruit or green-leafed salads, decorating cakes and desserts.

■ **Leaves**: Ripping into soups (such as cucumber, spinach and pea), tossing into salads (especially potato). Whole leaves can go with the flowers in a glass of Pimms.

USE INSTEAD Baby spinach leaves (only for savoury dishes).

Chervil

One of the more delicate herbs, its fine stems hold up sprigs of feathery leaves. It is used mostly in European cooking, particularly French, and is sometimes called French parsley.

CHOOSE Available fresh.

TASTE Delicate in appearance and flavour, so use quite generously. Has a hint of parsley and anise about it.

STORE Fresh chervil stores for up to 2 days in the fridge (see Storing Fresh Herbs, page 128).

PREPARE A rough chop is all that is needed, stems can be used too as they are very fine.

COOK Stir into sauces or any other hot dish at the end of cooking for the most flavour, or throw over warm cooked vegetables just before serving.

USE FOR
■ Combining with parsley, chives and tarragon for the classic *fines herbes* mix in French cooking.
■ Adding to salads, omelettes, creamy sauces and dressings.
■ Mixing with melted butter, lemon zest and juice for pouring over fish.

BORAGE

CHERVIL

GOES WITH Eggs, fish, seafood, chicken, asparagus, peas, carrots, potatoes, beetroot, broad beans.

USE INSTEAD Parsley, dill, chives, tarragon, fennel leaves (all offer different flavours, though).

Chives

A delicately flavoured member of the onion family. The pale purple flowers can be used as well as the stems, which look like plump long blades of grass. Chives were used in China thousands of years ago and there is a variety called garlic chives that is also known as Chinese chives.

CHOOSE Fresh, dried or freeze-dried. For fresh, the stems should look pert and crisp. Garlic chives are broader and flatter and traditionally used in Chinese and Indian cooking.

TASTE Use chives generously for a mild, slightly sweet and spicy onion flavour. Garlic chives taste initially mild and grassy, then suddenly hit you with a mighty garlic kick that lingers. Use these more cautiously.

STORE Keep in the fridge (see Storing Fresh Herbs, page 128) for up to 3 days.

PREPARE The easiest way is to gather a bundle of stems together and snip with scissors – cut them short and fine for mixing and sprinkling, long for using as an edible garnish.

COOK To keep their crispness and oniony flavour, snip them over food at the end of cooking rather than during.

USE FOR
Flowers:
■ Scattering over salads. They are edible, but used more as a garnish.
Stems:
■ Livening up the flavour of omelettes, sauces, soups, rice, salsas and salad dressings.
■ Making flavoured butter (see Herb Butters, page 133).
■ Stirring into savoury scone, pancake and muffin mixes.
■ Mixing with soured cream and folding into crushed potatoes, or into soft cheese for baked potato toppings.

GOES WITH Eggs, potatoes, tomatoes, smoked fish (especially salmon), green salads, chicken, soured cream and cream cheese, avocados, beetroot, carrots, globe artichokes.

USE INSTEAD Green tops of spring onions.

Coriander

Every last bit of this herb gets used: even the root is a prized part of the plant in Thai cooking. It's a global herb, cropping up in Mexican, Latin and North American, Thai, African, Indian, Middle Eastern, Asian and Mediterranean (especially Portuguese) cooking. It looks a little like flat-leaf parsley only floppier, and is also known as Chinese parsley.

CHOOSE Fresh, freeze-dried, dried or in sunflower oil. The spice comes in the form of dried seeds and powder (see page 174).

TASTE Coriander is a mix of flavours – hints of lemon, sage, mint, pepper and ginger – all of which give a unique refreshing taste. If you love it, add loads. The root is more pungent than the leaves and stems.

STORE Keeps in the fridge for up to 4–5 days (see Storing Fresh Herbs, page 128). Outer leaves can turn yellow, so check regularly and discard.

PREPARE A large bunch may need a good rinse to get rid of any gritty soil. Chop the tender part of the stems along with the leaves, or just tear the leaves off the stems and scat-

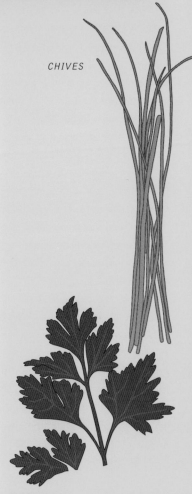

CHIVES

CORIANDER

ter in whole. The roots are tradition-ally pounded in a curry paste.

COOK Roots and stems are cooked in curry pastes or dishes that simmer away. The more fragile leaves are best stirred in at the end so their distinctive flavour is not lost.

USE FOR
■ Adding flavour to Thai curry pastes (the root) and *chermoula* – a spicy Moroccan marinade (leaves and stems).
■ Flavouring Indian lentil dishes, such as *dhal* (stems).
■ Stirring into salsas (good with tomato or mango), fresh chutneys and relishes (goes well with sweetcorn), also hummus.
■ Tossing at the last minute into stir-fries, noodle and rice salads and slow-cooked braises.
■ Making a coriander pesto.
■ Piling in profusion on to noodle soups for a garnish.

GOES WITH Coconut milk, chillies, ginger, garlic, lime, rice, noodles, chicken, lamb, pork, fish, prawns.

USE INSTEAD Flat-leaf parsley – you'll get the look and colour but not the flavour.

Curry leaf

This looks a bit like a miniature bay leaf, but is less sturdy and is used in greater quantities. It grows mainly in India and Sri Lanka where it is used to flavour curries. Also found in Malaysian and Indonesian cooking.

CHOOSE Fresh (from good Indian speciality stores) or freeze-dried.

TASTE When very fresh, the leaves are incredibly aromatic with a sweet, spicy taste of curry. They give a mild curry flavour to dishes rather than heat. The flavour becomes more muted after drying.

STORE Keep fresh ones for 3–4 days in the fridge. They freeze well, so if you have too many, pack the rest flat in a plastic bag and store them in the freezer for up to 3 months.

PREPARE Simply strip the leaves from the stems in a single motion.

COOK Curry leaves may be fried, often with mustard seeds, at the start of a dish to bring out their aroma, or sprinkled in at the end as a flavouring and garnish. As the dried leaf tastes milder than the fresh, you may need to use more.

coriander–dill

USE FOR

- A flavour base for curries.
- Chopping and mixing into fresh chutneys and relishes (fresh only).

GOES WITH Chicken, lamb, fish, most vegetables (especially root ones), mangoes.

USE INSTEAD No substitute.

DILL

Curry plant

Has silvery-green leaves that look a little like those of a rosemary plant. If you rub them between your fingers, or brush past the plant, the curry aroma is intoxicating – far stronger than the taste.

USE FOR

- Flavouring rice, vegetables or salads.

Dill

Dill has long been associated with Scandinavian cooking where it is popular with fish, but is also used a lot in Russia, Iran, Germany and Turkey. Its light, feathery sprigs are similar to those of fennel, just a little spikier.

CHOOSE Fresh, dried or freeze-dried. The spice is available as seeds (see page 176).

TASTE Mild with a touch of aniseed.

STORE Fresh in the fridge for up to 3 days (see Storing Fresh Herbs, page 128). Once it starts to droop, it is past its best.

PREPARE Strip the fronds from the tougher main stalk and tear, snip or chop.

COOK Will lose its flavour if added too early to a dish.

USE FOR
- Stirring into creamy sauces for fish and chicken.
- Marinating for pickles or with salmon for gravad lax.
- Salad dressings – goes well in a potato salad.
- Snipping over vegetables just before serving – try on buttered carrots or beans.
- Stuffing whole sprigs into fish before baking.

GOES WITH Fish (especially salmon, mackerel, trout, tuna), eggs, beetroot, broad beans, green beans, potatoes, cucumber.

USE INSTEAD Fennel fronds or tarragon (different flavour).

Elderflower
see EDIBLE FLOWERS, *page 161*

Fennel

Green fennel has frond-like leaves that look much like dill, though the foliage is a bit more dense on thicker stalks. Not to be confused with the fennel bulb which is a vegetable.

CHOOSE Fresh, as green or bronze fennel (leaves are best when young). The spice is available as seeds (see page 176).

TASTE Fennel has an even more defined aniseed taste than dill. Bronze fennel is milder.

STORE In the fridge for up to 3 days (see Storing Fresh Herbs, page 128).

PREPARE Chop, using stalks as well as leaves.

COOK Stirring it into a dish towards the end of cooking will soften it as well as bring out the flavour.

USE FOR
- Livening up sauces for fish, chowders and fishy soups.

- Roasting fish – make a herb bed with the whole stalks.

GOES WITH Oily fish, (especially mackerel, trout, sardines, salmon), potatoes, rice, beetroot.

USE INSTEAD Dill, or fronds from the fennel bulb.

FENNEL

Fenugreek

Used a lot in Indian and Iranian cooking, fenugreek (or *methi* as it is called in India) has a leaf shape that is similar to clover, but with larger gaps between the leaves. In Indian cooking, the leaves are often used in salads.

FENUGREEK

CHOOSE Fresh (usually available in Indian and Iranian speciality stores). The spice is available as seeds (see page 177).

TASTE This leaf has a very mild, slightly bitter, grassy flavour when raw.

STORE Fresh fenugreek will keep in the fridge for up to 3 days (see Storing Fresh Herbs, page 128).

PREPARE A simple bit of chopping is all that's required.

COOK Bitterness is reduced by cooking which also releases a curry-powder aroma and taste.

USE FOR

- Stirring into fish curries and *dhal*.
- Giving a spicy flavour to burgers and Indian *seekh* kebabs.
- Mixing into a herb omelette.
- Tossing with cooked potatoes or into salads.
- Adding to Indian bread such as *chappati*.

GOES WITH Potatoes and rice, lamb, chicken, cauliflower, green beans, tomatoes, mushrooms, prawns, yogurt, garlic and ginger.

USE INSTEAD Fresh curry leaves.

Filé powder

see SASSAFRAS, *page 155*

Lavender

Not just a pretty flower that is found in the garden, lavender is popular in cooking in Mediterranean countries as well as England. It is used mainly to give flavour to sweet dishes, but also to some savoury recipes. You can eat both leaves and flowers, but the flowers are the best.

CHOOSE Fresh. For use in cooking, it's best to grow your own if you can, as plants bought in a florist or garden centre may have been sprayed with pesticides.

TASTE Lavender has a powerful flavour and sweet fragrance that is a mix of floral with citrus. The flowers are stronger than the leaves, and more commonly used. Use very cautiously – too much will give an overpoweringly perfumed taste to your food.

STORE Will keep for up to a week in the fridge (see Storing Fresh Herbs, page 128).

PREPARE Rinse and carefully dry the lavender on kitchen paper. Chop leaves finely (if using); finely chop the flowers or pull the petals out separately.

USE FOR

- Flavouring caster sugar for use in cakes, biscuits, meringues, chocolate cake or muffins, ice cream, jellies, rice pudding, custard and *crème brûlée*. Nestle a few dried flower heads into the sugar and leave for a week or two for the flavour to develop. Sift them out before using.
- A substitute for rosemary (the

spiky leaves) for adding to bread, or
use the lavender stems as skewers for
fruit or lamb kebabs.

- A flavoursome decoration in salads
(the flowers), scattered on desserts,
or dropped into a chilled glass of
champagne.

- Chopping and adding just a few
sprigs straight into cake and biscuit
mixes.

- Infusing in milk or cream for
creamy desserts.

GOES WITH Lamb, game
(especially good with pheasant),
rabbit, cream, raspberries, strawberries, apricots and other summer
fruits, rhubarb.

USE INSTEAD Rosemary, though
the flavour is different.

Lemon balm

This herb is a member of the mint
family, and looks a lot like it.

CHOOSE Fresh only. Leaves will
either be variegated with splashes of
yellow, or plain green. Younger leaves
have a better flavour.

TASTE A mild combination of lemon
and mint.

LEMON
BALM

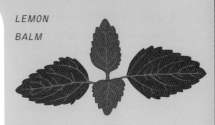

STORE Will keep in the fridge for about 4 days, or freeze in ice cubes for dropping into drinks (see Storing Fresh Herbs, page 128).

PREPARE Chop, shred or use the leaves whole or as sprigs (like mint) for adding to drinks.

COOK Best used with cold dishes, as heat kills its flavour, although it can also be added to a dish at the end of cooking.

USE FOR

■ Tearing or chopping into tomato salsas or salads, or whole in mixed leaf salads.
■ Scattering over cooked vegetables such as carrots and courgettes.
■ Adding chopped to sauces, stuffings or marinades.
■ Infusing a sugar syrup for use in fruit salads.
■ Making herbal tea.
■ Decorating and giving flavour to a glass of iced tea or other summer coolers.

GOES WITH Chicken, fish, creamy sauces, tomatoes, vegetables, summer fruits.

USE INSTEAD Lemon zest.

Lemon grass

Adds the exotic fragrance to Thai, Indonesian and Vietnamese food, but it crosses the culinary divide well and is wonderful in Western dishes too. It looks a bit like a drier, firmer version of a spring onion stalk, and it is the pale green part of its stem that holds the key to the flavour.

CHOOSE Fresh or freeze-dried. Also available crushed in sunflower oil, a convenient and concentrated way to buy it. Fresh stalks should feel firm and heavy – if they feel light, chances are the whole thing has dried out too much.

TASTE Unique. Not exactly lemony, more like a refreshingly tart per-fumed citrus essence. Not added for its looks, just for its flavour.

STORE Keeps in the fridge in a plastic bag for about a couple of weeks. Or freeze, tightly wrapped in clingfilm, for several months.

PREPARE Lemon grass is used whole, sliced or pounded to a paste. First get inside the stalk to release the flavour. Slice off the bottom, then peel off any dry outside layers. Give a hefty bash with a rolling pin to bruise

lemon balm–grass

it and you will smell the scented oils being released. If using to flavour a stew or curry, the whole stalk can be dropped in, then removed at the end as you would a bay leaf. For adding to marinades or salads, cut the bottom part of the stalk into very fine slices. As soon as it starts to feel hard stop slicing, as the top bit can be rather woody. Or, for a curry paste, pound the sliced stalk to a paste using a pestle and mortar. If using dried lemon grass, it helps to soak it in hot water for an hour or so before using to soften it, unless it is going to be cooked in liquid for a longish time.

COOK The whole stalk is added at the beginning of slow-cooked dishes for the flavour to infuse, then removed at the end.

USE FOR
■ Flavouring Thai curries, especially with fish and chicken.
■ Adding to the water used for steaming fish, chicken or vegetables, along with some ginger and other aromatics such as star anise, for a gentle scent.
■ Flavouring marinades (finely chopped), soups (goes well with tomato), noodle broths, or stocks.
■ Mixing raw finely chopped into salads (especially chicken or shellfish) – use the lower tender white part of the stem.

LEMON GRASS

■ A skewer for kebabs – wrap minced meat around a whole stem for grilling or barbecuing. Or cut each stem into four lengthways and use as a skewer for threading food on.

■ Flavouring cream for *crème brûlée*.

■ Bringing a fragrance to fruit salads, especially tropical fruit ones by flavouring a syrup (see opposite).

GOES WITH Chicken, fish, shellfish, pork, beef, chilli, tomato, coconut, ginger, galangal, lime leaves, coriander, basil, most fruits and vegetables.

USE INSTEAD Lemon zest – though don't expect the unique intense fragrance of lemon grass.

Lemon verbena

Native to Chile, lemon verbena is a plant worth growing. As well as having a herb to use, you can also enjoy its fragrance.

CHOOSE A fresh herb you are more likely to find in a garden centre.

TASTE Fresh, lemony and fragrant. Use generously.

STORE Once picked, the leaves last a couple of days in the fridge (see Storing Fresh Herbs, page 128).

PREPARE Use finely chopped or as sprigs.

USE FOR

■ Adding to rice to serve with chicken or fish.

■ Flavouring salads and drinks – whole leaves are especially good in iced tea.

■ Infusing in cream to make ice cream.

GOES WITH Chicken, pork, duck, fish, carrots, rice.

USE INSTEAD Lemon grass or lemon zest.

Lime leaf (kaffir lime)

Gives a special and unique citrus flavour to the cooking of South-East Asia. The leaf is dark green and glossy, shaped like an elongated heart and grows on an evergreen tree which also bears the fresh kaffir lime fruit used in Asian cooking.

CHOOSE Fresh and freeze-dried.

TASTE Aromatic with an intensely fragrant citrus flavour, and a strong scent of lime.

lemon grass–lime leaf

STORE The fresh leaves will keep for several weeks in a plastic bag in the fridge and freeze well too for up to a year.

PREPARE Use whole, or shred very finely with a pair of scissors.

COOK Use lime leaves as you would bay – drop them in at the beginning of cooking, and take them out before serving. Shred as above for adding more last-minute flavour to a stir-fry.

USE FOR
- Scattering into stir-fries (good with pork and chicken).
- Adding to Thai fish cakes, curries and stir-fries (finely chopped).
- Tossing into salads (shredded).
- A garnish for soups and curries – very finely shredded.
- Dropping into cool summer drinks.
- Infusing with milk or cream for custards and other creamy puddings.

GOES WITH Chicken, pork, salmon, prawns, fish, rice, coconut, lemon grass, Thai basil, coriander, ginger, blueberries.

USE INSTEAD Strips of lime zest – will give the citrus taste but not the unique perfume.

LEMON GRASS SYRUP
Stir 250 ml (8 fl oz) boiling water into 100 g (3½ oz) golden caster sugar and stir until the sugar has dissolved. Add 1 bruised, halved lemon grass stalk and leave to cool. You can pour into jars and chill for 2–3 days. Remove the lemon grass before serving. Use for fruit salads.

LEMON VERBENA

LIME LEAF

Lovage

This looks a bit like celery leaves, and is used mostly in European dishes. You will probably have to grow it.

CHOOSE Fresh is not often available commercially, but it is easy to grow in a pot.

TASTE Like celery, only much stronger. If added in large quantities it can overpower, so use sparingly.

STORE Fresh will keep for 3–4 days in the fridge (see Storing Fresh Herbs, page 128).

PREPARE Both leaves and stems are used, but if the stems are thick they will be tough, so discard. Use chopped or finely shredded (see page 129).

COOK Despite its similarity to celery, it is not so robust when cooked, so prefers to be added at the end.

USE FOR
- Adding to chowders, especially fish ones.
- Tossing a few leaves into an apple and cheese or leaf salad.

GOES WITH Pulses, lamb, pork, fish, root vegetables, apples, rice.

USE INSTEAD Parsley or celery leaves, or an equal mix of both.

Marigold

see EDIBLE FLOWERS, page 161

Marjoram and oregano

These herbs are closely related, and look similar with a similar taste. They are popular in Italian, Greek and Mexican cooking, especially when tomatoes are involved.

CHOOSE Fresh, freeze-dried and dried.

TASTE A warm, aromatic spiciness pervades both herbs. Marjoram tends to be milder and sweeter; oregano is a bit stronger and more peppery.

STORE Fresh will keep for about 3 days in the fridge (see Storing Fresh Herbs, page 128), dried for up to a year in an airtight container.

PREPARE Use the leaves whole or chopped. Sprigs of the little pink or white flowers make a pretty garnish.

lovage–mint

COOK Add towards the end of cooking to preserve their flavour.

USE FOR
- Chopping into Greek salad.
- Scattering over pizzas, into sauces (popular in souvlaki) and over roast vegetables.
- Stuffings, especially for chicken and lamb.
- Roasting with lamb – just sit the joint on top of a big bunch.
- Making a marinade for chicken by mixing with olive oil, lemon juice and crushed dried chillies.

GOES WITH Lamb, tomatoes, olives, garlic, lemons.

USE INSTEAD Use marjoram and oregano interchangeably.

LOVAGE

MARJORAM/OREGANO

Mint

Traditionally a familiar herb in British cooking (think of roast lamb and mint sauce or jelly), though it's also used in other countries, such as India (mixed into raw chutneys), Morocco (mint tea) and France (crème de menthe liqueur).

CHOOSE Fresh, freeze-dried or dried, though dried lacks that refreshing minty flavour. Dried mint is used more in Mediterranean countries, often mixed with oregano. There are numerous mint varieties, but the one most commonly grown is spearmint, also known as garden mint. Peppermint and apple mint are popular too. Moving away from Europe, there is Moroccan mint with its smaller leaves. For Vietnamese mint, see opposite.

TASTE Spearmint is menthol-fresh, a little bit sweet and a little bit sharp. Peppermint and apple mint are milder, apple mint combining mint and the sweetness of apple. Moroccan mint is spicy but not as sweet as spearmint.

STORE Keeps for up to 3 days in the fridge (see Storing Fresh Herbs, page 128), or keep in water like a small bunch of flowers.

PREPARE Strip the leaves from the stems (which can be tough, so discard) and use whole or torn, shredded or chopped. Smaller leaves at the top of the stem tend to be sweeter and tastier, so good to save for garnishing.

COOK Best scattered on to food raw at the end of cooking, although used for flavouring while boiling potatoes or peas.

USE FOR
- Mixing into yogurt with grated cucumber and a little cumin for a spicy raita dip or without the cumin for tzatziki.
- Tossing into an omelette with crumbled feta.
- Adding a sprig or two to boiling water as you cook new potatoes or peas.
- Flavouring salads (great with couscous, tomatoes and new potatoes) and fruit or vegetable salsas.
- Stirring into mince for meatballs, kebabs or burgers.
- Dropping into a glass of Pimms or a jug of punch.
- Scattering over slices of sweetened strawberries.

GOES WITH Lamb, chicken, duck, prawns, feta and halloumi cheese, beetroot, spring vegetables (especially new potatoes, peas and broad beans), courgettes, tomatoes, cucumber, strawberries and raspberries, peaches, oranges, watermelon, apples, chocolate, yogurt, oregano.

USE INSTEAD No real substitute.

Nasturtium
see EDIBLE FLOWERS, *page 161*

Nettle

This ancient herb is collected wild, so take care when picking and make sure it has not been sprayed with pesticides.

CHOOSE Young, tender leaves in the spring.

TASTE Similar to spinach. Not to be eaten raw because of its sting.

STORE Best used as soon after picking as possible as it quickly wilts.

PREPARE AND COOK Cook as you would spinach (see page 312). The leaves lose their sting after they have been cooked.

USE FOR
- Adding to soups.
- Mixing into bread dough – gives a lovely green fleck to the bread.

USE INSTEAD Spinach.

Oregano
see MARJORAM AND OREGANO, *page 148*

MOROCCAN MINT TEA
Mint tea is a national drink in Morocco. To make enough for 6, heat the teapot with boiling water first. Throw out the water, add 2–3 tsp green tea leaves, ½ tsp dried mint and 4–5 sugar cubes, then tuck in several sprigs of washed fresh mint so the pot is tightly filled. Fill up with boiling water, let it infuse for about a minute, then serve immediately (traditionally in small, heatproof glasses) – if the tea sits too long it starts to taste bitter.

VIETNAMESE MINT
This is not actually mint, it is an Asian herb that tastes more like coriander, and is spicy and aromatic. It is quite hard to find, but traditionally used a lot in salads and noodle dishes and for wrapping inside spring rolls. It is also called Rau ram and Vietnamese coriander.

Parsley

A real all-rounder and a useful herb for adding a splash of colour as well as flavour to many European and Middle Eastern dishes. It is both hardy and readily available.

CHOOSE Fresh – between curly and flat-leaf. Curly is the traditional British parsley and is brighter green than the darker, more open, flat-leafed parsley that is often referred to as Italian or continental parsley. Dried and freeze-dried are also available.

TASTE Curly parsley has a fresh, grassy flavour, flat-leaf parsley has a stronger flavour.

STORE Keeps for about 5 days in the fridge, or freeze (see Storing Fresh Herbs, page 128).

PREPARE Leaves are used finely chopped if you want to have just background flavour and texture, or whole or roughly chopped for something like a salad where it is an important part of the taste. Stalks can flavour stocks.

COOK For the best flavour, add at the end of cooking.

USE FOR

■ Mixing with grated lemon zest and finely chopped garlic for Italian gremolata – sprinkle over fish, veal, chicken or lamb before serving.
■ Bulking out basil for making pesto.
■ Scattering into soups, stews and sauces (the most traditional being parsley sauce) at the end of cooking, for colour and tangy taste.
■ Stirring or tossing into meatballs, hamburgers, fish cakes, omelettes, marinades, salsas.
■ Adding flavour to salads, especially tabbouleh.
■ Chewing if you've eaten garlic or onion to help get rid of the smell.

GOES WITH Most things, especially chicken, ham, fish, rice, pasta, eggs, tomatoes, most vegetables (goes well with crushed potatoes), garlic, lemon, chives, basil.

USE INSTEAD To be authentic, curly goes with British recipes, Italian with other cuisines – but there are no hard or fast rules. Chervil makes a good substitute, as does coriander.

Rosemary

A hardy herb that loves the warmth of the Mediterranean where it grows, but also does well in cooler parts of

parsley–rosemary

Europe and America. It is a vital ingredient in *herbes de Provence* (a French blend of herbs which also includes marjoram, tarragon, thyme, savory, bay, lavender and basil).

CHOOSE Fresh and dried are available all year round. Dried keeps its flavour quite well.

TASTE A very aromatic herb, with hints of pine and a bitter-sweet taste.

STORE For 5–6 days in the fridge (see Storing Fresh Herbs, page 128), or put stems in a jug of water.

PREPARE Sprigs and leaves are used whole to give flavour, but are hard and tough to eat, so chop finely if the herb is to be eaten. Use cautiously and taste when adding, as it can be overpowering if too much is used.

COOK Unlike that of other herbs, the taste does not fade with cooking.

USE FOR
Chopped: Flavouring Mediterranean stews, sauces and gravies, sprinkling over pork and lamb chops or joints before cooking, adding sparingly to shortbread.
Individual leaves: Scattering over breads before baking, especially

FLAT-LEAF PARSLEY

CURLY PARSLEY

ROSEMARY

Italian ones like focaccia, also over meat and vegetables for roasting.

Sprigs and stems: Make brushes with the sprigs and use to brush olive oil over vegetables, then drop the brushes on to the vegetables as they roast or barbecue. Use sprigs to flavour oil or vinegar, or infuse in cream or sugar syrup for desserts and fruit salads; throw on to barbecue coals and let the fragrance flavour the food above them. Use older, firmer stems, stripped of leaves, as skewers for kebabs, scallops, or bacon rolls to serve with turkey.

Flowers: Adding to drinks for decoration by freezing in ice cubes (see Storing Fresh Herbs, page 128).

GOES WITH Lamb, pork, duck, game, sausages, oily fish (especially salmon), monkfish, scallops, goat's cheese, potatoes, pulses, tomatoes, olives, mushrooms, aubergines, pumpkin, squash, garlic, oranges, apricots, nectarines and peaches.

USE INSTEAD Dried instead of fresh, or fresh thyme – though the taste is different.

Sage

Sage is a popular herb in British and Italian cooking. It goes really well with oily foods and fatty meats as it cuts the richness.

CHOOSE AND TASTE Fresh, freeze-dried or dried. There is a number of fresh varieties, the most well-known being common sage (silvery green leaves) which is strong and earthy. Other varieties include purple sage (milder in taste), pineapple sage (smells more of the fruit than it tastes) and tricolour sage (variegated leaf with pink, cream and green patches, milder taste).

STORE Best used freshly picked, but keeps in the fridge for 2–3 days (see Storing Fresh Herbs, page 128).

PREPARE Use leaves whole, or strip from the stems and chop finely.

COOK Only used cooked – its flavour develops and doesn't disappear over time. Because of its strong taste, it is not a herb to be added in large handfuls.

USE FOR
■ Being traditionally Italian – to flavour butter for tossing with pasta (drop a few leaves into butter as it melts), mushrooms or squash.
■ Being traditionally British – to flavour meat and poultry stuffings.

- Being traditionally Greek – stirring into meat stews.
- Frying the leaves for a crisp fragrant garnish (see Frying Herbs, page 130) – it goes really well on risotto and pasta, especially with pumpkin and squash.

SAGE

GOES WITH Pork, duck, goose, sausages, bacon, cheese, pulses (especially lentils), onions, pumpkin or squash, mushrooms, apples, thyme and parsley.

USE INSTEAD Dried is a good substitute for fresh. Or use another hardy herb such as rosemary or thyme – but expect a different taste.

Sassafras (filé powder)

The North American sassafras tree bears the leaves that are ground to make filé powder which is used in Cajun and Creole cooking, a speciality of Louisiana.

CHOOSE Dried filé powder, sometimes called gumbo filé.

TASTE Citrus and sour. It gives gumbo (a spicy meat, fish or vegetable stew) its distinctive taste.

STORE Will keep for up to 6 months in an airtight container.

COOK Cooking or boiling makes the texture of filé powder go stringy, so stir it in off the heat just before serving. Doesn't reheat well.

USE FOR
- Cajun cooking when you are thickening and flavouring soups and gumbos.
- Serving separately as a flavouring like salt.

USE INSTEAD No substitute.

Savory

In Germany this herb is referred to as the 'bean herb' – it is happy to be paired with broad beans, butterbeans and lentils. Winter savory is robust and tough with thin, glossy leaves to see it through the cold; summer savory has longer, softer leaves.

CHOOSE Between summer and winter savory. You will need to look for it in a garden centre.

TASTE As its name suggests, savory is full of flavour. It has a slight, not unpleasant, bitter taste, so shouldn't be used with a heavy hand, especially winter savory. Summer savory is a bit more delicate, tastes a little like thyme with a hint of marjoram, and is tender in texture. Winter savory is altogether more robust, has tougher leaves and a stronger flavour that is more similar to sage.

STORE Winter savory is hardier and will last for about 10 days in the fridge, twice as long as summer savory (see Storing Fresh Herbs, page 128).

PREPARE Use finely chopped, or as sprigs to give flavour to bean dishes as they cook.

COOK The taste is powerful raw, but mellows and improves with cooking.

USE FOR
- Enhancing slow-cooked, robust, meaty stews and vegetables.
- Flavouring stuffings along with other herbs such as thyme, mint and marjoram.
- Stirring into bean or potato salads.

GOES WITH Lamb, pork, rabbit, oily fish (good with trout), most beans, peas, mushrooms, cabbage, root vegetables, beetroot.

USE INSTEAD Thyme or marjoram.

Sorrel

A member of the dock family (it looks similar to spinach) that grows wild in parts of Asia and Europe.

CHOOSE Between garden sorrel and the smaller French sorrel (also called buckler leaf sorrel). You are unlikely to find sorrel in supermarkets, but try looking in garden centres as it is an easy herb to grow.

TASTE A bit like spinach, with a slight tartness and a bitter edge.

STORE For a day or two in the fridge (see Storing Fresh Herbs, page 128).

PREPARE Only the large leaves are used (stripped from the stalks), often shredded into ribbons (see page 129).

COOK You can cook it like spinach (see page 312) – briefly, until wilted and losing its vibrant-green colour. Also like spinach it loses a lot of its volume when cooked.

USE FOR
- Shredding into omelettes.
- Adding younger raw shredded leaves to a green salad.
- Flavouring creamy soups, sauces and purées for fish.

WINTER SAVORY

SUMMER SAVORY

GOES WITH Chicken, eggs, fish (especially salmon).

USE INSTEAD Spinach.

Tarragon

One of those herbs that some cooks just can't do without. The French love it and it's essential in *sauce béarnaise*. Though the slender, floppy leaves appear delicate, it's a herb with great flavour.

CHOOSE Available fresh, freeze-dried and dried. French tarragon is the preferred variety – there is also a Russian tarragon which lacks the subtle, refined flavour of French.

TASTE Strongly aromatic with a touch of spicy pepper and liquorice. You need only a little of this delicate-looking herb to give a lot of flavour to a dish, so use cautiously and taste as you go.

STORE Fresh keeps in the fridge for up to 5–6 days, or it freezes well (see Storing Fresh Herbs, page 128).

PREPARE Use whole leaves stripped from the stalks, chopped leaves, or as sprigs. Eat raw or cooked.

COOK Cooking tarragon brings out its best side and the flavour remains whether it is cooked in a dish for a long or short time.

USE FOR
- Most things with chicken – they are a great combination. Try tucking a few sprigs under the skin before roasting.
- Adding to a potato salad.
- Stirring into mayonnaise and serving alongside cold chicken or poached salmon.
- Mixing 2–3 chopped leaves with chives and chervil or parsley for a fresh herb omelette – or with a few fried mushrooms.
- Laying a sprig or two in the cavity of a fish such as trout or salmon with lemon slices before cooking, or on top when cooking fish or chicken fillets in paper parcels.
- Flavouring white wine vinegar.
- Making herb butter (see Herb Butters, page 133).

GOES WITH Chicken, prosciutto, fish (especially salmon and trout), shellfish, eggs, cream, potatoes, asparagus, tomatoes, mushrooms, beetroot, carrots, mayonnaise, lemon, mustard.

USE INSTEAD Fennel leaves, though the flavour is different.

Thyme

A herb for many dishes, favoured
by cooks around the world including
British, Caribbean, Mediterranean,
Mexican, Middle Eastern and North
American. It's a perfect flavouring
for rich, earthy dishes.

CHOOSE Fresh or dried. There
are many varieties, the most familiar
being common or 'garden' thyme.
The next most popular is lemon
thyme. Unlike many other herbs,
dried thyme keeps its flavour well.

TASTE The tiny thyme leaves give
off a sweet fragrance and a spicy,
earthy taste. Lemon thyme blends
the flavour of thyme with the fresh
taste of lemons.

STORE Fresh will keep in the
fridge for about a week (see
Storing Fresh Herbs, page 128).
Dried keeps for about a year in
an airtight container.

PREPARE As the leaves are very
small, they can be stripped from the
stems and thrown straight into a dish,
or whole sprigs can be added. The
little flowers can also be used as a
garnish.

TARRAGON

THYME

COOK Thyme is one of the few herbs that can survive in the cooking pot for a long time. Stems can be a bit tough and twig-like, so remove prior to serving.

USE FOR

■ Enhancing the taste of robust dishes (such as Irish stew, steak and kidney pie, Cajun gumbos, French *cassoulet*), soups, sauces, casseroles and roasts.

■ Adding to stuffings with other herbs such as parsley and rosemary.

■ Stirring into marinades or dropping a few sprigs into stocks.

■ Giving flavour to fried or roast potatoes or onions – scatter in a handful of leaves, or a few sprigs as they cook.

■ Stuffing into whole fish before cooking (lemon thyme).

■ Flavouring biscuits (lemon thyme) and bread.

■ Mixing with goat's cheese.

GOES WITH Most meats (especially lamb, pork and game), poultry, fish and vegetables, beer and wine, pulses, feta, goat's cheese.

USE INSTEAD Dried instead of fresh, or *herbes de Provence* which includes thyme.

Verbena
see LEMON VERBENA, *page 146*

Vietnamese mint
see MINT, *page 149*

EDIBLE FLOWERS

Before using edible flowers, make sure they are clean and dry and haven't been sprayed with pesticide.

■ **Borage:** See page 134.

■ **Elderflower:** Catch elder while you can – it is in flower for a few weeks only in May. If picking from the hedgerows, choose elderfower as far away as possible from the road to avoid any pollution, and use on the day of picking. Whole heads can be used to make elder-flower cordial, or they can be infused in sugar syrup to extract their perfumed taste before using the liquid to make desserts such as sorbets and jellies.

USE INSTEAD: Elderflower cordial.

■ **Marigold:** Pluck off the bright-yellow petals (don't use the centres) and use straight away for sprinkling over salads. But don't stop there – they can add taste and colour to custard or rice, instead of saffron.

■ **Nasturtium:** The flowers have a peppery taste, a bit like cress, and look pretty tumbled into salads, or tossed into summer fruit punches. The leaves are even more peppery, like watercress, and can be used in salads too.

■ **Rose:** Scatter petals on to poached peaches or apricots for a Middle Eastern dessert, or over cakes and creamy desserts for an instant decoration. For a longer-lasting decoration individual petals can be frosted. Gently brush each petal with lightly beaten egg white using a clean paint brush. Sprinkle all over with caster sugar, shake off any excess, then lay the coated petals on greaseproof paper to dry and become crisp. They will keep for a week or more in an airtight container.

SPICES

FROM THE EXOTIC TO THE FAMILIAR, SPICES GIVE AUTHENTICITY TO CUISINES FROM AROUND THE WORLD. ALL HAVE A UNIQUE FLAVOUR, AND IT'S GOOD TO KNOW HOW THEY CAN BE USED TO BRING OUT THEIR BEST CHARACTERISTICS. TO HELP YOU USE THEM UP BEFORE THEY LOSE THEIR POTENCY, THERE'S ALSO QUICK IDEAS FOR SPICING UP YOUR COOKING. AND IF YOU DON'T HAVE THE RIGHT SPICE, YOU'LL FIND SUGGESTIONS FOR ALTERNATIVES.

GRINDING WHOLE SPICES

Bought ground spices are convenient, but their flavour disappears quickly. For top taste and aroma you can't beat freshly ground. It's best to grind just the amount you need or can use quickly, as the flavour soon fades after grinding. Dry-roast first (see right) if you wish, then use any of the following grinding methods:

■ Pestle and mortar – easy to crush as coarse or fine as you like.

■ Rolling pin or heavy pan – put the whole spices into a strong freezer bag, seal the end and bash them with a rolling pin or pan until crushed.

■ Electric grinder – if you want to grind whole spices on a regular basis, buy a special spice grinder or keep a small coffee grinder just for this purpose so you don't get spicy coffee.

BRINGING OUT THE FLAVOUR

Heat brings out the flavour of spices, whether they are to be used whole or in preparation for grinding.

Dry-roasting (dry-frying): To get the fullest flavour from spices or seeds they are often dry-roasted first, which means in a pan with no oil. Heat a small, heavy-based frying pan (without any oil), tip in the spices and fry them over a medium heat, stirring or tossing around frequently for a minute or two, lowering the heat if they brown too quickly. When they start to turn brown and smell rich and nutty, remove from the heat and cool. Use whole or crushed.

Tarka: A special Indian technique where spices such as mustard and cumin seeds are fried in hot oil. This intensifies the flavour of both the seeds

cajun spice

and the oil. Heat a thin layer of oil in a heavy-based pan until very hot. Add the seeds – they will sizzle and jump around in the pan. Watch carefully and remove once they start to deepen in colour. This takes only a few seconds.

SPICE MIXES

Ready-blended spice mixes bring the exotic flavours of other countries to your food and save you having to buy lots of different spices. Use them to sprinkle into food or as a spice rub on meat or fish before pan-frying, grilling, roasting or barbecuing.

Cajun spice

A blend of herbs and spices that usually includes pepper, chilli, paprika, garlic, thyme, oregano and cumin.

TASTE Bold and hot with chilli, sweet with herbs for a Louisiana-style taste.

USE FOR Flavouring gumbos and jambalaya, rubs for fish and meat, or stirring into yogurt to make a quick dip for raw vegetables or roast potato or sweet potato wedges.

TOP 10 STARTER KIT

When starting to build up a spice collection, these will give your food plenty of global flavours.

- Cinnamon
- Chilli
- Chinese five spice
- Cumin
- Garam masala
- Mustard seeds
- Paprika
- Peppercorns
- Saffron or turmeric
- Vanilla

Chinese five spice

Made of star anise, Sichuan pepper, cinnamon, fennel and cloves.

TASTE Oriental, with a complex blend of sweet, bitter and pungent.

USE FOR Tossing into stir-fries or rice, or in oil and soy sauce marinades.

Dukkah

An Egyptian mix which usually includes roasted sesame, coriander and cumin seeds and hazelnuts.

TASTE Adds Middle Eastern flair with its spicy, nutty flavour.

USE FOR Sprinkling over salads, coating meats, fish and vegetables before roasting, nibbling on its own as a snack, dipping (dip bread into olive oil, then into the dukkah mix), mixing with honey for a sandwich filling.

Garam masala

This Indian blend literally translates as 'hot spices'. Recipes vary, but it usually includes chilli, coriander, fennel, cardamom, black pepper, cumin, cloves, nutmeg and cinnamon.

TASTE Gives an authentic Indian taste to your food.

USE FOR Adding to curries as they cook, but it is more often sprinkled over at the end as a seasoning, a bit like salt and pepper.

Jamaican jerk seasoning

A blend of allspice and hot chilli peppers with thyme, bay, cinnamon, cloves or nutmeg for using in Caribbean cooking. 'Jerk' refers to the dry mix of herbs and spices used to flavour meat and fish, as well as describing the style of cooking, usually on the barbecue.

TASTE Hot and spicy Caribbean taste.

USE FOR Sprinkling over oiled meat (especially pork), chicken or fish before cooking to give a dark crust. Marinate first to enhance the taste.

Mixed spice

A traditional English blend of cinnamon, coriander, cloves, cassia, ginger, nutmeg and caraway. Commonly used in baking.

TASTE Warm and spicy – reminds you of Christmas.

chinese-seven-spice

USE FOR Adding to rich fruit cakes and puddings (especially Christmas ones), gingerbread, also winter fruit compotes.

Ras-el-hanout

A Moroccan blend of rose petals or buds, black peppercorns, ginger, cardamom, nigella seeds, cayenne, allspice, lavender, cinnamon, cassia, coriander seeds, mace, nutmeg, cloves.

TASTE Complex mix of spicy, herbal and floral flavours.

USE FOR Tossing into rice, tagines and couscous for an aromatic Moroccan hit.

Seven-spice powder
(shichimi togarashi)

This Japanese mix of spices, flavourings and seeds can contain white sesame seeds, pieces of dried mandarin zest and nori (seaweed), poppy seeds, hemp seeds, chilli flakes and pepper. Look for it in Oriental shops.

TASTE Hot and aromatic, peppery.

USE FOR Seasoning meat, fish and noodles.

SPICES A–Z

Allspice

Sometimes called Jamaican pepper, the berry is similar but slightly bigger than a peppercorn and mostly comes from Jamaica where it grows on an evergreen tree native to the Caribbean and Central America. Europeans use it whole in pickles and ground in baking and desserts, whereas Caribbean cooks grind it to make jerk seasonings and rubs (see Spice Mixes, page 164).

CHOOSE Whole berries or ground.

TASTE Tastes of a combination of spices, cloves being dominant, with a hint of cinnamon, nutmeg and pepper.

STORE The berries keep almost indefinitely in an airtight jar.

USE FOR
- Flavouring Jamaican jerk dishes and giving authentic flavour to other Caribbean dishes, plus grilled pork chops, poached fish and stewed fruit.
- Flavouring the meat for moussaka.
- Mixing into pickles (whole).
- Adding to marinades for meat.
- Spicing up your Christmas cooking – sprinkle some into mincemeat for mince pies, Christmas pudding or cake, mulled wine (whole) or spiced red cabbage.

GOES WITH Beef, pork, chicken, sausages, root vegetables, fruit (especially oranges), honey, chocolate.

USE INSTEAD Equal parts of cloves, cinnamon and nutmeg.

Asafoetida

Sometimes called 'stinking gum' because of its strange smell when raw. Asafoetida is a gum resin from the stem and roots of a giant, fennel-like plant which grows in India and Iran, and is used mostly in Indian cooking.

CHOOSE In its whole solid form it resembles lumps of shiny brown sugar, but is mostly available dried and ground as a beige, brown or mustard coloured powder.

TASTE When the solid pieces are crushed, they smell quite unpleasant, but once fried asafoetida has a nice garlicky-onion aroma. The ground version is milder in flavour as it is mixed with a starch to stop it sticking together. Use only in small amounts.

STORE Whole asafoetida lasts for many years, ground for up to 1 year.

allspice–caraway

Keep in a very tightly closed container or the smell will overpower your kitchen cupboard.

PREPARE Grind the solid version before using.

USE FOR
- Enhancing the flavour of Indian dishes (especially curries and pickles) and spice mixes.
- A replacement for onion and garlic.

GOES WITH Fish, pulses, vegetables.

USE INSTEAD Garlic or onions.

Caraway

A curvy little seed with ridges that finds itself flavouring cakes, biscuits and breads in North European cooking and in spice blends in North African cuisine (essential to harissa, see page 89).

CHOOSE Dried whole seeds.

TASTE Aromatic, warm and nutty, with a hint of anise and citrus.

STORE Keeps for about 6 months in an airtight jar.

COOK If you dry-roast the seeds for a minute or two in a small frying pan, this will bring out their aroma (see Bringing out the Flavour, page 162).

USE FOR

- Flavouring breads and seed cakes.
- Adding to stews such as Hungarian goulash.
- Stirring into cheese scone or cheese biscuit mixtures.

GOES WITH Pork, beef, cabbage and other vegetables, cheese.

USE INSTEAD Fennel or dill seed (milder).

Cardamom

These pale green pods grow on bushes in the rain forests of southern India, Sri Lanka and Guatemala. They are hand-picked, then dried, and this personal attention means they cost a bit more than most spices. Russians and Scandinavians tuck them into pastries, cakes, biscuits and breads, Indians into tea, rice and meat dishes.

CHOOSE Pale green pods (white ones have been bleached) that contain about a dozen tiny black seeds. The stickier the seeds, the fresher they are. Ground cardamom is available but harder to find.

TASTE The seeds have a perfume and flavour that's all their own – hard to describe but they have quite a strong taste of eucalyptus, with hints of ginger and citrus, slightly bitter and sweet all at the same time. The outer pods merely protect the seeds, so should not be eaten.

STORE Will keep for about a year in an airtight jar. For ground cardamom, crush the seeds just before you need to use them as the flavour will diminish quickly once they are ground.

PREPARE When adding cardamom pods whole to dishes, give them a quick sharp bash with a rolling pin first to crush lightly or bruise and expose the seeds and their flavour. The pods are usually thrown away after cooking, or left in for decoration only. For just the seeds, slit the papery pods lengthways with a sharp knife so you can then open them up and tease out the seeds.

USE FOR

- Flavouring rice dishes (especially pilafs or rice pudding) and slow-cooked meat dishes.
- Giving fragrance to vanilla ice cream or Indian ice cream (kulfi) and to lassi, Indian tea and mulled wine.
- Adding to fruits being poached in sugar syrup.

GOES WITH Lamb, rice, cream, yogurt, chocolate, coffee, apples, pears, figs, mangoes, oranges.

USE INSTEAD No real substitute.

Cassia
see CINNAMON, *page 171*

CARDAMOM

Cayenne
see CHILLI, BELOW

Chilli

One of the most widely used spices around the world, chilli is particularly popular in the cuisines of India, Mexico, South America, South-East Asia, the Caribbean, Africa and southern Italy, especially Sardinia and Sicily.

CHOOSE AND TASTE Chillies vary in taste from mild and sweet to scorchingly hot. As a general rule with fresh chillies, the plumper the chilli, the milder the taste. But chillies aren't only about heat: each variety, of which there are hundreds, has its own unique flavour.

Fresh: These should be firm and glossy. For mild heat try the large, sweet-tasting, green Anaheim or greeny-yellow banana chilli, for medium heat

TIPS & TRICKS: CHILLI
Cool it – if your mouth burns from using too much chilli in a dish, water or beer won't cool you down. Instead reach for something dairy, such as a glass of milk or some yogurt. If the dish itself is too hot to eat, mellow the flavour with a spoonful or two of yogurt or cream.

the torpedo-shaped jalapeño, and for fiery heat the fruity habanero (Scotch bonnet) or the tiny Thai bird's-eye.

Whole dried: For adding whole or broken in pieces to a cooked dish.

Dried crushed: Made from crushed whole chillies including the seeds, they have a concentrated taste that gets more intense with cooking. Add early on for the hottest heat; sprinkle over at the end for a milder effect.

Cayenne: Made by grinding the smallest chillies to a hot powder, it is pure chillies, which Indians call chilli powder. This causes confusion with Western chilli powder, which is milder, being a blend of spices originally devised for Mexican dishes. Hot and strong, cayenne packs a mighty punch. Use cautiously, in pinches.

Chilli powder: Whereas cayenne is pure chilli, this is a diluted blend of chilli peppers with spices, oregano and salt that is available hot or mild.

STORE Fresh chillies will keep in a plastic bag in the fridge for up to 2 weeks. Dried chillies will keep for ages in an airtight container, the powder for up to 6 months as it loses its strength over time.

PREPARE
It's the inside bits of the chilli – the ribs and seeds – that hold the heat, so remove them if you want to cool things down. These parts can burn sensitive skin, so deal with them carefully. Halve the chilli lengthways, then lift and scrape out the central rib and seeds with a sharp knife (see illustration, opposite). Slice or chop the chilli, then wash your hands. If you put your hands to your face or eyes, it can sting.

COOK Start timidly by adding small amounts and get braver as you find out how much heat you enjoy. To add flavour, not heat, drop whole chillies into your cooking at the start, then lift them out at the end.

USE FOR
■ Stirring into salsas, salads, mash; scattering over fish and chicken before roasting to add a spicy kick.
■ Grinding fresh to make Thai curry paste (green or red).
■ Dropping whole (fresh or dried) into stews, curries and casseroles for a spicy flavour, or into sugar syrups to make sorbet (fresh).
■ Adding a pinch whenever you want to turn up the heat, especially good in chowders, kedgeree, smoked salmon, sauces, pasta (cayenne, dried crushed chillies).
■ Giving a spicy flavour to Mexican dishes such as tacos, chilli con carne, tortillas; to Bolognese and tomato-

chilli–cinnamon

based sauces; to marinades, dips and dressings (fresh, chilli powder).

■ Flavouring a mild cooking oil such as groundnut before using to stir-fry vegetables. If you drop a couple of whole dried chillies with a few slices of garlic and ginger into the hot oil and let them fry for a couple of minutes, they flavour it beautifully (see page 102).

■ Serving as a special seasoning – offer dried crushed chilli in a little dish as an alternative to salt and pepper.

GOES WITH Chicken, beef, lamb, prawns, fish, coconut, coriander.

USE INSTEAD Tabasco adds a kick.

SEEDING CHILLI

CINNAMON

Cinnamon and cassia

Native to Sri Lanka, cinnamon is the inner bark stripped from an evergreen tree which curls into sticks (quills) as it dries. It is used in sweet and savoury dishes all over the world from India and Morocco to North America and Mexico. Cassia is very similar, but is native to Burma. It is most important in Chinese cooking, and one of the spices that make up Chinese five spice (see Spice Mixes, page 164).

CHOOSE Either the curled-up, thin sticks of bark, or ground powder. The paler the colour, the better the quality. Cassia is closely related to cinnamon but looks and tastes a bit coarser – less curled and more bark-like. It is harder to get hold of than cinnamon.

TASTE The flavour and aroma of cinnamon are easily recognizable, being sweet and fragrant and a bit woody. Cassia has a slightly stronger taste.

STORE Sticks of cinnamon keep for several years in an airtight container. Ground cinnamon loses its flavour more quickly, but keeps for several months.

COOK When cooking with cinnamon, use whole sticks when you want a subtle flavour without the flecks of spice, or release more flavour from them by breaking them in pieces. Use ground for a spicy look and extra flavour.

USE FOR
- Flavouring desserts such as apple pie, poached pears, fruit crumbles, rice pudding, ice cream, fruit and spice cakes, breads and biscuits (sticks or ground).
- Stirring hot chocolate (sticks).
- Dropping into mulled wines, punches, fruit salads and compotes (sticks).
- Adding spicy fragrance to fruit and vegetable chutneys (sticks or ground).
- Bringing sweet spiciness to savoury dishes such as Indian curries and pilafs, Greek moussaka, Moroccan tagines, Mexican stews (sticks or ground).
- Livening up French toast or buttermilk pancakes (ground).
- Pairing with more robust flavours such as duck and pork, figs and prunes, root vegetables (cassia).
- Tying in bundles to decorate the Christmas tree (sticks).

GOES WITH Poultry, lamb, rice, couscous, beetroot, bananas, oranges, apricots, apples and pears, figs, rum, chocolate, coffee, red wine.

USE INSTEAD Cinnamon and cassia can be used interchangeably.

Cloves

These unopened buds of the small tropical evergreen clove tree get their name from the French word *clou*, meaning nail, which is what they look like. As well as being used in their own right, cloves also crop up in several spice mixes, including Chinese five spice and Indian garam masala (see Spice Mixes, page 164).

CHOOSE Whole cloves or ground. When buying whole, look for plump ones that haven't been broken up.

cinnamon–cloves

TASTE Quite pungent and over-powering with hints of camphor and pepper, a taste that numbs the mouth if too much is used. Whole ones aren't eaten, so fish them out before serving, or warn people that they are in there. Use cautiously.

STORE Whole cloves for up to a year in an airtight jar, ground for up to 6 months.

USE FOR
■ Flavouring Middle Eastern, Indonesian, African and Indian rice dishes, also curries and other meat dishes.
■ Poking into onions to flavour milk for savoury sauces such as bread sauce, into gammon to flavour and decorate, into oranges or apples to float in mulled wine or cider (whole).
■ Spicing up apple pie (add 2–3 at the most) and pickles (whole).
■ Adding ground to baking recipes in many countries.

GOES WITH Pork, gammon, lamb, chicken, root vegetables, onions, red cabbage, apples, oranges, dried fruits.

USE INSTEAD Allspice (instead of ground cloves). Or ground mixed spice for baking and desserts.

CLOVES

SPICES A–Z

Coriander

see also HERBS, *page 137*

These little round brittle seeds from the herb coriander get included in spice mixes such as Moroccan harissa, Egyptian dukkah, and Indian garam masalas (in India it is called *dhaniya*), as well as being used worldwide in their own right.

CHOOSE Dried seeds and ground.

TASTE Unlike the fresh leaves of the herb, the spice is mild and sweet with floral and orange touches.

STORE The seeds will keep for about a year in an airtight container, ground for several months.

COOK The seeds benefit from being dry-roasted before use to enhance their flavour (see Bringing out the Flavour, page 162).

USE FOR
- Adding to casseroles (especially pork and chicken), soups (root veg) and curries (dry-roast first, see page 162).
- Flavouring pickles and chutneys.
- Mixing into marinades and stocks.
- Crushing the seeds and sprinkling over potatoes before roasting, or mixing with cumin for a spicy crust for roast lamb.

GOES WITH Pork, chicken, fish, carrots, parsnips, swedes, pulses, cumin.

USE INSTEAD Cumin.

Cumin

These little oval seeds, similar in looks to caraway only less curvaceous, find themselves spicing up chilli recipes in Tex-Mex cooking, in Indian curries (in India it is referred to as *jeera*), as well as North African and some European dishes.

CHOOSE Seeds or ground.

TASTE Strong, slightly sweet as well as bitter – nice and spicy. Best used in small amounts.

STORE The seeds will keep in an airtight container for up to 6 months, but ground cumin loses its flavour more quickly.

COOK Dry-roast the seeds (see Bringing out the Flavour, page 162) before grinding, or fry them whole in oil briefly before using to bring out their flavour.

USE FOR
- Flavouring kebabs (great with lamb) and couscous dishes.

coriander–curry

- Making Indian lamb curries such as rogan josh.
- Scattering over potatoes, or chunks of pumpkin or other root vegetables when roasting.
- Spicing up meatballs and burgers.
- Mixing with yogurt to make *raita*.

GOES WITH Most meats especially lamb, chicken, cheese, lentils, rice, couscous, potatoes, cabbage, cauliflower, aubergine, yogurt, coriander.

USE INSTEAD Coriander.

Curry powder

A convenient blend of spices used for Indian cooking in the West. It is not used in India where cooks blend their own spices.

CHOOSE Ground powder – mild, medium or hot.

TASTE Blends vary, but all usually include coriander and cumin, and sometimes fenugreek, along with other spices such as turmeric, ginger and mustard. The hotter ones have ground chillies added. All are aromatic.

STORE Keeps in an airtight jar for several months.

USE FOR

- Mild curries such as korma and tikka masala (mild powder).
- Medium curries such as rogan josh (medium powder).
- Spicier curries such as madras and vindaloo (hot powder).
- Sprinkling into sauces, marinades, soups, or over vegetables as they roast.

USE INSTEAD Garam masala.

Dill seeds

see also HERBS, *page 139*

Flat, oval dill seeds are popular in European and North American cooking.

CHOOSE Seeds.

TASTE A bit like caraway, but milder and sweeter.

STORE Keeps in an airtight jar for about 2 years.

USE FOR

- Pickling, as in American dill pickles.
- Adding to breads and cakes.

GOES WITH Shellfish, cured fish, vegetables, especially beetroot, cabbage and cucumber.

USE INSTEAD Caraway seeds.

Dukkah

see SPICE MIXES, *page 164*

Fennel seeds

see also HERBS, *page 140*

This is one of the spices that is used to make Chinese five spice (see Spice Mixes, page 164), as well as the Indian five-spice mix *panch poran*. The dried seeds come from the fennel plant that can be found growing in India and Asia, South America, Australia and the USA, as well as the Mediterranean. They look like a greener version of cumin seeds.

CHOOSE Seeds only available.

TASTE Have an aniseed flavour.

STORE Will keep in an airtight container for about 2 years.

COOK Dry-roasting them (see Bringing out the Flavour, page 162) will draw out the sweetness.

USE FOR

- Flavouring savoury breads, pickles and chutneys.
- Meat, fish and vegetable curries.
- Chewing at the end of a meal as a mouth freshener.

GOES WITH Oily fish such as salmon, chicken, lamb, lentils, tomatoes.

USE INSTEAD Caraway or dill seeds.

Fenugreek seeds
see also HERBS, *page 141*
These mustard-yellow seeds look a bit like miniature corn kernels and come from the fresh fenugreek herb. They are widely used in Middle Eastern cooking. In India they are called *methi* and are often fried in oil with onion, cumin and mustard seeds to bring out the flavour at the start of making a curry.

CHOOSE The seeds are found in Indian speciality stores.

TASTE Smell similar to curry powder (they are often part of the blend in commercial curry powders) and give a nutty, earthy and bitter taste.

STORE Will keep in an airtight container for about a year.

COOK A brief spell in the frying pan to dry-roast (see Bringing out the Flavour, page 162) is important to bring out their nutty taste. If they outstay their welcome in the pan or get too hot in there, they turn bitter.

USE FOR

- Flavouring curries.
- Adding to Indian pickles, chutneys and sauces.
- Sprouting the seeds for salads (see Get Sprouting, page 261).

GOES WITH Fish, lamb, rice, potatoes and other root vegetables, tomatoes.

USE INSTEAD No substitute (not even the fresh leaf) just leave it out if you can't find it.

Five spice, Chinese

see SPICE MIXES, *page 164*

Galangal

This is the South-East Asian cousin of root ginger, sometimes called Thai ginger, that is used a lot in Thai, Malaysian and Indonesian cooking. It has the same knobbly look as root ginger but its shoots are tinged pink when young, and it has a more translucent skin, whiter flesh and tougher texture.

CHOOSE Fresh roots, dried (sliced) and powder. The one most available in the West is 'greater' galangal, which is native to Java. The smaller 'lesser' galangal is native to China. Look for galangal in speciality greengrocers or Oriental stores.

TASTE A mild blend of ginger and pepper with a hint of citrus.

STORE Keep fresh galangal in the fridge in a perforated plastic bag for at least a week, possibly two. Or freeze for 2–3 months. Dried will keep for about a year, powdered for up to 3 months.

PREPARE Peel fresh galangal first, then pound, grate, thinly slice or chop according to the recipe, as you would root ginger (see following page). Dried needs soaking in hot water for at least 10 minutes.

USE FOR

- Dropping a few slices into Oriental noodle soups, or the classic Thai chicken and coconut soup *tom ka gai*.
- Pounding with other flavourings such as chillies, lemon grass and coriander to make Thai curry pastes.
- Adding to sauces for fish.

GOES WITH Chicken, fish and seafood, noodles, coconut.

fenugreek–ginger

USE INSTEAD Fresh root ginger
(but the taste is not quite the same –
it is more gingery).

Garam masala
see SPICE MIXES, *page 164*

Ginger

Ginger is one of those spices that
has never been out of fashion, and is
prized for its medicinal as well as
culinary virtues. It was once so popular in Europe that it was put on the
table just like salt and pepper. Though
fresh ginger is called root ginger, it is
really a stem (rhizome), and its irreg-
ular knobbly shape gives each piece a
lively character all of its own.

CHOOSE Fresh root, ground and
dried, or crystallized. Or stem
ginger in syrup and pickled ginger
(see page 88). Fresh gives the best
ginger flavour, but ground is used for
baking. Fresh root ginger should be
plump and heavy rather than light
and wrinkled. Choose pieces with
not too many knobbles on as they are
easier to work with. Once wrinkled
they are more likely to be fibrous
inside. Ready-grated ginger in sunflower oil is also available in jars.

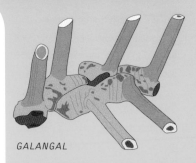

GALANGAL

TIPS & TRICKS:
GALANGAL
1 tsp powdered galangal is equiva-
lent to about 5mm (¼ in) piece of
the fresh root.

TASTE Fresh ginger is warm and rich with a hot, tangy bite. Ground ginger is hotter, more potent and less aromatic, very different from fresh.

STORE To stop fresh from drying out or going mouldy, put in a perforated plastic bag in the fridge and it will keep for at least 2 weeks. Or freeze whole (or peeled and grated into ice-cube trays) for up to 2 months. Ground keeps for about 6 months.

PREPARE The knobs are easy to snap off in pieces, so you can prepare the size you need. Peel off the brown outer skin with a sharp knife (not necessary if the ginger is to be discarded after cooking), then slice, grate, shred or chop (see opposite).

USE FOR

■ Storing in sherry (fresh), then using both the ginger and the sherry in Chinese cooking.

■ Adding to marinades, jams and marmalades (fresh, stem in syrup and crystallized).

■ Livening up ice cream mixtures or fresh fruit salads (chopped stem in syrup and crystallized).

■ Shredding fresh into matchsticks, then briefly frying with thin slices of garlic and spring onion, for scattering over Chinese-style steamed fish.

■ Partnering with garlic for a sweet-pungent combination at the beginning of Chinese stir-fries or Indian curries (chopped fresh).

■ Baking – goes well in shortbread, flapjacks, fruit cakes and puddings, crumble toppings (mostly ground, but other types too).

■ Making a soothing cup of ginger tea – grate a small knob of peeled ginger into a cup. Pour boiling water over and let it infuse for 5 minutes. Strain if you want, add a squeeze of lemon juice and sweeten with honey.

■ Dipping into melted chocolate for a sweet treat (crystallized).

■ Sprinkling over fresh melon chunks or wedges as a starter (ground).

GOES WITH Pork, beef, duck, chicken, prawns, scallops, fish (especially salmon), onions, rhubarb, pears, apples, lemons, oranges, melons, chocolate, honey.

USE INSTEAD Galangal for fresh. Ground ginger doesn't make a good substitute for fresh.

Juniper

British gin would be nothing without the dark purple juniper berry that flavours it. Other Europeans find many different uses for juniper

ginger–juniper

berries – Germans mix them into sauerkraut, while Scandinavians add them as an aromatic when pickling beef. The berries, which also grow in North America, look like small dark blueberries, and have a smell similar to that of a pine forest when they are crushed.

CHOOSE Dried berries. They should be plump with a chalky bloom a bit like blueberries.

TASTE Reminiscent of gin, and slightly bitter with a refreshing hint of pine. You don't need many to add the flavour: 4–6 are usually enough.

STORE In an airtight container where they will keep for a couple of years. You will know when they are past it as they will go hard and dry.

PREPARE Crush first to release their flavour.

USE FOR
■ Giving rich flavour to game dishes (including pâtés), beef casseroles and stews.
■ Giving a venison-like flavour to other strong-flavoured meats such as beef or pork.
■ Adding to marinades, especially robust red wine ones for game.

PREPARING FRESH ROOT GINGER

PEEL: Snap off the size you need, then peel away the skin with a small, sharp knife.

SLICE: For rounds, cut across the piece of ginger in thin slices. For shredding into sticks, make a small pile of the rounds then cut across them in thin sticks.

CHOP: For finely chopped, cut as for sticks, then continue chopping as for finely chopped herbs (see page 128).

SHREDDING GINGER

TIPS & TRICKS: GINGER

If fresh ginger is particularly fibrous, it's easier to grate rather than slice or chop. It's even easier to grate if you freeze it first.

■ Making a rub for meats, mixed with garlic and salt.

GOES WITH   Game, venison, pork, goose, cabbage, apples, cider.

USE INSTEAD   If adding to sauces or marinades, use 1 tsp of gin for every couple of berries required.

Mace

see also NUTMEG, *page 184*
This is the lacy orange helmet that fits snugly over the hard nutmeg seed, part of the fruit of the tropical nutmeg tree. Once picked, the nutmeg seed dries and shrinks in its protective sheath, and the mace can then be cracked and removed. In Britain it is traditionally used to flavour potted meats and fish.

CHOOSE   As blades (pieces of the lacy sheath) of mace, or ground.

TASTE   Like a slightly bitter version of nutmeg.

STORE   The blades have a long life span if kept in an airtight container.

COOK   If using the whole blades in cooking, remove prior to serving.

USE FOR
■ Adding a pinch to melted butter when making potted shrimps.
■ Flavouring milk puddings, fruity chutneys and quiches.
■ Infusing in milk for béchamel, onion or cheese sauces, or adding to stock liquid for soup (especially fish and shellfish).
■ Giving a warm spiciness to mulled wine or tropical punches.

GOES WITH   Lamb, fish, shellfish, onions, carrots, spinach, cheese, red wine.

USE INSTEAD   Ground nutmeg.

Mustard seed

Little, round seeds that are popular in both European and South-East Asian cooking. Crush them and their flavour leaps out at you; fry them whole and they can be very subtle and sweet. Used to make a variety of mustards (see page 96).

CHOOSE   Dried yellow (sometimes referred to as white), brown or black seeds.

TASTE   The brown seeds have a hotter and more bitter taste than the sweeter yellow ones. The tiny black

juniper–mustard

ones are the strongest and most pungent of all of them.

STORE Mustard seeds have a long shelf life if kept airtight and dry.

COOK Many Indian recipes call for dry-roasting the seeds first or frying them in a little oil until they begin to pop, to help draw out their nutty flavour (see Bringing out the Flavour, page 162).

USE FOR
■ Adding to chutneys (particularly good in mango chutney), pickles and marinades.
■ Frying with garlic and ginger to start off a vegetable stir-fry.
■ Mixing into a syrupy glaze for spreading over gammon.
■ Scattering over potatoes, squash or root vegetables as they roast (coat with oil first).
■ Flavouring Indian vegetable and dhal dishes.

GOES WITH Chicken, pork, lentils, spinach, cauliflower, cabbage, root vegetables, mango, maple syrup and honey.

USE INSTEAD No real substitute.

MACE/ NUTMEG

TIPS & TRICKS: JUNIPER
An easy way to crush the soft juniper berries (if you don't have a pestle and mortar), is in a small bowl with the back of a spoon.

TIPS & TRICKS: MACE
Mace is extremely hard, so to grind your own, break the blades into smaller pieces and grind in a small coffee grinder. Or buy it ready ground.

Nigella (kalongi)

Also sometimes called black onion seeds, these tiny jet black seeds are mainly produced in India, and are used a lot in Indian and Middle Eastern cooking.

CHOOSE Dried seeds – you may see them labelled as black onion seeds, which look similar but are not exactly the same.

TASTE Slightly bitter and peppery with a crunchy texture.

STORE They will keep for a good 2 years if kept in an airtight container.

COOK Dry-roast first (see Bringing out the Flavour, page 162).

USE FOR
■ Sprinkling into or over bread doughs before baking or over savoury biscuits such as cheese biscuits.
■ Flavouring rice pilafs and curries.
■ Adding to pickles and chutneys.
■ Scattering over root vegetables as they roast.

GOES WITH Most vegetables, rice, lentils.

USE INSTEAD Cumin seeds, sesame seeds, cracked pepper (each will give a different character to your dish, however).

Nutmeg

see also MACE, *page 182*

England went crazy for nutmeg in the 18th century, and it was sprinkled into both sweet and savoury dishes. Today it is popular in many European dishes as well as North African ones, especially Moroccan and Tunisian. Fresh from the tree, nutmeg comes well padded. It is found snuggled inside a fleshy fruit with its own outer shell of mace. Nutmeg is more popular than mace partly because it is cheaper and easier to buy.

CHOOSE Whole nutmeg or ground. Ground is very convenient, but freshly grated has more flavour.

TASTE Warm, spicy and bittersweet.

STORE Whole nutmeg keeps for years in an airtight container. Ground loses its aroma and taste quite quickly (it keeps for about 6 months).

PREPARE The most efficient way to grate a nutmeg is to have a special nutmeg grater that gives you a fine,

nigella–paprika

fragrant powder. Use carefully – for most dishes, a pinch or two is enough.

USE FOR

■ Adding a little to a savoury quiche, fish pie or chowder.

■ Mixing into pasta sauces, especially creamy ones, or ones with spinach; also a must for a classic béchamel sauce.

■ Adding to Mediterranean meat sauces for lasagne, moussaka and Bolognese, and Middle Eastern lamb dishes.

■ Giving fragrance to mulled wine, punches and eggnog.

■ Flavouring milk-based desserts and sauces, especially rice puddings and custards.

■ Stirring a pinch into fruit compotes.

■ Perking up biscuits, fruit cakes and teabreads.

GOES WITH Chicken, lamb, cheese, eggs, milk, pumpkin and squash, carrot, broccoli, cauliflower, cabbage, spinach, honey.

USE INSTEAD Mace.

Paprika

Take some special sweet red peppers, dry, then grind them and you have paprika. It's the spice Hungarian cooking couldn't do without (think

TIPS & TRICKS: NUTMEG

■ *Nutmeg is quite oily, so tends to stick in clumps in the jar. If this happens, just give the jar a good shake before using.*

■ *From one whole nutmeg, you should get 2–3 tsp of ground.*

of goulash), and Spain has its own version which shows up in their chorizo and many fish, rice, egg and potato dishes. It also adds colour and spice to some Indian dishes and Moroccan tagines. In Europe, Spain and Hungary are the main producers.

CHOOSE Dried ground. Its degree of sweetness or heat depends on the type of peppers used to produce it, plus how much of the hot bits of the pepper (seeds and veins) are added. It's not as hot as chilli, though, as paprika's main purpose is to add colour and flavour, not heat. When recipes call for paprika they usually refer to Hungarian paprika. You can also buy Spanish paprika, smoked or not.

TASTE

Hungarian: Often called 'sweet paprika' as that is its taste – sweet and well balanced.

Spanish: Can be slightly milder than Hungarian. Spanish paprika is graded as *dulce* (sweet and mild), *agridulce* (bittersweet) and *picante* (hot).

Smoked: This striking, red Spanish paprika is made from peppers that have been wood-smoked before grinding, giving it a wonderful new depth of flavour. You may see it sold as smoked paprika or *picante pimenton*. It's easy to get addicted to its robust, smoky flavour.

STORE Will keep in an airtight container for a few months. Its colour can deteriorate quickly.

COOK Take care when frying with paprika, as overheating makes it bitter.

USE FOR

- Boosting the colour and taste of homemade tomato sauce, chilli con carne, meat stews or curries.
- Sprinkling a little over chunks of chicken or pork before stir-frying, or even over a whole chicken before roasting.
- Mixing with salt, rosemary sprigs and oil, then tossing with potatoes ready for roasting.
- Colouring and flavouring a salad dressing.
- Coating roasted almonds – after roasting, toss in oil, then paprika and salt, and eat as a snack.
- Scattering a pinch or two over soups, grilled fish, canapés, salads, sauces and dips (such as hummus) to garnish and flavour.

GOES WITH Chicken, sausages, beef, veal, pork, rice, most vegetables, yogurt.

USE INSTEAD Cayenne pepper (for heat and colour – not the flavour), but use a fraction of the amount called for as it is far hotter and not so sweet.

Pepper

see also SICHUAN PEPPER,
page 192

Pepper is a spice that can be black,
white or green. There are also pink
peppercorns which are similar, but
berries from a different plant, not
peppercorns at all. Green peppercorns
are picked while unripe, black ones are
picked when turning from green to red,
then dried in the sun until black, hard
and wrinkly. Pepper is grown mainly in
India, Vietnam, Indonesia and Brazil.

CHOOSE Whole dried peppercorns,
black, white, green (also in brine),
pink (also in brine), or as a mix. Or
as ground (black or white).
Black: Good all-rounder. Grind whole
peppercorns yourself for the freshest
peppery flavour.
White: Choose for lighter-coloured
dishes, such as fish, or where you
don't want the specks of black to spoil
the look, as in light sauces or soups.
Green: Often used for sauces with
steak, lamb or duck.
Pink: Popular for fish dishes in the
South of France, also goes well with
poultry and vegetables.

TASTE Black pepper is hot and fiery
(less so when used whole); white is
less aromatic and milder in taste, but

quite strong in heat; green is milder than black and fresher; pink is milder than green and sweeter.

STORE Peppercorns keep for ages in an airtight container.

PREPARE Peppercorns are used whole or crushed using a pestle and mortar (see Grinding Whole Spices, page 162, and Kitchen Kit, page 66). Pink peppercorns are a bit soft for grinding, so are usually used whole. Any in brine should be rinsed first.

COOK For the best flavour, add pepper towards the end of cooking.

USE FOR
- Flavouring soups or slow-cooked dishes (whole or freshly ground).
- Crushing and patting on to meat, especially steak, before grilling, barbecuing or roasting.
- Mixing into herb butters or anything that will benefit from a peppery taste.
- Elevating the taste of strawberries by sprinkling a good grinding of black pepper over the top.

GOES WITH Smoked fish, most vegetables, most meats.

USE INSTEAD No exact substitute.

Poppy seed

Versatile, minute seeds from the opium poppy (opium is not found in the seeds, though). Can be used in cooking, to be decorative, or to add crunch or flavour to both sweet and savoury dishes.

CHOOSE Seeds. The most common are dark bluey-black and easy to buy. Harder to find are the white ones favoured in Indian cooking.

TASTE Faintly nutty.

STORE Best in the fridge for up to a few months as they can go rancid, or in the freezer.

COOK Dry-roasting (see Bringing out the Flavour, page 162) enhances their taste.

USE FOR
- Adding to or sprinkling over muffins, biscuits, cakes, pancakes and breads.
- Tossing with noodles – great for noodle salads.
- Mixing into salad dressings (goes well with lemon) or sprinkling over steamed and buttered vegetables.

GOES WITH Breads, feta, salad leaves (especially spinach and water-cress), cauliflower, carrots, lemon.

USE INSTEAD Sesame seeds
(different flavour, though).

Ras-el-hanout
see SPICE MIXES, *page 165*

Saffron

The dried stigmas from the saffron
crocus may not look like much, but
introduce them to liquid and they
explode with colour and flavour.
Hand-harvesting the huge amounts
required makes it the most expensive
of spices. It is mainly produced in
Spain, India, Iran, also Greece and
Italy, although centuries ago it was
grown in Saffron Walden in Essex,
which took its name from the spice.
Use it for both sweet and savoury
dishes.

CHOOSE Stigmas (threads). As a
general rule, the deeper the colour,
the better the saffron – the best being
deep red with orange tips. Lack of
orange on the tips could indicate the
saffron has been dyed. Cheaper
saffron, apart from not having the
intense red-to-orange glow about it,
can also look a bit raggedy. Good
saffron will always be expensive, so
when buying unbranded cheap saffron
from markets in other countries, look

out for fakes – if it's too yellow, chances are it's not the real thing. Ground saffron is sometimes available, but has often been adulterated with other ingredients.

TASTE Easier to recognise than describe – but very pungent and aromatic, slightly bitter and almost musty with floral hints. You don't need to use much saffron to have an effect – a pinch (about a dozen threads) is usually enough for a dish to serve 4. Too much makes food taste too bitter and rather medicinal.

STORE Will keep in an airtight container for several years.

PREPARE To tease the colour from the threads and ensure the colour is evenly distributed, they are usually steeped in a few tablespoons of warm water, white wine, stock or milk for half an hour or so before using. You can then add the liquid with or without the threads, but straining them off is fiddly, and they look good too.

USE FOR

■ Giving flavour and colour to traditional dishes such as Spanish paella, Moroccan tagines, French fish stews (*bouillabaisse*), Italian risottos, Cornish saffron cake and Swedish saffron buns.

■ Zapping up a tomato sauce to go with pasta.

■ Sneaking some into a tortilla – soak a few threads in a spoonful of boiling water and add with the eggs.

■ Adding a pinch to a creamy sauce for fish or spaghetti, or to the water when boiling rice.

■ Infusing in a little butter and beating into mashed potato.

■ Mixing into a spiced syrup for fresh fruits such as figs, nectarines and plums.

GOES WITH Fish and shellfish (especially mussels), lamb, chicken, rice, polenta, carrots, fennel, garlic, white wine.

USE INSTEAD Turmeric is cheaper and will give you a yellow colour (fine for rice), but doesn't go with all food, and the flavour is very different.

Sesame seeds

These tiny, flat, oval seeds, from the seed pods of a tropical plant, certainly get around. You'll spot them being scattered into or over Asian dishes (stir-fries and sesame prawn toasts), Middle Eastern breads and sweetmeats (*halvah*) and crushed into pastes (tahini, the base for hummus), or sprinkled over American burger buns.

saffron–sesame

CHOOSE Seeds – white (the most common), black (hard to get) or brown (unhulled white) depending on the variety of plant the seeds come from. Or as sesame oil (see page 103).

TASTE Can be used raw but their wonderful nutty taste comes into its own after dry-roasting (see Bringing Out the Flavour, page 162). A lot of flavour is packed into each tiny seed; black sesame seeds contain the most.

STORE Best kept in the fridge for up to 6 months, or in the freezer.

COOK Dry-roasting is really worth it to release their nuttiness and fragrance (see Bringing out the Flavour, page 162). Heat the white and brown ones until just turning golden and starting to jump in the pan for the best flavour, and the black ones until you can start to smell the fragrance. Sesame seeds burn quickly, so watch over them. If sprinkling over food before baking, there's no need to fry first.

USE FOR
- Giving crunch to stir-fries.
- Coating tuna and salmon fillets before frying.
- Scattering over biscuits and breads.
- Mixing into Oriental dressings.
- Sprinkling over salads before

serving, especially ones with chicken.
■ Scattering over root vegetables, such as carrots or parsnips, after roasting.

GOES WITH Chicken, fish, prawns, Chinese greens, noodles, tofu, rice.

USE INSTEAD Poppy seeds (not so nutty, though).

Sichuan pepper
(*also spelt* SZECHUAN)

Though similar in looks to pepper, this isn't from the pepper family at all but is a dried berry from a shrub native to the Sichuan province of China. It is one of the ingredients used to make Chinese five spice (see Spice Mixes, page 164).

CHOOSE Whole berries or coarsely ground.

TASTE Fragrant, spicy and pungent, slightly peppery.

STORE Whole berries will keep indefinitely in an airtight container, ground for up to 6 months.

COOK Dry-roast to bring out their oils for 4–5 minutes until they start to smoke (see Bringing out the Flavour,

page 162), but watch the heat and throw away any that get too blackened.

USE FOR
■ Stir-fries.
■ Seasoning crispy duck.

GOES WITH Chicken, duck.

USE INSTEAD Black peppercorns (less pungent).

Star anise

Among the prettiest of spices (each one is a starry-flower-shaped, dried seed pod), star anise is native to China and Vietnam and one of the spices used in Chinese five spice (see Spice Mixes, page 164). Western cooks are latching on to its merits and drop it into all sorts of dishes, including syrups, preserves and even poaching broths, to give an exotic flavouring.

CHOOSE Whole star anise (shiny brown seeds within the pod), or pieces.

TASTE Like liquorice, with an added fragrance and warmth. The taste is fairly intense, so don't overdo it.

STORE If kept in an airtight container in the kitchen cupboard, whole star anise will keep for many months.

PREPARE Nothing to do – just drop the whole thing into whatever you are making. Fish it out before serving, or leave in as a decoration (but take care not to eat it).

USE FOR
- Infusing in a syrup for fruit salads.
- Flavouring marinades for chicken.
- Adding to broth for steaming fish or chicken with other aromatics, such as ginger, lemon grass or cinnamon, or into stocks for Oriental dishes.
- Dropping into rice while it cooks to accompany Chinese dishes.
- Giving flavour to stewed fruits such as pears and rhubarb.

GOES WITH Chicken, pork, duck, beef, rice, tropical fruits, peaches, pears, plums, rhubarb, leeks, soy sauce, lemon grass, ginger, Sichuan pepper.

USE INSTEAD Chinese five spice (see Spice Mixes, page 164) for savoury dishes where it's all right to use a ground spice.

STAR ANISE

Sumac

Used a lot in Arabic, Lebanese and Turkish cooking, sumac is the fruit of a small shrub. It is used to add sour-ness to a dish in the same way as lemon, vinegar or tamarind.

CHOOSE Ground powder (brick red) from Middle Eastern or Greek shops.

TASTE Tart, almost lemony.

STORE Will keep for several months in an airtight container.

USE FOR
■ Rubbing over cubes of fish, chicken or lamb for kebabs before grilling to add flavour and colour.
■ Flavouring stuffings, stews and casseroles.
■ Mixing the powder into yogurt with mint or coriander for a dipping sauce.

GOES WITH Chicken, lamb, fish and shellfish, rice, lentils and pulses, aubergine, sesame, yogurt, nuts.

USE INSTEAD Lemon juice or vinegar for an acidic flavour (only if adding to stews or salads). Lemon zest and salt if using for sprinkling.

Tamarind

Also known as Indian date, this is the fruit of the tamarind tree which grows inside pods that look rather like large peanuts in their shells. Inside the pods is a sticky, brown pulp wrapped around numerous seeds. Commercially this pulp is semi-dried and shaped into blocks or made into paste. Much loved in Indian, Middle Eastern and South-East Asian dishes, it is used to add an acidic tang much as lemon juice or vinegar is used in the West.

CHOOSE Pulp in various guises – as paste in jars, pulp in blocks and concentrate.

TASTE A complex mouthful of sour, sweet, fruity and tangy flavours.

STORE The paste and blocks will keep for up to a year in the fridge.

PREPARE
Paste in jars: This is the easiest – everything has been done for you as it is the crushed, sieved pulp. Just get your spoon out – the label or recipe will advise how much you need.
Pulp in blocks: Thai or Indonesian is moist and soft, so simply cut off a piece and mash it with hot water to make your own paste. Use as is or strain for just the liquid. If it is to go into something that simmers, just chop the tamarind finely, add as is and let it dissolve in the dish. Indian tamarind is harder and more compressed, so not as easy to work with. Cut off a 25 g (1 oz) piece and soak in 150–300 ml (¼–½ pint) hot water for half an hour. Strain in a sieve,

sumac–turmeric

pressing the tamarind well down to extract the liquid.

Concentrate: This is like a very dark syrup. Use sparingly and cautiously. Not so fresh-tasting as paste.

COOK The flavour softens when added early on in a dish.

USE FOR
- Giving a mild fruity taste to rice – add a little to the water as it cooks.
- Flavouring salad dressings instead of lemon juice or vinegar.
- Using in marinades, especially for chicken, pork or prawns.
- Adding a spoonful to tomato or mango relishes for a sweet-sour taste.
- Making chutney (tamarind has a lot of pectin, so helps it set).
- Stirring into curries, especially vegetable or chicken.

GOES WITH Fish and shellfish, chicken, pork, potatoes, cauliflower, pulses, mangoes.

USE INSTEAD Lime or lemon juice or vinegar (not such complex flavours).

Turmeric

This tropical root, a member of the ginger family, looks like root ginger but has an orange flesh. After drying it turns yellow, and will give a distinctive colour to many curry and rice dishes, that is deeper and more ochre yellow than saffron. The main producer is India, where it forms the basis of many masalas and curry powders. Turmeric is also used throughout South-East Asia and in Moroccan tagines and stews.

CHOOSE Ground. The whole root is available from Indian speciality shops, but the powder is more commonly used.

TASTE Musky and pungent, slightly harsh. If you add too much, both colour and flavour can get too intense.

STORE Ground will keep in an air-tight container for about 9 months.

PREPARE If using the root, peel it like root ginger, then slice, chop or grate.

COOK Turmeric is often fried with other spices to draw out the flavour, but be careful not to let it burn.

USE FOR

■ Giving colour and fragrance to both fish and meat curries.
■ Mixing a little into kedgeree and other savoury rice dishes.
■ Making spicy chutneys and pickles (it's what gives piccalilli its colour).
■ Adding a pinch or two to a fish chowder or to savoury pancake batter.
■ Sprinkling over potatoes as they roast for a golden glow.

GOES WITH Chicken, lamb, fish, vegetables (especially potatoes, cauliflower and spinach), pulses, rice, coconut milk, yogurt, ginger.

USE INSTEAD Saffron is more expensive and has a different flavour, so use it instead only when a yellow colour is needed and not the flavour of turmeric.

Vanilla

There's something exotic about vanilla. It's nearly as expensive as saffron but its tantalizing flavour makes it worth paying the price. The pods (or beans) are the fruit of a Mexican orchid which have been sun-dried so they shrivel and turn a deep brown. Vanilla is exported from tropical places such as Mexico, Indonesia, Tahiti and Madagascar (bourbon beans).

CHOOSE Between pods, extract and essence.
Pods: These give the true vanilla

turmeric–vanilla

taste. They should be shiny, slightly oily, supple, slightly wrinkled, but not brittle or dry – with a rich aroma. Length is a good indication of quality: about 15–20 cm (6–8 in) is best.

Extract/essence: Check the label for 'natural/pure vanilla extract', which is the real thing. It has been 'extracted' from the pods, which have been soaked and softened in alcohol to give a liquid with a powerfully concentrated vanilla flavour. Vanilla essence is a cheaper version that bears little resemblance to the genuine article.

TASTE Sweetly perfumed, rich and almost creamy.

STORE If kept well sealed in an air-tight container, the pods will keep for at least 2 years.

PREPARE For an intense vanilla flavour, both pods and seeds can be used. Slit the pod lengthways and open it. Using the tip of a small sharp knife, carefully scrape the pod to remove the tiny sticky seeds. When added to a dish, these seeds will appear as little black specks and are a sign of authenticity.

VANILLA

TIPS & TRICKS: VANILLA
- *If a recipe calls for the seeds only, scrape them from the pod but don't throw the pod away. Tuck it into a jar of sugar to give you vanilla sugar (see page 119).*
- *You can recycle a vanilla pod if it hasn't been used too vigorously to start with. Wash it, dry well and keep tightly wrapped for another time – if it has only been soaking in liquid it should still have a lot of flavour left.*

SPICES A–Z

USE FOR

■ Infusing in cream or milk for ice cream, custard (for making trifle, *crème brûlée, crème caramel* and *panna cotta*) and milkshakes.
■ Infusing in sugar syrup for fruit salads.
■ Flavouring meringues and other sweet things, such as cakes and biscuits.
■ Adding a subtle, unusual flavour to fish and shellfish sauces.

GOES WITH Mostly sweet things such as ice cream, cream, chocolate, coffee, most fruits, (especially tropical and summer ones).

USE INSTEAD Use vanilla pods and extract interchangeably.

TASTE Nutty, slightly coffee-like.

USE FOR

■ Mixing into meringues (especially good in a pavlova) and biscuit mixes or bread.
■ Beating into whipped cream – good with chocolate desserts.
■ Flavouring cake icings.

GOES WITH Chocolate, nuts, cream.

USE INSTEAD Leave out if not available, or mix a bit of finely ground coffee with a little mixed spice (see Spice Mixes, page 164).

Wattle seeds

An Australian ground spice that is available by mail order over the internet. It is made from the seeds of a certain type of acacia that is gathered by the Aboriginal people, then roasted and ground to a powder that has a resemblance to roasted coffee.

Fruit and Veg

FRUIT

FRUITS OFFER AN ABUNDANCE OF HEALTH-GIVING PROPERTIES, BEING HANDY-TO-EAT PACKAGES OF VITAMINS, MINERALS, FIBRE AND DISEASE-FIGHTING PLANT COMPOUNDS. USUALLY LOW IN CALORIES AND SODIUM, BUT CRAMMED WITH ANTIOXIDANTS, THEY PROVIDE AN OPTIMAL WAY TO IMPROVE HEALTH. WHETHER BUYING FRUITS FOR EATING RAW OR FOR MAKING INTO DESSERTS, THIS CHAPTER WILL BE A HANDY ALPHABETICAL GUIDE, WITH LOTS OF EASY SERVING SUGGESTIONS.

BUY IN SEASON

To get the best possible flavour and nutritional value from fruit, buy when it is in season and look at the label to check that it hasn't travelled too far.

FREEZING FRUIT

Fresh is best, but freezing is convenient if you are want to use fruit for cooking. Some fruits suit being frozen whole by open freezing (below), while others are better frozen as a purée, in a compote or in a sugar syrup.

CHECK LIST Choose fruit in peak condition – for fruit to be good quality after freezing, it must be good quality before it goes in.

■ For best flavour the fruit should be just ripe (not too hard or too soft).
■ Wash gently only if necessary and pat dry with kitchen paper.

Open freezing

This is a technique for freezing certain fruits whole, so they don't stick together in a big lump or get crushed or damaged. When ready to use, just pour or scoop them out of their container.

Fruits to choose: Summer berries and currants, cherries, cranberries.
How to do it: Lay the fruit in a single layer on a baking sheet lined with greaseproof paper and 'open freeze' (that is, put in the freezer uncovered) for a few hours or until the fruit goes solid. You can then tip the fruit into freezer bags or containers, seal, label and return to the freezer; they will keep for up to a year.

Freezing in syrup

Since freezing causes many fruits to discolour or lose their texture, especially stoned fruits such as peaches, plums and apricots, they benefit from immersion in sugar syrup for freezing. **Fruits to choose:** Peaches, pears, nectarines, plums, apricots, apples. **How to do it:** Make a syrup by dissolving one part sugar to two parts water (that is 100 g (3½ oz) golden caster sugar and 200 ml (7 fl oz) water to 500 g (1 lb) fruit), then simmer until it is syrupy. Add 1–2 tbsp lemon juice and leave to cool. Peel the fruit (see individual fruits, pages 202–249), halve or slice, removing any stones, seeds or cores, then pack into rigid freezer containers. Pour the cold syrup over the fruit to cover. If necessary, pack a piece of crumpled foil on top to keep the fruit immersed in the syrup. Seal, label, freeze – the fruit will keep for about 6 months.

BAKING EN PAPILLOTE

To seal in all the juices of a fruit completely when cooking, try baking in foil. For each serving, cut out a large square of foil. Pile the fruit in the centre, enrich with a knob of butter, sweeten with a sprinkling of sugar or a drizzle of honey or maple syrup, then add a splash of wine or other alcohol. Bring the sides of the foil up and fold over to seal tightly. Place on a baking sheet and bake at 180°C/350°F/Gas Mark 4 (160°C/325°F in fan ovens) for about 15 minutes or until just tender. Alternatively cook on the barbecue for 5–10 minutes.

INSTANT FREEZER DESSERT

For an instant freezer dessert, scatter frozen fruits straight on to serving plates and pour over a warm chocolate sauce made by gently melting 150 g (5 oz) white chocolate with 150 ml (¼ pint) double cream. The warm chocolate soon starts to thaw the fruits.

FRUIT A–Z

Apple

Although there are several thousand apple varieties, only a few are available commercially. If you see a variety for sale you haven't tried before, give it a go. Apples are divided into eaters and cookers. The main difference is that cooking apples are tarter; some eating apples can, however, also be used for cooking (see Use For, opposite).

CHOOSE

- Available all year round, but often cheaper and at their best in autumn.
- Firm fruit, with no wrinkles or bruises.
- Sweet-smelling fruit – apples should smell as well as taste sweet (apart from cooking apples).

STORE Keep in a fridge or cool place in a perforated plastic bag. If kept too warm they will lose crispness. FREEZE: Stewed or puréed (see opposite) or as apple sauce. Or slice and poach for a minute in sugar syrup, then freeze (see page 200).

PREPARE Use a vegetable peeler or sharp knife to peel (the advantage of a peeler is that it removes less flesh

than a knife). To core, cut the apple into quarters, cut out the core with a small, sharp knife, then peel, slice, dice or chop. To keep the apple whole, remove the core first using an apple corer; if you want to remove the peel too, do that after coring as the apple is less likely to crack. Grate, with peel on or off, using the broadest part of the grater, for adding to muesli, cakes or salads.

COOK

Bake: Core as above with an apple corer, keeping the apple whole, skin on. Score around the middle with a sharp knife, just over halfway up, then put in a shallow baking dish. Stuff with whatever you fancy, such as dried fruits, crushed amaretti or ginger biscuits, nuts, chunks of marzipan or crystallized ginger, or mincemeat, then sprinkle with a little muscovado or caster sugar, dot with butter and pour about 1 cm ($\frac{1}{2}$ in) water into the dish. Bake at 180°C/350°F/Gas Mark 4 (160°C/325°F in fan ovens) for about 40–45 minutes (depends on the size of the fruit) or until tender when tested with a skewer.

- Serve with ice cream, cream, crème fraîche or custard.

Poach: See Pear, page 240.

Pan-fry: Melt a generous knob of

apple

butter – about 30 g (1 oz), in a frying pan with 3–4 tbsp golden caster sugar until the sugar starts to colour. Tip in thickish wedges of apple and cook over a medium heat for a few minutes until starting to turn brown around the edges and soften.

■ Serve over ice cream or with clotted cream on their own or with pancakes or waffles.

Stew: Peel, core and slice or chop 500 g (1 lb) apples and put in a pan with a couple of spoonfuls of water, sugar to sweeten, a squeeze of lemon and a knob of butter. Butter a circle of greaseproof paper and place snugly on top of the apples, then cover with a lid. Cook over a lowish heat, stir-ring often, until the apples are soft, about 10–15 minutes. Boil to thicken, add water to thin, or purée to make the mixture smooth.

■ Serve as apple sauce, or when cold mix with equal amounts of ready-made thick custard and whipped cream for a quick dessert.

USE FOR

Eating: Crisp, fresh and juicy such as Cox, Braeburn, Pink Lady, Jonagold, Royal Gala, Fuji, Golden Delicious, Egremont Russet.

Salads: Golden Delicious, Pink Lady, Fuji.

Baking: Bramley (English cooking

TIPS & TRICKS: APPLES

To stop apples turning brown when cut, toss them with lemon juice. If you use an eating apple for cooking, you may not need to add as much sugar (as they are sweeter than 'cookers').

MATCHING FRUITS AND ALCOHOL

If you want to add a splash of something boozy to your fruits, here's a quick guide:

■ *BRANDY – cherries, apples, pears, oranges, peaches, apricots*
■ *CASSIS – summer currants and berries, plums*
■ *KIRSCH – cherries, summer berries*
■ *PORT – cherries, plums, cranberries, redcurrants*
■ *RUM – pineapples, mangoes, bananas, mandarins, clementines*
■ *VODKA – pears*
■ *WINE (white or rosé) – grapes, nectarines, peaches, apricots*
■ *WINE (red) – strawberries, plums, pears*

apple), Granny Smith, Fuji.
Dessert: Golden Delicious, Braeburn, Bramley, Granny Smith, Cox, Discovery, Jonagold, Royal Gala, Pink Lady, Egremont Russet.
Apple sauce: Bramley or other cooking apple.

GOES WITH Pork and gammon, cheese, blackberries, pear, lemon, nuts, cinnamon, cloves, thyme, cider, brandy.

GOOD FOR YOU A source of fibre and vitamin C, though the bulk is found in the skin and core.

USE INSTEAD Pear.

Apricot

This belongs to the family of stone fruits, along with cherries, nectarines, peaches and plums. Apricots began their life in China before being grown in the Middle East. Wherever they grow in the world they need warmth. During the summer they now come from hot European countries, mainly Spain, France and Greece, and for a few brief months in winter from South Africa and Chile.

CHOOSE
- Best during the summer months.
- You can't always go by the colour, but apricots should feel heavy and be reasonably firm, but with a bit of tenderness and no brown spots.
- They should smell fragrant when ripe.

STORE If they are not ripe when you buy them, leave them to ripen at home at room temperature for several days. When ripe, they will keep in the fridge for up to 4–5 days.
FREEZE: In sugar syrup (see page 201).

PREPARE No need to peel. To halve, using the dimple as a guide, go round the stone with a sharp knife. Gently twist apart with both hands, then scoop out the central stone. Brush any cut flesh with lemon juice as it goes brown quite quickly.

COOK The flavour is highlighted by cooking, so unless they are really fresh and ripe, apricots are often more popular cooked for desserts.
Poach: As for pears, see page 240, but poach for 10–15 minutes, using half white wine, half water, or all water.

USE FOR
- Making compotes, jams and chutneys.
- A fruit crumble.
- Poaching to use as a topping for cheesecake or sponge cake.

apple–banana

■ Mixing into a stuffing for lamb with nuts and herbs, or adding at the last minute to a Moroccan lamb stew.

GOES WITH Chicken, duck, lamb, almond, orange, chocolate, sweet white wine.

GOOD FOR YOU Contains high levels of the antioxidant beta carotene and vitamin A.

USE INSTEAD Peach or nectarine.

Banana

see also PLANTAIN, *page 243*
Bananas look like fat fingers, which is probably how they got their name, as banana comes from the Arabic word *banan* which means finger. This fruit originated in the Far East and the biggest exporter is now Ecuador in South America.

CHOOSE The familiar yellow, or the more unusual red or apple banana. Red bananas come from Ecuador, have a red-purple skin and a drier taste than yellow bananas (otherwise they can be used interchangeably), but are good for baking. Black patches on their skin indicate ripeness. Apple bananas are tiny in size and some-times known as dwarf bananas. They

TIPS & TRICKS: BANANAS
■ *If bananas get too ripe for eating, peel, mash and freeze them for using in cakes, muffins or smoothies.*

are sweeter than ordinary bananas, but are treated the same. The perfect size for pan-frying (see right).

■ They are available all year round.

■ Buy when yellow if you want to eat them straight away, slightly green if not (leave them for a few days at room temperature to ripen). Or buy a mix of yellow and greenish ones so you have some for now, some for later.

■ For baking, bananas that are over-ripe and brown-skinned are softer to mash and give the best flavour.

STORE Not in the fridge as the skin goes black, although the flesh can still be used for baking. Best kept in a fruit bowl on their own (or can help ripen other fruits, see Speedy Ripening, page 221).

FREEZE: In their skins. The texture of the flesh will not be the same but is handy to have for mashing and using in baking.

PREPARE Just peel and slice or mash with a fork. Use lemon juice to stop them going brown.

COOK

Bake: Peel 2 bananas, halve length-ways and lay them in a shallow baking dish. Squeeze with the juice of half a lemon, dot with a knob of butter, sprin-kle with 3 tbsp light or dark muscovado sugar and drizzle with 1–2 tsp of rum. Cover and bake at 180°C/350°F/ Gas Mark 4 (160°C/325°F in fan ovens) for about 20 minutes until softened.

■ Serve warm with cream, crème fraîche or yogurt.

Barbecue: Make a small slit in the skin to stop the banana bursting. Put on a hot barbecue and cook for about 10 minutes, turning often, until the skin is completely black. Take off the barbecue and slit open lengthways with a sharp knife.

■ Serve with barbecued meats, or sprinkle with cinnamon and light muscovado sugar as a dessert with cream or ice cream.

Pan-fry: Peel and halve lengthways. Put about 30 g (1 oz) each butter and golden caster sugar into a frying pan and heat until melted. Add the banana halves, fry until just softening, then splash in 2–3 tbsp rum and let it bubble to warm through.

■ Delicious with ice cream.

Grill: Peel and halve lengthways, lay the pieces on a baking sheet, brush with lemon juice and sprinkle with sugar. Grill under a hot grill for a few minutes until soft and caramelized.

■ Serve with chicken, gammon or fish.

USE FOR

■ Mashing and mixing into bakes such as banana bread and muffins, or into

flapjacks for a softer texture.
■ Puréeing for milkshakes and
smoothies.
■ Making a chocolate banana lolly –
peel and put on a small wooden skewer,
wrap tightly and freeze. Once frozen,
unwrap and coat in melted chocolate,
which will immediately harden.

GOES WITH Bacon, gammon,
cream, yogurt, honey, maple syrup,
lemon, rum, cinnamon.

GOOD FOR YOU Great source of
potassium and slow-release carbohydrate.

Berries

There are many members of the berry
family, with strong family resemblances
– all are small, juicy, simple to prepare
and bursting with vitamin C.

CHOOSE

Blackberry: Late summer–early
autumn; try also loganberry (part
blackberry, part raspberry) which is
longer in shape and sharper in taste,
so better cooked with sugar than raw.
Blueberry: All year round, but especially good in the summer.
Gooseberry: Early summer for green
cooking ones, midsummer for dessert
varieties.

Raspberry: Have most flavour in high summer.

Strawberry: Available all year round. Bigger fruit doesn't always have more flavour. Try also alpine or wood strawberries (*fraises de bois*), both smaller, extremely fragrant and sweet.

■ If they're sold in a carton, check the lower layers of berries for signs of mould or crushing – any that are past their best will quickly infect the rest.

■ All should look unblemished, plump and bright.

STORE Best eaten soon – they keep for no more than a couple of days after you buy or pick them, except for gooseberries (they will keep for up to 2 weeks if not fully ripe) and blueberries (4–5 days). Spread softer berries out on a plate so they can't crush each other, preferably on kitchen paper. If you are going to eat them fairly quickly, don't store in the fridge. If refrigerated, bring them out about an hour ahead of eating and serve at room temperature for optimum flavour.

FREEZE: By open freezing (see page 200), then freezing. Firmer berries, such as gooseberries and blueberries, don't need to be open frozen first, but can go straight into freezer bags. Strawberries go mushy after freezing, so are best frozen as purée.

PREPARE Berries need very little attention apart from the following.

Gooseberries: Top and tail them – snip off the bits at both ends.

Raspberries: Because they are fragile, these are best not washed. If you really want to, give a very quick rinse in a sieve or colander.

Strawberries: To prevent the fruit becoming waterlogged, wash briefly before hulling (see page 29) and dry on kitchen paper. With ripe or home-grown fruit, you can gently pull out the leaves and core. For imported and unripe strawberries, the centre isn't always as loose, so cut around the leaves and stalk with the tip of a small, sharp knife, and ease them out. Use strawberries whole, in halves, quarters or slices.

EAT All berries are wonderful eaten just as they are, apart from tart-tasting gooseberries which need cooking first with sugar (ripe dessert varieties can be eaten raw). Blueberries also benefit from a little cooking.

COOK

Gooseberries: Use early season green fruit. Put 250 g (9 oz) fruit in a pan with 150 ml (¼ pint) water and 125 g (4 oz) sugar and cook over a low heat until they soften and half have burst. Add more sugar if needed.

berries

Blueberries: Dissolve 30 g (1 oz) sugar in a pan with 1–2 tbsp water. Stir in 250 g (9 oz) blueberries and simmer for a few minutes, until they brighten in colour and start to burst and turn the syrup a deep purple.

USE FOR

■ Creating a simple dessert. Tip the berries into a large bowl, sprinkle with icing or caster sugar and an optional splash of red wine or balsamic vinegar for strawberries, cassis for blueberries, blackberries and raspberries. Leave for half an hour to create a flavourful juice, then serve with cream or just as they are.

■ Making a milkshake or smoothie. Blend a handful of berries (not gooseberries) with a sliced banana in a food processor or blender until smooth, then whizz in enough milk or apple juice to create the desired thickness.

■ Dropping whole or sliced fruits (raspberries, strawberries and blueberries) into glasses of chilled sparkling wine as an aperitif.

■ Mixing and matching. Make up your own combination of berries for a summer fruit salad and macerate in lemon grass syrup (see page 147).

■ Stirring a few blueberries or raspberries into a brownie mix or mixing with peaches after poaching.

■ Stewing blackberries or gooseber-

QUICK BERRY COULIS

To make an uncooked fruit purée or coulis, drop 150 g (5 oz) strawberries or raspberries, 1 tbsp each sugar and water into a food processor or blender, whizz until smooth, then check for sweetness.

■ Swirl through cream, yogurt or crème fraîche and use as a filling, spoon into glasses for a dessert, or sieve to make an instant coulis.

BERRIES ON ICE

For dropping into summer drinks and cocktails, put a few mixed berries in ice-cube trays with strips of lime zest, top up with water and freeze until solid. Pack into freezer bags and store in the freezer.

ries and serving with yogurt on your morning muesli.

GOOD FOR YOU

Blackberry: Rich in vitamin C and fibre.

Blueberry: Thought to be a real superfood because it contains a high concentration of phytochemicals which can help protect against many illnesses such as heart disease, some cancers and type-2 diabetes.

Gooseberry: Good source of vitamin C; some fibre.

Raspberry: High in vitamin ; the seeds add fibre.

Strawberry: Particularly high in vitamin C; contains fibre.

Cherry

A small stone fruit belonging to the same family as peaches, plums, apricots and nectarines.

CHOOSE Either sweet, or sour cherries such as Morello (these are very sour, so are used for cooking).

■ Home-grown are cheaper and sweeter during early to mid summer (also available at different times of the year from France, Turkey, Spain, the USA, Chile and South Africa).

■ Look for cherries with green fresh stems that are still attached, as they keep longer than ones without stems.

■ Go for plumpness and glossiness; avoid split or bruised fruit.

STORE Keep in a bowl on the kitchen worktop, or in a perforated plastic bag in the fridge for up to 2 days. If the bag has no air holes, the cherries will sweat and go bad quickly. Don't wash them until ready to eat.

FREEZE: Remove the stones first, then open freeze (see page 200).

PREPARE Rinse, then pluck the fruit from the stems. The easiest way to remove the stone is with a cherry pitter (see opposite). It keeps the cherry whole and you can use it for pitting olives, too. Another way is to score all the way round the cherry with a small, sharp knife, twist each half in opposite directions to separate, and pull out the stone.

COOK

Poach: For each 375 g (12 oz) cherries, dissolve 90 g (3 oz) golden caster sugar in 300 ml (½ pint) red wine or port in a wide, shallow pan. Throw in a couple of star anise if you like, then add the cherries, stoned or not, and gently simmer for a few minutes until tender.

■ Unbeatable with clotted cream or ice cream.

berries–cranberry

USE FOR
Sweet cherries
- Serving simply at the end of a meal in a pile, on a platter with big chunks of brie and goat's cheese.
- Dipping in melted chocolate.
- Stirring into cake mixes: they go well with chocolate and almond flavours.
- Chopping finely or coarsely to mix with lime juice and grated zest, some chopped coriander, a pinch of dried chilli flakes and some finely chopped shallot for a fresh salsa to serve with roast duck, grilled gammon or cold meats.

Sour cherries
- Making jam or adding to pies.
- Adding to fruity, red wine based, savoury sauces.

GOES WITH Duck, chicken, gammon, cheese, chocolate, almond, kirsch, port, cream.

GOOD FOR YOU Provides vitamin C and is packed with antioxidants.

USE INSTEAD Canned or in jars if you can't find fresh.

CHERRY PITTING
The easiest way to remove the stone is with a special cherry pitter. Just press the cherry pitter into the indent in the stem end and the stone should pop right out the other end.

Cranberry
Drop a cranberry and it should bounce if fresh: that's why they are sometimes

called 'bounce berries'. They grow on trailing vines, on boggy marshlands mostly in Canada and the USA, but can also be found in northern Europe.

CHOOSE
- An autumn/winter fruit.
- Should be dry, plump, not at all shrivelled.
- Look for bright red, about the size of a small grape.

STORE A sturdy fruit – it will keep for at least a month in the fridge.
FREEZE: Cranberries freeze beautifully, so best to buy when in season, then open freeze (see page 200) and freeze for up to 4 to 6 months. Can use straight from frozen.

PREPARE Just cook.

COOK Generally not a fruit for eating raw as they are so tart – cranberries benefit from being cooked with sugar to get the juices to flow.

USE FOR
- Mixing into stuffings with nuts (especially hazelnuts) and orange zest to serve with chicken or turkey.
- Making cranberry sauce (see opposite) or mixing into muffins or gooey steamed puddings.
- Folding sweetened, cooked and cooled fruit into whipped cream to fill a pavlova or orange or hazelnut-flavoured cake.
- Chopping and mixing into mincemeat for Christmas pies and tarts.

GOES WITH Poultry, nuts, mincemeat, orange, cinnamon.

GOOD FOR YOU Contains vitamin C and flavonoids (antioxidants that help fight heart disease and cancer).

Currant (red, black and white)

The three types, red, black and white, grow on low bushes and hang in little clusters on slender stalks. All are tart – blackcurrants have the boldest flavour, and white (redcurrants with no colour pigment) are sweetest.

CHOOSE
- At the height of summer.
- All should look clean and glossy and not squashy. White are harder to track down than red and black.

STORE In the fridge, unwashed, for up to 3 days.
FREEZE: Open freeze (see page 200) with their stalks on – they will easily become separated after freezing.

cranberry–currant

PREPARE Wash, then hold each stalk firmly at the top over a bowl. Run a fork down its length so the stalk goes between the prongs, allowing the berries to be released easily.

EAT White and red can be eaten raw, sprinkled generously with sugar. Black are rarely eaten raw.

COOK They are usually cooked with sugar to bring out their juiciness.
Poach: Pour 3 tbsp water into a pan with 60 g (2 oz) caster sugar. Heat, stirring, to dissolve the sugar, then add 425 g (14 oz) fruit. Simmer gently and briefly until just starting to burst.

USE FOR
■ Mixing with soft summer berries for summer pudding (all colours).
■ Combining colours for contrast in tarts or pies, or to decorate cheesecakes, pavlovas and creamy desserts.
■ Making fruit coulis and syrups, jams, cordials and jellies (red or black).
■ Making an instant sauce. Defrost frozen currants, then mash with sugar and a squeeze of lemon juice (or purée in a blender) and sieve until smooh.
■ Creating purées for sorbets, ice cream and mousses (black).
■ Freezing in tiny clusters in ice-cube trays, filled with water, for dropping into summer drinks (any colour).

QUICK CRANBERRY SAUCE
Tip 225 g (8 oz) cranberries into a pan with 5 tbsp water. Bring to the boil, cover and cook for 10 minutes until the skins pop. Tip in 125 g (4 oz) caster sugar, the finely grated zest of 1 orange and 2 tbsp red wine or port (optional). Cook, stirring to dissolve the sugar, then simmer for about 5 minutes or until the sauce reaches the thickness you want. Cool. It will keep for several days in the fridge, or for up to 3 months in the freezer.

■ Crushing and adding a few to oil and vinegar dressing (red or black).

GOES WITH

Blackcurrants: Duck, game, mint, red wine, cream, yogurt.

Redcurrants: Lamb, goose, raspberries, strawberries, melon, peaches, rosemary, cream.

White currants: Mix with red and black for summer desserts.

GOOD FOR YOU All contain vitamin C, blackcurrants the most.

Date (fresh)

for DRIED, see page 84

Fresh dates are moister but not as sweet as dried. Dates look dried even if fresh, so it is not always easy to tell which you are buying, but in supermarkets they are likely to be dried.

CHOOSE

■ All year round, but fresher in the winter months around Christmas.

■ Go for plump, shiny and a bit wrinkly, with dark brown skin.

■ Medjool dates are particularly good – they taste like toffee.

STORE Will keep in the fridge for several days in an airtight container, or at room temperature.

FREEZE: Remove stones from fresh dates, pack into freezer bags or containers and freeze for up to a year.

PREPARE Simply remove the stone by pushing it through the date. For a neater look, slit the date lengthways, open it, lift out the stone and close it up again. If you need to remove the skin, pull the stem off then hold the date by pinching it at one end and pushing the flesh so it squeezes out the other end.

USE FOR

■ Stuffing with cream cheese or curd cheese, after slitting lengthways and mixing with a little finely grated orange zest.

■ Making chutney.

■ Adding to cakes and puddings to make them moist and sticky.

■ Snipping over your breakfast cereal to sweeten instead of sugar.

■ Putting in sandwiches – just chop and mix with softened cream cheese.

■ Sweetening savoury stews, especially Moroccan lamb or chicken ones.

USE INSTEAD Dried figs, prunes or dried dates.

GOES WITH Lamb, chicken, creamy cheeses, honey, nuts, oats.

currant–fig

GOOD FOR YOU Great source of fibre, vitamin C (more than cranberries and cherries) and chloride.

Fig

Most of the inside of the fig is made up of wine-red edible seeds. Originally from western Asia, figs are now mainly produced in Mediterranean countries. They are delicate, so are often shipped unripe to prevent bruising. Treat gently.

CHOOSE

■ Available at different times depending on variety and country of origin.
■ Should feel soft, but not excessively so, with no blemishes or bruises which indicate they have been damaged.
■ Look for plump figs with no signs of shrivelling.
■ They range in colour from green to almost black, with shades of yellow, brown, red and purple in between.

STORE At room temperature for ripening, or loosely packed individually in kitchen paper in the fridge. They will only keep for a day or two, so eat them quickly.
FREEZE: Gently wash and remove the stems, pat dry, then open freeze (see page 200).

PREPARE Keep whole or cut into quarters, so their shapeliness can be admired. For a nice effect, cut through the skin and quarter the flesh without cutting all the way through; you can then open out the fruit like a flower to show off the juicy red flesh (see illustration opposite).

EAT Best eaten at room temperature, so if you've stored the figs in the fridge, get them out about an hour before you want to serve them. No need to peel; just tuck in or split open with your fingers first.

COOK

Grill: Cut in half lengthways, drizzle with honey and grill for a few minutes until lightly caramelised.

Poach: In red wine. Heat 600 ml (1 pint) red wine with 150 g (5 oz) sugar in a medium pan until dissolved. Bring to the boil, then lower the heat to a simmer. Add the figs (there is enough liquid for about 12). Put in as many as will fit in the pan in a single layer: do in batches if necessary. Cover and poach for 5–8 minutes or until softened. Lift the figs out with a slotted spoon into a serving dish and bubble the wine for another 5–8 minutes until reduced to a thin syrup. Cool, then pour over the figs.

Roast: Sit 6–8 figs in an ovenproof dish so they are upright and fit snugly. Drizzle with 2 tbsp each honey and orange juice. Roast at 220°C/425°F/ Gas Mark 7 (200°C/400°F in fan ovens) for about 8–12 minutes or until the skins start to crack.

USE FOR

■ Making kebabs – cut into quarters, wrap with Parma ham, thread on skewers, then serve, or lightly brush with oil and grill for a few minutes.
■ Adding quartered to salads with goat's cheese and rocket, drizzled with an olive oil dressing.
■ Serving raw or roasted as a simple dessert, drizzled with honey and served with spoonfuls of plain yogurt or fromage frais and a scattering of toasted nuts.

GOES WITH Parma ham, ricotta, goat's cheese, nuts, honey, cinnamon.

GOOD FOR YOU Has iron and potassium and is high in fibre; also high in calcium – dried figs have twice as much per 100 g (3½ oz) as milk.

Gooseberry
see BERRIES, *page 207*

Grape

One of the oldest cultivated fruits in the world, grapes have many uses. They produce wine, vinegar and verjuice and, when dried, shrivel to become currants, raisins and sultanas, as well as being a juicy fruit in their own right. They are grown mostly in Greece, Spain, Italy, the USA, India, South Africa and Chile.

CHOOSE

■ All year round, as varieties from around the world come into season. Choose from black, red and green (also called white), with or without seeds. Flavours vary – black, such as Ribier and Black Italia, tend to have more depth. Favourite green ones are Vittoria and Italia, and red-skinned are Flame and Muscat Rosada. Seedless grapes are convenient, but ones with seeds in are often tastier.
■ Check that they have a fresh bloom, the stalks are fresh and there are no bruised or small, shrivelled grapes.
■ Don't buy in bulk unless you are going to eat them quickly as grapes are closely packed on the bunch, so can squash and bruise each other if left sitting around too long.

STORE Pluck off any bad ones from the bunch, wash, then store in a fruit

OPENING FIGS
If you want to be fancy – open out the quartered fig like a flower (see Prepare, opposite).

FIX IT: FIGS
If your figs lack juiciness and flavour, drizzle with honey and roast or grill.

bowl for a day or two if you are going to eat them straight away. Otherwise they will last unwashed in a perforated plastic bag in the vegetable drawer of the fridge for up to a week. For best flavour take out about an hour before eating.
FREEZE: Not recommended.

PREPARE Wash before use and, unless they are seedless, halve and pick out the seeds. If a recipe calls for skinning the grapes, prick each end, drop into boiling water for 1 minute, then into cold water and peel.

COOK Not used a lot in cooking, but when you do, add towards the end to keep their shape and texture intact.

USE FOR

■ A healthy snack or serving in little clusters still on the stalks with cheese.
■ Adding to both sweet and savoury salads.
■ Classic cooked savoury dishes such as sole Véronique.
■ Decorating desserts by 'frosting' the grapes. Brush each grape all over with lightly beaten egg white, then sprinkle with caster sugar (or dip them in the sugar) to coat evenly, shaking off any excess. Lay on baking parchment to dry.

GOES WITH Chicken, pheasant, fish, cheese, white wine, tarragon.

GOOD FOR YOU Low in nutrients, but the red varieties particularly contain a lot of flavonoids (antioxidants).

Grapefruit

Grapefruit is a citrus fruit, a descendent of the sweet orange and the larger pummelo (see opposite). Grapefruit have been cultivated for centuries in hot places such as Israel, Morocco, South Africa, Cyprus and Jamaica, and the 1970s saw the sweeter pink grapefruit grown in Florida and parts of the Caribbean.

CHOOSE

■ All year round, though there is more choice and sweeter and juicier fruit in winter and spring.
■ Shiny, thin-skinned ones that feel heavy with juice – light ones usually indicate a thick peel and less flesh.
■ Between yellow (white) flesh, pink and ruby red. Pink is much sweeter.

STORE Can be left at room temperature (better served like that too). Will keep for a week or two.

PREPARE To serve at breakfast, see right. Alternatively, segment them

grape–grapefruit

as you would an orange
(see pages 234 and 235).

EAT Best raw. Pink and red ones
don't need sugar, but you might want
to sweeten the yellow-fleshed, tangier
ones. To prepare, cut in half widthways, dig out and discard any pips
and loosen the flesh from the pithy
shell with a small, serrated knife or a
curved grapefruit knife. Loosen each
fleshy segment from the membranes
that separate them (see illustration,
right). Serve in the shell.

COOK

Grill: Prepare each half as above, put
on a small baking sheet, sprinkle with
about 1 tbsp light muscovado or
caster sugar and a touch of ground
cinnamon or ground ginger. Put under
the grill until the sugar melts and
caramelizes.
- Serve as a refreshing breakfast.

USE FOR

- Making a tangy marmalade.
- Combining (segmented) with orange
segments for a lively fruit salad;
sprinkle with toasted chopped hazelnuts or pistachios.
- A side salad (segmented) with slices
of avocado and crisp salad leaves or
with baby spinach leaves or watercress, avocado and orange.

PREPARING A
GRAPEFRUIT FOR
EATING

WHAT IS A PUMMELO?
This is similar to a grapefruit,
but thicker-skinned and pithier.
It is less juicy, so serve sprinkled
with sugar.

■ Squeezing the juice to use for a dressing instead of lemon. Sweeten with a little honey.

GOES WITH Chicken, oily fish (especially trout and mackerel), shellfish, avocado, spinach, mango, other citrus fruits, ginger, honey.

GOOD FOR YOU High in vitamin C and potassium. Pink varieties are a good source of beta carotene.

USE INSTEAD Pummelo.

Guava

A fragrant tropical fruit – it looks like a smooth lemon and smells of an expensive perfume. Inside is a sweet-sharp flesh varying in colour from yellow to salmon pink.

CHOOSE

■ Available most of the year.
■ Yellow aromatic fruit indicates ripeness, though as they bruise easily guavas are often sold unripe – green and hard.
■ They should feel firm, but give slightly in your hand when gently squeezed.

STORE If they are unripe when bought, leave them to ripen at room temperature, then keep in the fridge in a perforated plastic bag.
FREEZE: Best as a purée.

PREPARE Peel first if you like, then slice or cut in chunks.

EAT Make sure it is ripe first – the perfumed smell (which is often more beguiling than the taste) will tell you; otherwise it tastes sharp. You can eat the whole fruit, with skin and crunchy seeds, though one way to eat it is to cut it in half, then scoop out the flesh and seeds with a spoon.

COOK Cooking lifts the flavour. Try chopping or slicing and mixing with apples or pears for a crumble or compote. Or stew in the same way as apples (see page 203) and purée to make a sauce for serving with meats.

USE FOR

■ Adding peeled, sliced or chopped to a fruit salad.
■ Squeezing like a lemon to make a drink with the juice.
■ Chopping to make a salsa for serving with rich meats.
■ Jams, jellies, ice creams and sorbets.

GOES WITH Rich meats such as duck, pork and game, pineapple, strawberries.

GOOD FOR YOU Extremely rich in vitamin C, containing much more than an orange. Also rich in potassium, niacin and beta carotene.

Kiwi

This furry, brown-skinned fruit, with bright green flesh and black seeds, is named after the national bird of New Zealand and is also grown there. Native to China, it used to be called Chinese gooseberry. The golden variety is less hairy and has yellow-gold flesh that is sweeter than the green, somewhere between mango and melon.

CHOOSE

- All year round.
- Look for slightly firm fruits which give a little when gently squeezed. Avoid overripe ones.
- Check there are no bruises, and the skin is tight-fitting, not shrivelled.

STORE When ripe they will keep in the fridge for about a week. To speed up the ripening process, if not ripe when bought, see right.
FREEZE: Not recommended as the flesh becomes mushy on thawing.

PREPARE

With a knife: Peel off the thin inedible skin with a knife or vegetable

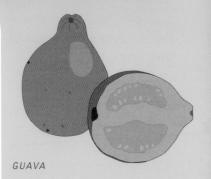

GUAVA

SPEEDY RIPENING
Fruit, especially kiwi, is often sold underripe. To ripen quickly at home, put the fruits in a paper bag along with an apple or a banana, giving them plenty of room so they don't get squashed. Leave at room temperature, away from direct sun.

peeler, then chop or cut the flesh in thickish slices or wedges (thin slices break up easily). The central white core is edible too, but if it is tough, just cut it out.

With a spoon: Cut a thin slice off each end of the fruit. Have a plate underneath to catch any juice, then, holding a dessertspoon in one hand and the fruit in the other, rotate the fruit with your hand, keeping the spoon flush with the peel as you go. When you get all the way round, the peeled fruit will plop right out. You can then slice it or cut it in wedges.

EAT Cut in half widthways and scoop out the flesh with a teaspoon.

COOK Heating destroys all the vitamin C as well as its colour, so don't.

USE FOR
- A filling for pavlovas or tarts.
- Chopping into salsas.
- Blending with a banana or other tropical fruits for a smoothie.

GOES WITH Chicken, pork, raspberries, papaya, banana, cream.

GOOD FOR YOU Eat one of these and you'll get your daily supply of vitamin C (for adults). It's also an effective natural laxative.

Lemon

Though it is not often eaten on its own, every bit of a lemon is a culinary treasure, and so this citrus fruit is loved around the world for its myriad uses. Its sour, tart taste makes it one of the most invaluable fruits.

CHOOSE
- All year round.
- Shiny ones with a real lemon-yellow colour. Darker, more orangy-yellow ones are less sour.
- Heavy, smaller lemons with thin, smooth skins have lots of juice – good for slices or wedges.
- Large ones can have more pith and skin – fine if you're making preserves or candied peel.
- Italian lemons are large with thick, knobbly skins, so have plenty of zest.

STORE Will keep for a couple of weeks or more in a perforated plastic bag in the fridge, or for a week or so in the fruit bowl. Check regularly for mould. Cut and wrapped in cling film, it will last 3–4 days in the fridge. FREEZE: Either whole or sliced. Whole – wash and dry, then pack into freezer bags, seal and label. Sliced – open freeze (see page 200).

kiwi–lemon

PREPARE Most lemons are waxed to preserve their skin, so unless they are organic, which are unwaxed, give them a scrub. If they have been in the fridge, let them reach room temperature before squeezing to get more juice.

Zest: This is the yellow outer part that holds the key to the lemon's flavour – if you go too deeply and take off the white pith too it can make a dish taste bitter. Fine for marmalade, but not for most other things. To release the aromatic oil in the zest, use a grater or zester for fine pieces (see pages 62 and 72), or for wider strips use a vegetable peeler.

Juice: Halve and twist the juice out with a lemon squeezer.

COOK Add towards the end of cooking as heat destroys the vitamin C.

USE FOR

- Stopping peeled or cut fruits and vegetables from going brown (see Acidulated, page 8).
- Flavouring desserts, biscuits, cakes (cuts through richness in heavy fruit cakes and mincemeat), risottos, pasta, couscous, sorbets, ice creams.
- Adding a little grated zest to sharpen the taste of mayonnaise, or making a salad dressing by mixing one-third lemon juice to two-thirds olive oil.
- Garnishing and flavouring. Sprinkle

TIPS & TRICKS: KIWIS

- *For really tender meat, lay a few slices of kiwi over it about an hour before cooking.*
- *Don't use kiwis in any recipe involving gelatine, as the same enzyme that tenderizes also inhibits gelatine from setting. The enzyme curdles milk and single cream too.*

slices with sugar, flash under the grill and use to decorate desserts such as cheesecake, lemon tart, sorbet.

- Deglazing a pan. After frying fish, add 1–2 tbsp juice, let it bubble in the fish juices, add some herbs and pour over the fish.
- Helping jams and marmalades set (it has a high pectin content).
- Roasting with wedges of potatoes. Coat the potatoes in oil, squeeze the juice from lemon wedges over the potatoes, then tuck in amongst them, season with pepper and roast.
- Cooking wedges on an oiled griddle pan to serve with fish, chicken, pork.
- Threading wedges on to skewers with wedges of onion and cubes of pork, chicken or fish.
- Adding fragrance to roast chicken. Halve a lemon and sit the halves inside the chicken cavity with a couple of bay leaves while roasting.

GOES WITH Any fish, chicken, salad leaves, honey, fruits, vegetables.

GOOD FOR YOU Contains lots of vitamin C.

USE INSTEAD Limes – but their flavour is stronger, so use about two-thirds the amount.

Lime

Looks like a small, green lemon but has a refreshing flavour all its own. Another member of the extended citrus fruit family, limes are particularly popular in South-East Asia where they are thought to have originally come from.

CHOOSE
- All year round.
- As with lemons, thin-skinned and heavy indicates lots of juice.
- Even, shiny, green skin, or with patches of yellow on too.
- Use kaffir limes for Thai cooking, though these are not readily available – look in Asian speciality stores. They are darker green, more knobbly-skinned, and used for their zest. Use ordinary limes if you can't find them.

STORE Will keep in the fridge for up to 2 weeks in a perforated plastic bag, or for about a week at room temperature.
FREEZE: Either whole or sliced.
Whole – wash and dry, then pack into freezer bags, seal and label.
Sliced – open freeze the slices (see page 200).

PREPARE The same as for lemons (see page 223), and take care when

lemon–lime

grating not to include the white pith as lime zest is thinner than a lemon's.

EAT Like lemons, not usually eaten as a raw fruit.

COOK Add towards the end of cooking as heat destroys the vitamin C.

USE FOR
- Making margueritas and daiquiris.
- 'Cooking' raw fish as in ceviche. When the juice is squeezed over raw fish, such as thin slices of salmon, and left to marinate, it has the same effect as cooking it and changes the appearance of the flesh from raw to opaque.
- Adding to many Thai dishes, especially soups, and Mexican guacamole.
- Bringing out the flavour of fruits – squeeze over chunks of papaya, melon, avocado or mango.
- Making salsas – the juice and zest are great with mango, a little oil and chopped chilli to serve with Mexican or Indian food, or fish dishes.
- Dropping slices into drinks such as gin and tonic, iced tea, fruit punch.

GOES WITH Chicken, fish, blueberries, tropical fruits such as mango and papaya, chilli.

GOOD FOR YOU Contains vitamin C, but less than lemons and oranges.

TIPS & TRICKS: LEMONS
Microwave your lemon on medium-high for 20–40 seconds or until just warm (the timing depends on the size of the lemon). This warms it a bit so you'll get more juice out (1 lemon generally gives about 2–3 tbsp juice).

If you haven't got a microwave, warm the lemon up by rolling it on the kitchen counter for a minute or two.

USE INSTEAD Lemons – use a bit more because of their milder flavour.

Lychee

With its brittle, pinky-red, bumpy shell, a lychee can look a hard nut to crack. But it is thin-skinned with a juicy, fleshy, translucent, white fruit that looks a bit like a swollen, jellied grape and tastes sweet and perfumed. It originated in China (hence its popularity with Chinese food) and now grows in tropical areas such as Madagascar, Mauritius, South Africa, Australia and Thailand.

CHOOSE
■ Available at different times of the year, especially in the winter.
■ Should look pinky red for freshness (green means not yet ripe, brown means they are past it). If they feel heavy they will be plump and juicy inside.

STORE At room temperature and try to use as soon as possible. FREEZE: Not recommended.

PREPARE Make a slit across the tight-fitting, brittle shell then peel it off, or just use your fingers. To keep the inside fruit whole, make a slit in the juicy, white flesh and pull out the stone. Or make a slit round the fruit's middle after peeling, twist to separate into halves and discard the stone.

EAT Just peel and eat your way around the shiny, dark stone as you would a plum. Or prepare as above.

USE FOR
■ Adding to fruit salads – goes well with melon, mango, pineapple, grapes in a lemon grass syrup (see page 147) especially after a Chinese or Thai meal.
■ Serving with vanilla ice cream.
■ Creating an instant dessert – put a few, peeled and stoned, in a bowl with a handful of blueberries and a squeeze of lime.

GOES WITH Other tropical fruits, blueberries, lemon grass.

GOOD FOR YOU Contains vitamin C and phosphorus.

USE INSTEAD Canned if you can't find fresh, but they taste less fragrant.

Mango

There are so many varieties of mango, there's no way to describe the perfect one. Not only can colour vary, but also texture, size and flavour.

lime–mango

Whatever the variety, when ripe a mango is the perfect-tasting fruit.

CHOOSE
■ Different varieties come into season at different times from the tropics, mostly Brazil, Mexico, Pakistan, India, Jamaica, South Africa.
■ Don't always go by colour – go by feel. When ripe a mango yields slightly when held and gently pressed.
■ For an especially tasty mango, try the small, golden Indian Alfonso mango, around only for a few weeks in late spring. Its soft texture when ripe makes it really easy to mash.

STORE A week or two in the fruit bowl, depending how ripe when bought. If underripe, keep at room temperature to soften. Eat as soon as ripe, or keep a couple of days in the fridge.
FREEZE: Sliced or cubed, in sugar syrup (see page 201).

PREPARE Using a sharp knife, cut down either side of the stone, feeling where the stone is with the knife and cutting close to it. This gives two mango 'cheeks'. For cubes, prepare 'hedgehog style' (see right).
Or slice off the peel and cut the flesh into slices or chunks. Slice off any flesh left on the stone too.

LYCHEE

PREPARING A MANGO

1 *Score evenly spaced lengthways lines through the flesh almost to the skin. Score across in the opposite direction to make cubes.*

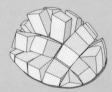

2 *Bend the mango back and the cubes will pop up making them easy to eat with a spoon or slice off into cubes.*

EAT On their own in slices, cubes, or halves or presented in halves 'hedge-hog-style' (see page 227).

COOK Mostly enjoyed raw, but if used in cooking, usually added at the end (except in chutney).

USE FOR

■ Adding cubes or slices to a turkey or chicken stir-fry at the last minute.

■ Buzzing in a blender, then folding into cream, crème fraîche or yogurt to use as a filling for pavlova. Or to pile on top of a trifle with tropical fruits.

■ Mixing up into a smoothie with a banana, milk and yogurt.

■ Combining with lime, chilli and coriander for a chutney or salsa. Serve with barbecued prawns.

■ Using unripe sour and crunchy mangoes in Asian salads or with chilli dips.

■ Making sorbets and ice cream.

GOES WITH Chicken, turkey, shellfish, Parma ham, coconut, chilli, orange, passion fruit, peach, cream, yogurt.

GOOD FOR YOU A great supplier of beta carotene and vitamins C and E.

Mangosteen

The thick, leathery skin of the mangosteen protects a delicate-tasting, white flesh which is segmented like an orange. It has a refreshing tang a bit like rhubarb and grows in tropical countries such as India, Thailand and Indonesia. Despite its name, it has nothing to do with a mango.

CHOOSE

■ All year round; best in the summer.

■ The skin should be dark purple, almost the colour of an aubergine. When green it is unripe.

■ It should feel heavy. If it's light the fruit inside has probably dried out.

STORE Will keep for a couple of weeks in the fridge wrapped, less at room temperature.

PREPARE Cut through the skin around the middle with a sharp knife, then twist it off in opposite directions to reveal the white segments.

EAT There is more skin than flesh. To get at the edible bit, cut it in half, then scoop out the flesh with a tea-spoon, avoiding the large seeds. Or remove the skin only, as above, then separate the flesh into segments and simply eat the flesh off the seeds.

COOK An expensive fruit which is best eaten on its own.

USE FOR
■ Mixing with other tropical fruits for a fruit salad.

GOES WITH Other tropical fruit.

GOOD FOR YOU Not especially nutrient rich, but is high in phyto-chemicals.

MANGOSTEEN

Melon

A member of the squash family this grows on the ground like a pumpkin. Melons come in many different sizes, colours, shapes and flavours.

CHOOSE
■ All year round, as different varieties are available at different times, but best at the height of summer.
Cantaloupe: Sweet, aromatic and juicy with a peachy-orange flesh.
Charentais: Small and round, deep orange, juicy, fragrant flesh and pale green skin.
Galia: Sweet, yellow flesh, thick, green skin.
Honeydew: Mild flavour, yellow or pale green flesh, sweet and refreshing.
Ogen: Small and round, delicate tasting, pale yellow flesh.

Piel de Sapo: Mild and sweet with a pale yellowy-green flesh.

Watermelon: Not a true melon, but used in a similar way. Looks stunning with bright red flesh and black seeds dotted throughout the flesh (seedless are also obtainable). Huge in size compared with other varieties, so often sold in big wedges rather than as a whole. It can lack flavour, but due to its juiciness is refreshing to eat on a hot day.

■ Test for ripeness by smell – melons can give off a lovely fragrance (Cantaloupe, Charentais, Ogen).

■ Test for ripeness by feel – the melon should give slightly when pressed with your thumb at the stalk end.

■ Ripe watermelons sound hollow when shaken.

STORE At room temperature until ripe, then use as soon as possible. Once peeled and cut, they will store in the fridge (well wrapped or the smell and taste will taint other foods) for up to 2 days.

FREEZE: Sliced or cubed in sugar syrup (see page 201).

PREPARE Cut in half – doesn't matter which way – and scoop out the seeds and any stringy, fibrous bits with a spoon. Cut in wedges and peel off the skin, then slice or chop. Or, while still in halves, scoop out little balls of melon with a melon baller.

EAT Small melons, like Ogens, can be served in halves with the seeds scooped out. Otherwise in wedges – to make it easier to eat, release each wedge from the skin by sliding a knife under the flesh close to the skin. Most refreshing if served chilled.

USE FOR

All types can be used for sweet or savoury dishes.

■ Serving in a salad – try watermelon and salty feta cheese, Galia with prawns and lime, or Charentais with avocado and crab.

■ Combining different colours of melon or making up a vibrant fruit salad or platter.

■ Making a purée for a juice mixed with orange.

■ Wrapping wedges with Parma ham for a starter, or serving wedges on a platter with Parma ham, rocket and Parmesan shavings.

■ Creating an instant dessert. Tip chunks of melon into a bowl with some grapes (red or white). Chill for an hour, then pour over some elderflower cordial diluted with fizzy apple juice and serve scattered with freshly torn mint.

melon–nectarine

GOES WITH Ham, prawns, feta cheese, mint, nectarines.

GOOD FOR YOU Melons are a great source of beta carotene – cantaloupe is really high; other melons have vitamin C and niacin.

Nectarine

see also PEACH, *page 237*

The rosy-cheeked nectarine bears a strong resemblance to its relative, the peach, but has thinner, smoother skin and firmer, often juicier, sweeter flesh. Mostly grown in the USA, South Africa and Mediterranean countries.

CHOOSE

- At their juiciest in midsummer.
- When ripe they smell fragrant and should feel fairly firm, just giving a little when pressed.
- Any bruising or mould is a sign the fruit is past its best.

STORE Ripen (if necessary) at room temperature for a couple of days. They will then keep for a couple more days, or in the fridge for longer.
FREEZE: In sugar syrup (see page 201).

PREPARE No need to peel unless you want to. Cut round the middle,

TIPS & TRICKS: NECTARINES

Nectarines discolour quickly once cut, so brush cut slices with lemon juice to stop them going brown.

FRUIT A–Z

until you reach the stone, and twist both halves in opposite directions to separate. Dig out and discard the stone, then keep in halves, or cut into slices or chunks.

EAT
Best eaten raw, just as is, skin intact.

COOK
Poach: This is a good idea if the fruit is unripe (see Peach, page 238).
Roast: In halves or chunks in a shallow dish with 150 ml (¼ pint) sweet white wine, a sprinkling of sugar and some grated orange zest for 15–20 minutes at 180°C/350°F/ Gas Mark 4 (160°C/325°F in fan ovens).

USE FOR
■ Tossing with fruits such as melon, mango and raspberries for a fruit salad.
■ Caramelizing (see page 14) to serve with cheesecake and other creamy desserts. Dissolve 125 g (4 oz) caster sugar with 4 tbsp water in a heavy frying pan. Cook until caramelized then stir in a knob of butter and add 3 nectarines cut in wedges. Cook gently until soft, turning to coat in the caramelized sauce.
■ Adding wedges or chunks to a stir-fry of chicken, turkey or pork.

GOES WITH Chicken, Chinese

flavours, mascarpone cheese, amaretti biscuits, rosé and white wine.

GOOD FOR YOU Contains beta carotene and vitamin C. More nutritious than peach.

USE INSTEAD Peaches.

Orange
Part of the citrus fruit family, oranges are mostly sweet, but you can also get bitter ones for cooking. Oranges come mainly from Israel, Spain, Morocco and South Africa.

CHOOSE
■ All year round; different varieties are available at different times.
■ You can never be sure how juicy an orange is until you cut it, but select small and heavy over large and light, as heaviness indicates they have a lot of juice.
■ The rind should look thin and be tight; if not, it may have excess pith.
■ Between the sweet eating orange and the bitter variety:
Sweet
■ Blood: Attractive for their wine-red colour, available only for a few months at the beginning of the year. Sweet, juicy and aromatic.
■ Navel: Popular for being seedless

nectarine–orange

and easy to peel, with a lovely flavour.

■ Valencia: Smooth-skinned and sweet with just a few seeds; a great orange to choose for juicing.

Bitter

■ Seville: The rougher-skinned, coarser-fleshed, bitter-tasting oranges used for making marmalade or in cooking, but not for eating raw. You need to look out for them at the beginning of the year when they are around for just a few weeks.

STORE Up to a week or two at room temperature.

FREEZE: The juice freezes well and keeps for about 4 months. Because of their short season, Seville oranges are worth freezing, which they do well – just wipe them and pack whole into freezer bags. Thaw before using.

PREPARE

Zest: Unless the oranges are organic and unwaxed, give them a quick scrub. Use a grater or zester to remove the zest only (see pages 62 and 72), not the white pith which has a bitter flavour. Or use a vegetable peeler to remove wider strips of zest. Add these to dishes like stews or soups for flavouring, or cut with a sharp knife into strips like very slim match-sticks to use as a decoration or for adding to sauces.

WHAT'S IN A NAME? SOFT CITRUS FRUITS

These easy eaters, all members of the mandarin family, have loose skins which make them so easy to peel.

■ *MANDARIN AND TANGERINE: These names are often used inter-changeably. It is hard to define the difference – and they refer to small, loose-skinned citrus fruits.*

■ *CLEMENTINE: A type of tanger-ine, small, virtually seedless, easy to peel, sweet and juicy.*

■ *SATSUMA: A variety of tangerine with a mild taste, sometimes a bit sharp, very easy to peel.*

Juice: Halve and squeeze out the juice with a lemon squeezer.

Segment: By doing this you eliminate pith and membranes at the same time, so it's an attractive way to prepare an orange and makes it nicer to eat. Trim a small slice off both ends of the fruit. Sit the orange upright on a board. Using a small, sharp knife, slice downwards through the skin and pith following the curve of the fruit, avoiding cutting into the flesh. This leaves a whole rindless, pithless orange. Hold the orange over a small bowl to catch the juice, and cut down both sides of each segment to release it from the membrane (see illustration opposite). Squeeze what's left of the membrane to get all of the juice.

USE FOR

■ Flavouring cake icings, whipped cream, mascarpone dessert fillings/toppings (zest or juice).
■ Making a salad with watercress or chicory, crumbled blue cheese and walnuts (segments).
■ Adding unpeeled slices to mulled wine, Pimms, sangria and other summer or winter punches.
■ Sevilles – making marmalade; adding zest and juice to dressings and marinades with honey, garlic and oil, or to orange sauces to go with duck and game; adding strips of zest to stews.

GOES WITH Many things, especially ham, duck, chicken, pork, game, beef, carrots, chicory, beetroot, watercress, nuts, peaches, apricots, plums, chocolate.

GOOD FOR YOU Contains potassium, vitamin C, folate and biotin.

Papaya

Also known as paw paw, this tropical fruit is shaped like an overgrown pear and has a subtle but sweet flavour, similar to peach and apricot. It is grown in tropical countries such as Hawaii, Brazil, Jamaica, Malaysia, Ghana, Peru.

CHOOSE

■ Available at different times of the year – best from spring to early summer, then again in autumn.
■ When ripe a papaya should feel slightly soft all over like an avocado.
■ The skin should be yellowy-green with orange tinges. Avoid any with pitted skin as the flesh could be bruised.
■ Green papayas (unripe) are used in Thai cooking as a vegetable or for shredding into salads.

STORE If not ripe when bought, leave at room temperature to ripen.

orange–papaya

Otherwise ripe papayas can be kept in the fridge.
FREEZE: In sugar syrup (see page 201).

PREPARE With skin still on, slice in half lengthways. Inside is an apricot-orange or deep salmon-pink flesh and clusters of sparkly black seeds. Scoop out the seeds with a spoon and discard. Peel off the skin with a sharp knife (easier if cut into quarters), then slice the flesh or cut into chunks. The flesh does not discolour, so this can be done ahead. To purée papaya, seed, peel and chop as above, then whizz in a blender or food processor with a squeeze of lime or lemon juice.

EAT Once it has been halved and seeded, squeeze each cut half with lime juice (to intensify the flavour) and eat out of the shell with a spoon.

COOK Cooking can spoil its delicate flavour, so it's best eaten raw.

USE FOR

■ Mixing into salads (goes well tossed with cold chicken, grapes and a curried mayonnaise or vinaigrette dressing), into green-leafed salads or with other tropical fruits in a fruit salad.

■ Puréeing for sorbets, or for a drink sweeten with sugar, freshen up with

SEGMENTING AN ORANGE and eliminating the pith and membranes at the same time, is an attractive way to prepare it, plus it makes it easier to eat.

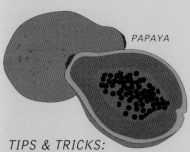

PAPAYA

TIPS & TRICKS: PAPAYA

■ *Papaya contains the enzyme papain that prevents gelatine from setting, so it's best not used for desserts that involve gelatine (unless the papaya has been cooked first as this destroys the enzyme).*

■ *When adding papaya to a fruit salad, put in just before serving as it goes soft if added too far ahead and can also soften other fruits.*

lime juice and thin with apple juice.

- A dessert – halve, seed, then fill each half with blueberries or raspberries and finish with a squeeze of fresh lime.
- A starter or light lunch – cut into wedges and wrap with Parma ham.
- Marinating and tenderizing meat (see pages 32, 242 and 331).

GOES WITH Chicken, grapes, blueberries, watermelon, lime, mango and other tropical fruits.

GOOD FOR YOU Has more vitamin C than oranges; also a good source of vitamin A, folate and fibre.

Passion fruit

A highly aromatic and flavoursome fruit. The wrinkled skin disguises what lies beneath – an intensely perfumed, juicy pulp surrounding lots of seeds.

CHOOSE

- All year round.
- The skin should be deep red or purple and not too wrinkly. Smooth skin means the fruit is unripe, so leave at room temperature until the wrinkles start to appear.
- Avoid fruit that are very light in weight, with dark, wrinkly skins, as they are dried out.

STORE Best kept at room temperature, not in the fridge.

PREPARE Cut in half and scoop out the seeds and pulp. If you want only the fragrant juice, sit a sieve over a bowl, tip in the pulp and seeds and press the juice through with a wooden spoon.

EAT Cut in half and scoop out the contents with a spoon – everything (apart from the skin) is edible.

USE FOR

- Scattering over puddings such as pavlovas and ice cream, or into fruit salads for an exotic fragrance.
- Mixing the strained juice or pulp and seeds with whipped cream to pile into meringues or use as a filling for cakes.
- Stirring the strained juice into unwhipped cream for a quick sauce, or blending with other fruits for a refreshing drink.

GOES WITH Pineapple, raspberries, mango, lychee, banana, orange, cream.

GOOD FOR YOU A great source of beta carotene, iron, niacin, phosphorus and fibre.

Peach

see also NECTARINE, *page 231*
Native to China, now grown worldwide, peaches have mottled, rosy-pink
skin and either yellow (more common)
or white flesh.

CHOOSE

■ Best and cheapest during the summer.
■ Peaches should smell sweetly fra-
grant and feel firm but give slightly
when pressed gently in your hand.
Avoid hard or bruised fruit.
■ If you can, buy them tree-ripened.
Underripe peaches will soften at room
temperature but will not be as sweet.

STORE   Once ripened, they will keep
for 1–2 days at room temperature.
FREEZE: As a purée or in sugar syrup
(see page 201).

PREPARE   Cut round the dimple of
the peach with a sharp knife, then
gently twist in opposite directions to
separate into halves. Remove the
stone. Slice or chop.
To skin: Try peeling it off with your
fingers, but if the skin is too clingy
drop the whole peach into boiling
water for about 15 seconds, or a bit
longer if it is large or less ripe.
Remove and immediately put briefly
into cold water. Peel off the skin with

PASSION FRUIT

TIPS & TRICKS:
PASSION FRUIT
There is only about 1 tbsp pulp in
each passion fruit – so you may
need to buy lots if serving a crowd.

your fingers. If that still doesn't work, resoak and try again, or use a vegetable peeler.

EAT Eat whole as is. You can eat the skin too, but if there is a fuzzy bloom, it is easy to rub off under cold running water. Peel if skin seems tough.

COOK

Poach: Pour a bottle of rosé or white wine (or half wine, half water) into a wide pan and add 150 g (5 oz) caster sugar. Stir over a medium heat until the sugar has dissolved. Lower the heat, add about 6 whole or halved stoned peaches (skins on) and flavour with a cinnamon stick, split vanilla pod or bashed lemon grass stalk. Cover and poach for about 10 minutes for whole, 4–5 minutes for halves, turning occasionally if they aren't completely covered in the poaching syrup. Lift them out with a slotted spoon and peel off the skins. Bring the syrup to the boil and bubble away for 10 minutes or so until it is nice and syrupy. Cool and pour over the peaches.

Roast: Place the halved stoned fruit cut-side up in an ovenproof dish and pour in 5–6 tbsp of a sweet white or rosé wine. Drizzle with honey or a sprinkling of icing sugar and roast for 15–20 minutes or until tender at 180°C/ 350°F/Gas Mark 4 (160°C/ 325°F in fan ovens). Serve hot or chilled.

USE FOR
- Same as nectarines (see page 232).
- Piling wedges into tall glasses with layers of whipped cream or ice cream, raspberries or strawberries and bought raspberry coulis.
- Serving simply in slim wedges with plain yogurt drizzled with honey.
- Making a salad with watercress, crumbled goat's cheese and a balsamic dressing.

GOES WITH Ham, chicken, goat's cheese, raspberries, almonds, ginger, cream, ice cream.

GOOD FOR YOU Contains beta carotene and vitamin C.

USE INSTEAD Nectarine.

Pear

There are thousands of varieties of pears. They grow well in cooler climates like that of the UK and Belgium, as well as in hotter ones such as those of Chile, Spain and South Africa. The basic pear shape varies from long and thin to round and bulbous, and colours range from

peach–pear

speckly brown through to bright green, yellow and blushing red.

CHOOSE

- At their juiciest in the late summer and early autumn.
- As they easily bruise when ripe, buy when slightly underripe, firm but not hard, then leave them to finish ripening when you get them home.
- Don't poke and prod to check when ripe. Pears ripen from the inside out, and when ready should give slightly at the base. Avoid ones that are too soft and squidgy at the bottom.

Some varieties available to buy are:

Anjou: Sweet, meltingly soft flesh, mild flavour. Grown a lot in the USA. Good for eating and cooking.

Bosc: Nice and juicy for eating, good texture for stewing.

Doyenné de Comice: From France, buxom and remarkably juicy and rich with a melting texture. Good for eating, especially with cheese; also good for cooking.

Concorde: A mix of Comice and Conference, juicy and sweet. Good for eating and cooking.

Conference: Slim and elegantly British, with a juicy, aromatic, sweet flavour and a firm, slightly gritty flesh. Good all-rounder.

Rocha: Firm, juicy and very sweet. Good for eating and cooking.

FIX IT: PEACHES

If the only peaches you can get are hard, poach them to bring out their flavour (see opposite).

TIPS & TRICKS: PEACHES

Toss cut peaches in lemon juice to stop them turning brown.

Packham's: Native to Australia and a favourite there; yellow with smooth, musky-tasting flesh. Good for eating.

Williams' Bon Chrétien (Bartlett): Very juicy and sweet, with tender flesh. Good for cooking and eating.

Asian pear: Firm and crunchy (more like an apple), very juicy and fragrant. Better eaten raw, unpeeled, as it doesn't soften as much as other varieties when cooked.

STORE If bought underripe, keep in a coolish place until ripe. Use as soon as possible.

FREEZE: Slice and poach for a minute in sugar syrup first (see page 201). Comice freeze particularly well.

PREPARE

After peeling or cutting, brush with lemon juice to prevent browning.

Whole: Keep the stems on, then peel lengthways (use a vegetable peeler for the smoothest look).

Halves: Halve lengthways and scoop out the core with a teaspoon. Use for stuffing, roasting or grilling.

In pieces: Cut into quarters lengthways, cut out the core, then peel with a sharp knife. Slice or chop.

COOK Use underripe pears as they keep their shape better.

Roast: Melt 30 g (1 oz) butter with 2 tbsp light muscovado sugar and 1 tbsp cider vinegar in a frying pan. Add 4 pears (halved and cored), coat well and cook for a minute. Put them in a small roasting tin (or around a roast) and spoon over the pan juices. Roast at 200°C/400°F/Gas Mark 6 (180°C/350°F in fan ovens) for 20–25 minutes.
■ Goes well with roast pork and game.

Grill: Lay wedges on a baking sheet, brush with lemon juice and sprinkle with caster sugar. Cook under a hot grill for 4–5 minutes, until golden.
■ Serve with cream or ice cream.

Pan-fry: Melt some butter in a frying pan, toss in pear wedges and cook until starting to soften. Sprinkle with a spoonful of sugar and cook carefully, stirring, until golden, for about 4–5 minutes.
■ Great with a green leaf salad and cheese.

Poach: Dissolve 100 g (3½ oz) caster sugar in a small pan with 600 ml (1 pint) red wine (or half wine, half water, or all water). Add 4–6 peeled pears (stalks on). Cover and gently poach for 15–25 minutes, or until tender, not soft. Remove with a slotted spoon. Thicken the syrup by bubbling for a few more minutes, then strain and pour over the pears.
■ Good with ice cream.

pear–pineapple

USE FOR

- Adding to salads (raw or grilled) with blue cheese such as Roquefort, toasted walnuts or pecans, crisp salad leaves and a dressing flavoured with walnut oil – or more simply with rocket and shavings of Parmesan.
- Chopping or slicing into cakes, teabreads, pies and crumbles.
- Cooking in chutneys – or using raw for a salsa mixed with apple, lemon or lime juice and zest, a squeeze of honey, chopped thyme and nuts, to go with roast pork.

GOES WITH Parma ham, pork, cheese (especially blue), crisp salad leaves, chocolate, vanilla, ginger, nuts, red wine, spices (see right).

GOOD FOR YOU Contains lots of fibre.

USE INSTEAD Apple.

Pineapple

This rather regal-looking fruit, with its crown of leaves, originated in South America. Pineapples are now grown a lot in Costa Rica and the Ivory Coast.

CHOOSE

- All year round.

TIPS & TRICKS: PEARS

To stop pears from toppling over when poaching whole, cut a thin slice from the bottom so they can stand up straight.

LIVEN UP THE POACHING LIQUID

Make your poaching liquid more spicy, fragrant or downright fruity by adding different flavourings:

- *NICE AND SPICY: Cinnamon stick, star anise, cloves, slices of fresh root ginger.*
- *FRAGRANTLY PERFUMED: Sprigs of lavender, rosemary or mint, bruised lemon grass, slit vanilla pod. (Use with all water poaching syrup only.)*
- *REALLY FRUITY: Strips of lime, orange, mandarin or lemon zest, pared off with a vegetable peeler.*

TIPS & TRICKS: PINEAPPLE

Because of the enzyme it contains, pineapple is best not used in conjunction with gelatine as it prevents it from setting, unless the pineapple has been cooked first – heat destroys the enzyme (so canned is fine).

■ Buy when ripe. It should smell sweet and strongly of pineapple. If you pull on a leaf at the top it should come out easily. The base should be slightly soft.

■ The rind should look fresh, not dry or shrivelled, the leaves green and perky.

■ Apart from the standard pineapple, others to try are Golden – ultra-sweet with a smooth flesh – and Queen. Very sweet and juicy, Queen is the perfect size for one or two people, plus the core is edible, so there is less preparation.

STORE At room temperature for up to 3–4 days. Or in an airtight container in the fridge once cut up. FREEZE: Sliced or cubed in sugar syrup (see page 201).

PREPARE

Slices: Slice the leafy top off first with a sharp knife, taking the slice a bit further down until you reach the fleshy fruit. Don't throw this away if you want to use it as decoration. Cut a slice from the base of the pineapple, then peel as described opposite. Cut into rings and stamp out the cores with an apple corer, or slice the pineapple in quarters lengthways and, holding each piece peeled side down, cut out the hard cores. Brushing with lemon juice will prevent browning.

Halves or quarters: Take the whole pineapple, leaves too, and cut through the centre lengthways in halves or quarters. Cut out the core, then the fruit, and use the shells as containers for serving fruit salad.

COOK

Pan-fry: Melt some butter in a frying pan, add pineapple slices and cook for a few minutes until starting to soften. Sprinkle 1–2 tbsp sugar over and cook, stirring, until golden. Pour in 1–2 tbsp of rum and bubble for a few seconds.

Grill: As for pears, page 240.

USE FOR

■ Threading chunks on to skewers with pork or chicken for kebabs.

■ Adding chunks to cakes, sponge puddings.

■ Sprinkling with sugar and kirsch or rum for a speedy dessert.

■ Topping a pavlova along with kiwi and passion fruit.

■ Tenderizing meat in a marinade – pineapple has an enzyme that breaks down protein, but don't leave in too long or the meat will go too soft.

■ Tossing into stir-fries near the end of cooking.

■ Chopping for salsa. Mix with chopped roasted red pepper and parsley or coriander, olive oil and lime juice. Serve with pork, gammon, chicken or prawns.

GOES WITH Gammon, chicken, cheese, coconut (think pina colada), rum, kirsch.

GOOD FOR YOU Contains lots of vitamin C – especially the Golden pineapple. The enzyme pineapple contains helps digestion, so is the perfect end to a meal.

Plantain

see also BANANA, *page 205*

Is a type of banana, but quite unlike it to eat. You wouldn't snack on a raw one, as plantains need to be cooked. Though technically a fruit, many parts of the world (particularly Africa, the Caribbean and Latin America) use it more as an accompanying vegetable, just like potatoes or rice.

CHOOSE

■ All year round.

■ Green unripe plantains for making plantain chips (like crisps).

■ Ripe, soft, black ones for roasting, frying or barbecuing. The softness of the plantain tells you how ripe it is - the softer and blacker it is the better, rather like an over-ripe banana. But unlike a banana, even when the skin of a plantain is completely black, the flesh is still fine to use.

■ If you can't find it in your super-

PEELING PINEAPPLE

Peel pineapple by sitting it upright on its base and slicing off the peel, working from top to bottom. As you go, nick off as many of the little brown 'eyes' as you can; any others can be dug out with the tip of the knife or the end of a vegetable peeler.

market, look in Caribbean or Latin American markets.

■ Allow about one medium plantain per person.

STORE Keep at room temperature if bought unripe – then leave to ripen in a paper bag for several days (see Speedy Ripening, page 221). Once blackened and softened, you can keep plantains in the fridge for a few days.

PREPARE

When green: the skin is too hard to peel off, so slice it off with a sharp knife. Cut the flesh into thin slices and make plantain chips (see right).

When soft and black: the skin is much easier to peel – use a knife to remove any fibrous bits. Can be cooked whole, or sliced straight or diagonally (thickness depends on how you are going to cook them, see below).

EAT Must be cooked first.

COOK Only when soft and black.

Barbecue: Keep their skins on and wrap in foil, then barbecue for about 20–25 minutes, turning occasionally until softened. Slit the skin open and serve whole, or peel and cut into 2.5 cm (1 in) chunks. Serve with a knob of butter and fresh black pepper.

Roast: Peel and cut into 2.5 cm (1 in) chunks. Toss with a little olive oil then roast at 200°C/400°F/Gas Mark 6 (180°C/350°F in fan ovens) for about 40 minutes, turning every 15 minutes, until golden and tender. Serve sprinkled with salt and pepper.

Fry: Peel and cut into 5 mm (¼ in) slices. Heat 2–3 tbsps of olive or sunflower oil in a pan, add the plantains and fry slowly in a single layer until golden, turning once, for 4–5 minutes each side. Sprinkle with salt and pepper.

USE FOR

■ An accompaniment to roast chicken, other roast or barbecued meats or fish, or with rice and peas.

■ Making plantain chips (see right).

GOES WITH Fish, chicken, Caribbean curries, lime, rice, butter, nuts, allspice, cinnamon.

GOOD FOR YOU Good source of beta carotene, folate and vitamin C.

USE INSTEAD Sweet potato or green unripe banana (sweeter, softer).

Plum

The juiciest of all stone fruits. The most famous British plum is the Victoria, sweet and good for cooking or eating. When not in season locally

plantain–plum

(in Britain), plums are available from Spain, Chile, South Africa and France.

CHOOSE

■ All year round; best in late summer–early autumn when in season locally.

■ Colour isn't a help to know when ripe, as there are many different coloured varieties ranging from dark purple to yellow. Look instead for the chalky-white 'bloom' on the outside of the skin which indicates freshness.

■ Pick plump ones – they should give a little when squeezed. Avoid if soft in the dimple near the stem.

STORE Keep at room temperature for 3–4 days once ripe, or in the fridge in a perforated plastic bag for 4–5 days. FREEZE: Stewed or sliced in sugar syrup (see page 201).

PREPARE Cut round the dimple of the plum with a knife, then twist apart and remove the stone, using the tip of the knife if it is stubborn. Leave as halves, chop or slice. Easier to skin after cooking.

EAT Sweeter varieties, such as Black Amber, Angelino, Victoria.

COOK Most plums are good for cooking with, especially Czar, Mirabelle, Victoria and Quetsch.

PLANTAIN CHIPS

Serve these instead of potato chips with fish or chicken, or with a spicy dip as a snack.

Peel a couple of green plantains and slice very thinly (like potato crisps), either with a sharp knife or a mandolin (see page 70). Heat enough sunflower or vegetable oil to come about 4 cm (1½ in) up the sides of a deep frying pan. Drop a cube of bread in the oil – if it browns quickly the oil is ready. Add the plantain slices in batches and fry until golden. Drain on kitchen paper then sprinkle with salt and pepper or a pinch of dried chilli flakes.

Stew: Melt 30 g (1 oz) butter with 30 g (1 oz) light muscovado sugar in a pan. Tip in 500 g (1 lb) plums, the finely grated zest and juice of an orange and simmer for about 10 minutes, until soft.
■ Serve with cream or ice cream.
Poach: As for pears (see page 240), but in halves (skin on) for 10–15 minutes.
Roast: As for peaches (see page 238), with red wine.

USE FOR

■ Adding to pies, tarts and crumbles.
■ Making a sauce for pork or duck.
■ Chutneys, jams and fruit compotes.
■ Tossing (raw) in slices into savoury salads with chicken and watercress or with tropical fruits in sweet salads.

GOES WITH Pork, duck, game, nuts, orange, Chinese spices.

GOOD FOR YOU Contains some iron, fibre, beta carotene, niacin and vitamin E.

Pomegranate

Originally from Iran, now grown mostly in the USA, India, Spain, Turkey and the Middle East, this fruit consists of a myriad of edible seeds within a sweet, juicy, ruby-red pulp.

CHOOSE

■ Best in autumn and winter.
■ Hard, deep-red-blushing (or yellowy) skins that are smooth and shiny.
■ Fruit should be heavy and plump.

STORE In the fridge in a perforated plastic bag for a week or two.
FREEZE: Not recommended.

PREPARE

Seeds and flesh: Cut the fruit in half widthways, hold each half over a bowl, hit the skin hard with a rolling pin and the seeds just drop out.
Juice: Tip the seeds and flesh into a sieve and press out the juice using the back of a spoon. Try not to crush the membranes and pith as they are both bitter.

EAT Best eaten as is. Cut in half or into quarters and eat the seeds and flesh straight from the shell with a teaspoon (or with a toothpick), avoiding the pith and membranes. You can just suck the flesh from the seeds, or crunch through the seeds too.

USE FOR

■ Scattering over savoury salads – refreshing with crab and fennel.
■ Sprinkling over grapefruit and orange segments for breakfast.
■ Serving the seeds splashed with gin,

or over lemon sorbet, cheesecake or ice cream.

- Adding the juice to marinades and salad dressings – good with chicken.
- Garnishing Middle Eastern dips, rice and other savoury dishes.

GOES WITH Duck, chicken, pork, white fish, lobster, other tropical fruits, salad leaves.

GOOD FOR YOU High in vitamin C.

Pummelo
see GRAPEFRUIT, *page 219*

Raspberry
see BERRIES, *page 207*

Rhubarb

Though technically a vegetable, with long stalks and large, dark green leaves, rhubarb is treated as a fruit. Though very British, it is also grown in cooler parts of Europe.

CHOOSE

- Between forced (indoor) and outdoor-grown crops. Forced is available at the beginning of the year; the main crop is in season from spring to early summer. Forced rhubarb is delicate in

FIX IT: PLUMS

Plums have a lot of juice, which can be a problem when making a pie or crumble. To overcome, toss them in 1–2 tbsp plain flour plus the sugar called for in the recipe. As the juice comes out in cooking, everything mixes together to create a syrupy sauce.

PLUMS FOR COOKING

- *DAMSON: Small and oval with a purply-blue skin. It has a very sour taste, so needs to be cooked, not eaten raw. It makes wonderful jam.*
- *GREENGAGE: A variety of green plum that came to Britain from France in the 18th century. Because of its colour, it goes well mixed with purple or red plums in compotes, pies, tarts, jams and crumbles.*
- *SLOE: Another member of the plum family, this fruit grows wild and looks similar to a blueberry. The fruits are pricked and soaked with gin and sugar to make sloe gin.*

TIPS & TRICKS: POMEGRANATE

Pomegranate juice stains, so watch you don't get splashed when preparing.

flavour and looks, being slim, pink and sweet. Outdoor rhubarb is more rugged, with sturdier, green and red stalks.

■ Stalks should not be limp and bendy.

STORE For a week or two in the vegetable drawer of the fridge. FREEZE: As a purée. Or cut into lengths, blanch in boiling water for 1 minute, cool quickly in cold water, drain, then open freeze (see page 200).

PREPARE

Remove the leaves – they are poisonous. **Forced:** No need to peel. Wash, then trim both ends of the stalks and cut into thin or chunky slices.

Outdoor: Scrape or peel off any tough skin with a small,sharp knife and prepare as above.

COOK Cook to soften and sweeten – outdoor rhubarb takes longer to cook. You can poach and stew rhubarb, but it falls apart quickly so it is best to roast in the oven. Don't add liquid, as rhubarb gives off enough of its own. **Roast:** Heat the oven to 200°C/ 400°F/Gas Mark 6 (180°C/350°F in fan ovens). Rinse, trim into pieces about 2.5 cm (1 in) long and arrange on a baking tray. Scatter with 90 g (3 oz) caster sugar. Cover with foil and roast for 15 minutes, then remove

the foil and roast for a further 5 minutes until the rhubarb is soft but has kept its shape and the juices are syrupy. (Timings are for outdoor rhubarb. Reduce by a few minutes if using forced.)

■ Serve warm or cold with clotted cream, ice cream or custard.

USE FOR

■ Making crumbles, pies, tarts and jam (alone, or mixed with strawberries).

■ Puréeing after roasting and cooling to fold into bought custard and whipped cream for an instant fool.

■ Piling (after roasting) on top of a pavlova, or to make a base for trifle.

■ Making a sauce to serve with pork (on its own or mixed with apples).

GOES WITH Strawberries, raspberries, orange, ginger, nuts.

GOOD FOR YOU Contains calcium and a little vitamin C and iron.

Strawberry
see BERRIES, *page 207*

Watermelon
see MELON, *page 229*

DECORATIVE AND EXOTIC FRUITS

- **Kumquat:** This looks like a baby elongated orange. The whole lot is edible, so can be scattered over or on dishes, sliced or halved.
- **Persimmon:** Also called Sharon fruit, this is grown in Israel and looks like a big orange tomato. Firm and smooth is best; look for ones with a bright orange glow. Unusual bittersweet taste, astringent if eaten underripe. Eat as an apple, or slice and chop for mixing into a fruit salad, or slice on to cheesecakes or pavlovas.
- **Physalis:** Also called Cape goose-berry, this orange-coloured fruit is enclosed in a flamboyant, inedible, papery husk. Peel back the husk, so it frames the fruit, and use as an edible decoration on desserts or cakes. Tangy but fragrant.

- **Prickly pear:** One of the cactus family, this has a mild taste like watermelon. Trim off the top and bottom, cut in half lengthways, peel and slice its brilliant-red flesh to liven up fruit salads.
- **Rambutan:** Similar to a lychee, though its outer coating of soft, curly spines has a bit more flam-boyance. Prepare and use as a lychee. Delicious with scoops of vanilla ice cream.
- **Star fruit:** When sliced, this fruit creates pretty star shapes. The flavour is very mild and can sometimes be bitter. Choose yellow ones, as green will be unripe and sharp tasting.
- **Tamarillo:** A very sleek-looking fruit, rather like an incredibly smooth oblong plum. Peel off the bitter skin, then slice into thin wedges. It can be eaten raw, but tastes quite sharp, so is best poached or stewed. Try adding some to a curry.

VEGETABLES

USING A VARIETY OF VEGETABLES IN YOUR DIET CAN BRING A
NEW DIMENSION TO YOUR COOKING. THEY ARE A GREAT SOURCE
OF NUTRIENTS AND CAN BE A HEALTHY NIBBLE, A DELICIOUS
SIDE ORDER OR AN IMPRESSIVE MAIN EVENT. AT THEIR PEAK,
VEGETABLES NEED LITTLE TO LIVEN THEM UP, BUT FOR VARIETY
YOU'LL FIND PLENTY OF IDEAS HERE FOR DIFFERENT WAYS TO
SERVE THEM AND A WEALTH OF HINTS AND TIPS ON CHOOSING,
STORING, PREPARING AND COOKING.

TOP VEGETABLE TIPS

- To ensure maximum freshness, taste and nutrient content, buy vegetables when in season, when they haven't had too long a journey, and eat as soon as possible after buying.
- Check vegetables regularly after storing for signs of deterioration. Once one starts to spoil, it can quickly infect others.
- Wash vegetables just before preparing, not before storing.
- Prepare vegetables just before cooking, as they can lose nutrients quickly once cut.
- Whenever possible, don't remove edible skins as they are a valuable source of fibre, nutrients and flavour.
- Cut into even-sized pieces for even cooking.

- It is hard to be exact when giving cooking times as there are many variables, such as the age of a vegetable, how it is cut and personal preference. To avoid overcooking, start checking sooner rather than later, then keep checking until cooked how you like it.
- Preserve as many nutrients as possible when cooking vegetables by cooking quickly with minimum water. Steaming and microwaving are two of the healthiest ways to maintain the nutrients, texture and flavour of a vegetable, as the juices are not lost into the cooking liquid.
- When cooking vegetables for salads, blanch them briefly, then plunge into cold water to keep their colour, freshness and nutrients.

artichoke

VEG A–Z

Artichoke (globe)

A globe artichoke is the edible, cultivated flower of a plant in the thistle family. When young, serve artichokes whole and enjoy the tender ends of each leaf with melted butter, hollandaise or a dip, along with the heart, or just serve the hearts in salads.

CHOOSE

■ Available all year round, but best in late spring and early autumn.
■ Those that are a perfect green (or purple) and tightly closed.
■ There should still be some stalk attached and the leaves should have a slight bloom to them.
■ Allow 1 artichoke per person.

STORE In the fridge in a perforated plastic bag for up to 3–4 days.

PREPARE It helps to know what is and isn't edible when preparing an artichoke. You can eat the tender bottom part of the leaves and the heart. You can't eat the tough outside leaves, the furry choke and inner leaves that enclose it.

It's up to you whether you remove the choke before or after cooking.

BABY VEG

Baby vegetables are more tender in texture and more delicate in taste than mature vegetables.

There are many available, such as aubergine, artichoke, beetroot, broccoli, carrot, cauliflower, courgette, corn and leek. They are a more expensive way of buying vegetables, but fun for certain occasions. Because of their smaller size and youth, they can often be eaten whole, needing little preparation and a shorter cooking time.

QUICK SERVING IDEA

For a quick way to liven up hot or cold green vegetables before serving, simply toss in a couple of spoonfuls of vinaigrette dressing.

If removing before cooking, break off the stalk at the base along with any tough bits attached or going into it. Trim off the top third of the artichoke with a sharp knife, about where it starts to taper in, then trim and discard any tough outer leaves. (If the artichoke is young, trim higher up.) Spread the leaves out a bit so you can get at the middle part. Pull the little cone of pale leaves out from the centre to reveal the fuzzy choke. Scoop the choke out with a spoon, being careful not to disturb the best bit underneath – the heart. As soon as you have prepared each artichoke, drop it into water with a little lemon juice to stop it browning.

If removing the choke after cooking, trim the raw artichoke and discard the tough outer leaves (see opposite), then cook the artichoke as below. Allow to cool slightly, then spread the leaves out so you can get at the middle part. Pull out the central cone of pale leaves and scoop out the hairy choke with a spoon, taking care not to disturb the heart.

COOK

Boil: Place the artichokes in a big pan, half fill with boiling water, add 3 tbsp lemon juice, return to the boil and simmer for about 25 minutes for medium or 30–40 minutes for larger ones. When they're ready, a leaf will come away easily from the base of the artichoke when pulled, and the heart will be tender when gently prodded with a sharp knife or skewer. Drain upside down in a colander or sieve, so any excess water runs out.

Steam: Follow the same timings as for boiling, adding a few extra minutes if necessary.

EAT After cooking, cool slightly and serve warm or cold. Pull off the outer leaves one at a time, starting at the bottom. Dip the tender end in melted butter and finely grated lemon zest, or in mayonnaise, sauce, or a dip, then pull it through your teeth to remove the tasty flesh. Discard the rest of the leaf. You then get to the best bit – the heart, which can be cut into and eaten with the accompanying sauce or dressing.

WAYS TO SERVE

- Wrap slices of Parma ham around cooked hearts and drizzle with a herb dressing for a starter or light lunch.
- Create a dipping sauce by thinning pesto with olive oil and mixing it with finely chopped tomatoes.

GOES WITH Hollandaise sauce, mayonnaise, tomatoes, butter, lemon, garlic, vinaigrette dressing, chives, thyme.

GOOD FOR YOU Contains vitamin C and folate.

Artichoke (Jerusalem)

First cultivated in North America, this knobbly little vegetable (an underground tuber) is a member of the sunflower family and not related in any way to the globe artichoke. It looks a bit like root ginger, and has a nutty, distinctive flavour. It is delicious roasted, boiled, steamed or pan-fried, cooked in a soup, or raw, thinly sliced, in a salad.

CHOOSE

- All year round, but best in mid-winter.
- The fewer knobbles they have, the better, as the more misshapen they are, the harder they are to peel.
- They should be firm.
- Allow 700 g (1½lb) for 4 people.

STORE For about 1 week in a cool, dark place.

PREPARE Fill a bowl with cold water and add a squeeze of lemon juice. Scrub the artichokes under running water, then, if peeling, cut off any of the more bumpy or knobbly bits that will make removing the skin difficult. Most of the nutrients are just beneath the skin, so leave it on when possible. Drop immediately into the lemon water to prevent browning.

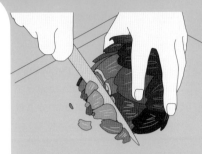

TRIMMING A GLOBE ARTICHOKE

1 Trim off the top third of the artichoke (or where it starts to taper in) with a sharp knife.

2 Then trim and discard any tough outer leaves

JERUSALEM ARTICHOKE

COOK Timing depends on size, but Jerusalem artichokes can be cooked like potatoes. Add lemon juice to cooking water to stop them discolouring.

Boil or steam: Cut into chunks and put in a pan. Pour over enough boiling water to cover, bring back to the boil, cover and cook for 12–15 minutes, or until tender. Drain. Alternatively, steam, allowing a few minutes longer.

Pan-fry: Cut into thickish slices. Heat about 5 mm (¼ in) sunflower oil in a frying pan. Add the slices and fry for 6–10 minutes, tossing occasionally until golden. Drain on kitchen paper and season.

Roast: Heat a few tablespoons of olive oil in a roasting tin in a 200°C/400°F/Gas Mark 6 oven (180°C/350°F in fan ovens) for 5 minutes. Add whole, unpeeled artichokes and toss in the oil. Tuck in a couple of bay leaves and roast for about 30–40 minutes or until golden and tender.

WAYS TO SERVE

■ Boil or steam and toss with butter or olive oil, salt and pepper.

■ Make a gratin as you would with potatoes, dot with butter and sprinkle with grated Parmesan cheese.

■ Use half and half with potato to make a silky-smooth mash.

GOES WITH Potato, cream, lemon, mustard, chives, parsley, tarragon.

GOOD FOR YOU Rich in carbohydrate and iron; a good source of vitamin C and potassium.

Asparagus

An elegant, versatile vegetable which can be served as a starter, main course or accompaniment. However you serve it, keep it simple, so the flavour is not masked.

CHOOSE

■ At its peak and best flavour when in season – in the UK for just a few weeks around the end of April, but available at other times of the year from countries such as Chile, Peru, South Africa, France and Spain.

■ Between the two main types – green, which is popular in the UK, America and Italy, or the white asparagus, favoured by the French, Germans and Belgians (this is cut below the ground – hence its lack of colour).

■ Very thin, wild asparagus (called 'sprue') is also available.

■ Stalks should look strong and firm, tips bright and perky.

■ Allow 500 g (1 lb) for 4 people.

STORE Wrap the stems in damp kitchen paper, put in a perforated plastic bag and store in the fridge for no more than 2–3 days.

artichoke–asparagus

PREPARE Small, young tips sold in packets require no preparation. For the bigger, tastier stalks, bend the spear until it snaps and discard the tough, woody ends. No need to peel. Leave whole, cut in half widthways or slice on the diagonal.

COOK

Boil: Lay the asparagus in a large frying pan, pour over boiling water to cover, add some salt and cook for about 3–5 minutes (depending on size) until the asparagus turns bright green. Left too long, it will go soft and dull-looking. (Sprue takes about 1 minute.)

Chargrill: Toss in olive oil, and cook on a preheated griddle pan for about 5 minutes, turning, until tender and marked with ridges from the pan.

Roast: Toss the asparagus in oil and roast at 200°C/400°F/Gas Mark 6 (180°C/350°F in fan ovens) for about 15 minutes.

Steam: Pile the spears into a steamer set in a large pan or frying pan over simmering water and steam for 4–5 minutes or until they feel tender if you stick a sharp knife into the stem. (Sprue will take 1½–2 minutes.) Season to serve.

Stir-fry: Trim and slice on the diagonal. Heat a little oil in a frying pan. Add the asparagus and stir-fry for a few minutes over a high heat until tender.

EAT Pick the spears up with your fingers and dip the tips in butter, or toss lightly in olive oil and lemon juice with a grind of salt and pepper.

WAYS TO SERVE

■ Serve simply with a good extra virgin olive oil, sea salt and freshly ground black pepper, or more traditionally with melted butter for dipping, hollandaise sauce or a soft-boiled egg.

■ Roast the asparagus with strips of prosciutto coiled around. Drizzle with a little olive oil, then roast as on page 255. Goes well with fish or chicken.

■ In a salad, toss with cooked new potatoes, broad beans and peas, and drizzle with pesto thinned with olive oil and a squeeze of lemon juice.

GOES WITH Fish (especially salmon), bacon and ham, tomatoes, green beans, new potatoes, roasted peppers, Parmesan cheese, pesto, eggs.

GOOD FOR YOU

Contains folate and vitamins C, A and B6.

Aubergine
(US: eggplant)

Like the tomato, the aubergine is really a fruit that is used as a vegetable.

It is native to South-East Asia but is used in many cuisines, including Indian, Mediterranean and Middle Eastern.

CHOOSE

■ Available all year.

■ The slightly bulbous, pear-shaped aubergine is the most common, and it should be shiny, deep purple, smooth and plump. You can also find white ones; small, round, green pea aubergines the size of grapes; and long, thin, purple ones (sometimes striped with white) the shape of a cucumber.

■ The stalk end, with its hood-like calyx, should be bright green and the vegetable should feel heavy.

STORE In a perforated plastic bag in the fridge for up to 3–4 days.

PREPARE To avoid discolouration, prepare just before cooking. No peeling is required: just trim off the green calyx and stalk at the narrower end, then cut into slices or chunks. Some traditional recipes advise salting aubergines to draw out bitterness (see opposite), but modern varieties are less bitter, so there's no real need. If you are going to fry the aubergine, however, salting will reduce the amount of oil needed.

asparagus–aubergine

COOK Aubergines soak up oil like a sponge when they are fried, so it is best to grill or roast them.

Chargrill: For ridge marks, cook on a griddle pan. Brush the aubergine slices with oil, heat the pan until very hot, then lay the slices on the pan, cooking a few at a time in a single layer. As they start to brown, turn over and cook the other side.

Grill: Lay slices on a foil-lined grill pan in a single layer, brush with oil and sprinkle on herbs such as thyme or rosemary, then grill until starting to turn golden. Turn over and grill the other side (brush and sprinkle again).

Roast: Place aubergine slices or chunks on a baking sheet in a single layer. Drizzle and toss with olive oil, scatter with herbs as before and roast at 200°C/400°F/Gas Mark 6 (180°C/350°F in fan ovens), for 20–25 minutes, or until golden and tender.

Stir-fry: Heat a little oil in a non-stick wok or frying pan, add small, chopped aubergine pieces and stir-fry, turning often, for 4–5 minutes until golden and tender, adding more oil if needed.

WAYS TO SERVE

■ Scatter roast aubergine slices with grated Cheddar or Gruyère cheese and grill until golden and bubbly.

■ Cut into chunks and fry in oil with garlic and ground cumin until golden.

TIPS & TRICKS:
SALTING AUBERGINES
Lay the prepared aubergine on a board or tray and sprinkle evenly with salt. Leave for about 30–45 minutes, by which time little beads of moisture will appear on the cut surfaces. Pat them off with kitchen paper.

VEG A–Z

Add a can each of tomatoes and chick peas, simmer for 10 minutes, add a handful of spinach leaves and cook until the leaves wilt. Serve with rice.
■ For 'crisps', slice the aubergine thinly, then salt and pat dry (see page 257). Heat about 1 cm (½ in) oil in a frying pan and fry in batches until golden. Drain on kitchen paper. Sprinkle with salt and serve with fish or chicken or as a snack.

GOES WITH Garlic, onions, tomatoes, peppers, cheese, lentils, spices such as cumin and coriander, yogurt.

GOOD FOR YOU Fairly low in vitamins and minerals but has a good amount of fibre.

Avocado

A tropical fruit, native to Central America, that is used as a vegetable. To enjoy at its best, eat raw, not cooked.

CHOOSE
■ Available all year.
■ The most popular varieties are Fuerte, with its smooth, green skin, and the almost black-green Hass with its thicker, more knobbly skin. You can also buy avocados without stones (see opposite).
■ A ripe avocado should give slightly when gently pressed with your thumb.

STORE At room temperature, not in the fridge. If an avocado is still hard when bought, leave to ripen in a paper bag for a couple of days.

PREPARE Once cut, the flesh of an avocado goes brown quickly, so prepare just before needed. Cut lengthways all the way round through the skin and flesh with a sharp knife until you meet the hard stone in the middle. Twist the two halves in opposite directions to separate. Either ease the stone out with a teaspoon, or stick a sharp knife firmly into the middle then pull it out, as opposite (top). Peel off the skin as opposite (centre). Keep as halves, slice, chop into chunky pieces or mash. Squeeze lemon or lime juice over to prevent browning.

COOK Not recommended.

EAT One of the nicest ways to eat an avocado is to halve and stone it as above, leaving the skin on, then serving with a drizzle of olive oil, a splash of balsamic vinegar and a sprinkling of salt and pepper. Allow one half per person and eat with a teaspoon.

WAYS TO SERVE
■ Wrap wedges of avocado with Parma ham, sit them on a bed of rocket or watercress and drizzle with a garlic and herb dressing.

■ To make a guacamole dip for serving with nachos or raw vegetables, mash 2 avocados with the juice of a lime, 1 or 2 finely chopped spring onions, chopped coriander, a pinch of crushed, dried chillies or Tabasco and salt.

GOES WITH Prawns, bacon, salad leaves, tomatoes, Parmesan cheese, grapefruit, lime, basil, balsamic vinegar, mayonnaise, soured cream.

GOOD FOR YOU Full of vitamin E and a source of iron, potassium and niacin. Unlike other fruits, avocados contain fat, but it's the healthy monounsaturated sort.

Bean sprout

The Chinese discovered the nutritional merits of bean sprouts, so you will find them in many Oriental dishes, especially stir-fries. The most widely available type is that of the mung bean. To sprout your own, see page 261.

CHOOSE
■ Available all year round.
■ They should look fresh and crisp with white roots — avoid those where the sprouting tips are wilting and brown.
■ Buy only as much as you need in one go as they quickly lose their crunch and fresh taste.

PITTING AN AVOCADO
Insert a sharp knife into the stone and lift it out.

PEELING AN AVOCADO
Score lengthways down the centre through the skin without cutting into the flesh. Peel the skin away from the flesh in two pieces.

STONELESS AVOCADO
Look out for stoneless 'baby' avocados. These can be eaten with a teaspoon and even the thin skin is edible.

STORE Loosely wrapped in kitchen paper inside a perforated plastic bag in the vegetable drawer of the fridge, for no more than a day or two.

PREPARE Quickly rinse in cold water and pat dry with kitchen paper.

COOK Mung bean sprouts will easily withstand brief cooking.
Stir-fry: Only for 1–2 minutes; any longer and they will lose their crunch.

WAYS TO SERVE
■ Add raw to salads with Chinese flavours or in spring rolls.
■ Scatter into a chicken or beef sandwich for a bit of crunch.
■ Toss into an omelette with a splash of soy sauce.

GOES WITH Chicken, beef, peppers, rice, ginger, chilli, coriander, garlic.

GOOD FOR YOU A good source of folate, iron and some B vitamins.

Beans

The good thing about beans is that you can eat the lot – pods and all. Like peas, beans belong to the legume family. Most are long and slender and hang elegantly from thin stalks as they grow.

CHOOSE
■ The pods of all beans should be firm and crisp. Avoid broad beans when they feel flabby with big pockets of air inside instead of plump beans. The most widely available types are:

Broad (US: fava): A plump bean which is available in summer, best early on. The pod that contains the beans can be eaten only when very young and tender. Allow 500 g (1 lb) in their pods for 2 people. Buy 1.5–2 kg (3–4 lb) beans in their pods for every 500 g (1 lb) of podded beans that you need.

Flat (helda): Similar to a runner bean, but flatter and smoother.

French (US: string): Also called *haricot vert*, this is a dwarf green bean variety that originally came from the USA. Available all year round. Allow about 225 g (8 oz) for 3 people.

Green: A general term used to describe French beans.

Runner: A popular British vegetable, but native to Central America. Larger, flatter and longer than a French bean. At their best in mid to late summer – small, younger ones are the most tender and sweet; later in the season they can become a bit tough and stringy. Allow about 700 g (1½ lb) for 4 people.

Yellow wax: A yellow variety of the green French bean. Allow about 225 g (8 oz) for 3 people.

bean sprout–beans

STORE Will keep in a perforated plastic bag in the fridge for up to 2–5 days. To check if they are still fresh, do the snap test. If a bean snaps in half easily when you bend it, it is still fresh.

PREPARE

Broad: First you need to pod the beans, as shown below right. Skinning the beans may seem fiddly, but is worth it if you have the time, as the skins can sometimes be tough. Cook the beans in boiling water (see below). Drain, tip into cold water, then slit open the skin of each one with your fingernail and pop out the shiny green bean inside.

French and yellow wax: Slice off the stalk ends, as on page 263.

Runner: Top and tail, then remove any stringy bits from both sides by pulling along the length of the bean with a small, sharp knife. Slice into long, slim, diagonal lengths, to show off the pretty pink seeds inside.

COOK Beans are best cooked quickly and briefly so they keep their bright colour. Test with a skewer or sharp knife – either should go in easily.

Boil: Put the beans in a pan, just cover with boiling water and return to the boil. Cook broad in their skins for 3–5 minutes (depending on their size), yellow for 4–5 minutes, French for

GET SPROUTING

To grow your own bean sprouts using dried mung beans, chick peas or Puy lentils, or a mix, follow these steps. The beans will expand so 3 tbsp dried beans will give you about a cup of sprouted beans.

- *Soak beans in plenty of cold water overnight. Drain and rinse.*
- *Tip them into a large jar and cover with tepid water. Lay a piece of cloth or muslin over the top, secure with a rubber band and drain off the water. Put the jar on a tray in a warm, dark place.*
- *Rinse with cold water and drain twice daily. The beans should start sprouting after 2–3 days and be ready to eat after 5–6. If you want a bit of green on the sprouts, expose them to the light for the last day.*

PODDING BROAD BEANS
Press the pod all the way along one of its seams, then open it out with your fingers. Push your thumb down the furry inside to release the beans.

4–6 minutes, runner for 3–5 minutes. Drain and season (see Tips & Tricks, opposite). When using in a salad, blanch first by cooking for 2–3 minutes, then tip into a colander or sieve and hold under cold running water so they cool quickly and remain crisp and green. Drain well.

Steam: For 4–10 minutes, depending on the bean.

WAYS TO SERVE

■ Toss boiled or steamed French or runner beans in butter or olive oil, salt and pepper.

■ Top boiled or steamed French or runner beans with a herb butter (see page 133).

■ Toss boiled or steamed French or runner beans while hot with olive oil and lemon juice, roughly chopped parsley and spring onions.

■ When broad beans are very young and tender, serve raw in their pods between courses, Italian-style, as a little bunch with a wedge of pecorino cheese and chunk of bread.

■ Briefly fry some chopped garlic in olive oil with 3–4 chopped anchovies, then toss with cooked, skinned broad beans.

GOES WITH Parma ham and bacon, chicken, tomatoes, pulses, herbs, anchovies.

GOOD FOR YOU Packed with protein, all beans are also blessed with fibre, potassium, calcium, niacin, beta carotene and some iron – so they are good in a vegetarian diet.

Beetroot
(US: beet)

A root vegetable loved for its earthy flavour, silky-smooth texture and vibrant red-purple colour. It is closely related to spinach and chard. Beetroot leaves can be eaten when cooked.

CHOOSE

■ All year round.

■ When raw, the roots should be firm and evenly shaped and the tops fresh and not wilting.

■ Also available ready-cooked.

STORE

Raw: In a cool, dark place for about 3–4 days.

Cooked: They will keep in the fridge for about 5–7 days. Pre-cooked vacuum-packed beetroot from the supermarket will last much longer – check the 'best before' date. Also check they're 'natural', not packed in vinegar.

PREPARE For raw beetroot, twist or trim off the stalks, leaving about 2.5 cm (1 in). Leave the whiskery bits

beans–beetroot

at the bottom. If you trim too close to the flesh before cooking, the beetroot will 'bleed' into the cooking water and lose their bright colour. Wash but don't peel (if you peel before cooking, they will bleed).

COOK

Boil: Place in a large pan and cover with boiling water, then bring back to the boil and cook for 1–1¼ hours, or until tender. When undercooked they can taste bitter. To tell if done, don't pierce with a knife but lift out with a slotted spoon and gently rub the skin – it should start to come away. Drain and plunge into cold water, then the skin will be easy to peel off. The peeled beetroot can be sliced, chopped or grated.

Roast: Pat gently dry after washing, then lay them whole in a roasting tin with 150 ml (¼ pint) water. Cover with foil and roast at 200°C/400°F/Gas Mark 6 (180°C/350°F in fan ovens) for 45 minutes–1 hour. Peel before serving.

WAYS TO SERVE

■ Cut roasted beetroot into quarters and serve tossed with olive or a nut oil and snipped chives.

■ Toss rocket leaves and crumbled feta cheese in a honey-mustard dressing. Arrange wedges of cooked beetroot on top, scatter with toasted walnuts and drizzle with a little more dressing.

TOPPING BEANS
The quickest way is to line the beans up on a chopping board, with the stalk ends all pointing the same way, then slice down the line in one movement.

TIPS & TRICKS: BEANS
Adding salt to beans while they cook toughens the skins, so it's best added later.

MORE UNUSUAL BEANS
YARD-LONG BEANS (also known as Chinese and snake beans): These originated in Asia and are not related to green beans but can be used in the same way.
BORLOTTI BEANS: One of the prettiest beans, with creamy-coloured pods splashed with pink. They need to be podded like broad beans. Popular in Italy for soups and stews, or served simply with olive oil and garlic.

■ Arrange cooked beetroot wedges or slices with sticks of cooked carrot. Drizzle with some olive oil, lemon juice, chopped garlic, chopped coriander and toasted cumin seeds for a Moroccan-style salad.

GOES WITH Smoked fish, horseradish, feta/goat's cheese, carrots, nuts, orange, cream/soured cream, mint.

GOOD FOR YOU A fantastic source of folate, and also contains potassium, phosphorus and fibre.

Bok choi

see PAK CHOI, *page 300*

Broccoli

A member of the cabbage family. Calabrese is a popular variety, from the Calabria region of Italy. This has tightly packed, dark green florets shaped a bit like cauliflower. Sprouting broccoli (see opposite) has purple-green florets on longer, more slender stalks.

CHOOSE

■ All year round.
■ Heads should be firm and bright green (avoid any that are turning yellow), with firm stalks, not at all limp.
■ Allow about 125 g (4 oz) per person.

STORE In the vegetable drawer of the fridge for up to 3 days.

PREPARE If the broccoli is bought already trimmed, just freshen up the ends of the stalks by taking off a slim slice. For non-trimmed pieces, neaten up stalks by trimming any tough outer parts with a vegetable peeler or sharp knife. Any tough leaves attached to the stalk should be discarded, but tender ones can be used. Divide the broccoli and cut into small florets with a little stem attached. The rest of the thicker part of the stem can be sliced diagonally (peel it first if the outside is dirty, discoloured or tough). Wash. If using in stir-fries or tossing with pasta, cut florets and stems into 1 cm (½ in) pieces.

COOK Don't overcook broccoli – cook until tender, but not soft. Test by pushing a sharp knife into the stem – the knife should go in easily, but the stem should still feel firm.

Blanch: If you are using broccoli for a salad, follow the instructions for boiling, but cook the broccoli for 2–3 minutes for sliced, 4–6 minutes for whole florets (depending on size), until tender-crisp. Drain in a colander or sieve and hold under cold running water to stop it cooking. Drain well.

Boil: Divide into individual florets with

beetroot–broccoli

a little stalk attached, then cut length-ways in half or leave whole. Put the broccoli in a pan, just cover with boiling water, bring back to the boil, then cover and cook for 4–6 minutes for small florets, 3–4 minutes for very small pieces. Drain well and season to serve.

Steam: Small florets for 4–6 minutes, for smaller cut pieces steam for 3–4 minutes, until tender.

Stir-fry: Heat 2–3 tbsp sunflower or groundnut oil in a frying pan until very hot. Add the broccoli (cut into 1 cm/½ in pieces) and stir-fry with the heat on high for a few minutes until the broccoli is turning golden and tender. Add a chopped clove of garlic and cook for about 30 seconds. Remove from the heat. For extra flavour, splash in some soy sauce and scatter with toasted flaked almonds, cashew nuts or sesame seeds.

WAYS TO SERVE

■ After cooking, drizzle with a little olive oil or melted butter, or add any or all of the following: a squeeze of lemon, a scattering of grated Gruyère or Parmesan cheese and a sprinkling of toasted almonds or pine nuts.

■ For a broccoli and pasta supper for 2, chop 225 g (8 oz) broccoli into 1.5 cm (¾ in) pieces. Put 200 g (7 oz) of pasta on to boil and drop the broccoli into the pan 4–5 minutes before the end of the

FIX IT: BEETROOT

Beetroot bleeds, so staining of other foods is almost inevitable. To reduce the amount of staining in a salad, add at the last minute when everything else has been tossed.

SPROUTING BROCCOLI

Also called purple sprouting broccoli, this has slimmer stalks and heads tinged with dark purple. It is sweeter and more tender than ordinary broccoli.

TO PREPARE, leave whole and just trim the stalk ends to freshen it up. TO COOK, steam or boil whole pieces (stalks and heads) for about 5–8 minutes or until tender. If stir-frying, parboil first for 2 minutes, then stir-fry for 4–5 minutes. For extra flavour add chopped garlic and chilli to the oil in the pan.

VEG A–Z

pasta's cooking time. Meanwhile fry some finely chopped garlic in olive oil with a seeded, finely chopped red chilli. Add some lemon juice and grated zest and toss with the drained pasta and broccoli, plus 200 g (7 oz) canned tuna, drained and flaked, and seasoning.

GOES WITH Tuna and other fish, chicken, cheese, eggs, peppers, mushrooms, tomatoes, lemon, almonds and other nuts, garlic, ginger, soy sauce.

GOOD FOR YOU Wonderfully nutritious – a good source of vitamin C (a 100g/4oz portion gives you your daily requirement) plus folate and other B vitamins, vitamin K, calcium, iron and beta carotene. Also packed with antioxidants called flavonoids. A true superfood.

Brussels sprout

Belonging to the cabbage family, sprouts look like miniature cabbages and grow clinging in rows to long, thick stems.

CHOOSE

■ Best in winter (after frost), but also available in autumn and spring.
■ Look for bright green colour, avoiding any that are going yellow round the bottom.

■ Choose plump, crisp sprouts with tightly packed leaves. They are sometimes sold on the stalk, which keeps them fresh for longer.
■ For sweetness, go for small sprouts.
■ Allow about 125–175 g (4–6 oz) per person.

STORE Keep in a cool place or in the fridge for up to 3 days.

PREPARE If they are still on the stalk, twist them off. Trim off any outer leaves that look old or are coming off of their own accord, then wash and trim off the bases. Cutting a cross in the base of sprouts will help them cook evenly – but there's really no need, especially when they're small, and it can make the insides go soggy.

COOK Timing is crucial, as under- or overcooking spoils their taste. They can overcook very quickly, so test often by piercing with the tip of a sharp knife or skewer. The tip should go in easily but the sprout will feel slightly crunchy and still have its bright green colour.
Boil: The classic cooking method for sprouts is to drop them (whole or halved) into a pan with a little salt, pour in enough boiling water to cover, bring back to the boil, cover and cook for 5–9 minutes, depending on size, or until just tender. Drain well.

broccoli–brussels

Steam: For 5–10 minutes (depending on size) over simmering water. Season.

Stir-fry: Either halve or finely slice, then heat a little olive oil in a frying pan or wok with a little chopped garlic and shallot. Add the sprouts and cook for 8–12 minutes. Top with a knob of butter and season to serve. If cooking a lot, add a splash of water or stock.

WAYS TO SERVE

■ Top cooked sprouts with butter and black pepper or a sprinkling of grated nutmeg. As an optional extra, toss with crispy fried bacon bits or lardons and toasted pine or pecan nuts or almonds (or with cooked chestnuts at Christmas).

■ Try them Italian style as a pre-meal snack. Boil whole until tender-crisp, then cool quickly in a sieve under cold running water, drain and serve seasoned and tossed with olive oil.

■ Add frozen peas to the pan a couple of minutes before the end of cooking time, then drain and toss with butter mixed with grated orange zest.

GOES WITH Poultry (especially turkey), game, bacon, chestnuts and other nuts, water chestnuts, oranges.

GOOD FOR YOU

Contains lots of vitamin C and fibre, plus beta carotene, vitamins E and K, folate and potassium.

Cabbage

The many varieties of cabbage range from the basic round red, white or green cabbage with tightly packed leaves, to the more sophisticated loose-leaved Italian *cavolo nero* and the slender Chinese cabbage.

CHOOSE

■ Different varieties are available at different times of year.

■ The leaves of all should look crisp and bright. The core shouldn't be split or dry. Red, green and white cabbages with tightly packed leaves should feel heavy.

■ Avoid cabbages that have holes in the leaves – a sign of intruders. Or those whose outer leaves have been removed – a sign of not being fresh.

■ Choose between loose-leaved (usually pointed in shape) or tightly packed (round).

■ 1 small to medium cabbage is plenty for 4 people.

TIGHTLY PACKED

Green: Round with very firm hearts, this is a later variety than green spring cabbage (see page 269), which has looser leaves.

Savoy: Has bright, dark green crinkly leaves that are mild and tender when cooked. Makes a colourful accompani-

ment to roasts, stews, casseroles and other wintery dishes. The leaves are also perfect for stuffing.

Red: Unique in the cabbage world for the wonderful colour it gives a dish. Its crisp, tightly packed leaves are finely shredded raw for salads, or chopped roughly and braised with spices and fruity flavours.

White: Round with pale, greenish-white leaves on the outside that get progressively whiter towards the centre. Crisp and crunchy, good shredded raw in salads, especially coleslaw, or boiled or steamed, then tossed in a little butter and freshly ground black pepper. Famous for being pickled in sauerkraut.

LOOSE-LEAVED

Cavolo nero: A dark green cabbage from Tuscany, with a pleasantly bitter taste. Sometimes referred to as kale. Use shredded in soups or stir-fried. If you can't find it, use Savoy or kale.

Chinese leaves: Also called Peking cabbage, it has elegantly long, pale green leaves with a crisp texture and milder cabbage flavour. Popular shredded for stir-fries or for dropping into soups for the last few minutes of cooking as it takes on other stronger flavours well.

Kale: See page 284.

Pointed: As its name implies, this is

cabbage

recognizable by its pointed head. The green leaves are softer and sweeter than tight-packed green cabbage.

Spring or cabbage greens (US: collard greens): Bright green leaves, the first of the season. Shred, steam and toss with butter to accompany winter comfort food. Or toss into stir-fries.

STORE In a cool place, or the vegetable drawer of the fridge. Tight-leaved cabbages, such as white and red, keep for up to a week or so, while looser-leaved ones keep for 2–3 days.

PREPARE

Tightly packed: Take off and discard loose or damaged outer leaves. Wash. Slice the cabbage lengthways into quarters, then cut out and discard the hard core from each quarter. Chop fairly roughly, or shred quite finely.

■ To shred by hand – lay one of the cut sides of each wedge on a board and cut across to make even-sized strips (see right).

■ To shred by machine – Use the shredding disc on your food processor. With the machine running, feed each cabbage quarter into the funnel.

Loose-leaved:

Take off and discard loose or damaged outer leaves. Separate the leaves from the tighter central bit and cut out the tough central stalks with a sharp

SHREDDING CABBAGE

knife, then chop or slice the leaves. A quick way is to pile several leaves on top of each other, roll them up loosely, then shred across with a sharp knife. Shred the tight central bit too.

COOK Cabbage should be cooked very quickly with only a little water so it keeps its crunch and vibrancy. The only exception to this is red cabbage, which is cooked for a long time, when it is braised with liquid and spices. Timings below vary depending on the type of cabbage used and how you have cut it. To test when done, check that it is tender with a bit of crunch, and that the colour is still bright.

Boil: Shred thickly and press into a large pan with a little salt. Add enough boiling water to almost cover, bring back to the boil, cover and cook for 4–6 minutes, stirring half way through. Tip into a large sieve or colander and press with the back of a spoon to remove as much water as you can.

Steam: For 4–8 minutes until wilted, depending how cut.

Stir-fry: Softer-leaved cabbages, such as Savoy and Chinese leaves, are best. Shred finely, heat vegetable or groundnut oil in a wok or frying pan, add the cabbage and cook on a high heat for 2–4 minutes or until tender, tossing often.

WAYS TO SERVE
- Stir-fry Savoy cabbage or Chinese leaves with chopped garlic and ginger and some soy sauce.
- Use different colours of tight-leaved cabbages. Mix finely shredded raw white, green and red cabbage with a little oil and lemon juice, some toasted sesame seeds, raw peanuts (unskinned), sultanas and a splash of sesame oil and serve as a colourful salad.

GOES WITH Ham, bacon, tomatoes, apples, mustard, sesame, garlic, ginger.

GOOD FOR YOU Contains lots of fibre as well as vitamins C, B and K, beta carotene and folate.

Carrot

A versatile root vegetable that is as good roasted in the oven for lunch as it is grated into a cake for tea.

CHOOSE
- Available all year round, but look out for tender young carrots in the spring, in bunches with their feathery leaves still on. Later in the year carrots become bigger and tougher.
- All carrots should be bright in colour, and feel hard. If they have leaves, these should be fresh and perky.
- Allow 500 g (1 lb) carrots for 4 people.

cabbage–carrot

STORE Will keep in a cool, dark place, or in a perforated plastic bag in the fridge, for a week or so.

PREPARE No peeling is needed for young carrots – just rinse, then trim off the stalks and the wispy bits from the narrower end. Older carrots should be trimmed and peeled with a vegetable peeler. Young, small carrots are usually cooked whole, but older ones can be cut in any of the following ways:
- Across into thin circles or thicker chunks, or sliced diagonally.
- Down the length of the carrot in slim strips, then chopped across into dice or matchsticks.
- Into ribbons – with a vegetable peeler, shave off thin strips down the length of the carrot. Use in salads.
- Grate for salads or baking (helps keep a cake mixture moist, such as carrot cake and rich fruit cake).

COOK To test when done, insert the tip of a sharp knife into the carrot. It should go in easily, but the carrot should still be firm in the middle.
Boil: For small, young carrots, put them whole into a pan with a little salt, add enough boiling water to just cover, bring back to the boil and simmer until tender, about 5–7 minutes. Boil sliced carrots the same way, allowing 4–5 minutes. Drain.

FIX IT: RED CABBAGE
Red cabbage can lose its natural colour once cut. To keep it red, pour 3–4 tbsp hot red wine vinegar over the shredded cabbage (this is enough for half a medium-sized cabbage), mix and leave for 5–10 minutes. Drain and serve raw with a dressing, or add to cooked dishes.

Roast: Heat a few tablespoons of olive oil in a roasting tin in a 200°C/400°F/ Gas Mark 6 oven (180°C/350°F in fan ovens) for 5 minutes. Add large chunks of carrot and toss in the oil with some salt and pepper. To spice things up a bit, add a sprinkling of ground cumin and coriander. Roast for 30–35 minutes or until golden and tender.

Steam: Small whole young carrots for 6–8 minutes, sliced for 5–6 minutes.

WAYS TO SERVE

- Toss boiled or steamed carrots in a little butter or olive oil, salt, pepper and chopped herbs such as chives, tarragon or parsley.
- Fry some chopped garlic, fresh root ginger and mustard seeds in a little oil. Add some cooked young whole carrots and stir to coat.
- Melt a knob of butter with a spoonful of maple syrup and a dollop of wholegrain mustard. Pour over boiled or steamed carrot slices.
- Boil the carrots and drain, or steam, then mix in the food processor to make a chunky purée with a knob of butter and freshly ground black pepper plus a little ground coriander to give it a touch of spice, or mash for a 'carrot crush'.
- Tuck some grated raw carrot into a pitta bread pocket filled with shredded lettuce and hummus.

GOES WITH Orange, beetroot, mustard, cumin, parsley, coriander, chives.

GOOD FOR YOU Very high in beta carotene; also has vitamin C, calcium and fibre.

Cauliflower

A member of the cabbage family, cauliflower is known for its creamy-white florets.

CHOOSE

- All year round.
- Those with pure white, densely packed heads and crisp, green leaves.
- Don't buy those where the white part is starting to discolour, or if you can see that the discoloured bits have been sliced off.
- Look at the base. The whiter it is, the more recently it has been picked.
- For an alternative, look out for small varieties with bright green heads (see Romanesco cauliflower, opposite).
- Allow 1 medium cauliflower for 4 people.

STORE In a perforated plastic bag in the vegetable drawer of the fridge for several days.

PREPARE Slice across the base, to release some of the outer leaves. Trim

carrot–cauliflower

away all the outer leaves, discarding any you don't want (if they are fresh and green they can be cooked too). Leave whole or cut off the individual florets from the main stem, and slice again if large. Aim to have similar-sized pieces so that they will cook at the same speed. Wash before use.

COOK The florets are cooked when you can push the tip of a sharp knife or skewer into the stalk. Take care not to overcook or they will disintegrate.
Boil: Put the florets in a pan with a little salt, cover with boiling water and bring back to the boil. Simmer, covered, over a medium heat for 5–10 minutes depending on the size of the florets. Drain well. If you are cooking whole, start testing after 10 minutes.
Steam: Florets keep their shape best when steamed. Put them into the steamer (with any leaves), with the heads facing up, for 5–10 minutes, depending on size.

WAYS TO SERVE
■ Top with a knob of butter, black pepper, some grated cheese and a pinch of grated nutmeg.
■ Heat 2 tbsp vegetable oil in a frying pan. Add a chopped garlic clove and 1 tsp each mustard and cumin seeds and cook briefly until the seeds start to pop. Stir in ½ tsp turmeric, then tip

TIPS & TRICKS: CAULIFLOWER
Squeeze a little lemon juice over cauliflower florets to keep them snowy white.

PERK UP CAULIFLOWER CHEESE
■ *Add some snipped chives or a spoonful of grainy mustard to the sauce.*
■ *Cook the cauliflower with some frozen peas or broccoli florets.*
■ *Give it a crunchy top – scatter with buttery fried breadcrumbs mixed with finely chopped anchovies or crispy pieces of bacon just before serving.*
■ *Lay slices of fresh tomato, roasted pepper or sundried tomatoes over the top, sprinkle with grated Parmesan cheese and grill until bubbly and golden.*

ROMANESCO CAULIFLOWER
This has a pointy shape and bright lime green colour. Smaller in size than the white cauliflower, it is also milder and sweeter in taste. Use as for regular cauliflower, raw or cooked. If you are looking for something to liven up a vegetable platter with dips, florets of romanesco do the job well.

in lightly boiled or steamed florets and stir for about a minute until well coated. Serve scattered with chopped parsley or coriander.

GOES WITH Ham, bacon, cheese (especially firm cheeses like Parmesan and Cheddar), potatoes, anchovies.

GOOD FOR YOU Contains vitamins C and B6, folate and biotin.

Celeriac

Beneath the uninspiring exterior of the celeriac lurk flavour, creamy texture and great potential. A member of the parsley family, this large, ungainly, bulbous winter root vegetable has a hint of celery in its taste and can be turned into mash, grated raw into salads, roasted or used to liven up the flavour of winter stews. It is traditionally cut into very thin sticks or grated for the French salad *rémoulade*.

CHOOSE

■ Available from early autumn through to spring.
■ Celeriac varies in size, and the outside skin can be rough and knobbly. It should feel firm and heavy. The smoother it is, the easier it will be to prepare and the less you will waste.
■ If you have a choice, go for small–medium size: about 700 g (1½ lb).
■ Allow about 1 kg (2lb) celeriac (unpeeled weight) for 4 people.

STORE It will keep in a cool, dry place for up to a couple of weeks.

PREPARE Slice off the top and bottom, then trim off any really knobbly bits. As the outside is quite tough, lay the celeriac cut-side down on a board and peel quite thickly down its length to reveal the creamy flesh, going all the way round with a sharp knife. Cut out any blemishes, then cut into whatever shape you like – chunks, slices, small dice, fine strips – or grate for using raw. Celeriac quickly discolours once peeled and cut, so unless you are using it straight away, drop the prepared pieces into water with a squeeze of lemon juice or a little wine vinegar.

COOK

Boil: Put the prepared celeriac into a pan with some salt, just cover with boiling water and add a squeeze of lemon juice. Bring back to the boil and cook for about 10–15 minutes, depending on size.

Steam: For about 15 minutes.

Roast: Heat a few tablespoons of olive oil in a roasting tin in a 200ºC/ 400ºF/Gas Mark 6 oven (180ºC/

350°F in fan ovens) for 5 minutes.
Add chunks of peeled celeriac (like
roast potatoes) and toss in the oil.
Season with salt and pepper and roast
for 40–55 minutes, turning occasionally or until golden. They taste good
but don't go crisp like potatoes.

CELERIAC

WAYS TO SERVE
■ Boil and mix with equal amounts of
potatoes for a different type of mash.
■ For spicy roast celeriac, instead of
tossing in oil as above, toss in melted
butter mixed with some curry powder
and mustard seeds.

GOES WITH Salmon, roast meats
(especially pork), mustard, mayonnaise.

GOOD FOR YOU It has minerals
such as calcium and potassium, as
well as some vitamin C.

USE INSTEAD Parsnip or potato,
but flavour and texture are different.

Celery
A good backdrop vegetable when
added to soups and stews, celery also
has many merits in its own right, pro-
viding flavour as well as crunch.
Bunches of celery range in colour from
white to green. The darker in colour,
the stronger the flavour.

CHOOSE

- All year round.
- The stalks should look fresh, firm and evenly shaped with no bruising.
- Select stalks with lively-looking leaves.

STORE In its plastic bag in the vegetable drawer of the fridge for up to 2–3 weeks.

PREPARE Remove any large, stringy outer stalks as they are often tough. You can add them chopped with onion and carrots to give flavour to stocks, stews or soups – peel off any tough strings with a vegetable peeler first. The slimmer inner stalks are tender, so are good for eating raw or stir-frying. Snap off the stalks as needed, and wash. Trim the ends, then leave the stalks whole or cut into slices. Leaves can be used in salads, or as a garnish for soups.

COOK Celery is mostly eaten raw, but it can also be cooked.
Braise: Fry whole stalks in a little butter for a few minutes, pour in enough water to cover and simmer for 10–15 minutes or until tender. Scatter with chopped parsley and serve with roast meats or chicken.
Stir-fry: Heat 1 tbsp oil in a wok or frying pan. Tip in diagonally sliced celery and stir-fry for 4–6 minutes until tender-crisp. Season.

WAYS TO SERVE

- Slice for a salad and toss with chicory leaves and thin shavings of fennel and Parmesan cheese.
- Add chopped to a stuffing for chicken or turkey, or to flavour stocks.
- Lightly fry stalks, then put into an ovenproof dish, cover with cheese sauce (see page 461) and a sprinkling of grated cheese and bake at 190°C/375°F/Gas Mark 5 (170°C/340°F in fan ovens) for about 15–20 minutes until golden and bubbly.

GOES WITH Cheese, beetroot, apples, mayonnaise, nuts, nut oils.

GOOD FOR YOU Has potassium and some fibre.

Chard (also called Swiss chard, ruby chard)

This leafy vegetable is a stunning version of spinach. Its stems are either vivid ruby red or pure white, and the crinkly leaves are dark green.

CHOOSE

- Available most of the year, though best in summer and autumn.
- Go for crisp, fresh-coloured leaves, with no brown marks on the stems.
- Small leaves don't necessarily indi-

celery–chard

cate tenderness. Big ones can be just
as tender as small (or more so).

■ Allow about 1 kg (2 lb) chard for
4 people.

STORE In a perforated plastic bag
in the fridge for up to 3–4 days.

PREPARE The stalks (or ribs) and
leaves are best cooked and served
separately. The leaves can be steamed,
boiled or pan-fried, like spinach. The
stalks are good chopped, then steamed
or boiled and added to a sauce or
soup, or fried.

■ Chop the stalks from the bottom of
the leaves (on older, bigger leaves you
may also need to cut the stalks out of
the leaves). Stalks can be left whole
or chopped.

■ Give the leaves a quick rinse, drain
well and leave whole, tear or shred
thinly.

COOK

Boil: Pack the leaves into a large
pan with a little salt. Just cover with
boiling water, bring back to the boil
and cook for 1–2 minutes or until
wilted. Drain well in a colander or
sieve and press out any excess moisture with the back of a spoon.

Stir-fry: Heat a little oil in a large
wok or pan. Add the chopped stems
and stir-fry for 2 minutes. Add the

FIX IT: CELERY
If celery has gone a bit limp,
bring it back to life by standing
it in a jar of water in the fridge.

TIPS & TRICKS: CELERY
When fresh, celery should
snap in two easily.

CHARD

shredded leaves and toss for another 2–3 minutes until wilted. Season and squeeze over a little lemon juice.

Steam: For 3–4 minutes or until just wilted. Press out the excess moisture with the back of a spoon. Serve with melted butter.

WAYS TO SERVE

■ Stir-fry the leaves with a little chopped garlic and crushed dried chillies, then scatter in some chopped tomatoes and parsley.

GOES WITH Tomatoes, lemon, cream, garlic, nutmeg, chilli.

GOOD FOR YOU High in fibre, plus vitamin C.

USE INSTEAD Spinach.

Chicory (US: endive or Belgian endive)

The tightly packed, crunchy leaves form the shape of a small torpedo. They can be eaten raw or cooked.

CHOOSE

■ All year round, though best in winter.
■ Between the more common white with yellow tips (Belgian endive) or red-leaved (see radicchio, opposite).
■ If choosing white chicory, make sure the tips are yellow – if green they can taste too bitter.
■ Allow 1 head of chicory per person.

STORE In a perforated plastic bag in the fridge for up to 4–5 days.

PREPARE Just trim the ends if necessary and discard any limp outer leaves. The inside leaves can then be separated for a salad, or the whole head can be cut lengthways into halves or quarters. If you cut the chicory, brush the cut sides with lemon juice to stop them going brown.

COOK

Pan-fry: Cut into quarters. Heat some olive oil in a frying pan and fry a little chopped garlic or shallot. Lay the chicory in the pan cut side down and fry for 3 minutes. Turn and fry for another 2–3 minutes, or until golden and tender. Season with salt and pepper and a splash of balsamic vinegar.

Roast: Lay halves in an oiled baking dish or roasting tin. Scatter with a few bay leaves and garlic cloves, drizzle with olive oil, cover with foil and roast at 200°C/400°F/Gas Mark 6 (180°C/350°F in fan ovens) for 30 minutes. Remove the foil and roast for a further 15–25 minutes until golden and tender.

WAYS TO SERVE

■ Toss raw leaves with crisp slices of apple and pear, a few green salad leaves and toasted pecans or hazelnuts with a lemon and nut oil dressing.
■ Serve pan-fried chicory scattered with grated or crumbled cheese and fresh thyme leaves.
■ Use the raw leaves as mini containers for canapés. Fill with salad such as chicken Caesar or ham and cheese.

GOES WITH Chicken, bacon, cheese (especially blue cheeses, Gruyère and crumbly cheeses), nuts, apples, pears, mustard.

GOOD FOR YOU Can contribute to potassium intake.

USE INSTEAD Radicchio (see right).

Chilli
see SPICES, *page 169*

Chinese leaves
see CABBAGE, *page 268*

Courgette
(US: zucchini)

One of the smaller-sized members of the squash family. Courgettes don't

CHICORY

RADICCHIO
The most common type of radicchio is Rossa di Chioggia. With its white leaves streaked with deep pink, this radicchio is similar in shape to a small cabbage. Its colour adds drama to salads and mixing it with other leaves will tone down its strong, bitter and peppery flavour. Use in Italian-style salads with other strong flavours such as anchovies, capers and red wine dressings. As it is quite sturdy, it can be cut into wedges and griddled. It is also delicious shredded and used with cream and garlic as a pasta sauce. Just wilt in the cream with some chopped garlic, then toss with cooked pasta. Other types of Italian radicchio include Radicchio Rossa di Treviso, which is grown in a similar way to Belgian endive.

VEG A–Z

have a lot of flavour of their own, but take on other flavours really well – try frying them with olive oil, onion and garlic, or simmering with tomatoes and other saucy ingredients. Their vibrant yellow flowers are very popular in Italy where they are served stuffed or deep-fried in a light batter.

CHOOSE

■ All year round – they tend to be cheaper during the summer.

■ Both green and yellow varieties are available.

■ Look for ones that aren't too big (they will be less watery), with shiny, bright, smooth and firm skin. (Any sign of softness or hollowness in the middle means they will be fibrous.)

■ Allow 500 g (1 lb) for 4 people.

STORE They will keep in the fridge for several days, but are best used as soon as possible.

PREPARE Wash, then trim both ends. There is no need to peel. Choose how you want to cut them:

■ Into round or diagonal slices.

■ Down the length of the courgette in slim lengthways strips, then chopped into dice or matchstick lengths.

■ Into ribbons – with a vegetable peeler, shave off thin strips down the length of the courgette to use in salads, or drop into boiling water with pasta at the end of cooking. For salads, ribbons taste better when blanched briefly first (see page 12), then plunged into cold water and drained.

■ Grated for a salad or for use in baking (helps keep some cake mixtures moist).

■ Halve lengthways through the middle, scoop out the seedy centre, then stuff and bake.

COOK Because courgettes contain a lot of water, steaming, frying or roasting in the oven are the best ways to cook them. Boiling just makes them more watery. Test when ready by piercing with a sharp knife – they should be tender-crisp, the colour still vibrant.

Stir-fry: Heat a little olive oil in a frying pan or wok (or use a mix of butter and oil). Add the sliced courgettes, but don't crowd the pan – you may need to cook them in batches. Stir-fry, turning occasionally, until golden on both sides.

Roast: Cut the courgettes into chunky pieces, put in a roasting tin, drizzle with oil and sprinkle with pepper and herbs. Roast at 200°C/400°F/Gas Mark 6 (180°C/350°F in fan ovens) for 25–35 minutes or until golden and tender, turning half way through.

Steam: For 3–5 minutes depending on their size.

WAYS TO SERVE

■ Steam, then toss with olive oil and basil or oregano, or fry and serve with grated Parmesan and black pepper.
■ For a salad, toss blanched courgette ribbons (see page 280), with an oil and vinegar dressing, some chopped garlic, herbs and halved cherry tomatoes.

GOES WITH Mozzarella and Parmesan cheeses, aubergine, tomatoes, onions, garlic, herbs such as basil, oregano, parsley.

GOOD FOR YOU Mostly made of water, but the seeds give fibre; also contain some iron and vitamin C, potassium and beta carotene.

Cress *see page 289*

Cucumber

Linked to the squash family, cucumber is a cooling vegetable to eat at the height of summer when it is at its best.

CHOOSE

■ All year round.
■ Best if it is plump and firm with a bright colour and no dents or bruises.
■ Between the long, slender English cucumber and the shorter, thicker ridge cucumber which has more seeds.

FIX IT: COURGETTE

If you have stir-fried courgettes and they are still watery and insipid, toss a handful of dried breadcrumbs into the pan. Turn up the heat and they will crisp up and remove the sogginess.

TIPS & TRICKS: CUCUMBER

To stop cucumber sandwiches from going soggy you can salt the cucumber like an aubergine. Just slice the cucumber, sprinkle with salt and leave for 20–30 minutes. This draws out the moisture. Pat dry with kitchen paper, removing the salt as you do so, and you will have crisp, less watery slices.

STORE In the vegetable drawer of the fridge for up to 4–5 days if uncut; about 3 days if cut.

PREPARE Peeling isn't necessary with fine-skinned English cucumbers, and the colour and texture of the peel contrasts well with the flesh. Smaller ridge cucumbers have quite tough, bumpy skins, which are better removed with a vegetable peeler. Trim both ends, wash the cucumber, then slice, dice, or cut in chunks or sticks. For a ridged effect, score down the length of the cucumber with the prongs of a fork before slicing. Or cut into thin, wide ribbons down the length using a vegetable peeler.

COOK Usually eaten raw.

WAYS TO SERVE
■ Cook slices of ridge cucumber briefly in melted butter, to warm them through. Season and serve with fish.
■ Grate coarsely and mix with yogurt, garlic and a little chopped mint to make a refreshing Indian raita.
■ Chop and mix with chopped avocado and spring onion, and toss with olive oil, lime or lemon juice to make a salsa for serving with salmon.

GOES WITH Fish (especially salmon), yogurt, dill, mint, fennel, chives and garlic. Cools down curries.

GOOD FOR YOU Cucumber is about 96% water.

Endive
see CHICORY, *page 278*

Fennel
Although it looks like portly celery, fennel's wonderful aniseed flavour sets it apart. It's loved by Italians and used in many Italian recipes. Whether it's cooked in attractive wedges or thinly shaved and served as crisp raw slices, its taste is distinctive. The herb fennel (see page 140) is a close relation but not to be confused with the vegetable.

CHOOSE
■ All year round, but it's at its best in the summer months.
■ Smaller bulbs are more tender and should be white and feel heavy.
■ Any feathery fronds should look fresh, bright and green, not yellow and floppy.
■ Allow 1 small or ½ large fennel per person.

STORE Will keep in a perforated plastic bag in the vegetable drawer of the fridge for up to 3–4 days.

cucumber–fennel

PREPARE Remove any feathery green fronds at the top and, if they are fresh, keep for garnishing. Trim off the top shoots and the root of the fennel, then peel off any damaged or brown-looking outer layers. To cook and serve whole, cut out the tough inside core in a cone shape from the bottom end with a small, sharp knife. Slices can be cut across or down the bulb. Alternatively, cut the whole bulb into wedges by slicing in half lengthways, then in quarters, then cut out the core from each wedge (take care not to remove all of it or the wedges will fall apart).

For a salad: Keep the slices really thin. The most effective tool for this is a mandolin which gives thin shavings, although a very sharp knife can also be used. Hold the fennel by its root end to slice, so it doesn't fall apart. To keep the raw slices crisp and white, soak in iced water with a little lemon juice.

COOK This brings out the sweetness of fennel.

Boil: Place the whole fennel, or wedges, in a saucepan with a little salt. Add boiling water to cover, and a squeeze of lemon juice. Bring back to the boil, cover and cook whole for 15–20 minutes, wedges for 8–10 minutes. Drain really well to get rid of any water trapped between the layers.

SIMPLE GREEK SALAD

Mix chunks of cucumber with chunks of red pepper, tomato and a little chopped red onion. Crumble over some feta cheese, scatter with dried or fresh oregano, then drizzle with olive oil, a squeeze of lemon juice or splash of wine vinegar, and season with plenty of freshly ground black pepper and a dash of salt.

TIPS & TRICKS: FENNEL

When boiling fennel, increase its flavour by dropping a star anise into the water.

Pan-fry/griddle: Boil or steam wedges until tender, then heat a little oil in a frying pan or on a griddle, add the fennel and cook until golden, turning occasionally.

Roast: Toss wedges or thick slices in olive oil with sprigs of rosemary in a roasting tin, and roast at 200°C/400°F/Gas Mark 6 (180°C/350°F in fan ovens) for 40–50 minutes.

Steam: Whole for about 20 minutes, quarters for 10–12 minutes.

WAYS TO SERVE

■ Lay steamed or boiled wedges on a buttered baking tray, dot with butter, sprinkle generously with grated Parmesan cheese and grill until golden.

■ Toss very thinly sliced raw fennel with olive oil, grated lemon zest and juice, salt and pepper.

■ Simmer fennel slices in a simple tomato sauce (see page 121), covered, for about 15 minutes, or until tender. Good with chicken or fish.

GOES WITH Chicken, white fish, salmon, smoked fish, tomatoes, Parmesan cheese, dill.

GOOD FOR YOU Has some beta carotene and B vitamins.

Garlic *see page 298*

Kale

Hardy members of the cabbage family, both kale and curly kale are available. Curly kale is the most familiar, with its robust, frilly leaves and strong, distinctive flavour. It is used in a similar way to cabbage.

CHOOSE

■ When in season – at its sweetest and best in winter and early spring.

■ Look for crisp leaves with a bright colour.

■ Curly kale – the leaves should be tightly curled.

■ Kale – this has smooth leaves, good for pan-frying when the leaves are young and tender.

■ Allow about 700 g (1½ lb) kale for 4 servings.

STORE In the fridge for up to 3 days – the longer it is kept, the more bitter the leaves become.

PREPARE Cut the leaves from the stalks. Cut out and discard any tough-looking rib parts of the stalks from the leaves. Wash, then chop or shred.

COOK

Boil: Don't cook kale in lots of water Pour about 1 cm (½ in) water into a large pan. Add some salt, bring to the

boil and add the washed, chopped or
shredded leaves. Cover and cook over
a medium heat, shaking the pan
occasionally, for 4–5 minutes, or until
wilted and just cooked. Drain and
press out any excess water with a
spoon. Serve tossed in butter and salt
and pepper.

Pan fry: Heat 2–3 tbsp olive oil in a
large pan. Rinse 500 g (1 lb) kale,
shred it, and add enough to make a thin
layer in the pan, then let it wilt before
adding more. Keep adding in this way,
then cover and cook for 5–10 minutes
depending on the tenderness and size
of the leaves.

WAYS TO SERVE
■ When pan-frying, add some chopped
garlic to the last of the leaves, and
serve scattered with chopped crispy
bacon and a drizzle of olive oil.

GOES WITH Chicken, bacon,
sausages, garlic.

GOOD FOR YOU Kale is full of
vitamins C, B, E and K and is a good
source of fibre, beta carotene, folate,
calcium and iron.

Kohlrabi
Although it belongs to a branch of
the cabbage family, kohlrabi has no

CURLY KALE

VEG A–Z

resemblance to cabbage. Instead of having layers of leaves, it looks a bit like a turnip and is sometimes called 'cabbage turnip' – its name derives from the German words *kohl* (cabbage) and *rabi* (turnip). It can be pale green or purple, stir-fries beautifully, and has a delicate, sweet flavour and a crisp and crunchy texture.

CHOOSE

■ All year round, though it's best from summer to early winter.

■ Small–medium size is best, about the size of a tennis ball, as some of the larger ones can be tough.

■ The bulb should feel firm and heavy, and the leaves should be crisp-looking.

■ Allow 1 small kohlrabi per person.

STORE In a perforated plastic bag in the fridge (leaf stems trimmed off) for up to 2 weeks.

PREPARE Trim off any leaf stems or leaves (these can be washed and cooked like cabbage or used in salads and stir-fries if tender). Trim off both ends, then peel with a potato peeler or small, sharp knife like an apple. Cut into chunks, wedges or thin slices. Slice into thin strips if using in a stir-fry or in a salad. (Blanch briefly for a salad.)

COOK

Roast: Steam wedges first for 5 minutes, then toss in a roasting tin with oil, salt and pepper and roast at 190°C/375°F/Gas Mark 5 (170°C/340°F in fan ovens) for 40–50 minutes, turning occasionally, until golden and tender.

Steam: For 8–12 minutes, or until tender-crisp.

Stir-fry: Cut into strips. Heat some oil in a frying pan, add the kohlrabi and stir-fry for 2–3 minutes. Toss in some thin slices of fresh root ginger and garlic and fry for another 2–3 minutes, or until tender-crisp. For extra flavour, finish off with a splash of soy sauce and sesame oil.

WAYS TO SERVE

■ Steam chunks or slices and toss with butter, lemon juice and dill or parsley.

■ Roast chunks with other root vegetables, such as carrots and parsnips.

■ Add strips to stir-fries, or cook chunks or slices in soups and stews.

GOES WITH Chicken, fish, bacon, cheese, carrots, leeks, peas and cream, and herbs like parsley, dill, chives and chervil.

GOOD FOR YOU A good source of vitamin C and potassium.

USE INSTEAD Turnip.

Leek

Related to the garlic and onion family, leeks taste similar to mild onion, but are more subtle and slightly sweet.

CHOOSE

■ All year, but best from the end of summer through to the end of spring.

■ Scrubbed, trimmed and ready to use for convenience, or loose and unwashed for more taste.

■ For tenderness and sweetness go for small to medium leeks.

■ The lower white part should be firm, the top green part, crisp and bright in colour.

■ About 875 g (1¾ lb) untrimmed leeks will serve 4 people.

STORE Wrap well in a plastic bag so their smell doesn't overpower other foods. They will keep for up to a week in the vegetable drawer of the fridge.

PREPARE Pre-packed leeks are already trimmed, so just trim the ends. For loose leeks, slice off most of the green part, or as far along as it appears tough or damaged. Slice off the roots, then peel off any damaged outer leaves. Dirt can collect inside the furled leaves, so insert a knife where the white part meets the green part and slice lengthways (going about half

KOHLRABI

KOHLRABI CRUNCH
Young kohlrabi can be used raw as a dipping veg, or you can nibble on wedges of it like an apple. It also makes a great salad: toss thin strips in a vinaigrette or mustardy dressing, or use it grated with finely shredded carrot and thin slices of apple.

way into the leek), almost down to the root end. Open it out and rinse the layers of leaves under cold running water. Leave whole, slice into circles (thick or thin) or lengthways into strips.

COOK Leeks can turn mushy if overcooked or cooked with too much water, so it's better to steam or panfry them. To test when done, prod with the tip of a sharp knife. The leek should feel tender but still be firm.

Steam: 4–8 minutes for sliced, 10–18 minutes for whole, depending on size.

Pan-fry: Melt a large knob of butter in a frying pan. Tip in sliced leeks and seasoning and simmer on a low heat for about 5–8 minutes, uncovered, stirring occasionally.

WAYS TO SERVE
- Crumble goat's or another cheese such as Cheshire over steamed leeks, sprinkle with chopped fresh oregano or thyme and serve drizzled with olive oil.
- Blanch sliced leeks first for a couple of minutes, drain well, then stir-fry with bacon lardons (see page 353).
- Toss hot steamed leeks with a mustard or herb dressing and chopped sundried tomatoes for a warm salad.
- Coat with cheese sauce (see page 461), top with grated cheese and grill

until golden. Nice with crispy bacon bits too.

GOES WITH Ham, bacon, chicken, fish, potatoes and other root vegetables, tomatoes, eggs, cheese, mustard.

GOOD FOR YOU Has plenty of fibre, plus some vitamin C and folate.

Lettuce

Lettuce can be crisp or floppy, various shades of green, or green with red highlights. Flavoursome dressings and sturdy ingredients bring out the best in crisp leaves, while floppy ones go well with more delicate accompaniments.

CHOOSE
- All year round.
- Leaves should be perky-looking, not limp or with signs of discoloration. Crisp lettuce may have fading leaves on the outside which can be removed.

Cos (Romaine): Recognizable by its long thin leaves. Its crisp texture goes well with thick creamy dressings, bacon, avocado and Parmesan. A classic choice for Caesar salad, it is also good stir-fried.

Curly endive (frisée): A member of the chicory family, it looks like a curly mop of hair. Its frilly, green leaves get progressively paler towards the centre, where they are pale yellow or white.

leek–lettuce

The outer leaves have chicory's slight bitter taste. Good mixed with milder leaves and blue cheese dressing.

Escarole: Pale green, floppy, soft leaves, which are curly, but less so than those of curly endive. Goes well with mild-flavoured dressings.

Iceberg (crisphead): What this lacks in flavour it gains in crispness. It is round with pale green, tightly packed leaves. Its mild taste is best in mixed salads with flavoursome dressings.

Little Gem: Small in size, with tight, crisp leaves, it tastes slightly bitter and is less tender than other lettuces. Good shredded or cut in wedges and served with something sweet or fruity such as apple slices or a creamy dressing to temper its bitterness. The leaves are also good as 'containers'.

Lollo rosso and Oak leaf: Both have soft and floppy, green leaves with splashes of plum red, but don't have much flavour, so are better mixed with other leaves. They go well with oil and vinegar dressings with herbs to sharpen up their taste.

Quattro Stagioni: Similar to escarole but has leaves with purply-red edges. Best with a mild dressing.

Round: Also called butterhead; the soft, buttery leaves are vibrant green with a mild taste. Good with a simple herb vinaigrette as well as a stronger, Thai-flavoured or creamy dressing.

A FEW MORE LEAVES

Salad leaves can be used alone or mixed and matched to give a variety of looks, tastes, textures and colours. Add some herbs too and you have the makings of a great salad.

- *LAMB'S LETTUCE (also known as* mâche *or corn salad): Comes in attractive bunches of long, oval leaves and mixes well with beetroot and rocket. Will take a slightly spicy dressing or a mild one that doesn't detract from its flavour.*

- *MIZUNA: Looks a bit like rocket, only more feathery and delicate. A Japanese leaf with a mild mustardy taste, it goes well with a sesame oil dressing.*

- *SALAD CRESS (also called mustard and cress): This has tiny, spicy leaves. Usually sold growing on fragile, thin white stems in punnets. Snip into sandwiches or over salads, or mix with other leaves. (See also Spicy Leaves, page 291.)*

Webb's Wonder: Another in the crisphead category, tight-packed in the centre like Iceberg, but a darker green colour.

STORE Don't wash before storing. Soft-leaved lettuces will keep in a perforated plastic bag in the vegetable drawer of the fridge for 1–2 days, crisp lettuce for 3–4 days.

PREPARE For optimum freshness and crispness, prepare just before serving. Separate individual leaves, then wash briefly, drain and shake well (or use a salad spinner). Treat gently as the leaves bruise easily. Use whole, torn or shredded. Lettuce leaves are best torn rather than cut with a knife as this can cause the edges to turn brown. If cutting wedges from crisp lettuce (such as Little Gem), brush with lemon juice immediately.

COOK Usually eaten raw, but can be shredded into soups at the last minute or braised with peas.

GOES WITH Other salad leaves, nuts, avocado, cheese, eggs, peas, fruit, herbs.

GOOD FOR YOU Has beta carotene, some B vitamins and vitamin K.

Marrow

A marrow looks like a giant courgette (a close relation). It can grow huge, but the bigger it gets, the more water it contains and the less flavour it has. It is also called vegetable marrow, and can be used in similar ways to courgette (see page 279), but its flavour is blander and it is more watery. You can add flavour to it by slicing and baking it, then piling a savoury stuffing on top (see opposite).

CHOOSE
■ Available in the summer months.
■ Best not to buy if more than 30 cm (12 in) long as the flesh will be watery.

STORE In a cool place for several weeks.

PREPARE
For chunks: Cut the marrow in half lengthways, scoop out and discard the seedy centre, then peel and chop into chunks.
For slices: Cut crossways into slices about 2.5 cm (1 in) thick, then remove the centre seeds and trim off the peel.

COOK Because marrow contains so much water, it is best to bake or pan-fry it rather than boil.

lettuce–marrow

Bake: Cut into slices as above. Place them in a shallow dish with a spoonful of water. Bake at 190°C/375°F/Gas Mark 5 (170°C/340°F in fan ovens) for 15 minutes, or until tender. Drain off any liquid. Serve seasoned and sprinkled with cheese. Alternatively, top with onion fried with garlic and tomatoes, lay slices of mozzarella cheese on top of that and grill until melted.

Pan-fry: Heat a little butter and oil in a frying pan. Add chunks of marrow and cook briefly, stirring occasionally, until softened but not going mushy. Season with salt and pepper.

WAYS TO SERVE

■ Fry some chopped onion and garlic in a little butter and oil. Pan-fry marrow chunks as above, then season and stir in some freshly chopped parsley.

GOES WITH Minced beef, pork or lamb, tomatoes, parsley, ginger (good for flavouring marrow jam).

GOOD FOR YOU Contains plenty of fibre, plus some beta carotene.

USE INSTEAD Large courgettes.

TIPS & TRICKS: LETTUCE

Add dressing to lettuce leaves just before serving, or the leaves will wilt and lose their crispness. If you want to prepare ahead, make the dressing in the salad bowl, lay the salad servers over it and pile the leaves on top. When ready to serve just toss everything together.

SPICY SALAD LEAVES

■ *ROCKET: For the true peppery flavour of rocket, choose organic wild rocket – it has smaller, more ragged leaves than regular rocket and a livelier taste. Toss into salads, wilt on top of pizzas or tarts as they come out of the oven, or into pasta at the end of cooking. It is also delicious tossed with a little olive oil, a splash of balsamic vinegar and a few shavings of Parmesan cheese.*

■ *WATERCRESS: This has a peppery flavour. Its bright, shiny, green leaves are good mixed with other leaves such as chicory, rocket, round lettuce or frisée. It contains lots of iron, calcium and vitamins A, C and some vitamin E plus a healthy dose of plant compounds that help protect against cancer. Toss with halved, warm new potatoes, so it wilts, and add a herb or mustard dressing.*

Mushroom

for DRIED, *see page 96*

The white mushroom is the most well known, but many edible fungi are now cultivated that were once available only in the wild, such as shiitake and oyster, so it's easier to mix different types together to liven up your meals.

CHOOSE

■ Cultivated are available all year round. True wild are seasonal, and are in the shops mostly in the autumn.

■ Caps should be fresh and firm, stems fleshy, not shrivelled.

■ Select from the many varieties, both cultivated and wild. The most common is the white mushroom which starts life as a button mushroom and, if left unpicked, doubles in size every 24 hours. It next becomes a closed-cup, then an open-cup mushroom, and finally, 5 days after being a button mushroom, a large, flat mushroom.

WHITE

Button: Small, white and very mild in flavour. Use raw or lightly cooked in sauces and salads, or increase the flavour by marinating in spicy dressings.

Closed-cup: A large button mushroom with a similar taste. Use for slicing into stir-fries, on to pizzas or cooking whole.

Open-cup: The radiating, pinkish gills are starting to show as the white mushroom finally opens up.

Flat/open: More developed still, with more flavour.

BROWN/CHESTNUT

Closed-cup/portabellini/crimini: This brown capped mushroom has more flavour and a meatier texture than the white cap. Use sliced raw in salads, or cooked in pasta and other sauces or chopped in stuffings.

Flat/portabello: A mature version of the chestnut mushroom. Completely open with dark gills, a gutsy flavour and meaty texture. Use for grilling or stuffing whole (remove the stalk first), slicing and stir-frying, flavouring stews and casseroles.

STORE Keep unwashed in a punnet or paper bag – if in a plastic bag they will sweat and quickly rot. Store in the vegetable drawer of the fridge for up to 3 days.

PREPARE All is edible. There is no need to peel: just rinse briefly in a colander and pat dry with kitchen paper. (Never soak mushrooms in water as they absorb liquid like a sponge and go soggy.) Trim the ends of the stalks and leave the mushrooms whole, halve, quarter, slice or chop.

mushroom

COOK Small, whole mushrooms can be added to dishes such as sauces and casseroles 5–10 minutes before the end of cooking. Otherwise they are best stir-fried or grilled.

Stir-fry: Slice or chop any that are large; leave small ones whole. To bring out their flavour, brown mushrooms first. Pour some oil into a frying pan (preferably non-stick) and get it hot before adding the mushrooms, or they will steam rather than fry. Keeping the heat high, stir-fry for 3–4 minutes until golden, tossing occasionally.

Grill: Brush with oil and cook whole under a preheated grill for 3 minutes. Turn and grill for another 2–3 minutes. Grill the larger, flat mushrooms for about 5 minutes on each side.

WAYS TO SERVE

■ When frying mushrooms, cook some finely chopped garlic and red chilli in the oil briefly before adding them to the pan. Add and stir-fry the mushrooms, season and finish with chopped parsley and a squeeze of lemon juice. Good with a mix of mushrooms.

■ Fry whole button mushrooms with chopped spring onions, then stir in crème fraîche or soured cream and sprinkle with paprika. Great with steak or chicken.

■ Thinly slice button mushrooms and serve raw as a salad tossed with sliced

FIX IT: MUSHROOMS

To give a wild mushroom flavour to fresh cultivated mushrooms, toss 425 g (14 oz) cultivated mushrooms (a mix is good) with 15 g (½ oz) soaked dried porcini or ceps. (Soak the dried mushrooms in 150 ml (¼ pint) warm water for about 1 hour, and use the flavoured liquid too.)

radish, watercress, crumbled crispy bacon and a full-flavoured dressing such as mustard, garlic or blue cheese.

■ Fry the mushrooms for 2 minutes, then add chopped shallots and garlic and fry for another couple of minutes. Stir in a few spoonfuls of double cream and heat. Season with salt and pepper and serve on toast scattered with chopped parsley.

GOES WITH Many things, especially beef, chicken, fish, tomatoes, bacon, pasta, cream, crème fraîche, soured cream, cheese, onions, spring onions, soy sauce, garlic, lemon, thyme, parsley.

GOOD FOR YOU Contains plenty of fibre and B vitamins. Has more vegetable protein per 100 g (3½ oz) than many other vegetables, so good for vegetarians.

Exotic and wild mushrooms

EXOTIC (CULTIVATED WILD)

A lot of the exotic-looking mushrooms available in the shops are actually cultivated and not truly wild.

Blewit: This has a purply-blue, tinted stem. It should be sliced and cooked thoroughly to bring out its distinctive taste. Delicious stir-fried with bacon.

Enoki: A tiny, creamy-white, mild-flavoured Japanese mushroom with a long, slender stem. Eat in salads, or stir-fry or scatter into soups at the last minute – it cooks instantly. Separate the joined-up stems before you use them.

Horse: When young and tender, these little, subtle-flavoured mushrooms with sturdy, long stems and helmet-like caps can be used interchangeably with white mushrooms. In the wild they grow quite large.

Oyster: These delicate-flavoured mushrooms require minimum cooking and are best flash-fried to prevent wilting. Pretty and shaped like fans, they come in pink and yellow as well as grey, although the colour disappears when they are cooked.

Shiitake: Used a lot in Chinese and Japanese cooking, these are enjoyed for their subtle flavour and unique texture. Tougher than most mushrooms, they need longer cooking to soften. Good in stews, or roasted with Oriental flavours. Trim off the tough stalks before using.

TRUE WILD

These are less easy to buy than cultivated mushrooms, as they are picked in the wild and available only when in they are in season.

Chanterelle: A pretty, apricot-coloured mushroom with a slightly frilly cap and pleasant flavour. Small ones are called *girolles* in France. Goes well with other varieties for a quick stir-fry, or on its own with scrambled eggs for breakfast. May need a brief wash before using. Dry with kitchen paper.

Morel: Highly prized and therefore expensive, this has a wrinkly, dark brown, dome-shaped cap. It is more likely to be found dried than fresh and goes well with creamy sauces.

Porcini (in Italy), cèpes (in France): Full of flavour with a meaty texture, these are difficult to find fresh, but are readily available dried (see page 96). To prepare fresh porcini, brush briefly under cold running water, but don't peel as all the flavour is in the skin. Dry with kitchen paper, then trim the end off the bulbous stalk. To get the benefit of the shape, slice them lengthways. Delicious quickly fried in butter.

Okra (bhindi)

Also known as ladies' fingers because of the elegant way it tapers to a point at one end, okra has a slightly furry, green-ridged skin and a creamy, seedy flesh with a pungent taste. Popular in Indian and Middle Eastern cooking and for making Cajun gumbos.

OKRA

FIX IT: OKRA

Okra can be glutinous and sticky when cooked for long – so will thicken soups and stews, but is not so popular when it is served as a vegetable. To reduce this texture you have two choices:
1 Use small, very fresh okra and cook very briefly.
2 Cook them whole, trimming around the stalks in a cone shape so the actual pod isn't pierced and able to release its sticky juices.

CHOOSE

- All year round.
- Should be firm and small, no longer than 7–10 cm (3–4 in) – the bigger and older it is, the tougher it is.
- Avoid those with brown markings on the skin – this indicates that the okra is not fresh.
- Allow 375 g (12 oz) for 4 people.

STORE In a perforated plastic bag in the fridge for up to 3 days.

PREPARE Wash, pat dry, then trim both ends. You can then leave whole, cut lengthways in half, or slice into pieces about 1.5 cm (¾ in) long.

COOK Okra is best fried or cooked with other ingredients.
Stir-fry: Heat a little oil or ghee in a wok or frying pan. Add the okra and fry for 6–12 minutes, depending on how it has been cut, until starting to brown.

WAYS TO SERVE

- Fry some sliced onion for a few minutes before adding okra (as above). When both are brown, stir in a pinch of turmeric and crushed dried chillies and cook a few more minutes. Serve scattered with chopped coriander.

GOES WITH Serve as a vegetable accompaniment to curries, or as part of a curry. Goes well with potatoes, tomatoes and coconut.

GOOD FOR YOU A great source of calcium, magnesium, iron, niacin, folate and vitamin C.

Onion

This has to be the most versatile vegetable in the world as it brings flavour to many dishes and can be used as a vegetable in its own right.

CHOOSE

- All year round.
- Those that are firm with no soft spots or shoots.
- From the following types:

Brown/yellow: The most common and a good all-rounder. It has golden-brown skin and white flesh.

Red: Mild and sweet-tasting, the pink-tinged flesh looks attractive and tastes good raw in salads and salsas. A good choice for roasting.

Spanish: This has a similar brown skin to the brown/yellow onion, but tastes milder and sweeter. It is also bigger. The mild flavour makes it good for salads, omelettes, salsas and stir-fries.

White: Strong in flavour, with white skin and flesh. Use raw in salads when you want the onion taste to dominate.

okra–onion

STORE Keep loose in a cool, dry place, where the air can move around them – they will keep for several weeks. Best stored on their own, as they are quick to take on moisture from other vegetables such as potatoes. Discard once they start sprouting. Don't store cut onion in the fridge or it will flavour your milk, unless wrapped well in cling film.

PREPARE Best prepared just before using. Cut a thin slice off the top of the onion, then peel by removing the papery outer skin and any soft or brown outer layers.

Chop: Keep the root end on so the onion doesn't fall apart as you chop it. Put the onion on its side on a chopping board and cut in half lengthways. Place the cut side down and make a series of horizontal cuts towards the root, stopping just short of the root end each time. Next, make a series of equally spaced vertical cuts down through the onion, again stopping short of the root end (see top right). Finally, hold the onion firmly with your fingers, then cut down across the vertical cuts so that the onion falls away in small pieces (see centre right). If you want smaller pieces still, carry on chopping or start with cuts very close together. Discard the root end.

CHOPPING AN ONION

1 *After making horizontal cuts through the onion stopping just short of the root, make a series of evenly spaced vertical cuts, again stopping short of the root.*

2 *Cut down through the onion across the vertical cuts so that it falls into small pieces.*

FIX IT: CHOPPING ONIONS

If cutting onions makes you cry, try the following:

■ *Chill the onions for 30 minutes (well wrapped), then keep the root end on while chopping (this contains the substance called allicin that makes your eyes water).*

■ *Put the onions in a bowl of cold water while peeling and keep the tap running while you chop them.*

Slice: Trim the root end. Hold the onion on its side on a board with your fingers across the centre. Slice down the onion into thick or thin slices, then separate each slice into rings or keep the slices whole (see opposite).

Cut into wedges: Slice off the top and root end and cut in half lengthways. Lay the cut side down and make lengthways cuts into quarters or eighths.

COOK Fry an onion well and it will bring lots of flavour to a dish – not only does the onion brown, it also creates sticky bits in the bottom of the pan which will flavour any added liquid. It's important to get the pan and fat hot before you start.

Pan-fry: Heat olive or sunflower oil in a frying pan, then add chopped or sliced onion. The oil should be so hot that it sizzles when the onion goes in, otherwise the onion will stew rather than fry. Cook on a medium heat for 7–10 minutes, moving the onion around occasionally so it doesn't burn. Aim to get it golden all over for the best flavour. The longer it cooks, the sweeter it will be.

Caramelize: This involves long, slow cooking until the onions reduce right down and become meltingly tender, so start with lots of them. Melt 30 g (1 oz) butter with 3 tbsp vegetable oil in a very large pan. Add about 1.25 kg (2½ lb) onions, sliced. With the heat very low,

cook for 40–50 minutes, stirring occasionally, until they are completely softened. Sprinkle in 1–2 tsp caster sugar, turn the heat up a bit and cook for another 10–15 minutes, until golden.

Roast: Lay wedges in a roasting tin, scatter with thyme sprigs and a couple of bay leaves, then drizzle with olive oil. Season and roast at 200°C/400°F/ Gas Mark 6 (180°C/350°F in fan ovens) for about 40–50 minutes, turning occasionally, until golden.

WAYS TO SERVE
■ Fry onion slices as above and toss with cooked new potatoes.
■ Mix chopped, raw red onion with sliced cherry tomatoes and chopped coriander. Add a squeeze of lemon juice and serve as a salad with curries.

GOES WITH
Most savoury ingredients, but especially meat, sausages and vegetables.

GOOD FOR YOU
Has niacin but is not particularly nutrient-rich.

USE INSTEAD
All onions can be used interchangeably, but use only red ones when you want a sweet taste.

More in the onion family
Garlic: Choose plump, firm bulbs with no green sprouts. Divide the whole bulb

onion

into separate cloves and peel off the skin (not necessary if it is to be crushed). If the garlic has a tiny, green shoot in the centre, take it out before chopping as it may have a bitter taste. CRUSH: Leaving the skin on, lay the flat side of a large chef's knife on top of the garlic clove and give it a heavy blow with your fist, then remove the skin. If you want the garlic more than just bruised, sprinkle a little salt on it and crush again. Alternatively, peel first and then use a garlic press. CHOP: Peel and slice the garlic, then move the knife back and forth in a rocking motion (like chopping herbs). COOK: Garlic can become bitter if cooked too long over too high a heat, so when frying, do so briefly and gently – don't allow it to get too brown. Or add towards the end of cooking when combining with other ingredients, so it doesn't burn. To roast, toss whole bulbs in olive oil and roast at 190°C/375°F/ Gas Mark 5 (170°C/340°F in fan ovens) for 20–25 minutes or until they feel soft. For separate cloves, throw a few unpeeled ones in with other roasting vegetables for the last 20 minutes of roasting time. To eat, separate the cloves and squeeze out the soft purée. Great with roasts and fish.

Pearl onion: A small sweet onion, also known as a baby or button onion, is perfect for dropping whole into

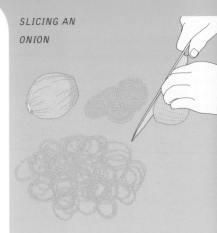

SLICING AN
ONION

TIPS & TRICKS: ONIONS

■ *If you want to reduce the strong flavour of raw onion, slice and soak in ice-cold water for a few hours.*

■ *To get rid of an oniony smell from your hands, rub them with lemon juice or vinegar.*

■ *If you are going to fry onions, chop them with a knife, rather than in a food processor. Using a machine can make them watery, causing them to steam rather than fry.*

slow-cooked dishes. Its thin skin makes it hard to peel, so soak for a few minutes in boiling water first to make it easier. Drain, rinse under cold water, then peel using a small, sharp knife. Keep the stem end on so the centre doesn't pop out.

Pickling onion: This is a regular onion picked when small, so is quite strong in flavour, and a bit smaller than a pearl onion. It is used for pickling as its name suggests, also for adding whole to stews. Soak as for pearl onion (see above) to make peeling easier.

Shallot: Closely related to the onion, the shallot is smaller, softer and sweeter in taste. Use when a hint of onion flavour is wanted. The longer banana shallot and the pinkish Thai shallot are also available. Trim off both ends and peel (if there is more than one bulb inside, pull apart to separate). To aid peeling, soak shallots in boiling water for a minute or two after trimming. Slice or finely chop. Like garlic, shallots need softening rather than browning as they can turn slightly bitter, so fry gently over a low heat, stirring often. They tend to cook more quickly than onions.

Spring onion/salad onion: Called green onion or scallion in the USA, this is mild in flavour and popular raw or in stir-fries. Trim off the root at the bottom, and any ragged green ends, then slice into rounds or shred by trimming off the top darker green part (this can be used separately), and cutting the lighter part lengthways in half, then lengthways again into thin strips. Use shreds in salads or for scattering over fish and chicken dishes, rice and noodles as a garnish. To make the shreds go curly, put into ice cold water for about 30 minutes. If you require a mild onion taste, use them like shallots by frying gently in a little oil or butter for a minute or two.

Pak choi
(also called bok choi)

A member of the cabbage family, this Chinese vegetable has bright white, chunky stems and dark green leaves, both of which are delicious to eat.

CHOOSE
- Available all year round.
- The smallest are the most tender.
- Avoid any with leaves that are starting to turn yellow.

STORE In a perforated plastic bag in the fridge for up to 4 days.

PREPARE Wash. Both leaves and stems are used, each having a slightly different texture and flavour. Steam them whole, or cut in halves or quarters

onion–pak choi

lengthways, or separate the leaves and stems and slice across finely or chunkily.

COOK Best cooked briefly to preserve taste and texture either by stir-frying or steaming.

Stir-fry: Heat 1 tbsp groundnut or vegetable oil in a wok. With the heat on high, add the stems and toss in the pan for a minute or two, then add the leaves which will wilt quickly. If you want to cook leaves and stems together, slice the leaves into wide strips and the stems more finely.

Steam: Lay whole or halved pak choi in the steamer and cook for about 4–8 minutes, or until the stems feel tender-crisp when pierced with a sharp knife. Or roughly slice the leaves and thinly slice the stalks so both cook at the same time, and steam for about 2–3 minutes.

WAYS TO SERVE

■ Serve drizzled with hoisin, oyster or soy sauce or sesame oil.
■ Use the leaves to line a steamer when cooking fish. They offer protection and flavour.
■ When stir-frying, add chopped garlic and fresh root ginger and finish with a splash of sesame oil.

GOES WITH Fish, chicken, hoisin/oyster/soy sauce, Chinese five spice.

ONION GRAVY

Quick and easy to make. Add grilled sausages and you have an instant supper.

Fry 2 peeled and sliced onions in 1 tbsp oil and a large knob of butter until softened and golden. Stir in 2 tsp flour and cook for 1–2 minutes to give a golden colour. Gradually pour in about 250 ml (8 fl oz) stock, stirring all the time, then add a pinch of dried rosemary and a good teaspoonful of redcurrant jelly. Bring to the boil, stirring, then simmer for a few minutes until it's the thickness you like.

PAK CHOI

GOOD FOR YOU Contains vitamins C and K and beta carotene.

USE INSTEAD Spinach or cabbage.

Parsnip

A root vegetable native to Britain that looks like a plump, cream carrot. It brings a delicate sweetness to winter soups, stews and roasts.

CHOOSE

- Available all year – but at its best in mid-winter. After a frost, its starch is converted into sugar which highlights the sweetness.
- Small and firm – large ones can be woody.
- Don't buy parsnips with lots of whiskery bits, or brown patches on the skin – this is a sign that they may be rotten inside.
- Allow 500 g (1 lb) parsnips for 4 people.

STORE In a perforated plastic bag in the vegetable drawer of the fridge for up to a week.

PREPARE Trim off both ends. Peel thinly with a vegetable peeler or sharp knife. Cut into even-sized chunks. If the parsnip is older and larger, you may need to cut out the central core if it is woody. Small ones can be left whole, or cut into lengths or chunks.

COOK Roast to bring out the natural sweetness, or boil and transform into a creamy mash.

Boil: Cut into chunks and put in a pan with a little salt. Cover with boiling water, bring back to the boil, then cook, covered, for 15–20 minutes until tender. Drain.

Roast: Heat a few tablespoons of olive oil in a roasting tin in a 200ºC/400ºF/Gas Mark 6 oven (180ºC/350ºF in fan ovens) for 5 minutes. Peel the parsnips, cut them into thickish long sticks and toss in the oil. Roast for about 40–55 minutes, shaking the pan occasionally, until tender and golden. Season.

WAYS TO SERVE

- Boil and serve with butter, salt, pepper, a pinch of grated nutmeg and a sprinkling of grated Parmesan cheese.
- Make a creamy mash using equal amounts of boiled parsnip and swede. After draining, roughly mash the vegetables, leaving some texture. Season and flavour with a little cream or soured cream, horseradish sauce and fresh thyme.
- Cut into chunks and roast with squash and wedges of onion, scattered with sprigs of rosemary, bay or thyme.

pak choi–peas

GOES WITH Roast meats, sausages and chops, most other root vegetables, cream, rosemary, thyme, curry spices.

GOOD FOR YOU Has folate, niacin, vitamin E and potassium.

Peas

Belonging to the legume family, peas (also called garden peas) are a summer vegetable with a very short season. They start converting sugar into starch as soon as they're picked, so freshness is crucial. Commercially frozen peas are frozen within 2½ hours of being picked, so are sometimes fresher-tasting than bought fresh peas.

CHOOSE

■ All year (in their pods and ready shelled from different parts of the world). British peas are in season from early to mid-summer.
■ The pods should be bright green, firm and plump.
■ There should be some air between each pea in their pod. If they feel too full and bloated, the peas may be hard and tough.
■ Allow about 225 g (8 oz) in the pod per person.
■ From 1 kg (2 lb) pods you should get 500–700g (1–1½ lb) shelled peas.

MINTED PEAS

For extra flavour, drop a couple of sprigs of mint into the water when boiling fresh peas.

STORE Use fresh peas as soon as possible afer buying or picking as they lose their sweet taste very quickly.

PREPARE Snap the pod open with your fingers at the top, then push the peas out along the pod with your thumb.

COOK The best way to tell if peas are cooked is to bite into one – the inside should be bright green in colour and not too soft.

Boil: Place peas in a pan and cover with boiling water. Cook in the minimum of water needed, so that nutrients aren't lost. Don't add salt as this can toughen the skins, but a pinch of sugar helps intensify their sweetness. Bring the water back to the boil, cover and simmer for about 2–3 minutes. Drain and season with salt and pepper.

Steam: For 1–2 minutes when young and in season, 3–5 minutes if older.

WAYS TO SERVE

■ After steaming or boiling, melt some butter in a pan, add chopped spring onions and cook briefly to soften. Tip in the peas and stir all together to warm through with some salt, pepper and a handful of chopped mint.

■ When cooking new potatoes, drop some peas into the cooking water for the last 3–4 minutes. Drain and toss with butter and chives.

■ Cook in stock with some chopped shallot and a handful of soft lettuce leaves to make the classic *petits pois à la française*.

GOES WITH Salmon, bacon and ham, duck, risotto, spring onions, garlic, mint, chives, basil, parsley.

GOOD FOR YOU Contain protein, fibre, B vitamins, vitamin C, iron.

USE INSTEAD Use fresh and frozen peas interchangeably.

More in the pea family

Mangetout/snow peas: This type of pea is picked while flat and undeveloped. It has a tender pod and tiny peas inside. You eat the whole thing like a bean. Break off the stalk end and pull along the length of the pod to remove the 'string' that runs underneath it. Trim off the other end. To preserve their crispness, boil in the minimum of water for about 2–3 minutes or steam or stir-fry for 3–4 minutes. If used in a salad they taste better when blanched briefly first.

Petits pois: The same variety as garden peas – just picked earlier so they are smaller and sweeter.

Sugar snap: A more developed version of the mangetout so plumper, but not quite as plump as a garden pea. Both pod and pea are eaten together, raw or cooked. No preparation is needed, apart from topping and tailing (see right). Boil or steam for 3–4 minutes so they still have some crunch left. Or slice very thinly lengthways and eat raw in a salad.

Pepper (sweet)
(US: bell pepper)

Related to chillies, peppers have a milder and sweeter taste. Most sweet peppers start off green (although some are purple), then, as they ripen, the colour changes to red, orange or yellow, depending on the variety.

CHOOSE
■ All year round, but especially good in the summer and autumn.
■ Those that are shiny and firm, not wrinkled or soft.
■ Between different colours, red, green, orange and yellow being the most common. Red, yellow and orange peppers tend to be sweeter than green, which have a less developed flavour but are good for long, slow cooking. Red, yellow and orange are better for eating raw or cooking quickly in stir-fries.

STORE In a perforated plastic bag in the fridge for up to 3–4 days.

TOP AND TAIL
This means to trim off both ends of vegetables or fruits, where only minimal trimming is required, as with beans, peas or currants.

PIMIENTO
Pimiento is the Spanish word for a sweet red pepper. It is used to describe red peppers, often sold in jars, that have been cored, seeded, peeled and cooked.

HALVING AND SEEDING
A PEPPER
Cut in half lengthways, then scrape out the seeds and pith with a sharp knife (see page 306).

VEG A–Z

Roasted and skinned, seeded and covered with olive oil, they keep in the fridge for up to a week.

PREPARE First you need to remove the core, pith and seeds.

For halving: Slice off the stalk end, then cut in half lengthways. Scrape out the seeds and white pith (see illustration, page 305). Usually used for stuffing or roasting.

For chopping or slicing: The easiest way is to sit the pepper upright on a board. Then, holding it by its stem end, slice the four sides away down its length, so you are left with the core and seeds in the centre. Cut each piece of pepper lengthways into thin, even strips for slices, and cut across the slices for small cubes. Start with bigger slices for bigger chunks.

To skin: see opposite.

COOK

Roast: Halve, core and remove the seeds, then drizzle with olive oil and put in the oven at 180°C/350°F/Gas Mark 4 (160°C/325°F in fan ovens), for 35–40 minutes. For more flavour, drop some sliced garlic and sprigs of thyme or oregano into the halves before drizzling with oil and roasting.

Stir-fry: Cut into even, thin strips, heat a little oil in a frying pan or wok, then add the peppers and cook over a high heat, tossing often, for 3–4 minutes until slightly blackened around the edges.

WAYS TO SERVE

■ Stir-fry pepper strips until softened. Add a splash of balsamic vinegar, some torn basil, chopped flat leaf parsley and finely chopped garlic. Serve with fish or roast chicken.

■ Skin the peppers, then tear them into bite-size pieces, lay them on a large plate and scatter with slices of anchovy, some torn oregano or basil, some sliced raw garlic, a few toasted pine nuts and a generous drizzle of olive oil. Serve at room temperature with French bread or ciabatta.

GOES WITH Chicken and fish (especially anchovies), olives, capers, cheese, rice, pasta, tomatoes, basil, coriander, garlic, balsamic vinegar, olive oil.

GOOD FOR YOU Contain lots of vitamin C and beta carotene. Raw red peppers have about 10 times the amount of beta carotene as raw and cooked green peppers.

More in the pepper family

Peppadew: This is a sweet and mildly spicy pepper from South Africa, available preserved and tightly packed

pepper–potato

whole in jars. Adds a spicy kick to salads, pizza toppings, stir-fries.

Romano: Perfect for roasting or stuffing, this long, narrow, red pepper is both sweet and tender. Prepare and use as regular peppers.

Plantain

see FRUIT, *page 243*

Potato

A favourite world staple, this native of South America is one of the most versatile of vegetables. Always served cooked, each variety has many different characteristics – whether light and floury for making the perfect mash or chips, or waxy for using in salads. Potatoes are also divided into early-growing varieties (new) and larger, older main-crop varieties.

CHOOSE

■ All year round, except for early-season new, such as Cornish New and Jersey Royals, which have a short season in late spring and early summer (to check true early potatoes you should be able to rub the skins off easily with your finger).

■ Potatoes should be firm.

■ Allow about 175–200 g (6–7 oz) raw unpeeled potatoes per person.

HOW TO SKIN A PEPPER

■ *This gives you smooth peppers, that are softer and sweeter with a slightly smoky flavour and are more digestible.*

■ *Lay whole peppers on a foil-lined grill pan. Put under a hot grill and turn once the skin starts to blacken. Keep turning until blackened all over – about 20 minutes. Place the peppers in a bowl and cover with cling film, or in a plastic bag and seal. The steam helps loosen the skin. When cool, peel off the skin with your fingers. Remove any stubborn bits with a sharp knife. Halve and remove the core and seeds.*

■ *QUICK FIX: If you only have one or two peppers to skin, blacken them quickly over a gas flame. Spear the pepper on to a long handled fork. Hold it over the flame, turning until the skin is blackened all over.*

GREAT MASH

After draining boiled potatoes, return them to the pan and pour over hot milk – allow 150 ml (¼ pint) per 1 kg (2 lb) potatoes. Mash with a big knob of butter and some salt and pepper until smooth and creamy, using a potato masher or electric hand mixer. For a smoother finish, use a potato ricer.

■ Select the type of potato that suits the way you want to cook it:

Waxy: Firm, keep their shape when cooked, but not good for mashing. Use for salads, boiling, steaming, baking (for cheesy-layered gratins), e.g. Cara, Charlotte, Carlingford New, Marfona, Nicola, Pink Fir Apple, Wilja.

Floury: Have a soft, dry texture when cooked. Use when you want the cooked potato to have a fluffy texture as in jacket potatoes, mash, roast and chips, but not for boiling (they will fall apart), e.g. King Edward, Maris Piper, Desirée (red skins).

Good all-rounder: Can be used when a recipe calls for no specific variety, eg: Wilja, Maris Piper, Desirée, Nicola, Romano.

Salad: Choose firm, flavourful ones such as Cornish New, Jersey Royal, Pink Fir Apple, Nicola New, Charlotte.

STORE In a cool, dark, well-ventilated place. Clear plastic bags can make them go mouldy, so transfer them to one that isn't see-through (e.g. a paper bag). Plastic also lets in light which causes them to turn green and sprout. Old potatoes will keep for a few weeks; new potatoes for only a few days.

PREPARE

Old: Give them a scrub and dig out any 'eyes'. When possible, leave the skin on (it is full of nutrients), or peel very thinly with a vegetable peeler. Wash.

New: No need to peel, just give them a wash and scrub.

COOK Use similar-sized whole potatoes, or cut into equal-sized pieces, to ensure even cooking.

Bake: Whole in their skins. Wash, then pat dry with kitchen paper. Prick all over with a fork, or lightly score round the middle of the potato. Put on a baking sheet or directly on one of the oven racks in a preheated oven at 200°C/400°F/Gas Mark 6 (180°C/350°F in fan ovens) for 50 minutes to 1¼ hours, depending on size. To bake in the microwave, stand one potato on kitchen paper and microwave on high for 6 minutes, turning once, then let stand for 2 minutes. Allow 8–10 minutes for 2 potatoes. When ready, the sides of the potato should feel soft when pinched.

Boil: Peel, cut into even pieces (not too small or they will go watery), put in a pan with a little salt and pour over boiling water to cover. Return to the boil, cover and boil gently for 15–20 minutes. Drain as soon as they are cooked. Cook new potatoes as above for about 12–15 minutes, with a sprig of mint in the water for extra flavour. When ready, the potato should feel tender when tested with a skewer or the tip of a sharp knife.

potato

Roast: Potatoes take on the flavour of the oil used for roasting – choose either light olive oil or sunflower oil (for a mild flavour) or goose or duck fat (for a rich flavour).

- Old: peel and cut the potatoes into big, even chunks. Put in a pan, cover with boiling water, bring back to the boil, then simmer for 3 minutes. Drain in a colander and shake it to rough them up a bit – this gives a crisper potato. Heat the oil or fat of your choice (allow about 2 tbsp per 450 g/1 lb potatoes) in a roasting tin in a 200°C/400°F/Gas Mark 6 oven (180°C/350°F in fan ovens) for 5 minutes. Tip the potatoes in, toss to coat with the oil, and roast for 45–60 minutes, turning once or twice. Season with salt at the end of cooking – they can go soggy if salted at the beginning. When ready, they should be golden and crisp on the outside, fluffy inside.

- New: Keep whole, tip into a roasting tin (tuck in some unpeeled garlic cloves and thyme sprigs if you like), drizzle with oil, season and roast at 200°C/ 400°F/Gas Mark 6 (180°C/ 350°F in fan ovens) for 30–40 minutes or until golden, turning a couple of times.

WAYS TO SERVE

- Old: Stir a spoonful or two of creamed horseradish or grainy mustard into mashed potatoes.

CRUSH – THE NEW MASH

Boil some whole new potatoes in their skins for 12–15 minutes or until tender. Drain well, tip back into the pan and crush roughly by pressing down with the back of a fork. Generously drizzle in some olive oil, season with salt and pepper and toss with one, two or three of the following herbs: chives, thyme, oregano, rosemary or parsley.

SAFE TO EAT?

Potatoes can have green patches from exposure to light – if these are small they can be cut away before cooking, but if they are extensive the potatoes should be thrown away as too much can make you ill. If the potatoes have sprouted, they are perfectly safe to cook and eat, but need using up quickly as they won't keep so well. Just slice off the sprouted bits before using.

FIX IT: POTATOES

- *Potatoes can discolour once peeled, so if you are not going to use them immediately, put in a bowl and cover with cold water.*
- *If you tip too much salt into a soup, curry or stew, add a chopped potato to soak up the salty taste.*

■ New: Toss when cooked with pesto, or a knob of butter or a splash of extra-virgin olive oil and a generous handful of chives or mint. For a spicy kick, add a pinch of crushed dried chillies or a little harissa.

GOES WITH Many things, including roast meats, fish, bacon, cheese, eggs, onions, mayonnaise and herbs.

GOOD FOR YOU Full of vitamin C, carbohydrate and fibre, as well as potassium. Most nutritious when eaten with skin on (increases iron content).

Pumpkin
see SQUASH, *page 314*

Radicchio
see CHICORY, *pages 278–79*

Radish

A root vegetable related to the mustard plant. Varieties include the common red-skinned (including the more elongated French Breakfast variety), which is eaten for its colour and crisp, peppery white flesh. Strongly flavoured black radishes are popular in eastern Europe and usually peeled; white radishes are also available (see opposite).

CHOOSE
■ All year round.
■ The leaves (if still attached) should be lively and bright green, the red part firm and not at all soft.
■ Smaller radishes are better – if they are too big, the white flesh goes spongy.

STORE In the fridge for 3–4 days, preferably without the leaves as these take the moisture from the radish.

PREPARE Do this just before eating, as radishes lose their potency after slicing. Trim off any leaves (unless you want to serve them with leaves on as part of a salad) and the root at the bottom. Leave whole, chop or slice.

COOK Red and black are usually eaten raw. For white, see opposite.

WAYS TO SERVE
■ Slice finely on the diagonal, mix with slender strips of cucumber, spring onion and seeded red chilli and toss in a dressing of lime juice, olive oil and a splash of soy. Serve Asian-style with grilled or roasted salmon or chicken.

GOES WITH Watercress, cucumber, lime juice, feta cheese.

GOOD FOR YOU Contains vitamin C, some iron and potassium.

Samphire

A true wild food, this is a European coastal plant that comes in two forms, rock and marsh. Marsh samphire is sold in fishmongers or on the fish counter in supermarkets; it grows wild by the sea on salt marshes and is crisp, juicy and salty. Rock samphire is a little shrub that is found growing on coastal rocks and cliffs.

CHOOSE
- In mid-summer.
- It should look fresh and perky – avoid any that looks slimy.

STORE   Best used on the same day.

PREPARE   Wash well to get rid of any mud or sand, then trim any tough bits from the stalks.

COOK
Boil: Put into a pan, cover with boiling water (no salt required – it's salty enough) and bring back to the boil. Cook for a minute, then tip into a sieve or colander to drain.
Steam: For a couple of minutes.

WAYS TO SERVE
- Boil or steam, then toss in butter, lime juice, chopped parsley and fresh black pepper, to serve with fish.

WHITE RADISH
Popular in Asia, these are bigger and milder in flavour than red skinned radishes and look like a white carrot. They are also known as mooli, *or* mouli, *or* daikon *in Japan. Use as an ordinary radish by slicing into salads. They can also be stir-fried, diced and added to soups or stews, or grated to serve with sushi.*

RADISH SALSA
Make a colourful salsa – finely chop some radishes and mix them with chopped cherry tomatoes and a little red onion and toss with some lemon juice, olive oil and a little chopped garlic and mint to taste. Serve with cold meats.

SAMPHIRE

- Raw in a salad with shellfish such as crab or prawns and a light vinaigrette.
- Toss into a fish stew at the end of cooking.

GOES WITH Fish and shellfish, especially crab, asparagus, Parmesan cheese, lime.

Spinach

With its dark green leaves, spinach just seems to ooze goodness. It is one of the fastest-cooking vegetables, and the very young leaves are good eaten raw in a salad (see opposite).

CHOOSE

- All year round, but at its best from late spring to early autumn.
- The leaves should be bright green, avoid any that are turning yellow.
- The stalks should look tender and crisp.
- Spinach contains a lot of water and reduces considerably in volume when cooked – you'll be surprised how much you need. Allow about 225 g (8 oz) per person for serving as a vegetable accompaniment.

STORE Keep in a perforated plastic bag in the fridge for up to 2–3 days. Don't wash until ready to use.

PREPARE Pre-washed bagged spinach will probably need only a quick rinse. Loose spinach, however, can have a lot of grit, and needs washing well. Remove any wilting leaves, then tip the spinach into a large bowl of cold water and swish it around, changing the water a few times, until all the grit has gone. Tip it into a colander and give it a good shake to drain. Don't leave it standing in the water. If using raw or to stir-fry, pat it dry with kitchen paper. If the spinach is young and tender, it may not need any more attention, but if the leaves are large and old, trim off any tough-looking stalks. If these are very thick in the leaf, fold each leaf lengthways along the central rib with the rib facing outwards, then tear the rib away from the leaf.

COOK Spinach cooks very fast and has its own supply of water, so you don't need extra for cooking. After washing, just shake off any excess water and the amount left on the leaves is all you need. As soon as the leaves have wilted, they are cooked.
In a pan: Melt a knob of butter in a large pan. Pack in the leaves, cover and cook over a medium heat for just under a minute. Give it a stir to get any uncooked leaves to the bottom of the pan, cover and cook for another

samphire–spinach

30 seconds or so, shaking the pan occasionally, until it has all wilted. Drain into a colander, then put a small plate on top (or use a large spoon) and press down firmly to squeeze out all the moisture.

In a bowl: With young, tender leaves you can simply tip the spinach into a large bowl, pour boiling water over it and leave for about 30 seconds until wilted, then drain and press out the excess moisture as above.

Steam: Pack the leaves into a steamer and cook for 1–3 minutes, depending on the amount, until the leaves have just wilted. Press out the excess moisture as above.

WAYS TO SERVE

■ After cooking and draining, toss with caramelized onions, or stir in cream or crème fraîche and a sprinkling of grated nutmeg and chopped parsley, chives or basil.

■ Fry some finely chopped garlic, toss in a handful of pine nuts and cook until toasty brown, then mix in cooked spinach with a handful of raisins.

■ Add raw to a salad with crispy fried bacon or Parma ham, croûtons, mushrooms and some crumbled blue cheese.

GOES WITH Fish (especially smoked haddock), chicken, bacon, ham, pasta, beans, mushrooms, pota-

BABY LEAF SPINACH

These are the tenderest of spinach leaves, so are the best choice for serving raw in a salad.

They are also good scattered on top of a pizza as it comes out the oven, so they wilt slightly in the heat of the pizza.

toes, cheese (especially Gruyère, Emmental and Italian ones such as Parmesan and ricotta), eggs, nutmeg, garlic, chives, lemon, curry spices.

GOOD FOR YOU Contains lots of iron and calcium; vitamins C and A.

Spring greens
(US: collard greens)
see CABBAGE, *page 269*

Squash
(including pumpkin)

There is a huge variety available – summer squash (thin-skinned with soft, moist flesh), such as courgettes and vegetable marrow (see pages 279 and 290), and the thick-skinned and firm, sweet-fleshed winter squash. Winter squash comes in many different shapes and colour combinations of orange, green and yellow.

CHOOSE

■ Certain squash are available all year; pumpkins usually only in the autumn.
■ They should feel firm, not hollow, and be heavy for their size.
■ Allow about 225–375 g (8–12 oz) unpeeled squash per person.
■ The following varieties are the most common:

Acorn: A ridged, small, dark green-(sometimes orange) skinned squash with a vibrant orange flesh that has a sweet flavour of chestnuts.

Butternut: Has a slim neck and curved base, which contains the seeds and fibrous bits; tan-coloured skin with an orange flesh and a nutty taste.

Crown prince: Bluey-grey in colour. Firm flesh, so good for roasting, cutting into chunks and threading on kebab skewers with lemon and red onion wedges, or in stews or curries.

Gem: Has dark green skin and is small and round, about the size of a large onion, perfect for stuffing. Leave whole to cook – no need to peel.

Kabocha: Dark green with pale markings and deep orange, sweet flesh.

Onion: A large, orange squash, so named because of its onion-like shape.

Pumpkin: As well as being useful for Hallowe'en decorations, pumpkin is great roasted, puréed for a soup, stuffed into pasta, or in a traditional pumpkin pie where it gives a silky-smooth texture and the flavour is enhanced with spices. Smaller ones are sweeter and easier to prepare than large ones, which can be extremely hard to cut into as the skin is so tough.

Spaghetti: This is a one-off in the world of squash. When you open it up after cooking, the flesh pulls out like strands of spaghetti, hence its name.

spinach–squash

STORE In a cool, dark, well-ventilated place for a few weeks. Once cut, pumpkin keeps for up to a week in the fridge, as long as it is well wrapped.

PREPARE Some squash, especially pumpkins, have very tough skins, so you need brute force to get into them. Put the squash on a towel to keep it steady, then use a strong, heavy knife to cut in half. For a pumpkin, you may need to use a rolling pin or hammer to hit the knife into the skin. Pull the knife out and work down in sections until you get to the bottom. Start again on the other side so you can cut it in half. Scoop out the seeds and any fibrous, stringy bits. Take a small, sharp knife and cut off the skin. You may find it easier to cut the squash in smaller pieces to do this. (If roasting you can leave the skin on.) Cut the flesh into wedges or chunks.

COOK

Boil: Peel and cut into even chunks, put into a pan with a little salt and cover with boiling water. Bring back to the boil, cover and cook for 10–15 minutes, depending on size, or until tender. Serve scattered with grated cheese and grilled, or mash with butter, salt and pepper. For Gem squash, prick all over with a skewer, then boil whole for about 25 minutes or until

SEEDING BUTTERNUT SQUASH

Once you have cut your squash in half, remove the seeds and any stringy bits with a spoon.

SPICED SQUASH
Serves 4
Fry an onion in 2–3 tbsp vegetable oil in a frying pan, until golden. Add 500 g (1 lb) peeled, cubed squash and fry for 5 minutes. Season with a sprinkling of ground cinnamon, add a handful of raisins, cover and cook for another 10 minutes or so until tender, turning every now and then. Season and serve scattered with toasted almonds.

tender. Halve, scoop out the seeds and serve with a knob of butter, salt and pepper. For spaghetti squash, cut in half lengthways and scrape out the seeds. Put in a large pan and cover with boiling water. Boil for about 20 minutes or until tender. Scrape the flesh out with a fork. It will look like fine strands of spaghetti.

Roast/bake: Roasting is one of the best ways to cook winter squash. Have the skin on or off (it's easier to leave it on), then cut in wedges or chunks, toss in olive oil and season with salt and pepper. Roast at 200°C/400°F/ Gas Mark 6 (180°C/350°F in fan ovens) for 30–40 minutes or until tender and brown at the edges. For spaghetti squash, cut in half lengthways and scrape out the seeds. Put in a roasting tin, drizzle with olive oil and season with salt and pepper. Roast at 190°C/375°F/Gas Mark 5 (170°C/340°F in fan ovens) for 40–45 minutes, or until tender. Scrape out the strands with a fork.

WAYS TO SERVE

■ Roast wedges or chunks of your favourite winter squash. Heat some olive oil in a small pan, briefly fry some chopped garlic, then throw in some dried sage leaves (or rosemary or thyme). As soon as they sizzle and go crisp, pour over the squash and season.

■ Boil or roast spaghetti squash, see left, and serve like spaghetti with a drizzle of oil or a knob of butter, grated Parmesan cheese, salt and black pepper.

GOES WITH Roast meats and poultry, bacon, pancetta, pasta, chick peas, orange, cream, sage, thyme, curry spices, nuts.

GOOD FOR YOU Contains lots of fibre, vitamins and minerals.

USE INSTEAD Use different squashes interchangeably, except for spaghetti squash.

Swede
(US: rutabaga)

This root-like vegetable, a member of the cabbage family, answers to several different names – yellow turnip, Swedish turnip, Russian turnip. In America it is called rutabaga and in Scotland, where it is a traditional accompaniment to haggis on Burns Night, it is known as 'neeps'. A swede looks like a colourful version of a large turnip except the flesh is more yellowy-orange and the skin purple.

CHOOSE

■ Best in late autumn to early spring.
■ When it gets too big it can become

quite tough, so pick out the smallest
ones with smooth, undamaged skins.
■ Allow about 750 g (1½ lb), unpeeled,
for 4 people.

STORE In a perforated plastic bag
in the fridge for up to a week.

PREPARE Cut off the root end, then
prepare like a potato: remove the peel
with a peeler and cut into chunks.

COOK

Roast: Heat a few tablespoons of olive
oil in a roasting tin at 200°C/400°F/
Gas Mark 6 (180°C/350°F in fan ovens)
for 5 minutes. Add chunks of peeled
swede and toss in the oil. Roast for
40–55 minutes until golden round the
edges. Or roast around a joint of meat.
Boil: Cut in chunks like potatoes and
put into a pan with a little salt. Pour
boiling water over to cover, bring back
to the boil and cook, covered, for about
12–15 minutes or until tender. Drain.
Steam: In small chunks for about 10
minutes, larger ones about 15 minutes.

WAYS TO SERVE

■ After boiling or steaming, mash
with butter and a spoonful of horseradish sauce. Good with beef.
■ Make up a mixed crush. Boil equal
quantities of swede and carrot, drain
well, then crush roughly with a fork or

VEG A–Z

potato masher. Season and add a splash of olive oil or butter if you prefer. To take it a step further, purée in a food processor either chunkily or smoothly. ■ Add chunks to soups, stews and winter casseroles – swede takes on other flavours well.

GOES WITH Beef, poultry, sausages, haggis, other root vegetables such as carrot, potato.

GOOD FOR YOU Has vitamins B and C and fibre.

USE INSTEAD Turnip – but this is smaller and not so sweet tasting.

Sweet potato

Not a true potato, this looks like an elongated old potato. It can have a thin yellow or white skin, but the most commonly available is the thicker-skinned, dark orange type. Prepare just as a regular potato (see page 308), but it is softer fleshed so will cook a little more quickly. The flesh is also sweeter-tasting, more like squash than potato, so goes well with spicy flavourings such as garlic, cinnamon and chilli.

COOK
Roast: Cut in wedges, peel on (scrubbed first), and lay them in a roasting tin. Drizzle with oil, season, toss together and roast at 200°C/400°F/Gas Mark 6 (180°C/350°F in fan ovens) for 25–30 minutes, turning half way through, until tender (the skin can be eaten as well as the flesh). Bake: Peel the whole sweet potato and cut into thickish slices, keeping the potato in its whole shape. Lay it on a large square of foil, drizzle all the slices with olive oil, scatter with crushed dried chillies, salt, pepper, and thyme and rub them all in, then reshape. Wrap the foil around to make a parcel and bake at 190°C/375°F/Gas Mark 5 (170°C/340°F in fan ovens) for about 40 minutes or until tender.

GOES WITH Chicken, pork, nuts, chilli, cinnamon.

GOOD FOR YOU Packed with beta carotene.

Sweetcorn
(US: corn)

Also called corn on the cob, this is actually a grain which is used as a vegetable. It is native to the Americas, where it is very popular. In Mexico the husks are used as a wrapping to make spicy *tamales*. A real summery vegetable. For canned sweetcorn see page 119.

swede–sweetcorn

CHOOSE

■ Through the summer into early autumn.

■ Preferably still in its husk.

■ The corn kernels should look plump, shiny and pale golden yellow, and the outside leaves (husk) a healthy green. You'll know just how fresh the raw corn is when you cut into it, as the kernels should release a milky-looking liquid.

■ Allow 1 head (cob) of corn per person.

STORE
In the fridge (best unhusked and wrapped in damp kitchen paper) for no more than a couple of days, less if possible as the natural sugars in corn quickly start to change into starch after picking, which makes the kernels less tender and not so sweet.

PREPARE
Holding the cob at its base, pull the outer leaves down from the top to expose the kernels, leaving them still attached, or remove, depending how you plan to cook. Pull away any of the whispy threads (silks) clinging to the cob. Trim off the ends of the cob with a sharp knife, then give the whole thing a wash. You can serve sweetcorn whole or cut into chunks. If you want to serve them in chunks, it's best to cook whole first then cut, as they are hard to cut through raw. To cut off the kernels, see page 321.

SWEET POTATOES

YAM

A tropical vegetable that is similar in texture to a potato, but starchier and much bigger in size. In the West Indies, South America and Africa it is a staple food, just like potatoes are in other parts of the world. In the USA the orange-fleshed sweet potato is often referred to as a yam, but it is not the same thing, though it can be cooked in much the same way with similar flavouring partners such as spices and nuts. See sweet potato, opposite.

COOK It's best to cook them as soon as possible (see Store, page 319). To test when done, a kernel should be tender, but still have some bite.

Barbecue: There are three ways:

■ Husks off in foil: This gives the least barbecue taste but is the most convenient. Remove the husks and silks. Toss the cobs with a little oil or butter and wrap them in foil. Place on the barbecue rack for 8–15 minutes, turning occasionally, until tender.

■ Husks on without foil: Peel the husks back (don't remove) and pull out the silky bits. Cover the corn with the husks again. If you have time, soak the corn in cold water for an hour or two – this creates steam during cooking, making the corn juicier; it also helps stop them from burning, but reduces the barbecued taste. Lay each cob straight on the barbecue rack and cook for 8–15 minutes depending on size and heat, turning with tongs, until toasty brown and tender.

■ No husks, no foil: This gives the most intense barbecue flavour. Remove the husks and silks as described (left), then put the cobs on the barbecue rack, turning often for even browning, for 5–7 minutes. Serve with butter, salt and freshly ground black pepper.

Roast: prepare and time as for barbecuing, but cook in a 220°C/ 425°F/Gas Mark 7 oven (200°C/ 400°F in fan ovens).

Boil: Whole in boiling water for about 3–6 minutes, depending on the age of the corn. Never add salt to the cooking water as this will toughen the corn. Start testing after 3 minutes. (Kernels will take no more than a couple of minutes.) Drain well.

EAT If serving whole, pick up and hold both ends and nibble your way along the cob. It's easier to hold if you use corn-on-the-cob 'handles' or you can stick a small fork into each end; or cut the cob into pieces after cooking and pick up to eat that way.

WAYS TO SERVE

■ Serve Cajun-style, cooked whole (by boiling or barbecuing) and topped with butter mixed with crushed dried chillies and some fresh or dried thyme.

■ Make a salsa by mixing cooked sweetcorn kernels with some chopped spring onion, chopped red pepper, some grated lime zest and juice and a drizzle of olive oil. Great with fish and shellfish.

GOES WITH Chicken, ham, fish (especially with smoked haddock in a chowder) and shellfish, peppers, chillies, tomatoes, thyme, basil.

GOOD FOR YOU Rich in fibre; small amounts of B vitamins.

USE INSTEAD Frozen or canned corn when fresh is not in season.

Swiss chard

see CHARD, page 276

Tomato

There are many varieties to choose from, with colours ranging from red to orange, yellow, green and even white, and shapes ranging from tiny and round to big and beefy. A tomato is technically a fruit, but is used and eaten as a vegetable.

CHOOSE

■ Different varieties are available all year round. The best flavour is during the summer months.

■ Look for smooth, firm tomatoes with healthy-looking, wrinkle-free skin and a strong tomato smell.

■ When using tomatoes out of season, cherry or good-quality canned will give you the best flavour.

■ The type of tomato you need depends what you want to do with it:

Beef steak: The biggest one with the meatiest texture. Great for stuffing, grilling or slicing for salads. To

CUTTING OFF THE KERNELS
Instead of eating sweetcorn whole, you can cut off the kernels and eat them as a side dish, or add them to dishes such as chowders, salads and stews.
HOW TO DO IT:
After removing the green husks and wispy silks as on page 319, stand the whole cob stalk-end down on a board. Cut down it in smooth strokes to release the kernels, going all the way round. Keep the knife as close to the hard centre as you can so that you keep the kernels whole.

prepare for stuffing, take a thin slice off the stalk end, then scoop out the centre with a teaspoon.

Cherry: Small and sweet. Serve whole or halved in salads. Also good for pasta sauces and roasting on the vine.

Green: This can mean unripe tomatoes, but there is also a tangy-tasting variety available which is ripe and green. Green tomatoes are firm, so good for slicing and frying, tossed in polenta to give a crunchy coating. Unripe green tomatoes are too sharp to eat raw, but make great chutney and are good fried for breakfast.

Plum: Oval in shape, its firmness and flavour, plus the fact it has fewer seeds, makes it popular for cooking in sauces and stews. You can get baby plum too.

Salad tomato (round): The traditional tomato, this varies in size. A good all-rounder – use in salads and cooking.

Yellow: Subtle in taste, looks pretty when mixed with other colours in salads, good for chutney too.

STORE Best kept at room temperature, as the fridge spoils their flavour. If you want to keep ripe ones in the fridge, put in a perforated plastic bag in the vegetable drawer and they will last for up to a week, but take out of the fridge half an hour before serving to get them to room temperature.

PREPARE Wash them, then remove the stalks. They may be left whole, halved, quartered, sliced, chopped, and seeded and/or skinned.

How to seed: Sometimes the seeds and juice need to be removed as they can make a dish watery and dilute its flavour, such as in fresh tomato salsa. Seeds can also add a bitter taste to a dish. To remove the seeds, halve the tomato widthways if round, lengthways if oval. If you want to chop the flesh, hold each half cut side down over a bowl and squeeze out the seeds and juice. To keep the shape of the tomato, scoop out the seeds with a teaspoon.

How to skin: Chewy bits of skin floating around in tomato sauces and other cooked tomato dishes can look unsightly and are not to everybody's taste. To remove the skins, score a cross in the base of the tomato with a sharp knife. Put into a bowl and pour over enough boiling water to cover completely. Leave for about 15 seconds for smallish tomatoes, 30–40 seconds for larger ones, just until the crosses start to peel back and the skin splits in places. Don't leave any longer or the tomatoes will start to soften. Lift out of the hot water with a slotted spoon and plunge into iced water, then drain and peel back the loosened skins with the tip of a small, sharp knife.

tomato

COOK

Grill: Cut in half, drizzle with olive oil, season with salt and pepper, then cook under a hot grill until starting to soften and brown around the edges. No need to turn over.

Pan-fry: Heat a little oil or butter (or use half oil, half butter) in a frying pan. Add thick slices of tomato, season and fry for a minute or two until starting to brown around the edges. Turn and repeat.

Roast: Drizzle with olive oil and a splash of balsamic vinegar and roast at 200°C/400°F/Gas Mark 6 (180°C/350°F in fan ovens) for about 15 minutes for cherry, 15–20 minutes for round, or until they are starting to burst and soften. Season with salt and freshly ground pepper.

WAYS TO SERVE

■ Add 2 tsp grainy mustard and a handful of snipped chives to an oil and vinegar dressing. Pour over thickly sliced tomatoes and serve as is or scattered with crisply fried bacon.

■ Chop some tomatoes with garlic and pile on to slices of toast. Scatter with some torn basil and freshly ground black pepper, and drizzle with olive oil.

■ Scatter halved cherry tomatoes on a large plate, sprinkle with a little finely grated lemon zest and chopped garlic, and drizzle with oil.

MAKE YOUR OWN SUNBLUSH TOMATOES

Roast the tomatoes long and slow in the oven and they will come out almost as if they had been dried in the Italian sun. If you store them in a jar covered in olive oil, they will keep in the fridge for a couple of weeks.

■ *USE FOR: Tossing into pasta and salads, serving with pan-fried chicken or fish, adding one or two to tomato sauces to concentrate the flavour.*

■ *HOW TO DO IT: Use medium-sized plum or round tomatoes, cut in half (cut plum ones lengthways), then seed. Toss with olive oil, salt and freshly ground pepper and a pinch of sugar, then lay them cut side up on a baking sheet. Bake at 110°C/225°F/Gas Mark ¼ (90°C/200°F in fan ovens) – or the lowest setting you have – for 4½–5 hours until chewy but not tough.*

Heat 1–2 tbsp olive oil in a frying pan, add some chopped garlic and several chopped tomatoes. Cook for a few minutes until the tomatoes have softened. Throw in a good handful of basil, then toss with freshly cooked pasta and a spoonful or two of the pasta water to moisten. Serve scattered with toasted pine nuts and drizzled with oil.

GOES WITH Chicken, fish, bacon, cheese, avocado, peppers, balsamic vinegar, olive oil, basil, oregano, chives, thyme, garlic, olives.

GOOD FOR YOU It is super-healthy, having lots of lycopene which is thought to fight certain cancers and heart disease, and is even more effective after cooking so canned tomatoes are excellent too. It also has lots of vitamins C and A, plus E when eaten raw, and there's plenty of fibre and beta carotene.

Turnip

Turnips were as a major staple food in Europe before potatoes became popular. Their skin is creamy white, tinged either purple or pale green, and they have a nutty taste.

CHOOSE
All year round.

The skin should be smooth without blemishes, and the turnip should feel heavy for its size.
Small turnips, about the size of a small apple, have a more delicate flavour than large, which can develop a very strong taste and woody texture.

STORE In a perforated plastic bag in the vegetable drawer of the fridge for up to a week.

PREPARE Older turnips need trimming and peeling. Young tiny ones with tender skins need only scrubbing and trimming and can be left whole. Both young and old turnips can be chopped, sliced, diced or cut into matchsticks.

COOK To test when done, pierce with a skewer or sharp knife – it should go in easily with no resistance.
Boil: Chop into chunks (small ones into quarters), then put in a pan with a little salt and cover with boiling water. Bring back to the boil and cook for 8–10 minutes or until tender. Drain and serve, or mash or purée with butter and milk or cream.
Roast: Small ones can be roasted whole, large ones are best in wedges. Toss with olive oil and pepper, then roast at 200°C/400°F/Gas Mark 6 (180°C/350°F in fan ovens) for

35–45 minutes or until tender.
Roasting makes turnips taste sweeter.
Steam: Cubes of turnip should be
steamed for 8–12 minutes; young
small whole ones take 30–35 minutes.

WAYS TO SERVE
■ Caramelize drained, boiled turnips
by frying with a knob of butter and
a little sugar for several minutes,
until golden.
■ Eat young turnips raw in salads in
very thin slices or grated with a soy-
based dressing, or cut in sticks and
serve with a dip.

GOES WITH Most roast meats and
root vegetables, bacon, cheese, nutmeg, parsley, garlic.

GOOD FOR YOU Turnips have vitamin C, potassium and calcium.

USE INSTEAD Swede (rutabaga) –
though this is larger and sweeter and
takes longer to cook.

Watercress
see SPICY SALAD LEAVES,
page 291

VEG A–Z

FIVE A DAY

Fruit and vegetables are loaded with vitamins, minerals, fibre and can help reduce the risk of heart disease and some cancers. So if you aim to eat at least five portions a day, it can help keep you healthy.

■ **What is one portion?** This can be 80 g (2¾ oz) of fresh fruit or vegetables (such as 1 medium apple or banana, 2 satsumas, 3 heaped tbsp cooked peas, sweetcorn or carrots, 1 cereal sized bowl of salad), 3 dried fruits such as apricots, a 150 ml (¼ pint) glass of pure fruit juice (this counts only once a day however much you drink). Potatoes do not count in the five a day, but sweet potatoes do. Beans and other pulses such as chick peas and kidney beans count only as one a day however much you eat.

■ **How can I eat them?** If you include one or two portions of fruit or vegetables in your main meal of the day, a glass of pure juice between meals and the occasional piece of fruit or vegetable to snack on during the day, you'll have no trouble. The fruits and vegetables can be fresh, frozen, canned or dried.

■ Go by colour. It is important to eat a good variety of fruit and vegetables, and choosing ones of different colours will give you that. Think of a rainbow of colours to help – green (e.g. kiwi fruits, broccoli, watercress and leafy greens), red (e.g. tomatoes, strawberries, peppers), blue and purple (eg blueberries, grapes, plums, aubergines), orange (e.g. citrus fruits, carrots, peppers), yellow (eg bananas, pineapple).

■ **What about fruit and vegetables in ready-made meals?** They count, but this type of meal is best served in moderation as the foods themselves can contain a lot of added salt, fat and sugar.

Meat, Poultry and Game

MEAT

AN IMPORTANT SOURCE OF PROTEIN FOR MOST OF US, MEAT
IS THE MAIN INGREDIENT IN MANY OF THE DISHES WE COOK –
BOTH FOR EVERYDAY MEALS AND SPECIAL OCCASIONS. USING
THE RIGHT CUT OF MEAT FOR A RECIPE OR COOKING METHOD
IS ESSENTIAL FOR TENDER, JUICY RESULTS, AND TO ACHIEVE
THIS, TODAY'S LEANER MEATS REQUIRE EXTRA CARE.

CHOOSE

Always buy meat from a reputable source – a good supermarket, butcher, farm shop or farmers' market, or a tried-and-tested website that has been recommended to you. It pays to shop around until you find an outlet or butcher you can trust.

Traceability

If you buy from butchers, farm shops and farmers' markets, they can usually tell you everything you want to know about their meat – where it comes from (and perhaps even what breed it is), the way it was reared, fed and slaughtered, and whether it has been matured and for how long. Labels on packaged meat in supermarkets are governed by law. They will tell you some, but not all, of these things, so take care to read them before you buy. To feel reassured about the traceability, quality and safety of the meat you are buying, the more information you get the better. One thing is certain – animals that have been allowed to feed and grow as naturally as possible, and that have been slaughtered without the stress of a long journey, will give the best quality meat in terms of flavour and tenderness.

Buy the best

Cooking meat can be tricky, especially if you are new to it. Buying good quality will help ensure successful results.

■ Organic meat is expensive, and so is meat from special breeds, but quality and flavour will be good.

■ Most important is the length of time that meat has been allowed to mature after slaughter, as this develops its flavour and makes it more tender. Meat bought from a reputable source will have been matured for the requisite amount of time for optimum flavour and tenderness – 10–14 days for beef, 8 days for lamb, 4 days for pork.

What to look for

■ Flesh that is moist and a tiny bit sticky, not dry, wet or slimy.

■ Beef and lamb should be dark red – the colour of claret wine – not bright red. A dark red colour indicates that it has been matured, and will be tender and flavourful. Veal should be creamy pale pink, pork should be a darker pink.

■ Light marbling (thin streaks of fat) throughout the meat is a good sign. During cooking, these will melt and give the meat succulence and flavour. Meat that is totally lean can be the opposite of this – dry and tasteless.

■ Any fat on the outside of the meat should be firm and creamy white, not yellow. White fat indicates freshness, yellow fat may be rancid or 'off'.

■ Don't buy meat that looks grey, or that has a greenish tinge – it will be past its best. If you see this with packaged meat, it is a sign that the meat is nearing its use-by date or that there is air inside the wrapping.

SAFE HANDLING

Common sense prevails.

■ Always wash hands, boards and utensils in hot, soapy water before and after handling meat.

GOOD FOR YOU

Meat, especially red meat and offal, is packed with nutrients:

■ *PROTEIN – essential for growth, good health, and well-being.*

■ *VITAMINS A, D and B – for healthy eyes, skin, bones, teeth, nerves and blood cells.*

■ *MINERALS, especially iron and zinc. Iron for healthy red blood cells, zinc for growth, healthy immune and reproductive systems, and skin.*

Many of the important nutrients are found in the lean part of meat, so you can reduce fat content by buying lean cuts or trimming off excess fat without losing nutritional benefits.

- Never deal with raw and cooked meats together. Ideally, keep a separate board for each.
- Meat cooks best when it is at room temperature, not taken straight from the fridge to the pan or oven. To safeguard against bacteria, especially in summer, remove the meat from the fridge 30–60 minutes before cooking, and keep it well-covered in a cool place.
- Leftovers of meat, or dishes containing meat, should be cooled as quickly as possible, then stored, well-covered, in the fridge for up to 2 days maximum, or they can be frozen. To serve, reheat thoroughly until piping hot in the centre (any liquid should be bubbling) and eat straight away. Frozen leftovers should be thawed slowly – in the fridge – before reheating. Don't reheat meat leftovers more than once.

STORE

Always keep meat in the fridge.
- Remove all wrappings and, before throwing them away, check for any use-by dates. The exception to this is vacuum-packed meat, which should be kept in its original wrapping – the storage time should be given on the label, or ask the butcher.
- Place unwrapped meat in a sealed container in the bottom of the fridge, so that it can't touch or drip on to other foods, and keep raw meat away from cooked meat.
- Fresh meat will keep for up to 2 days, unless it is minced or ground meat or offal, which is best cooked within 24 hours.
- Don't eat meat that smells high or 'off'.

Freezing

Meat freezes well, provided it is very fresh when it goes in the freezer.
- To prevent ice crystals forming in the meat, which will spoil its texture, freeze small amounts at a time, and prepare the freezer by switching it to fast-freeze or super-freeze beforehand (consult the handbook for timings and amounts).
- Wrap tightly, excluding all air. If not properly wrapped, meat will get freezer burn (see page 26).
- Double wrap any bones before freezing, to stop them piercing the packaging.
- Wrap chops, steaks and escalopes individually, or separate them with film or foil, so they don't freeze together and you can take them out singly as required.
- Store minced meat in the freezer for up to 3 months, small cuts up to 6 months, and joints and large cuts up to 9 months.

handling–**p**repare

■ Always thaw frozen meat before cooking, either slowly (in its wrappings on a plate in the bottom of the fridge) or quickly in the microwave, and cook it as soon as possible after thawing.

■ Never refreeze raw meat after it has thawed, but if you cook it after thawing, it is safe to refreeze.

PREPARE

Sometimes meat needs a little help before cooking, to improve both its flavour and texture. The simpler the technique, the better.

Marinating

Flavour and juiciness are given to meat by marinating, which can help tenderize it too. It is ideal for lean, boneless meat like steaks and escalopes, for cubes that are to be cooked by dry heat such as grilling or barbecuing, and for tough cuts on or off the bone that will be pot roasted, braised or stewed.

■ To marinate meat, coat or steep it in olive oil or natural yogurt with lemon juice or wine vinegar, herbs and/or spices and other flavourings. Fresh pineapple and papaya contain enzymes that tenderize, so for tough cuts of meat, mix in the juice from these (see also pages 32 and 242).

FRESH VERSUS FROZEN

There is nothing wrong with commercially frozen meat, but its texture when cooked is never as good as that of fresh meat. This is because there are so many factors that can affect it – its original quality (which you have no control over), how it was frozen and stored, and how you thaw it. Getting this combination right is tricky, so it is easy to see why frozen meat is not always on a par with fresh.
If you freeze meat yourself at home (see opposite), you will have more control over the process.

Pounding

This tenderizes meat by breaking down tough connective tissue, and it also makes the meat thinner so it will cook more quickly. It is good for lean, boneless meat like steaks, escalopes and fillets.

■ To pound meat, cover with cling film and bash with a meat mallet or rolling pin (or the base of a saucepan). Don't be too heavy-handed or you will tear the meat, and try to keep it the same thickness so that it will cook evenly.

Roasting times for meat

It is impossible to be entirely accurate with roasting times because individual ovens vary, and no two pieces of meat are exactly the same. Also bear in mind that bones are good conductors of heat, so joints on the bone cook slightly more quickly than boneless joints.

Whether the joint is on or off the bone, preheat the oven, and start by roasting at 200°C/400°F/Gas Mark 6 (180°C/350°F in fan ovens) for the first 15 minutes, then continue at 180°C/350°F/Gas Mark 4 (160°C/325°F in fan ovens) for the remainder of the time given below.

Beef	RARE	15 mins per 450 g (1 lb) + 15 mins
	MEDIUM	20 mins per 450 g (1 lb) + 20 mins
	WELL-DONE	25 mins per 450 g (1 lb) + 25 mins
Veal	MEDIUM	20 mins per 450 g (1 lb) + 20 mins
Lamb	RARE	15 mins per 450 g (1 lb) + 15 mins
	MEDIUM	20 mins per 450 g (1 lb) + 20 mins
	WELL-DONE	25 mins per 450 g (1 lb) + 25 mins
Pork	MEDIUM	20 mins per 450 g (1 lb) + 20 mins
	WELL-DONE	25 mins per 450 g (1 lb) + 25 mins

roasting

How to roast a joint of meat

When buying a joint on the bone, allow 225–375 g (8–12 oz) per person, raw weight; for boneless joints, allow 175–225 g (6–8 oz) per person, raw weight. Joints of meat don't always come with cooking instructions, but roasting is one of the easiest of cooking techniques, so you don't have to consult a recipe. Check the weight of the joint and calculate the cooking time according to the chart opposite. If you are going to stuff the joint, weigh it after stuffing.

■ Meat should be at room temperature when it goes in the oven, so take it out of the fridge 30–60 minutes before cooking.

■ Just before roasting, massage the joint with vegetable oil or olive oil, sea salt and freshly ground black pepper, plus any other spices, rubs or seasonings you like.

■ Baste frequently during roasting, unless it is a pork joint with crackling (see page 347).

■ After taking the meat out of the oven, cover it loosely with foil and let it rest for 15–20 minutes. This will make carving easier and allow you time to make gravy and cook the vegetables.

TIPS & TRICKS: SEASONING MEAT

Don't season meat until just before cooking because salt draws out moisture. If you sprinkle salt over meat and leave it for a while before cooking, the juices will be drawn out and the cooked meat will be dry.

HOW DO YOU KNOW THE JOINT IS COOKED?

Pierce the meat in its thickest part (away from any bones) with a metal skewer, and leave it there for about 30 seconds. When you take the skewer out, the tip should feel warm for rare meat, fairly hot for medium, and very hot for well-done.

For greater accuracy, use a meat thermometer (see page 58) to check the internal temperature of the meat. Beef and lamb can be cooked rare, but veal and pork should be either medium or well-done.

TEMPERATURES SHOULD BE:

■ *RARE*   *60°C (140°F)*
■ *MEDIUM*   *70°C (160°F)*
■ *WELL-DONE*   *80°C (175°F)*

BEEF

British beef is renowned for its quality, and breeds like Aberdeen Angus, Hereford and Longhorn are highly prized. Most cuts come ready-prepared for cooking. The only thing you may need to do is trim off excess fat, but be careful not to trim off too much – fat is good for basting and keeping the meat moist.

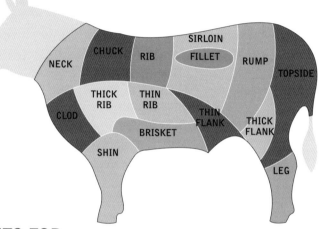

JOINTS FOR ROASTING

Top-quality, tender meat is best for roasting. For temperatures and times, see the roasting chart on page 332.

Fillet

■ The thick end cut from a whole fillet weighing 1.5–2 kg (3–4 lb) makes a neat, plump joint for 4–6 people that is easy to carve. For 2 people, you need a Châteaubriand (see page 15).
■ Fillet is very expensive, lean meat with a good flavour. The best are deep burgundy red with a marbling of fat. It is meltingly tender, especially when served rare, with little or no waste.

Rib, on the bone

■ This looks like huge chops joined together. There are two types, the wing rib and the fore rib. The wing contains the sirloin, has three bones and serves 6–8 people. The fore has four bones and will serve 8–10, but is often cut in half to give two joints, each serving 4–6.
■ For easy carving, rib joints must be chined (see page 16).

fillet–top rump

- Rib is tender and full of flavour, but expensive. The natural layer of fat and the marbling in the meat make it very succulent.

Rib, boned and rolled

- Fore rib that has been boned, rolled and tied with a layer of fat on top makes an easy-carve joint.
- The meat is the same quality as rib on the bone (see opposite), but costlier. Don't overcook or it may be dry.

Sirloin

- A rolled and tied boneless joint from the wing rib, with a light marbling of fat through the meat. It has a natural layer of fat on top that bastes the meat during roasting and helps keep it moist.
- Easy-to-carve, lean meat with lots of flavour and little waste. Pricier than rib.

Top rump

- A boneless, good-quality, good-value joint of lean meat. Usually sold tied with a layer of fat on top, to help prevent dryness.
- Has good flavour and succulence, and very little waste. Best served rare or medium, as well-done can be dry.

BEEF STOCK

Makes 2.5–3 litres (4–5 pints) and keeps in the fridge for up to 3 days, or in the freezer for up to 3 months.

1.5 kg (3 lb) beef bones, chopped
   into pieces by the butcher
2 onions, peeled and quartered
2 carrots, peeled and quartered
2 celery sticks, cut into large pieces
1 large bouquet garni (see page 129)
10 peppercorns
4 litres (7 pints) water

Preheat the oven to 220°C/425°F/ Gas Mark 7 (200°C/400°F in fan ovens) Place the bones in a roasting tin and roast for 30 minutes. Add the vegetables and roast for a further 20 minutes. Transfer everything to a stockpot or large pan. Skim the fat from the juices in the roasting tin, then stir 250 ml (8 fl oz) boiling water into the juices that are left and pour into the stockpot. Add the rest of the ingredients and bring to the boil. Half cover and simmer very gently for 4–5 hours, skimming occasionally, and topping up with water as necessary. Strain and cool, then refrigerate or freeze.

JOINTS FOR POT-ROASTING

Less tender cuts that aren't suitable for roasting can be pot roasted – boned, rolled and tied joints are best. Pat the meat dry with kitchen paper and season, then sear in hot oil until browned. Put in a pan with 500 g (1 lb) browned chopped onions, celery and root vegetables and 300 ml (½ pint) liquid (stock, wine or beer). Cover and cook slowly on the hob, or in the oven at 160°C/325°F/Gas Mark 3 (140°C/275°F in fan ovens). A 1.5 kg (3 lb) joint takes about 2½ hours and serves 6 people.

Brisket

■ Quite fatty, but with a good flavour.
■ The fat melts during cooking to give tasty meat that is easy to carve.

Silverside

■ Similar to topside, but slightly tougher.
■ Needs slow cooking to become tender.

Topside

■ Very lean meat with no marbling. Usually tied with a layer of fat.
■ Good flavour with little waste. Cook gently and slowly to avoid dryness.

CUTS FOR STEWS AND CASSEROLES

For a casserole or stew for 4–6 people, you will need 700 g–1 kg (1½–2 lb) meat. Brown it in hot oil, then cook gently in a covered pan, with 500 g (1 lb) browned, chopped onions, celery and root vegetables and 300 ml (½ pint) liquid. Cooking can be done on the hob, or in the oven at 160°C/325°F/Gas Mark 3 (140°C/275°F in fan ovens), and the usual timing is 2–3 hours.

Braising steak

■ Boneless meat, usually slices of chuck or blade, although top rump can also be used. The ideal thickness is 2 cm (¾ in), or cut into 5 cm (2 in) cubes.
■ Tender and full of flavour when slowly cooked.

Stewing steak

■ This boneless beef may be shin (from the fore leg) or leg (from the hind quarter), cut into 2.5–5 cm (1–2 in) cubes.
■ Connective tissue visible in the raw meat breaks down during cooking to give tender meat and rich gravy.

STEAKS FOR QUICK COOKING

All steaks (except for braising, stewing and minced steak) can be chargrilled, grilled, barbecued or pan-fried (see right). Steak is also good cut against the grain into strips or cubes for sautés and stir-fries. Cooking time for these is 2–4 minutes, from rare to medium.

Fillet steak

■ A round slice from a whole fillet, usually 2.5–5 cm (1–2 in) thick. Expensive, prime-quality meat.
■ Very lean and very tender, with no waste. Best served rare.

Sirloin steak

■ Boneless, cut from above the fillet. About 2.5 cm (1 in) thick, with a thin border of fat. If part of the fillet is included and it is left on the bone, this is a T-bone steak. A porterhouse is on the bone from the rib end of the sirloin and entrecôte steaks are sirloin steaks cut from between the ribs.
■ Lean, tender and flavoursome, with little waste. Good cooked any way, from rare to well-done.

HOW DO YOU LIKE YOUR STEAK COOKED?

For chargrilling, grilling or barbecuing, get the pan, grill or barbecue very hot before cooking. Lightly oil the steak and season with salt and pepper. For pan-frying, heat 1–2 tbsp oil in a heavy frying pan and season the meat just before cooking.

Cook the steak according to the times given below, turning once. Timings are approximate, for a steak cut about 2.5–5 cm (1–2 in) thick. Fillet steak takes the least time, rump the most. For success when pan-frying, don't overcrowd the pan. Keep the steak flat by pressing down on it with a fish slice or palette knife.

After cooking, let the steak rest for a few minutes before serving so that it is juicier and easier to cut.

■ *BLUE (bleu) or very rare: 1–1½ minutes each side*
■ *RARE (saignant): 1½–2 minutes each side*
■ *MEDIUM RARE: 2–2½ minutes each side*
■ *MEDIUM (à point): 2½–3 minutes each side*
■ *WELL DONE (bien cuit): 3–3½ minutes each side (To prevent charring, turn the heat down after the initial searing on each side.)*

Rib eye steak

- The 'eye' of the meat from the fore rib, about 2.5–4 cm (1–1½ in) thick.
- Cheaper than sirloin and fillet. Marbled with fat, so tender and juicy with lots of flavour.

Rump steak

- Large, boneless slice of quality meat, with a thick border of fat. Usually about 2.5 cm (1 in) thick.
- Not quite as tender as other steaks, but has a good 'beefy' flavour and firm texture.
- Can be fatty. Trim before or after cooking.

VEAL

The meat from calves that are no more then a year old, veal is lean and tender and requires careful cooking. Availability is patchy, so you may have to order in advance if you need a specific cut. If you are concerned about animal welfare, ask which country the veal has come from and how the animal was reared. Welfare varies from one farmer or producer to another, and from country to country – a good supplier should be able to give you this information.

THE BEST JOINT FOR ROASTING

For temperatures and times, see the roasting chart on page 332.

Loin

Other joints can be roasted, but this is the most readily available and will give good results.

- Prime-quality meat with a thin layer of fat sold boned, rolled and tied.
- Very lean meat, so the joint is best stuffed and wrapped in bacon, or smothered in butter (seasoned with herbs, spices or mustard), to give flavour and succulence.

CUTS FOR QUICK COOKING

Loin chops

- Lean, tender meat on the bone, with a border of fat. They look like pork loin chops, only larger and thicker. Pan-fry or grill, 6–7 minutes each side.

Escalopes

- Slices of lean meat, usually cut from the leg or rump, pounded very thin.
- Pan-fry in hot oil (or oil and butter) for 2–3 minutes each side, coated in

egg and breadcrumbs to make schnitzels, if you like. Also good cut into strips for sautés and stir-fries – cooking time will be 3–4 minutes in total.

CUTS FOR SLOW COOKING

Cubes

■ Sometimes called 'pie veal', these are boneless pieces cut from the shoulder, leg or neck that require long, gentle cooking to become tender. They can be quite fatty, but this is good as the fat breaks down during cooking and helps make the meat moist. Use in casseroles (especially goulash), for braising and stews, and in pies.

Osso buco

■ Thick slices of shank, with a round bone in the middle. Most often used for the braised Italian dish of the same name.
■ With long, gentle cooking in liquid, osso buco becomes the most tender and succulent of all the veal cuts, and the marrow in the centre of the bone (right) is a delicacy.

MARROW

The marrow in the centre of osso buco bones melts during long, slow cooking. In Italy it is highly prized in the stew of the same name, with diners traditionally saving it until last and eating it with a spoon. You can buy beef marrowbones from the butcher (they may have to be ordered) and extract the marrow to serve as a garnish for grilled meat, or to eat on garlic toast with salt. Ask the butcher for pieces of marrowbone cut about 7.5 cm (3 in) thick, and dig out the marrow from the centre with a teaspoon or small, sharp knife. Poach in lightly salted water for 2 minutes, drain and serve.

LAMB

Good-quality lamb, much of it free-range, is available all year round. The season for British lamb starts around Easter, and continues into autumn and early winter. Chilled fresh New Zealand lamb then takes over in the winter months. Bear in mind that the size of the cuts varies according to the time of year – small in spring, getting larger until autumn. Welsh and French salt marsh lamb are both prized for their flavour. They are expensive, but worth it.

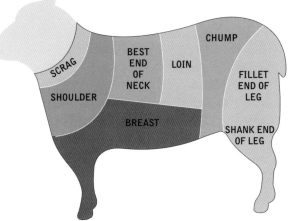

JOINTS FOR ROASTING

There is a good choice of different cuts for roasting, but they can be quite fatty. Trim well before cooking and remove any skin. For temperatures and times, see the roasting chart on page 332.

Best end

■ Also called best end of neck and rack of lamb. Consists of six to nine cutlets (the rib bones) joined together.

One rack serves 2–3 people. When the bones are scraped clean, it may be described as a French rack, or French-trimmed. Two racks with their bones locked to form an arch shape are a guard of honour (see opposite) and a crown roast is when two racks are tied in a circle (see opposite).

■ Prime-quality, juicy nuggets of meat form the 'eye' of each cutlet.

■ Expensive, but easy to cook and carve if the backbone has been chined (see page 16) – just slice in between the bones.

Breast

■ Inexpensive, thin cut from the belly, sold boned, rolled and tied. There is a high proportion of fat, so check that the joint has been well trimmed before buying.

■ Excellent flavour and succulence. To make the meat go further and counteract fattiness, slow roast or pot roast with a fruity stuffing.

GUARD OF HONOUR

Leg

■ A favourite for roasting, though pricey. A whole, bone-in leg weighing about 2.75 kg (5 lb) will feed 6. To feed 8, ask the butcher to leave the chump end on. Often the leg is halved into two smaller joints – the fillet end (top of the leg) and knuckle end (the bottom), each of which serves 4. Legs are also sold part-boned, or boned, rolled and tied. A 'butterflied' leg has been boned and opened out. It can be rolled and tied for roasting (with or without a stuffing).

■ Prime-quality, lean meat that is tender and flavourful with little waste. The fillet end is more tender, although the knuckle (shank) has a very good flavour.

■ When buying a leg, ask the butcher to loosen or remove the aitchbone to make carving easier, and to saw through the shank bone and fold it under so the joint will fit in the oven.

CROWN ROAST

Loin

- Sold on the bone (chined), or boned, rolled and tied. Boneless joints are good for stuffing and easy carving. A whole loin will serve 2–3 hungry people.
- Good-quality meat with a layer of fat on that is succulent and full of flavour with little waste. A good choice between lean leg and fattier shoulder, both for quality and price.

Rump

- A small joint for 1–2 people, from between the loin and the leg (known as the chump). Often sold boned and tied.
- Good value, with little waste. Tender, flavoursome meat that is easy to carve.

Saddle

- Two loins joined by the backbone. Best bought boned so that it can be stuffed and rolled for easy carving.
- A large, expensive joint for a special occasion – a whole saddle will serve 8–10 people. Remove excess fat before stuffing and rolling to get juicy, tender, flavoursome meat with no waste.

Shoulder

- A whole shoulder should serve 5–6 people. It is often halved and sold as two joints (the blade and the knuckle end), each of which will serve 3–4. A boned, rolled and stuffed shoulder will serve 6–8.
- Has quite a lot of fat, which gives it succulence and flavour. A well-trimmed boned joint is best for stuffing and easy carving with little waste. Some boned joints are sold rolled, others are tied into 'cushion' roasts.

CUTS FOR QUICK COOKING

Prime-quality cutlets, chops and boneless meat can be grilled, pan-fried, chargrilled or barbecued. Cooking instructions are the same as for steaks (see page 337).

Best end cutlets

- An 'eye' of meat attached to a long, curved bone surrounded with fat. Usually cut quite thin. Look best when they are French-trimmed.
- Juicy, tender and flavoursome, especially when rare (cook for 2–3 minutes each side). Allow 2–3 cutlets per head.

Butterflied leg

- A whole boneless leg, cut so that it has flaps on either side like butterfly wings. It will serve 5–6 people.

loin–fillet

■ Flavoursome meat with little fat. Juicy and tender if not overcooked – grill or barbecue for 30 minutes max, turning once, then leave to rest for 10–15 minutes. Cut across into thick slices to serve – there will be no waste.

Chump chops

■ Meaty slices, cut about 2 cm (¾ in) thick. Available on or off the bone (boneless chops are called chump or rump steaks), sometimes with a thick border of fat along the top.
■ Good flavour, but meat can be chewy and there is a fair bit of fat. Cook for 3–4 minutes each side or braise (see page 12).

Fillet

■ Expensive, lean meat sold in long, thin pieces; each one weighs about 300 g (10 oz) and serves 2. It is the eye of the loin, not to be confused with middle neck fillet (see page 345).
■ Can be cooked whole as it comes, or cut lengthways and opened out (butter-flied). Can also be cubed for kebabs, or sliced and pounded for escalopes, sautés or stir-fry strips.
■ Juicy and tender, with little waste. A whole or butterflied fillet cooks in 10–15 minutes, kebabs take 6–8, and escalopes and strips 2–3 minutes each side.

TIPS & TRICKS: KEBABS
When threading cubes of meat on to skewers for kebabs, push the cubes as close together as possible. This helps prevent them from over-cooking and drying out.

Leg steaks

■ Large slices cut from the top of the leg, sometimes with a piece of bone left in, surrounded by a thin layer of fat. A good thickness is 2.5–4 cm (1–1½ in); any thinner than this and they will be dry.

■ Lean meat with a good flavour, firm texture and no waste. Undercook for succulence, allowing about 3 minutes each side. Can also be cut into strips for sautéing or stir-frying.

Loin chops

■ A large nugget of meat on the bone, with a flap of meat and fat attached. Double loin chops are cut across the saddle, so they have a central bone (they are also called Barnsley chops, or butterfly chops because of their shape). Noisettes and medallions are boneless loin chops surrounded with fat, tied into neat rounds with string.

■ Lean, tender meat that has just enough fat to be self-basting, which helps make the chops juicy. As they are usually quite thick, 4–5 cm (1½–2 in), they take 5 minutes each side to cook.

■ Medallions and noisettes are very easy to eat and have hardly any waste.

CUTS FOR SLOW COOKING

Gentle braising or stewing suits lamb well. Prime, lean cuts benefit from the extra moisture that slow cooking brings, and fattier, tougher cuts become meltingly tender. For 4–6 people, you will need 700 g–1 kg (1½–2 lb) meat. Brown the meat in hot oil first, then cook with about 500 g (1 lb) browned chopped onions, celery and root vegetables and 300 ml (½ pint) liquid. Cook on the hob or in the oven at 160°C/325°F/Gas Mark 3 (140°C/275°F in fan ovens) for 2–3 hours or until tender.

Chump chops

■ Slices on or off the bone are good for braising.

■ Meat has enough fat to make it tasty and tender. With long, slow cooking, the fat melts off, leaving little waste.

Leg

■ Whole or half leg joints, or boneless cubes. Can be braised as a piece on the bone, or boned and cubed for casseroles, curries, couscous and tagines.

■ Lean meat with very little fat can be dry and chewy – don't overcook.

Neck

■ Scrag end comes in thick, fatty chunks on the bone, called neck end chops. Middle neck is less fatty and sold on or off the bone. Boneless middle neck comes either as one long piece called a fillet, or cut into cubes.
■ Fatty scrag needs trimming before cooking, so there is some waste. It makes good stews, but chill and degrease (see page 20) before serving. Middle neck is juicy and tender – use on the bone for Lancashire hotpot, or as boneless cubes for curries, couscous, casseroles and tagines.

Shank

■ The lower shin from the fore leg, on the bone. Allow 1 shank per person.
■ Very tender, gelatinous meat that literally falls off the bone when slow cooked in liquid. Full of flavour, with little waste. Cubes can be stewed.

Shoulder

■ Whole or half joints on the bone, or boned and rolled. Also diced meat. Needs excess fat trimmed off before cooking, so some wastage.
■ Has enough marbled fat to make it juicy and tender. Joints are good for pot roasts, cubes for casseroles and curries.

MUTTON

Meat from sheep that are over 2 years old is usually described as mutton. You can buy it at some farm shops and farmers' markets, or order it from your butcher or mail order over the web.
■ *If it has been properly matured, mutton has an excellent flavour, and is worth seeking out. The cuts are similar to those of lamb, but they must be cooked slowly for a long time to become tender.*
■ *Joints, chops and meat on the bone can be pot roasted, chops and boneless cubes can be used in casseroles and stews – they are especially good in curries.*

PORK

Most pigs are bred leaner than they used to be, which is good from a health point of view, but special breeds such as Gloucester Old Spot, Tamworth, Saddleback and Hampshire have a good amount of fat. Both are equally good, but for succulence and flavour, lean meat needs careful cooking.

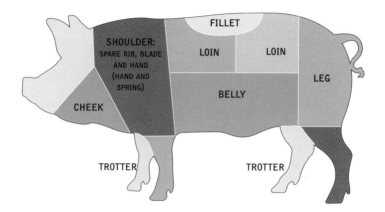

JOINTS FOR ROASTING

Roast pork should not be served rare or underdone – for temperatures and times, see the roasting chart on page 332. Check that the juices run clear, not pink or red, from the middle of the joint. If using a thermometer (see page 58), the internal temperature should be at least 70°C (160°F).

Belly

■ The cheapest joint. Comes as a large rectangle of fatty, streaky meat containing rib bones and topped with rind.

Best bought boned as a whole piece or in rashers, or boned, rolled and tied.

■ Well trimmed of fat and slow-roasted, belly is sweet and tasty, with melt-in-the-mouth succulence.

Chump end

■ From the rump, between the loin and the leg. Sold on the bone, or boned and rolled. Good amount of marbling and fat under the rind, and moderately priced.

■ The meat is quite succulent with little wastage, though slightly difficult to carve into neat slices.

belly–loin

Fillet

■ Very lean, boneless, prime-quality pork, also called tenderloin (it comes from the loin), without fat or rind. Looks like a thick sausage. Weighs 375–500 g (12 oz–1 lb), enough for 2–3 people. Expensive, but needs little trimming, so there is no waste.

■ Tender, but can be dry and bland. Best wrapped in bacon or Parma ham to protect and moisten during roasting, or butterflied and stuffed, then wrapped or tied. Don't overcook.

Leg

■ Expensive prime-quality meat with rind, best bought boned and rolled, or tied into shape with string. Whole legs are huge and rarely cooked at home, so legs are usually cut into 1.5–1.75 kg (3–3½ lb) joints to serve 4–6.

■ Lean and tender, easy-carve meat with good flavour and little waste. Don't overcook.

Loin

■ Prime-quality meat, with little waste. Sold on the bone as a rack like a row of chops (sometimes French trimmed), or boned and rolled, with or without rind.

■ Lean, tender and flavoursome, with just enough fat to be self-basting.

HOW TO GET CRISP CRACKLING

Crisping the rind on pork during roasting can be a bit hit-and-miss. A lot depends on the animal itself, but there are a few things you can do to increase your chances of success.

■ *Score the rind at about 5 mm (¼ in) intervals. Ask your butcher to do the scoring, or do it yourself with a very sharp knife or a scalpel. Work from the middle of the joint out to one side, then from the middle out to the other side – you will find this much easier than trying to score in one long continuous line.*

■ *Make sure the rind is absolutely dry before cooking by wiping and patting it with kitchen paper or a tea towel.*

■ *Massage the rind with a little vegetable oil, then with salt.*

■ *Roast according to the chart on page 332, but don't baste at all during roasting. The drier the rind during roasting, the better.*

■ *If the crackling is not crisp at the end of the cooking time, turn the oven up to its hottest temperature for about 10 minutes. If this doesn't work, you can try crisping up the crackling with a blowtorch, or lifting it off the meat and popping it under a hot grill.*

Racks on the bone should be chined (see page 16) and any rind scored so you can slice easily between the chops. Rolled joints carve easily with minimal waste, but have little room for stuffing.

Ribs

■ Chinese-style rib bones, also called spare ribs (not to be confused with spare rib chops and steaks, see opposite). Usually sold cut into ribs, but can be joined in a sheet.

■ Inexpensive. If necessary, separate bones by chopping between them. Tasty meat becomes tender-sweet and crisp when simmered in stock and then roasted.

Shoulder

■ A huge piece of meat that can serve 15–20 people, but is usually cut into three joints – spare rib, blade, and hand (also called hand and spring). All can be bought on the bone, with rind, but are difficult to carve, so boned, or boned, rolled and tied joints are better. Spare rib is the most useful size to serve 6–8 people, while blade comes smaller and will serve 4–6. Hand is the cheapest of the three. It is a very large cut, best slow-cooked. Some butchers use it for sausages and mince.

■ Price-wise, shoulder is good value compared to leg and loin and, as the meat is fattier, it tends to be juicier and sweeter.

CUTS FOR
QUICK COOKING

Prime, tender pork such as chops, escalopes and steaks can be grilled, pan-fried, chargrilled or barbecued. Cook in the same way as steaks (see page 337) but use the timings given below.

Chump chops/ steaks

■ From the rump, and sometimes called rump chops/steaks. Usually boneless and rindless. Best cut 2.5–4 cm (1–1½ in) thick.

■ Lean, flavoursome and moderately priced. Trim off any fat for healthy cooking and cook for 6–8 minutes each side. Don't overcook.

Fillet (tenderloin)

■ Boneless meat that is cut crossways into round slices to make medallions and noisettes. When pounded flat, they are called escalopes.

loin–spare ribs

■ Very lean and tender meat with no rind and no fat, so no waste. Cook 2–4 minutes each side. Can be cut into strips for sautés and stir-fries, which will cook even quicker.

Loin chops/ steaks

■ The most familiar-looking of the pork chops, with a large eye of meat on the bone, usually bordered by a layer of fat and rind. Occasionally the kidney is included. Loin steaks are simply the chop with the bone and rind removed.
■ Lean meat that needs careful cooking or it can be dry. Trim off any fat and rind for healthy cooking and cook no longer than 6–8 minutes each side. Steak meat can be drier than chop meat as the bone helps keep the meat moist. It can be cut into strips against the grain for stir-frying – cooking time is 4–5 minutes.

Spare rib chops/steaks

■ Sometimes called shoulder chops/ steaks, because this is the part of the animal they come from. Untidy-looking, with seams of fat running through. The chops have a bone along

SUCKLING PIG

You can buy a whole suckling pig by mail order or from the butcher – it makes an unusual roast (and a good talking point) for a special occasion. Suckling pigs, correctly called sucking pigs, are piglets that have been fed on nothing more than their mother's milk. The meat is pale and sweet-tasting, and very tender. The usual weight is about 3.5–5 kg (7½–11 lb), which is enough to feed 12 people and will just about fit in a standard oven (you may need to lay it diagonally in the roasting tin), or it can be barbecued on a spit. Look in Spanish, Portuguese and Italian cookbooks for recipes.

one side, the steaks are boneless.

■ Inexpensive, juicy and full of flavour. Cook for 6–8 minutes each side.

CUTS FOR SLOW COOKING

Pork is a lean meat with no marbling of fat like beef and lamb. Marinating and cooking with vegetables and liquid help make it moist – use the slow cooking instructions for lamb on page 344.

Belly

■ Comes as a slab of belly pork, or boned, rolled and tied as a joint. Also sold as thick rashers or slices, cut crossways from a boned slab.

■ A fatty cut that is tender, moist and full of flavour. Best slow-roasted.

■ Trim off rind and excess fat before cooking.

Chump chops/ steaks

■ From the rump end of the pig, a lean meat with enough fat to make it moist and flavoursome.

■ Trim off rind and excess fat before cooking. Chops are good braised, steaks can be cut into cubes for casseroles and curries.

Leg

■ Boned meat is sold diced for casseroles, curries and stews.

■ Good and lean. Keep the heat low and don't overcook or the meat can be dry.

Loin

■ Boned and rolled joints, chops on the bone and boneless steaks.

■ Very lean. To counteract any dryness, look for a good covering of fat between the rind and the meat. Braising with vegetables and liquid is a good way to make loin moist.

Shoulder

■ On the bone, or boned and rolled joints (either the spare rib or hand).

■ Meat becomes sweet and succulent when pot roasted or braised. Skim off excess fat or degrease (see page 20) before serving.

Spare rib

■ Chops and steaks.

■ Fatty meat is the best pork for braising on or off the bone, and for casseroles, curries and stews when boned and cubed. Degrease (see page 20) before serving.

spare ribs

BACON

Bacon is pork that has been cured with either a wet or a dry cure.

■ When pork is wet cured it is steeped in a brine of salt and water.

■ Dry-cured pork is rubbed with a mixture of salt and sugar.

■ After curing, bacon can be left as it is, in which case it is called unsmoked or 'green', or it can be smoked. Unsmoked bacon is paler in colour and milder in flavour than smoked, which can taste quite salty.

CHOOSE There are many different cures, and it is a matter of personal taste which you choose to buy.

■ Dry-cured bacon gives less shrinkage and wastage than wet-cured, and rashers will be crispier.

■ It is easy to see when bacon is fresh – it looks bright pink and damp, not dark, discoloured or dry. When checking for freshness, look at the fat as well as the meat – it should be white or creamy white, not yellow, greasy or curling at the edges.

■ Wet, sticky, smelly or slimy bacon is not good, so don't buy it.

STORE All bacon must be kept in the fridge, and storage times on any packaging should not be exceeded. If the bacon rashers are bought loose, keep

CAUL

If you see this at the butchers, you may wonder what it is – it looks like lacy curtain material. In fact it is the membrane that surrounds a pig's stomach, used in cooking for wrapping meat to help keep it together and make it moist.

■ *Two sheets of caul are enough to wrap most joints of meat, or up to 8 burgers, sausages or patties (crêpinettes in French).*

■ *Soak for a few minutes in cold water, then lift out gently and lay flat on a board.*

■ *Wrap meat in one piece of caul, then double wrap with the second piece to cover any tears or holes.*

■ *Roast, fry, grill or barbecue in the usual way – the caul will melt and disappear.*

them in an airtight container or wrapped in foil – unsmoked will keep for up to 7 days, smoked for up to 10 days. Bacon joints, raw or cooked, will keep fresh for up to 3 days. Vacuum-packed bacon freezes well, for up to 2 months.

PREPARE Mild-cured and unsmoked bacon joints need no preparation, but if you buy a smoked joint it will need soaking before cooking to remove excess salt (if you are in doubt, soak it anyway).

■ To soak a joint, put it in a large bowl or pan and cover with fresh cold water from the tap. Leave overnight in a cold place (the fridge is best). Drain, then cover with fresh water if the bacon is to be boiled, or dry it thoroughly with kitchen paper if it is to be baked or roasted.

■ Bacon rashers can be trimmed of any rind and excess fat with scissors, either before or after cooking, if you prefer them without.

COOK

JOINTS

These can be boiled and/or roasted, according to individual cuts and recipes. Boiling times are calculated at 20 minutes per 500 g (1 lb) plus 20 minutes, roasting is best at 180°C/350°F/Gas Mark 4 (160°C/ 325°F in fan ovens), allowing 30 minutes per 500 g (1 lb) plus 30 minutes. Allow all joints to rest for 15–20 minutes before serving.

Collar: From the shoulder, this is an economical joint that is usually cut in two and sold boned and rolled. Prime collar is a large joint, while end of collar is about half the size. Both are good for boiling and braising.

Hock: This comes in various sizes, including the knuckle end, all cut from the front leg of the pig. This is the best cut for soups (especially split pea and ham) when the meat is stripped from the bone and diced or shredded. It is also good in casseroles and stews.

Gammon: From the hind leg of the pig, this comes in three sizes. The largest, prime-quality joint is the hock (knuckle end), the one for boiling and baking and serving as ham on the bone, traditional at Christmas. Middle gammon, from the top end of the leg, is a lean and meaty joint that is sold on the bone or boned and rolled. It is good, lean meat that can be boiled and baked, braised or roasted (it is also cut into steaks and rashers – the one for 'ham and eggs'). Corner gammon is a small, boneless joint from the top of the leg that is corner-shaped, hence its name. Its lean meat is good boiled or roasted and served hot or cold.

joints–rashers

RASHERS

There are three different types, all of which are sold with or without rind. They come from the middle (the back and the belly) of the pig, and are suitable for grilling or frying. Cooking time is 2–3 minutes per side, longer if you like it crispy.

Back: This comes from the loin – the leanest, meatiest and most expensive cut. It comes with varying degrees of fat – look for the leanest – and is the one for big British breakfasts and bacon sandwiches.

Middle: This is two types of bacon in one – back and streaky together – and is a useful cut as you can divide it into back and streaky, as and when you need them. It is sold as long rashers or slices from a rolled joint. Rolled rashers look good on the breakfast plate.

Streaky: This comes from the belly and is the fattiest, but often the tastiest, cut. It is an inexpensive alternative to back bacon for breakfast, and is good for making BLTs. You can also use it for wrapping neatly round lean meat and delicate fish (pork fillet, turkey, chicken and monkfish) to flavour and moisten. Streaky bacon is also used to line tins and to make lardons (see right).

TIPS & TRICKS: GAMMON

To prevent curling during cooking, snip the edge of thick gammon steaks and rashers at right angles with scissors.

TIPS & TRICKS: BACON

Use rindless streaky bacon to line tins and moulds for pâtés and terrines. Before lining, stretch the rashers by pressing them with the flat side of a large knife blade. This makes a little bacon go a long way.

PANCETTA & LARDONS

Pancetta is Italian for cured pork belly. You can buy it in straight or round rashers, or diced. Lardon is the French word for diced bacon.

■ *Pancetta rashers can be used in place of streaky bacon – you may prefer their milder, sweeter flavour. They come both smoked and unsmoked, and can be quite fatty.*

■ *Diced pancetta and lardons are interchangeable in recipes. They are sold in packets, which are quite expensive. It is far cheaper to dice rashers yourself, although the meat will not be as thick. Use for flavouring and adding protein to soups, stews, stuffings, casseroles, quiches, risottos, pasta sauces, salads, pizzas and omelettes.*

SAUSAGES

Size, shape, flavour – there is such a bewildering array of sausages for sale. Personal taste will dictate which ones you buy.

CHOOSE Pork, beef and lamb are the main meats used in sausages. Ingredients and flavourings vary enormously, and many sausages are high in fat, but there is an increasing number of speciality sausages being made with other meats such as venison, buffalo and ostrich that are lower in fat. Always check labels for meat, fat, cereal and salt content, or ask the butcher what is in the sausages if they are made on the premises. Sausages with 75–90% meat, additive-free and with no artificial ingredients are the healthiest choice.

BEST SAUSAGES

Black pudding: Also called blood sausage, this is made from pig's blood and cereal, with varying amounts of fat. The French *boudin noir* is generally good quality, if you can get it. Slice and grill or fry, or crumble or chop and use in stuffings.

Chorizo: An orangey-red, spicy sausage from Spain, both fresh and dried are available. It is the fresh one you need for grilling and pan-frying. Chorizo is used in paella, and it is also good with eggs, and in risotto, pasta sauces and stuffings.

Cumberland: A traditional British banger, often sold in a long coil. A good breakfast choice, or when you want to cook bangers and mash with onion gravy. Good brands will have a high meat content. Grill, fry, barbecue or roast (see opposite).

Italian sausage: Fresh from the deli, these are generally very meaty with punchy flavourings (fennel and garlic are particular favourites). Good halved lengthways and grilled, fried or barbecued, but also excellent chopped in stuffings and pasta sauces.

Lincolnshire: A tender, moist sausage for grilling, frying and barbecuing. Traditional recipes use only pork, bread, sage, salt and pepper.

Loukanika: A good, meaty pork sausage from Greece, flavoured with herbs, spices, garlic and orange rind. Good grilled, fried or barbecued.

Merguez: A spicy hot, thin sausage made with lamb, from North Africa. Good grilled or fried, or chopped in pasta sauces, risotto and couscous.

Toulouse: The classic cassoulet sausage, also good for frying and grilling. Very meaty and garlicky, also excellent barbecued.

STORE Sausages are highly perishable. Always keep them well wrapped in the fridge and don't eat after the use-by date on the packet. Freshly made sausages from the butcher should be eaten within 2 days. Cooked sausages should be refrigerated and eaten within 24 hours of cooking. Sausages can be stored in the freezer for up to 3 months, and should be thawed in the fridge before cooking.

PREPARE AND COOK

- If sausages are in links, snip them apart with scissors.
- Grill or fry in a little hot vegetable oil in a non-stick pan. Slow cooking for 15–20 minutes is recommended, turning frequently. Check they are cooked through by cutting one in half lengthways.
- Sausages are also good cooked in the oven at 180°C/350°F/Gas Mark 4 (160°C/325°F in fan ovens) for 20–25 minutes, turning once.
- If you are barbecuing sausages it is a good idea to start them off in the oven for 10 minutes (temperature as above), then finish them cooking on the barbecue. This ensures they cook through without overcharring.

TO PRICK OR NOT TO PRICK?

If you prick sausages with a fork or toothpick before cooking, this will make the fat run out.

- *THE UPSIDE – it will prevent the casings from bursting, and give you less fatty sausages, especially if you drain them well before serving.*
- *THE DOWNSIDE – the sausages will be less moist and less juicy.*

MINCE

Versatile, inexpensive and quick to cook, mince is an invaluable ingredient for the busy cook. For dishes like Bolognese, shepherd's pie, keema curry and moussaka, first brown the meat in a little hot oil (or dry-fry in a non-stick pan) for 4–6 minutes, then cook according to your recipe for 20–30 minutes. Burgers, meatballs and patties should be cooked for 4–6 minutes on each side. All mince can be kept in the fridge for up to 24 hours, or frozen for up to 3 months (see page 330).

Beef

■ Tough cuts like neck and flank are often used to make minced beef, but it won't say this on the label if you buy it at the supermarket. If it is described as 'ground steak' it is likely to be made from better-quality meat than ordinary minced beef, and will be good for burgers, meatballs, Bolognese sauce, and stuffing vegetables.

■ Minced beef can be coarsely or finely ground, with varying amounts of fat – check the label. Standard mince may have 10–20% fat, lean or extra-lean mince 5–7%. Lean is healthier, but it can be dry. Ground steak is very finely minced, and usually the least fatty.

■ To be sure of what you are getting, ask your butcher to mince meat for you – chuck steak, top rump and topside are all good cuts for mincing.

Veal

■ Topside or pie veal may be used for minced veal, which makes good lean burgers and meatballs.

■ For extra flavour, mix it with another mince such as beef or pork.

Lamb

■ Usually made from breast, shoulder or middle neck fillet, richly flavoured cuts with a fair amount of fat (minced lamb can contain up to 25% fat). Good for burgers and meatballs that are to be grilled or barbecued, as the fat helps to keep them moist.

■ Dishes like shepherd's pie, keema curry and moussaka are traditionally made with minced lamb, but they can be fatty. Ideally, skim off fat during cooking, or chill after cooking and lift off the solidified fat before reheating.

Pork

■ Minced pork may have up to 30% fat. This makes it a good choice for making juicy burgers and meatballs. To make them less fatty, mix half and half with lean minced beef or veal.

OFFAL

Delicious when properly cooked,
offal deserves to be eaten more often.
You will find more choice at butchers
and farmers' markets than at the
supermarket, and a good supplier
will advise you on cooking methods
if you are keen to try out different
kinds. Traditional dishes made with
kidneys, liver and oxtail are quintes-
sential comfort food. They are also
cheap and nutritious, and easy to
prepare and cook.

CHOOSE Three types of offal are
readily available.
Kidneys: Calf's (veal) and ox, lamb's
and pig's.
Liver: Pig's, lamb's and calf's.
Oxtail
When buying kidneys and liver,
look for a fresh and glossy sheen,
and absolutely no smell. Lamb's and
calf's (veal) kidneys from the butcher
may have thick fat (suet) around them
– it should be off-white and crumbly,
not yellow or greasy.

Oxtail should look freshly cut, with
plenty of deep red meat surrounded
by white fat.

STORE Offal is best eaten fresh, on
the day of purchase if possible, but it
can be kept in a covered container in

the fridge for up to 24 hours. It doesn't freeze particularly well.

PREPARE Very little preparation is needed.

Kidneys: If you have bought the ones encased in suet, pull it away carefully. The kidneys themselves are covered in a thin membrane. Nick it with scissors or the tip of a small, sharp knife, then peel off with your fingers. Now cut out the white cores, halving the kidneys or cutting them into pieces according to the type of kidney and the way you are going to cook them.

Liver: Pull away any covering membrane, taking care not to tear the liver itself. With a very sharp knife, slice the liver as thinly as possible – 5 mm (¼ in) is the best thickness for quick cooking and tenderness. If you see any ducts or blood vessels while you are slicing, cut them neatly away.

Oxtail: Comes cut into joints ready for cooking. You can buy them individually (a tail usually cuts into 4 joints), or tied together as a crown roast. Trim away excess fat from the outside of each piece, if this has not been done by the butcher.

COOK All offal is richly flavoured, so portion sizes generally only need to be small.

Kidneys

■ Calf's (veal) and ox kidneys come joined together as lots of 'lobes', sometimes surrounded by suet. A whole calf's kidney usually weighs about 500 g (1 lb) and will feed 3–4 people. Tender and sweet, it is the chefs' favourite for sautéing. Cut it into bite-sized pieces and cook for 3 minutes max. Ox kidney is the traditional one for steak and kidney pudding. Strong and tough, it needs braising or stewing for a long time to become tender.

■ Lamb's kidneys are the smallest and mildest, and the most readily available – the best ones to try if you have not eaten kidneys before. They weigh 50–85 g (1¼–2¾ oz) each, so allow 2–3 per person. Grill whole or halved on skewers (to keep them flat) for 2–3 minutes each side. Or pan-fry them in butter, then coat in a Dijon-style sauce made with white wine, cream and mustard. They can also be used in steak and kidney pie or pudding if you don't like the strong flavour of pig's or ox kidney.

■ Pig's kidneys are larger and stronger in taste than lamb's, and they can be tough. They are best soaked in lightly salted water for a few hours to make them milder, then halved or sliced and used in pies and steak and kidney pudding.

Liver

■ Calf's liver is the most expensive, and the most tender. Its delicate flavour is almost sweet. For 2 people allow 225 g (8 oz). Thin slices are best seasoned and pan-fried over a high heat in olive oil (or oil and butter for extra flavour) for only 60 seconds on each side. Lemon, lime and sage are good flavours with calf's liver, so too is balsamic vinegar.

■ Lamb's liver is good fried, as long as it is thinly sliced and not over-cooked – 3–4 minutes each side is the recommended time. Allow 1–2 slices per person. It's stronger in flavour than calf's liver, but not too strong. Fried onions are the classic accompaniment – their flavours complement each other perfectly.

■ Pig's liver is strong and robust, and dark in colour. To make it milder, soak it in milk for an hour or two, then drain and dry. The best use for pig's liver is chopped or minced in pâtés and terrines.

Oxtail

■ This needs to be browned in hot oil, then braised very gently in liquid for at least 2 hours, during which time it becomes so tender that the meat literally falls off the bones. Allow 2 pieces per person (there is a lot of waste) and cook with wine and/or tomatoes to help cut the fat. Cook the day before serving so you can chill in the fridge overnight and then lift off the solidified fat before reheating.

Other offal

Heart: Size varies according to the animal the heart comes from. Lamb's heart has a good flavour and texture, and 1 small heart per person is the usual portion size. They can be sliced and pan-fried, but one of the best ways to enjoy them is stuffed and braised (they need long, slow cooking for 2–3 hours). When sliced, the stuffing gives them an appealing shape and the meat is juicy, tender and sweet.

Sweetbreads: Lamb's sweetbreads are a real delicacy, with their mild flavour and melt-in-the-mouth texture. They need to be soaked in cold water and blanched to remove impurities, then skinned and poached in milk or stock for 8–10 minutes until tender. After this initial cooking, they are good swiftly pan-fried to give them colour, and are often served in a cream and white wine sauce with chopped fresh herbs. Always cook and eat sweetbreads on the day you buy them as they are highly perishable.

Tongue: Whole ox tongue is sold salted or cured in brine. It needs poaching in liquid for 3–4 hours, then peeling and pressing (you can buy special presses at kitchenware shops, or use a cake tin). Home-pressed tongue is very good served well chilled and thinly sliced.

Tripe: The white, spongy stomach of cows and pigs is a great delicacy in Europe, where it is often slow-cooked with tomatoes and pungent garlic and onions – look for recipes in French and Italian cookbooks. It is sold blanched or 'dressed' ready for cooking, and you will need 175 g (6 oz) per person.

Trotters: Pig's trotters are prized for their jelly, and are sold split down the middle. Pop one in a long-cooking casserole or stew and you will notice how it enriches the gravy.

SPECIALITY MEATS

Farmers' markets, farm shops and specialist butchers sell some unusual meats that are worth buying, and you can also order them fresh or frozen over the web. When you buy the meat, ask the supplier for cooking instructions – he or she will know all about the meat they are selling.

■ **Buffalo:** The same as bison, and also sold under this name, buffalo is a red meat that is like beef, but contains about a third less fat. It can be used in any recipe for beef – the cuts are similar. Steaks can be grilled, chargrilled or pan-fried like beef steaks, but because they are so lean and low in fat, they benefit from being marinated before cooking, and they should not be overcooked. Buffalo burgers, grills and sausages are tasty and good.

■ **Ostrich:** Fillet and rump roasting joints and steaks are the most popular cuts, but burgers, sausages and meatballs are also made from this rich meat. Like all red meats, ostrich is a good source of protein and iron, but it is lower in saturated fat than beef, lamb or pork. As they are so lean, steaks are best cooked rare or they can be dry.

■ **Wild boar:** Boneless joints for roasting are popular, together with steaks, sausages, bacon and burgers. Marinating and long slow roasting are essential to make this mature, gamey meat tender and juicy. Roasting time is 35–40 minutes per 500 g (1 lb), and the oven temperature should be no more than 160°C/325°F/Gas Mark 3 (140°C/275°F in fan ovens).

POULTRY

CHOOSE

The majority of chickens and turkeys on sale in supermarkets have been reared indoors. This information won't appear on the label, but the price will be a good indicator – indoor-reared birds are generally the cheapest, with organic the most expensive and free-range in between.

Organic birds are free-range, allowed to roam outside in the day-time. Most (but not always all) of their feed is organic. The flesh will be tender yet firm, with a tasty, satisfy-ing flavour, because these birds are allowed to mature slowly. Chickens are reared for up to 14 weeks (indoor-reared birds are matured for up to 6 weeks), and some will have the name of the farm or producer on the label, which may give you extra reassurance. Don't be put off if organic chickens look scrawny compared to those reared indoors. Slower-growing breeds are less plump than indoor-reared birds, and the amount of exercise they have can also make them leaner and longer in the body.

Free-range birds are those that have had some access to the open air. They are less expensive then organic free-range birds.

Corn-fed birds – these golden yellow chickens are fed on a diet containing corn or maize. The colour makes them look appetizing, but the feed makes very little difference to the flavour.

What's in a name?

Organic and free-range poultry with the name of the breed on the label is generally more expensive than ordinary kinds, but these top-quality birds are well worth paying extra for.

Chicken: Look for slower-growing British breeds such as Devonshire Red and Devonshire Gold, Oakham White, Cotswold White and Cotswold Gold.

choose

These will have firm flesh with plenty of good, old-fashioned taste. The French *poulet de bresse* has an AOC like wine. It is reared under strict conditions, and is highly prized for its succulence and gamey-flavoured flesh. You may also see *poulet d'or, poulet noir* and *poulet anglais,* three other excellent French breeds.

Turkey: Norfolk Black and Cambridge Bronze are free-range, slow-maturing birds with densely textured meat that has more flavour and succulence than indoor-reared turkeys. Traditional 'farm fresh' birds have been dry hand-plucked and hung for 2 weeks. These turkeys will have a good, gamey flavour.

Duck: Aylesbury ducks are a good traditional breed with plump, meaty flesh. Gressingham duck is a cross between the domestic duck and the mallard, and is renowned for its distinctive flavour, which is similar to wild duck. It has crisp skin and moist flesh, and a good meat-to-fat ratio. Goosnargh, from the village of the same name in Lancashire, is another excellent duck, especially the succulent and tasty corn-fed kind. Last but not least, Barbary and Nantais ducks are two French breeds worth seeking out for their tasty meat.

GOOD FOR YOU
Poultry contains similar nutrients to red meat:
- *PROTEIN, essential for growth, good health and well-being.*
- *B VITAMINS, especially niacin, B6 and B12, for healthy blood cells and nervous system.*
- *ESSENTIAL MINERALS, especially iron (for healthy red blood cells), zinc (for growth, healthy immune and reproductive systems and skin) and selenium (an antioxidant essential for a healthy immune system, fertility and thyroid metabolism).*

Chicken and turkey are low in fat; their livers are rich in iron, and in vitamin A (good for eyes, vision, skin and growth).

Buying frozen poultry

■ It is always best to buy fresh rather than commercially frozen poultry. Fresh poultry has a better texture, and you can be more sure of what you are buying, but it is handy to keep a pack or two of your favourite pieces in the freezer. Wrap them individually (see opposite) so you can use them as you need. Whole birds use up a lot of room and need a long time to defrost, so are hardly worth the freezer space, but pieces defrost rapidly in the microwave, or in about 4 hours in the fridge.

■ If you buy a frozen bird, defrost it properly before cooking. For defrosting instructions and times, refer to page 379.

SAFE HANDLING

All of the safe handling criteria for meat on page 329–30 apply, but with poultry (especially chicken) there is some risk of salmonella contamination. If you have bought from a reputable source, the risk is minimal, but you should always follow these guidelines.

■ Refrigerate poultry as soon as you can (see right) and eat within the recommended guidelines.

■ Wash work surface, hands and utensils with hot, soapy water before and after dealing with raw or cooked poultry. Don't deal with the two together.

■ Keep a separate chopping board for raw poultry if you can, and wash it well in hot, soapy water immediately after use. When preparing raw poultry don't let it come into contact with other foods, especially foods that will not be cooked or reheated before being eaten.

■ Bacteria are easily killed by cooking, as long as you make sure poultry is properly cooked through before eating. This is especially important with whole birds (see page 367).

■ Refrigerate leftovers as soon as they have cooled, and eat within 2 days.

■ Leftovers should not be reheated more than once.

■ If you are dealing with frozen poultry, or freezing it yourself, see the guidelines opposite.

STORE

Fresh poultry is highly perishable, especially in warm weather, so you should keep it in the fridge.

■ Remove all wrappings, then wipe the poultry all over with kitchen paper (including inside any cavities). If there are any giblets, remove them and keep in a covered bowl in the fridge.

choose–store

■ Place the poultry on a tray or a large, deep plate and cover loosely with foil before storing in the bottom of the fridge (this will prevent any blood dripping on to other foods).

■ Birds and pieces keep fresh for up to 2 days; livers and minced poultry should be cooked within 24 hours.

Freezing

Small amounts of poultry can be successfully frozen at home, provided it is very fresh when it goes in the freezer. General guidelines are the same as for freezing meat (see page 330).

■ All poultry can be stored in the freezer for up to 6 months, apart from minced poultry, which should be stored for a maximum of 2 months. Nothing bad will happen after this time, but the texture of the meat will not be so good.

■ The best poultry for home freezing is portion-sized pieces such as breasts, legs, drumsticks and thighs, and packs of cubes or strips. Wrap pieces individually in cling film, then overwrap them with foil or in an airtight plastic bag – poultry is delicate and susceptible to freezer burn (see page 26).

■ Whole birds are an awkward shape to store, and take a long time to defrost, so they aren't really worth it.

GRAVY
Makes enough for 6–8 people

If roasting a bird, thickening the juices from the roasting tin is a good way to make a delicious gravy.

Remove the bird from the tin and pour off all but about 1 tbsp fat. Put the tin over a low heat, add 1 tbsp plain flour and stir well.

Slowly whisk in 500 ml (¾ pint) hot water or stock, turn up the heat and bring to the boil. Simmer, whisking, for 1–2 minutes, then season with salt and pepper to taste, and serve.

CHICKEN

Versatile, quick and easy to cook, chicken is lower in fat than most meats (especially without the skin). Choosing, preparing and cooking the different cuts is simple when you know how.

Whole birds

CHOOSE

■ Oven-ready chickens weigh from 1.5–2.5 kg (3–5 lb). A good average weight for a bird to serve 4–6 people is 1.75–2 kg (3½–4 lb).

■ Very small birds, called poussins, are baby chickens no more than 4 weeks old. They weigh about 425 g (15 oz) each, enough for 1 per person.

■ Large 'roasters' weigh from 3.5–5 kg (7½–10 lb). They are usually available to order from the butcher throughout the year, and at Christmas you may see them in the supermarket – they have replaced capons (castrated cockerels) that were a traditional alternative to turkey. Prepare and roast as for turkey (see pages 379–80).

■ Boiling fowl are old laying hens, good for making stocks and soups – they require long, gentle simmering to become tender. They are hard to come by – ask your butcher whether he can get one for you, or try a halal or kosher butcher.

PREPARING A CHICKEN FOR ROASTING

Whole chickens and poussins can be poached with liquid and vegetables but they are more usually roasted. They can also be barbecued (see page 368).

■ Take the bird out of the fridge and bring it to room temperature before cooking. Allow 1 hour for this.

■ Remove any trussing strings that are tied around the body of the bird. These keep the chicken in a neat, compact shape, but they slow down the cooking and prevent the bird from cooking evenly.

■ Wipe the bird inside and out with kitchen paper, removing the bag of giblets if there is one. The giblets are the neck, gizzard, heart and liver. They can be used to make stock (see page 371) although the liver is best left out as it can give a bitter taste.

■ For easy carving, remove the wishbone before cooking. Pull back the skin from the neck cavity to expose it, then cut around it with the tip of a small, sharp knife and cut it free at the bottom.

■ To add flavour and make the chicken more succulent, push a quartered onion or lemon, or a few chunks of garlic, into the body cavity. During cooking, the juices of these ingredients will flow, flavouring and basting the chicken from within.

whole birds

■ Sprigs of herbs, such as tarragon, rosemary, thyme and sage, can also be pushed into the cavity.

■ Stuffing can be pushed in the neck end (see right), but don't stuff the body cavity. If the cavity is stuffed, the heat may not penetrate right through to the centre of the bird and this will prevent it cooking all the way through.

■ To make the breast meat moist, lift up the skin at the neck end and insert your fingers between the skin and the flesh of the breast to create a pocket, then push in flavoured softened butter or soft cheese to cover the breast. Grated citrus zest, chopped fresh herbs, ground spices or crushed garlic make good flavourings for the butter or cheese.

■ Turn the bird upside down and pull the neck skin over the neck cavity (and any stuffing). Cut off any excess skin with scissors. Twist the wings round so the tips secure the neck skin in place, then tie the legs together with string (see right), if this has not already been done.

■ Weigh the bird and calculate the cooking time, allowing 25 minutes per 500 g (1 lb) plus an extra 25 minutes. The bird is now ready for roasting.

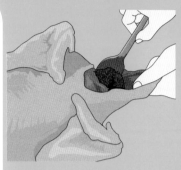

STUFFING A CHICKEN

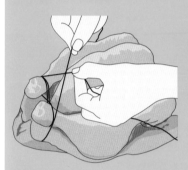

TYING THE LEGS WITH STRING

IS IT COOKED?

Do this simple test at the end of the recommended roasting time – don't go by the time alone.

■ *Ease one of the legs away from the body and pierce the thigh at its thickest point with a knife – the juices that run out should be clear. The juices between the thigh and the body should be this colour too. If any of the juices are pink or red, return the bird to the oven and test again after 20 minutes.*

ROASTING A CHICKEN

■ To help the bird cook more quickly, make two or three deep diagonal slashes across the tops of the thighs and into the back of the bird before roasting. This will allow the heat to penetrate right from the start.

■ Massage the bird liberally all over with softened butter or olive oil, then season with sea salt and freshly ground black pepper. This will make crisp, flavoursome skin.

■ A rub of paprika will give the skin a good colour, or you can use dried herbs for a different flavour.

■ Roast in a preheated oven at 190ºC/ 375ºF/Gas Mark 5 (170ºC/340ºF in fan ovens) for the calculated cooking time (see page 367).

■ For succulent, golden-brown flesh, lay the bird on one of its sides in the roasting tin and cook for 10–20 minutes, then turn it onto its other side for the next 10–20 minutes. Turn it breast-side down for another 15–20 minutes, then sit it breast-side up for the remainder of the cooking time to crisp and colour the skin. If you nestle the bird in a cradle-style rack in the roasting tin, it will be easier to manage and stay in position more securely, but if you don't have one, use some scrunched-up foil instead.

■ Make sure the bird is thoroughly cooked – see page 367.

■ Leave the bird, covered with foil, in a warm place for 10–15 minutes after roasting. This resting time is essential for the juices to settle in the meat and make it easy to carve. Carve in the same way as a turkey (see page 381).

BARBECUING A CHICKEN

If you have a kettle barbecue, you can cook a whole chicken on it with the lid down, but it will cook faster and more evenly if it is spatchcocked (split open along its back and splayed flat, see pages 46 and 47). You can buy spatch-cocked chickens and poussins, or spatchcock the bird yourself (see page 387) – cut along either side of the back-bone and remove it, then press down hard on the breast to flatten it. For ease of handling and to keep the bird flat during cooking, insert skewers through the wings and legs before cooking.

Breasts
CHOOSE

■ Available boneless (with skin or skinless), part-boned/on the bone (called suprêmes when part of the wing bone is attached), and cut into cubes or strips.

■ Allow 1 breast, on or off the bone, per person. The usual weight is 125–175 g (4–6 oz).

■ Meat is lean and tender, but can be dry. Bone-in breasts are the juiciest.

whole birds—breasts

PREPARE

- Strip off any skin, if you prefer (see Cutting the Fat, below right).
- Pull away the tender strip of fillet from underneath, and set aside.
- Use a small, sharp knife to cut out the silvery-white tendon from beneath, as this can be chewy.
- Marinate to make the lean meat more moist, slashing the flesh so the marinade can penetrate better (see page 41). Leave in the fridge for at least 4 hours or overnight.

COOK

- Whole breasts can be pan-fried, grilled, chargrilled or barbecued. Cook on a high heat for 7–10 minutes, turning once. They can also be roasted for 15 minutes in a preheated oven at 190°C/375°F/Gas Mark 5 (170°C/ 340°F in fan ovens).
- Cubes or strips are good for stir-frying, sautéing, grilling and barbecuing on skewers. They are also good in Mexican fajitas and Japanese teriyaki and yakitori. Cook for 5–7 minutes.
- Tender fillet strips (detached from underneath the breast) cook much more quickly then the rest of the breast, so add them at the end of the cooking time – they need about 3 minutes.
- Cubes and strips can be used in Thai and Indian curries and casseroles, but not if the recipe calls for long cooking. If it is more than 20 minutes, use thighs.

TIPS & TRICKS: COOKING CHICKEN

- *FOR PAN-FRYING and CHAR-GRILLING: To make boneless skinless breasts cook faster, and to help tenderize them, cut horizontally in half through the thickness of the meat, cover with cling film and pound with a meat mallet or rolling pin until thin. Pounded halves will cook in 5–6 minutes, turning once.*
- *FOR GRILLING: To keep meat moist, keep the skin on during cooking (the fat underneath will melt and baste the meat). Rub the skin with melted butter or oil, dried herbs or spices and seasoning, or make three diagonal slashes in the skin on each breast and insert flavoured butter or herbs. If the fat content concerns you, remove the skin before serving.*
- *FOR ROASTING: Do the same as for grilling (above), or wrap skinless breasts in thin slices of Parma ham or bacon, tucking herbs such as sage, tarragon or basil in between. For breasts with skin, push flavoured butter or soft cheese between the skin and the flesh.*

CUTTING THE FAT

- *Chicken breast meat with the skin on contains 12 g fat per 100 g.*
- *Skinned chicken breast meat contains 2 g fat per 100 g.*

Drumsticks

CHOOSE

- Drumsticks are the bottom end of the leg, with the bone in, covered with skin.
- Allow 2 per person.
- Drumsticks have dark meat, which is more succulent than white meat (breast) because it contains more fat.

PREPARE

- Chop off the bottom joint, to neaten the knuckle.
- Make several slashes through the skin, deep into the flesh.
- Marinate to make more succulent and tasty, if you have the time (at least 4 hours or overnight).
- Rub with oil, then with dried herbs and/or spices and seasoning.

COOK

- Grill or barbecue for 25–30 minutes, turning a few times. Or roast at 190°C/375°F/Gas Mark 5 (170°C/340°F in fan ovens) for 35 minutes, turning two or three times. Eat with your hands, wrapping the knuckle end in a napkin or foil.

Quarters/joints

CHOOSE

- These may be the leg quarter (the thigh and drumstick) or the wing quarter (the wing with part of the breast attached). The skin is always intact.
- Allow 1 per person.
- Legs are all dark meat, while wings have some white breast meat, so check what you are buying, especially if they are sold in packs rather than as individual joints.

PREPARE

- To reduce fat content, pull the skin away from the flesh with your hands.
- Slash and marinate for 4–24 hours, for extra flavour and succulence.

COOK

- Rub with oil and seasonings and barbecue or roast at 190°C/375°F/Gas Mark 5 (170°C/340°F in fan ovens) for 40 minutes, turning two or three times.
- Season and brown in hot oil before using in casseroles and stews.

Thighs

CHOOSE

- There are three types – on the bone with skin, boneless and skinless, and boneless skinless 'mini' fillets.
- Allow 2 thighs or 4 fillets per person.
- The dark meat of thighs is more succulent and tastier than breast, and more tender than drumstick.

drumsticks–**w**ings

PREPARE

- Pull off skin if necessary, and trim off visible fat.
- Slash and marinate for 4–24 hours for extra flavour and succulence.
- Boneless thighs can be stuffed.

COOK

- Brown in hot oil, then use in curries and casseroles. Whole thighs take 40–60 minutes, fillets 25–30 minutes.
- Barbecue boneless, skinless meat on skewers for 25–30 minutes, turning often.
- Roast stuffed thighs for 40 minutes at 190°C/375°F/Gas Mark 5 (170°C/340°F in fan ovens).

Wings

CHOOSE

- These are the bony wing joints that are sold in packs or loose. The meat is tasty and dark, with crisp skin.
- Allow 4 per person.

PREPARE

- Marinate for 4–24 hours, for extra flavour and succulence.

COOK

- Barbecue or roast for 40 minutes at 190°C/375°F/Gas Mark 5 (170°C/340°F in fan ovens). Best eaten with your hands.

CHICKEN STOCK

Makes about 1.5 litres (2½ pints)

*about 700 g (1½ lb) chicken bones
  and carcass*
*chicken giblets, without the liver
  (optional)*
*150 g (5 oz) mixed onion, celery
  and carrot, roughly chopped*
1 bouquet garni
6 peppercorns

Blanch the chicken bones, carcass and giblets in boiling water for 2 minutes, drain and rinse. Place in a pan with the remaining ingredients and cover generously with water. Bring to the boil, then simmer for 2–3 hours, skimming often and topping up with water as necessary. Strain the stock and leave to cool, then refrigerate for up to 3 days or freeze for up to 3 months.

CHICKEN LIVERS

*These are sold in tubs, often frozen. They are rich in iron and vitamin A and have a very mild flavour.
Use in pâtés and terrines, or pan-fry in oil and/or butter with herbs and seasonings for 5–7 minutes and toss with green leaves and fresh herbs for a warm salad.*

DUCK

Weight for weight, there is less meat on duck than on chicken or turkey. This is because duck has a higher bone-to-meat ratio, and more fat underneath the skin. On the plus side, duck meat is rich and tasty, so portion size can be smaller.

Whole birds

■ Ducks and ducklings weigh from 1.75 to 3 kg (3½ to 7 lb). Duckling is a bird under 6 months old. Roasting is the best cooking method for a whole bird, and you should allow 700 g (1½ lb) raw weight per serving.
■ A duck or duckling weighing 1.75–2 kg (3½–4 lb) will serve 2 people, a 2.5–3 kg (5–7 lb) bird will serve 4 people.

ROASTING A WHOLE DUCK

■ Take out of the fridge and bring to room temperature for 1 hour.
■ Cut away all visible fat from inside and around the body cavity and neck.
■ Stuff the neck end if you like, and secure in place with a skewer. A sharp-flavoured, citrussy stuffing will counteract fattiness and help the meat go further.
■ Preheat the oven to 200ºC/400ºF/ Gas Mark 6 (180ºC/350ºF in fan

ovens) before you put the duck in. A hot oven from the start will help crisp the skin.
■ Just before roasting, prick the skin all over with a fork and rub liberally with salt – this will allow the fat to run out and make the skin crisp.
■ Sit the duck breast-side down on a rack in the roasting tin. This will help the fat drain off quickly, and keep the duck out of the fat that melts off.
■ Roast for 25 minutes, then pour off the melted fat from the bottom of the tin and turn the bird breast-side up. Roast for another 20 minutes.
■ Pour off the fat again, baste the duck, and reduce the oven temperature to 180ºC/350ºF/Gas Mark 4 (160ºC/325ºF in fan ovens).
■ Continue roasting for 1½ hours for a duck weighing 1.75–2 kg (3½–4 lb), or for 2 hours for a duck weighing 2.5–3 kg (5–7 lb).
■ Pour off the duck fat from the bottom of the tin several times during the final roasting time, to prevent smoking and help keep the skin crisp.

SERVING After roasting, lift the duck on to a carving board and leave it to rest for 15–20 minutes. Don't try to carve a duck – it is far easier to joint it.
■ For 2 people: cut the duck in half lengthways, then cut each half diago-

nally across the breast so that each person has a leg and a wing portion with breast meat attached.

■ For 4 people: cut off the legs, then cut away the breast meat in two pieces, one on either side of the breastbone. Slice the breast meat on the diagonal. Serve each person some breast meat together with either a leg or a wing.

Breasts

Without the skin and fat, duck breast meat is quite lean, containing 6% fat. Marinating before cooking will help make it moist and juicy, so too will not overcooking it – duck breast is best served pink.

CHOOSE

■ Boneless breasts with the skin on are sold individually. The French *magrets* are excellent for flavour, and are often sold in vacuum packs for long keeping.

■ The average-sized duck breast weighs 125–175 g (4–6 oz), and is a generous portion for one person. Larger duck breasts can serve 2 people, depending on appetite and other ingredients cooked with them. For a stir-fry to serve 4, you will need only 2 duck breasts.

■ The meat is richly flavoured, so a little goes a long way.

GOOD FOR YOU
Duck meat contains more B12 vitamins than chicken, and almost as much iron as beef.

■ *Eaten together, cooked duck meat, fat and skin contain 29% fat, but you can reduce this considerably if you remove the fat and skin before cooking.*

■ *If you cook duck with the skin on, drain it well before serving and pour the fat off into a small container. It will keep for up to a month in the fridge, and is excellent for frying and roasting, especially for potatoes and parsnips.*

FLAVOURS TO GO WITH DUCK
Many Chinese and Thai recipes use duck with spices and sweet-and-sour flavours, while in European cooking duck is often cooked with fruits to offset its richness. The following fruits go especially well with duck:

■ *BLUEBERRIES*

■ *CHERRIES*

■ *CRANBERRIES*

■ *ORANGES*

■ *RASPBERRIES*

PREPARE

- Leave breasts whole for pan-frying, grilling or roasting. If the skin is left on, score it through to the fat in a diamond pattern.
- For sautéing or stir-frying, remove skin and fat and cut meat into strips, working diagonally against the grain.

COOK

- Season and dry-fry or chargrill whole breasts skin-side down for 3 minutes, pressing hard with a fish slice or spatula to keep the breast flat and squeeze out the fat. Turn the breast over and cook for another 3–4 minutes.
- Season and grill whole breasts skin-side up for 3 minutes, turn over and grill for another 3–4 minutes.
- Roast seasoned whole breasts in a preheated oven at 200°C/400°F/Gas Mark 6 (180°C/350°F in fan ovens) for 30 minutes.
- Leave whole breasts to rest for 10 minutes before serving.
- Sauté or stir-fry strips for 5–7 minutes.

Legs

CHOOSE

- Duck leg portions are sold singly on the bone, with the skin on.
- Allow 1 leg per person.
- Dark meat needs long cooking to make it tender.

PREPARE

- Prick the skin all over with a fork.

COOK

- Dry-fry until the fat runs and the skin is browned. Drain and use in casseroles and stews with vegetables and liquid. The cooking time is 1–1¼ hours at 180°C/350°F/Gas Mark 4 (160°C/325°F in fan ovens).

Smoked duck breast

- Cured and oak-smoked duck breast is sold sliced and ready to eat in the deli chiller cabinet in supermarkets.
- The lean meat edged with fat is tender and full of flavour. The fat is easy to remove before serving.
- Use slices for antipasti platters or sandwiches, or snip into salads.

Confit

Duck legs that have been cooked and preserved in their own fat are called *confit de canard*. You can make confit yourself, or buy it in cans and jars at supermarkets and delis.

- All it needs is reheating, and the quality is excellent – juicy, tender leg meat on the bone. Serve with potatoes or French bread, or add to cassoulet.

breasts–confit

GOOSE

Rarely available other than at Christmas time, goose is a real treat and a welcome change from turkey for the festive meal, especially if you are hosting a small gathering. The meat is rich, tasty and succulent, but the bird is fattier and bonier than turkey, so weight for weight it will not feed as many people.

CHOOSE Go for a free-range, traditionally reared bird from a reputable farm (there are many to choose from by mail order and on the web), or order from your farmers' market or butcher. Some good supermarkets and food halls also sell geese, so check availability with these too, in plenty of time for Christmas – geese are in limited supply from Michaelmas (29 September) until New Year.
■ For 6–8 people, the ideal weight is 4.5 kg (10 lb). This size will have the best meat-to-bone ratio.

PREPARE Take the goose out of its wrapping and remove the giblets, keeping all trussing strings intact as they will keep the goose in shape while cooking.
■ Store the giblets in a covered bowl in the fridge until you are ready to use

them for stock or gravy (they will keep for 24 hours).

■ The liver comes as part of the giblets, but it should not be used for making stock or gravy because it may make them taste bitter. Separate it and either fry it on its own as you would chicken livers, or use in the stuffing for the goose.

■ If there is any white fat with the giblets, save this separately (see opposite).

■ Put the goose on a tray, cover loosely with foil and keep at the bottom of the fridge (or in a cool place at no more than 13°C/56°F) until 1 hour before you are ready to roast. It will keep for 2 days.

ROAST This tasty bird can be roasted just as it is, but a fruity stuffing suits it well because it cuts the richness of the meat and helps it go further. There are plenty of ready-made fresh stuffings available at Christmas time – those with dried apricots or prunes and fresh apples flavoured with orange or lemon go especially well with goose.

■ Bring the goose to room temperature for 1 hour before roasting, during which time you can wipe inside the body cavity with kitchen paper and push the stuffing inside (you can do this with the legs still tied).

■ Weigh the bird after stuffing. The timing given below is for a 4.5 kg (10 lb) bird with stuffing in the cavity. If your bird is a different weight from this, allow 15 minutes per 500 g (1 lb), plus 30 minutes.

■ Preheat the oven to 190°C/375°F/ Gas Mark 5 (170°C/340°F in fan ovens).

■ Prick all over the breast with a fork and sprinkle with coarse sea salt.

■ Put the goose on a rack in a roasting tin and cover with a large, loose tent of foil, scrunching and tucking it tightly around the edges of the tin.

■ Roast for 1½ hours.

■ Carefully take the tin out of the oven and slowly pour off the fat. Use some to baste the goose, then cover with foil again and return to the oven for another hour.

■ Repeat the draining and basting with the fat and put the tin back in the oven for another 30 minutes, with the breast uncovered so the skin becomes crisp and golden.

■ Remove the goose from the rack and hold it with the legs facing downwards so that the fat drains off.

■ Leave the goose to rest, covered loosely with fresh foil, for 30 minutes before serving.

SERVE Carving is best done in the kitchen, but you may like to show off

roasting–fat

the whole bird on a platter first.

■ Cut the breasts away from either side of the breast bone and set aside.

■ Cut off the legs. Holding them one at a time by the knuckle end, thinly slice off the meat down to the bone.

■ Cut off the wings.

■ Remove the oyster fillets from the underside where the legs meet the body.

■ Carve the breast on the diagonal and serve alongside the other meat.

WHAT TO DO WITH THE FAT

There is a lot of fat on a goose. Although it is predominantly the mono-unsaturated kind, at least one-third is saturated fat, so it is best not to eat too much of it. On the plus side, goose fat is a good source of niacin and vitamin B6.

■ Before stuffing and roasting the bird, cut away any excess fat you find inside, particularly around the openings, and add to any white fat that was supplied with the giblets. This can then be rendered (melted very slowly) in a pan over a low heat, strained through muslin into a bowl or jar and kept in the fridge or freezer for up to 6 months. Use it for roasting and frying at high temperatures (it has a high smoke point), or for sealing the tops of pâtés and terrines.

■ Don't throw away the fat that is produced during roasting. It will not be as pure as the rendered white fat, but it is still excellent for frying and roasting, especially for potatoes, and it will keep in the fridge for up to a month.

■ If you like goose fat, you can buy it in jars and cans, and in chilled packs, at most good supermarkets and delis. A lot of goose fat is imported from France – look for *graisse d'oie* on the label.

Foie gras

■ This is the liver of ducks or geese that has been artificially fattened by force feeding the bird – *foie gras* means 'fatty liver'. Its texture is melt-in-the-mouth soft, and its flavour mild and delicate, unlike any other liver.

■ In France, pan-fried thin slices of foie gras are a delicacy, eaten hot at the start of a meal, and accompanied by Monbazillac or Sauternes wine, or a sweet Sauternes jelly. The raw liver is also used chopped in stuffings, and to enrich classic sauces.

■ You can buy foie gras at good delis and food halls, and over the web – a lot comes from south-west France. It is very pricey. Look for *foie gras de canard* (duck) and *foie gras d'oie* (goose).

■ For the ultimate luxury burger, add a little chopped raw foie gras to minced beef. It may seem extravagant, but it will melt into the meat during cooking to give a juicy result.

TURKEY

Available all year round in many different forms other than the festive bird at Christmas and Easter, turkey is an inexpensive, healthy choice for everyday meals. It is slightly lower in fat than chicken, has all the other nutritional attributes (see Good for You, page 363), and is just as versatile, quick and easy to cook.

Whole birds
CHOOSE

■ From October until Christmas, fresh and frozen birds start coming into the shops, then they appear again at other bank holiday times, especially at Easter.

DEFROSTING A FROZEN TURKEY

■ Whole birds must be completely defrosted before cooking or they will not cook through. Defrosting takes longer than you think, especially for large birds, so it is important to allow plenty of time, calculating backwards from the time you are planning to put the bird in the oven.

■ Once the turkey is thoroughly defrosted, it can be kept in the fridge for up to 2 days before cooking, so it is always best to start defrosting earlier than necessary, to be sure

foie gras–**w**hole birds

that the bird is completely defrosted.

- Remove all wrappings, place the turkey on a tray or a large, deep plate and cover loosely with foil.
- Leave to defrost in a cool place – no warmer than 13°C (56°F).
- Remove any giblets once loose.
- Check there are no ice crystals in the cavity before cooking, and pat dry inside and out with kitchen paper.

MINIMUM DEFROSTING TIMES

If your bird is a different weight from the ones listed here, calculate the defrosting time by allowing 1 hour 48 minutes per 500 g (1 lb). Put the bird in the fridge immediately after defrosting if you are not going to cook it straight away.

2.5 kg (5 lb)	10 hours
3.6 kg (8 lb)	16 hours
4.5–5.6 kg (10–12 lb)	21 hours
6.75 kg (15 lb)	30 hours
9 kg (20 lb)	39 hours

ROAST

- Take out of the fridge and bring to room temperature for 1 hour.
- Put any stuffing in the neck end.
- Secure the neck skin (and any stuffing) with the wing tips and a skewer.
- Season inside the body cavity and push in a few orange and/or lemon

SHORT OF TIME TO DEFROST THE TURKEY?

All is not lost – there is a short cut. It is perfectly safe to use the following defrosting method, as long as you stick to the guidelines.

- *Calculate the defrosting time at 44 minutes per 500 g (1 lb).*
- *Unwrap the frozen bird and immerse in cold water. Leave in a cool place (no more than 13°C/ 56°F) for the calculated time, changing the water regularly.*
- *At the end of the time, check inside the body cavity that no ice crystals remain. If there are still some there, hold the bird under the cold tap and rinse it thoroughly, letting the water run through the bird, then immerse in fresh cold water again until all the ice crystals have gone.*
- *Drain and dry thoroughly, inside and out, before cooking.*

WHAT SIZE TURKEY?

These quantities are generous, allowing for plenty of leftovers.

2.5 kg (5 lb)	serves 4–6
3.6 kg (8 lb)	serves 6–8
4.5–5.6 kg (10–12 lb)	serves 8–10
6.75 kg (15 lb)	serves 10–12
9 kg (20 lb)	serves 12–15

quarters and sprigs of herbs (thyme, parsley and bay are good).

■ Tie the legs with string.

■ Weigh the bird (you may need to use your bathroom scales) and work out the cooking time, allowing 18 minutes per 500 g (1 lb). Calculate the time you need to put it in the oven by working backwards from the time you want to serve the bird, building in extra time for preheating the oven and the resting time at the end.

■ Preheat the oven to 190°C/375°/ Gas Mark 5 (170°C/340°F in fan ovens).

■ Sit the bird on a rack in a roasting tin (or on a bed of quartered red onions that will give flavour to both the turkey and the gravy).

■ Massage plenty of softened butter or olive oil all over the breast and legs.

■ Season well and cover loosely with foil.

■ Roast for the calculated time, basting the bird with the tin juices every 30 minutes and removing the foil for the last 30 minutes to brown the breast.

■ When the turkey is done (see Is it Cooked?, page 367), transfer it to a carving board, cover with a loose tent of foil and leave to rest in a warm place for 30 minutes. This allows plenty of time to make the gravy with the tin juices (see page 365), finish off any roast vegetables and cook other vegetables. To carve, see opposite.

■ Roast turkey can be kept, covered, in the fridge for up to 3 days.

Breast joints

Oven-ready breast joints (on the bone and boned and rolled) are available all year round, and come in many different shapes and sizes. They are a convenient and quick alternative to a whole turkey, especially if you are catering for a small number of people, or if you aren't used to carving a whole bird. The quality of these joints is generally high, and the meat is usually succulent, but read the label carefully – not only for accurate cooking instructions but also for the ingredients. Some butter-basted turkeys and joints contain unhealthy hydrogenated oil.

Crown joint is the most popular turkey joint, and is simply the bird without its legs and wings. Legs take longer to cook than breast, which is why the breast is often overcooked and dry on a whole bird. This problem is solved with a crown, and since most people prefer white meat to dark, there is less waste.

CHOOSE

■ Crowns weigh between 3.5 and 4.5 kg (5 to 10lb), and provide 4–10 portions.

whole birds–breast

PREPARE As for a whole turkey (see page 378).

COOK As for a whole turkey (see page 380), allowing the same roasting time – 18 minutes per 450 g (1 lb).

Breast steaks
CHOOSE
- Skinless, boneless slices of breast, 2.5–4 cm (1–1½ in) thick.
- Allow 1 slice per person.
- Lean, tender, white meat.

PREPARE
- Use whole, or in cubes or strips.
- Marinate if time allows, to increase succulence and flavour (see page 383). A minimum of 4 hours is required to have an effect, although overnight marinating is best.

COOK
- Season the slices, then pan-fry them in hot oil (or a combination of oil and butter), or brush with melted butter or oil and then grill them. The cooking time for pan-frying or grilling is 6–8 minutes, turning once, halfway through cooking.
- Barbecue whole slices, or cubes or strips on skewers. The cooking time is 20 minutes for whole slices, 10 minutes for cubes or strips.

HOW TO CARVE A TURKEY

You need a very sharp knife for slicing, and a carving fork to steady the bird on the board.

- *Cut off the legs. Stand each leg on the board with the knuckle end facing up and cut between the thigh and the drumstick.*
- *Holding the knuckle end of each drumstick, slice downwards to remove the meat until you reach the bone, working all the way round. Slice the thigh meat.*
- *Cut off the wings, then cut them in two at the joint.*
- *Slice the breast meat neatly on either side of the breastbone, using the fork to steady the bird underneath.*

- Use cubes in sautés, casseroles and curries, strips in sautés, stir-fries and fajitas. The cooking time is 5–6 minutes.

Cubes
CHOOSE

- Boneless thigh or breast meat is sold ready-cubed.
- Allow 125–175 g (4–6 oz) per person.
- Dark thigh meat is more succulent than breast, but it contains more fat and takes longer to cook.

PREPARE

- Use straight from the packet, or marinate first (see opposite) for 4–24 hours.

COOK

- Brown in hot oil before using in casseroles, stews and pies.
- Or thread on skewers and grill or barbecue. Cooking time is 15 minutes for thigh meat, 10 minutes for breast.
- Use cubes of turkey breast in stir-fries and fajitas – they will cook in 7–10 minutes.

Drumsticks
CHOOSE

- This is the bottom joint of the leg, the same as a chicken drumstick only much larger.
- The cheapest cut, but not always available all year round.
- Each drumstick weighs about 625 g (1¼ lb) and will serve 2 people.
- Dark meat is more succulent than breast, though higher in fat.

PREPARE

- Slash and marinate (see opposite) for 4–24 hours, for extra flavour and succulence.

COOK

- Brush with oil or marinade, season and roast; or braise with vegetables and liquid. The cooking time is 1¼ hours at 190°C/375°F/Gas Mark 5 (170°C/340°F in fan ovens), turning once half-way through cooking.

breast–minced

Escalopes

CHOOSE

- Very thin slices of breast meat (sometimes called quick-cook steaks), also sold as strips.
- Allow 1 escalope, or 125–175 g (4–6 oz) per person.
- Lean and tender white meat.

PREPARE

- Use straight from the packet.

COOK

- Pan-fry in hot oil and/or butter for 3–4 minutes each side
- Sauté or stir-fry strips for about 5 minutes.
- Good with Mexican spices in fajitas.

Minced turkey

- Low-fat, as long as it is 100% lean breast meat without skin and fat.
- Use as a substitute for minced beef, veal, pork or lamb (see page 356) or mix half-and-half with one of these to lower the fat content.

TIPS & TRICKS:
TURKEY MARINADES

Turkey pieces are low in fat, but they can be bland and dry, especially the white breast meat. Marinating before cooking is one of the best ways to inject flavour and moisture.

- *A good marinade base is 3 parts olive or sunflower oil to 1 part lemon, lime or orange juice, wine or balsamic vinegar.*
- *To the base, add fiery ingredients like chilli, ginger, pepper, paprika and mustard seeds – they will quickly pep up any blandness, so too will pungent Indian spices such as cumin, coriander and cardamom, perfumed Moroccan spices like cloves and cinnamon, and spice blends such as Chinese five spice.*
- *Mexican flavours go especially well with turkey, as in the famous mole made with onions, garlic cloves, tomatoes, chillies and chocolate.*
- *Mix the marinade and meat until the meat is well coated and keep in a covered glass or ceramic bowl in the fridge. The marinating time should be at least 4 hours for the marinade to have a good effect; overnight or 24-hour marinating is ideal, and often more convenient.*

GAME

READY-TO-COOK GAME IS AVAILABLE FRESH IN SEASON
AND FROZEN ALL YEAR ROUND AT MANY SUPERMARKETS,
BUTCHERS, FARM SHOPS AND FARMERS' MARKETS, AS
WELL AS BY MAIL ORDER AND ON THE WEB. GENUINE
GAME IS HUNTED IN THE WILD FOR SPORT AND IS AVAILABLE
ONLY IN THE SHOOTING SEASON, BUT MANY BIRDS AND
ANIMALS ARE BRED FOR THE TABLE AND SOMETIMES
RELEASED 'INTO THE WILD' FOR THE SEASON.

STORAGE

Game is traditionally matured or
'hung' for several days before selling,
although young farmed game is often
eaten fresh. Check with your supplier,
as this will affect the storage time.

■ Keep game wrapped in the fridge
until about 1 hour before cooking.

■ Immersing joints and pieces of game
in a marinade (see opposite) will preserve the meat, tenderize it and give
it flavour. Store for 2–3 days in a
covered container in the fridge, or
up to 6 months in the freezer.

GAME A–Z

Grouse

Available from 12 August (the
Glorious Twelfth) to 10 December,
grouse is a small bird with dark red
meat and a pronounced gamey flavour.

CHOOSE Available only as whole
birds. Allow 1 bird per person.

PREPARE

■ Remove the wishbone (see page
366), and cut the legs and wings at
the second joint to neaten them.

■ Wipe the bird with kitchen paper
inside and out.

■ Season inside, and insert slices of
orange, lemon or apple and a few
sprigs of fresh sage and/or thyme.

■ Tie the legs together with string.

■ Season the bird all over and brush
liberally with softened butter or oil.

■ To prevent the breast meat drying
out, cover with streaky bacon,
pancetta, Parma ham or vine leaves.

COOK Roast at 190°C/375°F/Gas
Mark 5 (170°C/340°F in fan ovens)
for 30 minutes. Leave to rest for
10–15 minutes.

Guinea fowl

Originally wild game birds, most guinea fowl are now farm-reared all year round, and are classed as poultry. The meat has more flavour than chicken, which it most resembles (some say it tastes like pheasant), and is slightly darker. There is more leg meat than breast.

CHOOSE Available as whole birds, usually weighing about 1.2 kg (2½ lb), perfect for 2.

PREPARE
- As for chicken (see page 366).
- Guinea fowl is drier than chicken; covering it with streaky bacon or pancetta rashers before roasting helps moisten it.

COOK
- Roast at 190°C/375°F/Gas Mark 5 (170°C/340°F in fan ovens) for 15 minutes per 500 g (1 lb), plus 15 minutes. Rest for 10–15 minutes before carving.
- Serve carved like turkey (see page 381), or spatchcocked (see page 387) so that each person gets half a bird.

Hare

Larger than rabbit (see page 388) and with darker, stronger-tasting meat. It needs to be young (it's best from August to February) and well-hung to be tender.

GOOD FOR YOU
Lower in fat than most red meats, game is an excellent, healthy source of protein, vitamins and minerals. Because it is richly flavoured, portion sizes need not be large.

MARINATING
Game is lean, and can be dry. The best way to avoid this is to marinate the meat in the fridge for 2–3 days before cooking. The marinade should contain an acid such as lemon juice, wine or wine vinegar to help break down tough fibres, oil to moisten, and herbs and/or spices for flavour (see page 32).

AT-A-GLANCE SEASONS FOR GAME

Grouse	*Aug–Dec*
Guinea fowl	*All year round*
Hare	*Aug–Feb*
Partridge	*Sept–Jan*
Pheasant	*Oct–Jan*
Pigeon	*All year round*
Quail	*All year round*
Rabbit	*All year round*
Venison	*All year round*
Wild duck	*Sept–Jan*

CHOOSE

■ A dressed (skinned and cleaned) whole hare will serve 6–8 people, and is best bought jointed.

■ You can buy specific joints such as bone-in legs, and shoulders.

■ Saddle of hare is a prime cut, sold on the bone for roasting, or as fillets.

PREPARE

■ Marinate joints before cooking for up to 2 days, to make them more moist.

COOK

■ Sear joints, then braise with vegetables and liquid at 180°C/350°F/Gas Mark 4 (160°C/325°F in fan ovens) for 1½–2 hours. Traditional recipes thicken and enrich the gravy with the hare's blood.

■ Roast the saddle at 200°C/400°/Gas Mark 6 (180°C/350°F in fan ovens) for 30 minutes. Leave to rest for 10–15 minutes before carving.

■ Fillets are best pan-fried – allow 3–5 minutes per side.

Partridge

Available from 1 September to 1 February, this is paler, smaller and less gamey than pheasant. Redleg partridges weigh only 225–300 g (8–10 oz) – perfect for an individual serving.

CHOOSE

■ A whole bird serves 1 person.

■ Boneless partridge breasts can be bought in packs. Allow 2 per person.

PREPARE

■ Prepare whole birds for roasting as for grouse (see page 384), or spatchcock (see pages 46, 368 and opposite) for grilling or barbecuing, leaving the skin on.

■ Breasts are very lean – marinating for 4–24 hours before cooking will help prevent dryness.

■ Breasts can be skinned, although skin protects the meat and keeps it moist.

COOK

■ Roast whole birds at 190°C/375°/Gas Mark 5 (170°C/340°F in fan ovens) for 25–30 minutes. Leave to rest for 10–15 minutes before serving.

■ Brush spatchcocked birds with butter or oil, season, and grill or barbecue for 15 minutes, turning several times.

■ Pan-fry breasts in hot oil and butter for 5–7 minutes, turning once.

Pheasant

In season from 1 October to 1 February, this is the largest and the most widely available game bird. Traditionally sold in pairs (a cock and a hen) called a 'brace', but can be bought individually.

hare–pheasant

CHOOSE

- A whole bird serves 2 people.
- Boned and tied birds called 'pheasant cushions' are available at some specialist butchers – they look good and are easy to carve with no waste.
- Boneless breasts can be bought in packs. Allow 1–2 breasts per person.
- Bone-in thighs and whole legs are available. Allow 2 pieces per person.

PREPARE

- Prepare young whole birds for roasting as for grouse (see page 384). If you don't know the bird's age, pot roast it or the meat may be dry and tough. You can pot roast it whole or jointed.
- Breasts, thighs and legs benefit from being marinated for 4–24 hours before cooking to prevent dryness.
- Breasts are best cooked with skin on, to protect the meat and keep it moist. It can be removed before serving.

COOK

- Roast whole young birds as for grouse at 190°C/375°F/Gas Mark 5 (170°C/340°F in fan ovens), but for 40–50 minutes. Leave to rest for 10–15 minutes before serving.
- Brown whole birds and pot roast with red wine and vegetables. For 4 people, allow 2 birds, and cook, covered, at 160°C/325°F/Gas Mark 3 (140°C/275°F in fan ovens) for 1¼–1½ hours.

A ONE-OFF: KANGAROO

Kangaroo is available by mail order and on the web. It is a lean, low-fat red meat that can taste quite gamey if it has come from a mature animal.

- *Cuts from virtually the whole animal are available, and you can use them in any recipe for chicken or rabbit.*
- *Don't overcook or the meat will be dry.*

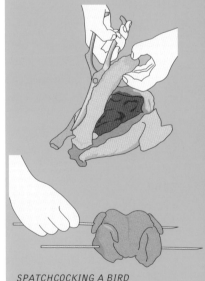

SPATCHCOCKING A BIRD
Cut out the backbone (top), then flatten the bird and push two skewers through the wings and legs (above). The skewers will keep the bird flat when cooking, and make it easy to handle.

- Pan-fry breasts in hot oil and butter for about 7 minutes, turning once.
- Thighs and legs are good casseroled – cook for 40 minutes. They can also be barbecued (most successful after marinating). Cook for about 30 minutes.

Pigeon

Most oven-ready pigeons are bred for the table and are available all year round. Rarer wild wood pigeons are at their best from May to September.

CHOOSE

- A whole bird is enough for 1 person.
- Boneless pigeon breasts are sold in packs, or slice them off the whole bird yourself. Allow 2 breasts per person.

PREPARE
As for pheasant (see page 387).

COOK

- Pot roasting is best for whole birds. Follow the instructions for pheasant (see page 387), allowing 45–60 minutes.
- Pan-fry breasts as for pheasant (see above), for 4–6 minutes.

Quail

This tiny bird is bred for eating, and is available all year. It tastes delicate and is best bought boned and stuffed.

CHOOSE As a whole bird – you will need 2 each. A stuffed boned bird will serve 1.

PREPARE Wipe and season inside and out. Tie the legs and wrap the whole bird in streaky bacon, pancetta or vine leaves.

COOK Roast at 180°C/350°F/Gas Mark 4 (160°C/325°F in fan ovens) for 20 minutes. Rest for 10 minutes.

Rabbit

Farmed rabbit is pale in colour and tastes like chicken; wild rabbit is darker, tastier and a bit tougher. Both are available all year round.

CHOOSE

- A dressed (skinned and cleaned) whole rabbit will serve 3–4 people if it is stuffed.
- Joints – you can buy a whole jointed rabbit, or specific joints such as bone-in legs, shoulders and saddle.
- Boneless rabbit meat is sold by weight, cubed ready for cooking.

PREPARE

- Soak wild rabbits in lightly salted or acidulated water for 2–3 hours to whiten the flesh and reduce strong flavours, then drain, rinse and pat dry.

■ A lean, dry meat, rabbit benefits from being marinated for 4–24 hours.

COOK

■ Whole rabbit can be roasted, but it needs to be boned, stuffed and barded (covered with strips of fat) – best left to the professional cook.

■ Braising is the best option for cooking rabbit at home. Sear bone-in joints on all sides, then braise with vegetables and liquid on the hob or in the oven at 180°C/350°F/Gas Mark 4 (160°C/325°F in fan ovens) for 1¼–1½ hours.

■ Boneless diced rabbit is good in casseroles and stews – it takes 50–60 minutes when cooked over a gentle heat, or in the oven at 160°C/320°F/Gas Mark 3 (140°C/275°F in fan ovens). Also good in pâtés, terrines and pies.

Venison

Farmed venison is available all year round, and offers flavour and tenderness. Wild venison is seasonal and its quality variable. The animal's age, and whether the carcass has been matured, will affect its quality.

CHOOSE

■ Red deer are most common; fallow and roe deer give smaller cuts. Allow 225–375 g (8–12 oz) meat on the bone,

ROASTING A JOINT OF VENISON

For perfectly cooked, juicy roast venison, undercook it and then let it rest in a warm place to finish cooking. Sear the joint in hot oil, then roast at 220°C/425°F/Gas Mark 7 (200°C/400°F in fan ovens) for 10 minutes per 500 g (1 lb). Use a meat thermometer for best results, as follows:

■ For rare venison, remove the meat from the oven when the internal temperature is 35–50°C (95–122°F) and let it rest until it has risen to 60°C (140°F).

■ For medium venison, remove it when the internal temperature is 50–55°C (122–130°F) and let it rest until it has risen to 65°C (150°F).

LEAN & LOW-FAT

■ Venison is very rich in iron and has less fat than other red meats.

■ Venison mince is really lean; use it to replace beef in sauces and for children's meals. It makes tasty burgers and sausages, too, but check the label as pork and beef fat may be added.

GAME A–Z

or 175 g (6 oz) boneless per person.

■ For roasting, use saddle (bone-in), loin (boneless saddle), haunch (back leg, on the bone or boned and rolled), whole fillet, or shoulder (boned and rolled from young venison).

■ For pan-frying, grilling or barbecuing – haunch steaks: topside and silverside, 125–300 g (4–10 oz) each; loin steaks: medallions, 60–150 g (2–5 oz); filet mignon 225–500 g (8 oz–1 lb); shoulder steaks 150 g (5 oz) max; stroganoff/stir-fry strips (from any of the above); sliced liver.

■ For pot-roasting and braising – shoulder (on the bone/boned and rolled); shank (foreleg); haunch (on the bone/boned and rolled).

■ For casseroling and stewing – diced boneless shoulder; diced shin; osso buco (shin with marrow bone).

PREPARE

■ Cuts are sold ready for cooking.

COOK

Venison is lean, with no marbling of fat, so needs careful cooking. Serve roasts and steaks rare or pink – overcooked venison is dry and tough. Cooking times depend on thickness rather than weight; use the following as a guide.

■ To roast a joint of venison, see page 389.

■ To pan-fry, grill or barbecue, sear

steaks quickly in hot oil/butter, then cook for 1 minute on each side. Leave to rest for a few minutes before serving.

■ Sauté or stir-fry stroganoff strips.

■ Shanks can be pot roasted, as lamb.

■ Diced shoulder can be used in stews.

■ Liver is tender and sweet, excellent sautéed, and good in pâtés and terrines.

Wild duck

Most wild duck is mallard, although sometimes widgeon and teal are available in the autumn and winter months.

CHOOSE

■ Whole duck – most will serve 2, although smaller teal will serve only 1.

■ Boneless breasts – 1–2 per person.

PREPARE

■ Whole ducks are oven-ready.

■ Breasts can be dry, and benefit from marinating for 4–24 hours.

COOK

■ Roast whole birds at 200°C/400°F/ Gas Mark 6 (180°C/350°F in fan ovens) for 40–45 minutes. Leave to rest for 10–15 minutes before serving.

■ Pan-fry breasts for 3–4 minutes on each side.

Fish and Shellfish

FISH

SUPERMARKETS WITH FISH COUNTERS AND INDEPENDENT FISH-MONGERS SELL A WIDE VARIETY OF FRESH AND FROZEN FISH ALL YEAR ROUND. MAIL ORDER AND WEB-BASED COMPANIES ALSO OFFER AN INCREASINGLY LARGE SELECTION OF DIFFERENT FISH – FRESHNESS AND QUALITY ARE HIGH, AND YOU WILL OFTEN FIND MORE CHOICE THAN IN THE SHOPS. THERE IS ALSO THE ADDED ADVANTAGE OF HAVING IT DELIVERED DIRECT TO YOUR DOOR.

CHOOSE

When buying fish, it is important to know where it has come from, and how it was caught. Over-fishing and the resulting decline in fish stocks are major issues, as are badly managed fisheries and fish farms, and irresponsible fishing methods. Read labels carefully and look for suppliers who support sustainable fishing and environmentally responsible methods, and who source their fish from well-managed stocks. For up-to-date information and advice on choosing fish, visit the Marine Conservation Society's website, www.fishonline.org.

What to look for

All fish should have a clean, fresh smell of the sea and seaweed (or river weed in the case of freshwater fish). A strong fishy smell is a sign of staleness. These are the other pointers for optimum freshness and quality:

Whole fish
- Clear, bright eyes that are slightly bulging.
- Gills that are red or rosy pink.
- Shiny, moist and slippery skin with no missing scales.
- Firm-looking body and stiff tail.

Fillets and steaks
- Firm, springy translucent flesh with no discoloration.
- Neat and trim, with no ragged edges.

Buying frozen fish

If fish is commercially frozen straight after it is caught, quality is usually good. Frozen fish is convenient too, and available all year. To be sure of the best quality when buying, check the following:
- Fish is frozen solid, with no sign of thawing.
- Packaging is undamaged.
- No sign of freezer burn (see page 26) or dark discoloration.

SAFE HANDLING

Fresh fish is highly perishable and should be handled quickly and carefully. Oily fish keep less well than white fish, and whole fish keep longer once they have been gutted.

- Always wash your hands, boards and utensils in hot, soapy water, both before and after handling fish.
- Don't prepare raw fish on the same board as cooked or preserved fish.
- Cool cooked leftovers quickly and refrigerate as soon as possible, for up to 24 hours only.

STORE

Fresh fish: Remove any packaging/wrappings and wipe the fish dry with kitchen paper, then lay it on a plate and cover with cling film. Place in the bottom of the fridge and store for no more than 24 hours.

Frozen fish: White fish will keep for up to 3 months. Oily and smoked fish, and cooked fish dishes will keep for up to 2 months.

GOOD FOR YOU

Nutritionists recommend eating fish and/or shellfish two to three times a week, including at least one portion of oily varieties like herring, mackerel, salmon and sardines.

- *All fish contain protein (they contain all of the essential amino acids that the body requires but can't make), but with less fat than meat. Protein is essential for good health and well-being.*
- *White fish is a good source of B vitamins, especially B12, essential for healthy growth.*
- *Oily fish is an excellent source of omega-3 fatty acids, which help lower cholesterol and prevent heart disease and strokes, and which play a large part in the healthy development of the brain (which is why fish is sometimes called brain food).*
- *All fish provide a healthy supply of minerals, especially phosphorus and calcium that are good for your bones and teeth – eating the bones of small fish like sardines and whitebait will give you an instant dose. Fish is also a good source of iodine (which controls thyroid hormones) and the antioxidant selenium (which guards against harmful free radicals).*

Freezing fish at home

Fish is delicate and best frozen commercially, but there are times when it is convenient and useful to freeze a small quantity at home.

■ Check with your supplier whether the fish is genuinely fresh, or whether it is thawed frozen fish (you will not be able to tell the difference just by looking at it).

■ If it has been frozen and thawed, don't refreeze it while it is raw, but you can refreeze it after it has been cooked and cooled – say in a soup, stew, lasagne or pie, or in fish cakes.

■ Fish can be frozen whole (gutted and cleaned) or as fillets or steaks.

■ First get the freezer as cold as possible by switching to 'fast freeze' or 'super freeze' according to manufacturer's instructions.

■ Freeze the fish in individual packages so you will be able to take out as few or as many portions as you need. Double wrap in cling film and foil, then pack in an airtight freezer bag.

■ Store in the freezer for up to 3 months (oily fish are best eaten within 2 months).

■ To thaw frozen fish, unwrap and place on a plate, then cover loosely with cling film or foil. Put in the bottom of the fridge and leave for at least 4 hours, or overnight, until no ice crystals remain (for more rapid defrosting, use the microwave). Before cooking, pat thoroughly dry with kitchen paper.

PREPARE

The fishmonger will scale, gut and clean fish for you. He will also fillet it, or cut it into steaks, if this is what you want, at no extra charge. This is better than buying ready-cut fillets or steaks because the fish will be fresher: it also leaves very little for you to do.

Whole round fish

Not everyone likes the look of a whole fish on their plate, so the neater and tidier it is the better. Prepare along the following guidelines, no matter which cooking method you choose.

Trim: Cut off the fins along the stomach and back with scissors, as close to the body as possible. To make the tail look more attractive, cut it into a V shape. This is called vandycking after the pointed shape of the painter Van Dyck's beard. Leave the head on for cooking, as it helps to keep the fish in good shape and gives it flavour, but cut it off before serving if you prefer, or cover the eyes with a garnish.

Scale: This is something the fishmonger should do, but it is useful to know how to do it yourself. Scaling is particularly necessary with mullet, sea bass and sea bream, as these are very scaly fish. Grasp the fish by the tail on a board and scrape a fish scaler or the back of a large knife blade from the tail to the head (see right).

Wash and dry: Hold the fish under cold running water and rinse well inside and out, rubbing off any scales. Pat dry with kitchen paper.

Score: This is optional, but it makes the fish cook more quickly and look more attractive, and if you are using a marinade, it will penetrate the fish faster. Make three or four diagonal slashes in each side of the fish, cutting right down to the bone, as shown on page 41 .

SCALING

Fillets and steaks

These are usually ready for cooking, but check the following just in case. It is best not to wash fillets and steaks before cooking as this can make them waterlogged. Simply pat them dry with kitchen paper.

Scale: Use the same technique as for whole round fish (see above), working from the narrow tail end to the head end with fillets, against the direction of the scales with steaks.

Skin: If you leave the skin on, it will hold the fish together during cooking, but many recipes call for skinless fillets. You can ask the fishmonger to remove the skin, but packaged fish from the supermarket is often sold with it on. To skin a fillet, lay it skin-side down on a board and dip your fingertips in salt to give you a good grip. Grasp the tail end or corner of the fillet with your salted fingers and insert the blade of a sharp knife between the skin and the flesh. Work the knife away from you, using a sawing action, until you reach the end of the fillet, gripping the tail end tightly as you go (see illustration opposite).

Remove pin bones: Run your fingers over the fleshy side of the fish to feel for any tiny bones sticking up. If you find any, pull them out with tweezers or your fingertips.

Trim: Cut into serving portions if necessary (it is easier to control the cooking time of small pieces of fish than one large fillet), and square off any untidy edges or fat so the fillets look as neat as possible.

Score: If fillets and steaks are to be cooked with their skin on, scoring helps them cook faster. It is very effective if the fish is thick and/or being marinated. Make two or three diagonal slashes in the skin, cutting deep into the flesh (see page 41).

COOK

There are many ways to cook fish, but they should all have two things in common – simplicity and speed. Fish is naturally tender and delicately flavoured, so almost without exception it needs the briefest of cooking and the minimum of fuss to be enjoyed at its best. This is good news when you are in a hurry.

How to tell when fish is cooked

Undercooking is better than overcooking (the exception to this is monkfish, which needs slightly longer than most other fish). Overcooked fish will be dry, and may be tough and chewy. Timings given with the following cooking methods are approximate – it is impossible to be exact, because much depends on the freshness and thickness of the fish, the type of pan and degree of heat used.

■ A whole fish is done when the eyes turn white and opaque.

■ Fillets and steaks are done when the flesh turns from translucent to opaque.

■ As an extra test, tease a section of the flesh apart with a fork. If cooked, it will separate easily into flakes (see page 24).

Bake

An oven method suitable for whole
fish, fillets and steaks, which are
wrapped in a parcel (*en papillote*,
see page 34) made of foil, greaseproof paper or baking parchment,
or vine, plantain or banana leaves.
Pastry also makes a good wrapping,
but it isn't as healthy as the others
because of its fat content. During
baking, fish cooks in its own juices
that moisten the flesh, so very little
extra fat is required. The parcel also
protects delicate fish from the heat,
and locks in the flavour of the ingredients that are baked with it. If
leaves are used, the dish becomes
scented with their perfume.

*REMOVING THE SKIN
FROM A FISH FILLET*

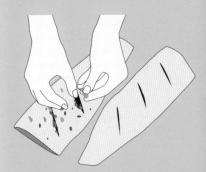

ADDING FLAVOUR TO FISH

Whole fish on the bone: Score
(see page 41), then brush with a
little olive oil and season lightly
inside and out. Push any flavourings,
such as lemon or lime slices, sprigs
of herbs, lemon grass, fresh ginger
slices, inside the body cavity and any
slashes (see above right). With whole
boned fish, the body cavity can be
filled with a stuffing.

**Fillets or steaks (with or without
skin):** Score (see page 41), and insert
flavouring ingredients as for whole
fish, above. Brush the fish with a little
olive oil and season lightly.

To cook: Lightly brush the inside of the wrapping with olive oil to prevent sticking, then sit the fish in the middle on a bed of herbs or vegetables for extra flavour. Wrap loosely, place on a baking tray and bake at 190°C/375°F/Gas Mark 5 (170°C/340°F in fan ovens). Large whole fish take 30–35 minutes, medium whole fish 20–25 minutes and small whole fish 15–20 minutes. Fillets and steaks take 10–15 minutes.

Barbecue

Hot and fast, barbecuing is one of the very best ways to cook fish, and is suitable for whole fish, fillets and steaks. Oily fish like sardines, mackerel and trout are especially good, as their natural oils make them self-basting. The most successful fillets and steaks are the thick, meaty kinds such as monkfish, tuna, swordfish and shark, as their firm flesh holds together well.

■ Marinating before barbecuing is beneficial, to add flavour and moistness (the fierce heat of the barbecue can make lean fish dry). Maximum marinating time should be 4 hours (see Marinades for Fish, page 417).

■ To prevent sticking, get the barbecue and grid really hot before cooking.

■ For easy lifting and turning, use a fish cage, or wrap the fish *en papillote* in foil (see Bake, page 397).

■ For cooking straight on the grid, fillets and steaks are best with their skin on, to help hold the flesh together, and they are also good cut into chunks and threaded on to oiled skewers.

■ If fish isn't marinated, brush with a little olive oil and season lightly just before cooking.

■ Don't overcook or the fish will be dry. Small whole fish take 5–7 minutes, medium whole fish 7–10 minutes, chunky fillets and steaks 7–10 minutes.

Braise

This is to cook fish in a covered dish in the oven – a cross between baking and steaming (see page 12). It is a good method for fish, whether whole, fillets or steaks.

■ Score any skin (see page 395).

■ Thin skinless fillets are best coiled round or folded over, to prevent drying out (see illustrations, opposite).

■ Put the fish in an ovenproof dish on a bed of thinly cut or shredded vegetables and either sprinkle with liquid or coat with a sauce.

■ Cover the dish with oiled or buttered foil or greaseproof paper and braise at 180°C/350°F/Gas Mark 4 (160°C/325°F in fan ovens).

■ Braising times are 20–30 minutes for whole fish, 10–15 minutes for fillets or steaks.

Chargrill/Griddle

A healthy, indoor-barbecue-style method, suitable for firm-fleshed fillets and steaks, especially salmon, thick cod loin, monkfish, red mullet, sea bass, shark, swordfish and tuna. The fish sits on the ridges of the chargrill/griddle pan (see page 54), above any fat, and becomes imprinted with charred lines.

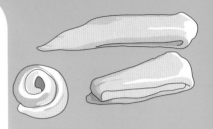

FOLD THIN SKINLESS FILLETS OF FISH BEFORE BRAISING

- Keeping the skin on during cooking will help hold the flesh together, but you can cook skinless fish this way too.
- Put the empty (unoiled) pan over a moderate to high heat and leave until very hot – you should feel the heat rising when you hold your hand about 7.5 cm (3 in) above it.
- Brush the fish with olive oil and season lightly. Do this just before cooking or the salt will draw moisture out of the fish and make it dry.
- Put the fish on the pan with its skin or skinned side facing up. Leave undisturbed for 2–3 minutes, pressing down firmly on the fish with a fish slice or palette knife (this helps make the charred lines more distinct – moving the fish too soon will cause it to stick). Turn over and repeat on the other side.
- For criss-crossed charred lines, give the fish a quarter turn once it has become charred.

Deep-fry

Deep-frying is an excellent way to cook fish – the fast speed and intense heat ensure moist, juicy flesh, while the coating protects the delicate flesh and gives a crisp contrast.

To deep-fry, heat groundnut or sun-flower oil to 190°C (375°F): drop in a cube of stale bread – it should turn golden brown in 30 seconds. Fry in small batches or the oil temperature will drop and the coating and fish will be soggy. Lift out with a slotted spoon and drain on kitchen paper before serving. Here are two of the most suc-cessful ways to deep-fry fish.

Goujons: Strips of white fish, best for delicate and thin fillets like sole or plaice. Dredge the strips in seasoned flour, dip in beaten egg and coat with fresh breadcrumbs. Spread in a single layer on a plate or tray and chill uncov-ered in the fridge for 1–4 hours to crisp up the coating. Deep-fry as above for 2–3 minutes until crisp and golden.

Tempura: Instant tempura batter mix is available in Japanese super-markets and the oriental sections of supermarkets. It is crisp and light, perfect for thick fillets of white fish such as cod, haddock, hake and rock salmon. Dip the fish into the batter, then deep-fry for 3–4 minutes until crisp and golden.

Grill

A fuss-free, ultra-healthy method using either no added fat, or a bare minimum. Ideal for whole fish, and for fillets and steaks, with or without skin.

- Oily fish such as herring, mackerel, red mullet, sardines, salmon and trout need only to be seasoned before grilling. Other fish, especially skinless white fish fillets, should be lightly oiled and seasoned, or coated with a crust or rub (see opposite) to protect their delicate flesh.

- Whole fish, fillets and steaks with skin on should be scored (see pages 41, 395 and 396)

- If time allows, marinating for 1–2 hours before cooking will help moisten and flavour the flesh (see Marinades for Fish, page 417).

- Preheat the grill to very hot before cooking, and put the grill rack about 7.5 cm (3 in) away from the heat.

- Grill thin fillets on one side only, with the skin or skinned side facing upwards. Turn whole fish and thick steaks once during grilling. Keep the flesh moist by brushing or basting once or twice with oil or cooking juices.

- Grilling times are 4–5 minutes for fillets, 5–7 minutes for steaks and 8–10 minutes for whole fish.

Microwave

This is one of the healthiest and best ways to cook fish – it retains juices and nutrients, without added fat.

■ Best suited to fillets and steaks.

■ Small whole fish can be microwaved, but the skin must be scored or it will burst.

■ For even cooking, make sure pieces are of a similar size and thickness. A turntable will help cook the fish evenly so use one if you have one.

■ Place the fish on a plate, season and sprinkle with a little citrus juice, light fish stock, white wine or water, plus a sprinkling of chopped fresh herbs if you like. Cover with cling film and microwave on High, turning the fish over halfway. For fish that is about 2.5–4 cm (1–1½ in) thick, the usual cooking time is 2–3 minutes, plus 1–2 minutes standing time, but ovens vary so you should consult your hand-book for exact timings.

Pan-fry

A no-fuss, quick and easy method for whole fish, fillets and steaks. Thick, meaty monkfish, tuna, swordfish and shark are good cooked this way, but so too are fish with less firm flesh such as cod, haddock, red snapper, sea bass and salmon, and even delicate flat fish

CRUSTS AND RUBS

Before pan-frying or grilling fish fillets, coat them with a flavour-packed crust or rub. It will look and taste good, and protect the flesh from the heat. When pan-frying, cook with the coated side down first; when grilling, start with the coated side facing up.

■ *FOR FISH WITHOUT SKIN – mix chopped fresh herbs such as dill, fennel, parsley and mint with grated lemon, lime or orange zest and seasoning to taste. Press thickly on to the skinned side of fish, after brushing lightly with oil.*

■ *FOR FISH WITH SKIN – mix spices such as chilli, cayenne or paprika with dried thyme, salt and coarsely ground black pepper. Rub over the skin and cook until crisp.*

such as sole and plaice, as long as they are cooked with care.

■ Whole fish can be pan-fried as they are, or lightly dusted with seasoned flour. Fillets and steaks are best protected with a light dusting of seasoned flour or a coating of bread or matzo crumbs or cornmeal, especially if they are skinless. A crust or rub (see page 401) is an even tastier option.

■ Season and/or coat the fish, then heat 1–2 tbsp oil in a non-stick or heavy frying pan until very hot. The temperature of the oil is important – if the oil isn't hot enough, the fish will absorb it and become soggy and greasy. Groundnut, sunflower and olive oils are all good for pan-frying, and you can add a knob of unsalted or clarified butter for colour and flavour if you like (not too much or it may smoke and burn).

■ Once you see bubbles breaking gently over the surface of the oil (any butter will start to foam at this stage), lower the fish into the pan with its skin or skinned side facing up (unless you want crispy skin – see opposite). Don't overcrowd the pan – leave plenty of space between each piece or the temperature of the oil will drop and the fish will stew rather than fry.

■ Cook over a moderate to high heat without moving, turning only once. The fish is ready to turn when it has changed colour up to the halfway mark. Don't be tempted to turn more often or the flesh may fall apart. Total cooking time for thin fillets is 2–4 minutes, thick fillets and steaks 5–7 minutes, small to medium whole fish 8–10 minutes.

■ Lift the fish out with a fish slice (see page 62) and drain well before serving.

Poach

A moist and gentle, fat-free method for whole fish and fillets, poaching can be done on the hob or in the oven, and is especially suited to salmon and delicate white fish. Once the fish is cooked and lifted out with a fish slice or slotted spatula, the liquid can be strained and used to make a sauce.

■ Poaching time is 5–7 minutes for fillets, 7–10 minutes for steaks. Small to medium whole fish take 15–20 minutes.

On the hob: Pour enough water, cold fish stock (see page 409), court bouillon (see page 411) or milk to just cover the fish into a wide, shallow pan and bring to a gentle simmer. Lay the fish, skin or skinned side down, in a single layer in the liquid, cover the pan and poach over a low heat.

In the oven: Lay the fish, skin or skinned side up, in a shallow baking dish or roasting tin and just cover

pan-fry–roast

with cold liquid (as for on the hob, above). Cover with foil or greaseproof paper and poach at 180°C/350°F/Gas Mark 4 (160°C/325°F in fan ovens).

In a kettle: Large fish such as a whole salmon or sea bass are best poached in a fish kettle, which can be hired from good fishmongers, supermarkets and kitchenware shops. You can then serve the fish hot or cold. Measure the thickest part of the fish and calculate the cooking time, allowing 10 minutes for each 2.5 cm (1 in), then lay the fish on the rack in the kettle. Pour in cold court bouillon (see page 411) to just cover the fish and bring to the boil over a moderate heat. Lower the heat, cover and simmer gently for the calculated time. If the fish is to be served cold, let it cool down in the kettle.

Roast

A quick and easy method best suited to whole fish like red snapper, sea bass and salmon, and to fillets with the skin on. Also good for robust fish without skin like monkfish tails, tuna steaks and thick cod loin. The technique is the same as for roasting meat, but extra care must be taken or the delicate flesh of the fish may dry out.
■ Preheat the oven to 190°C/375°F/Gas Mark 5 (170°C/340°F in fan ovens).

CRISPY FISH FILLETS

Chefs like to serve fish fillets with their crisp skin facing up, often on a bed of mash or seasonal vegetables:
■ *Score the skin on the diagonal (see page 41) and lightly dust it with seasoned flour.*
■ *Heat 1–2 tbsp oil in a frying pan over a moderate to high heat until very hot.*
■ *Put in the fish skin-side down.*
■ *Leave undisturbed for 6 minutes, until the skin is crisp.*
■ *Turn the fish over, switch off the heat and leave for 3 minutes.*
■ *Drain well and serve.*

■ If there is skin on the fish, score it (see pages 41, 395 and 396).

■ Brush olive oil all over the fish and season lightly, or coat with a crust or rub (see page 401).

■ Place the fish on a lightly oiled baking tray and roast uncovered.

■ Roast whole fish for 25–35 minutes, 10–20 minutes for fillets and steaks.

Steam

One of the healthiest cooking methods for fish as no fat is used and maximum nutrients are retained. Suitable for all types of fish – whole, fillets and steaks – but especially good for those with delicate flesh like plaice and sole.

■ Put the fish in a single layer in the steamer basket. For more flavour, lay it on herbs, or leaves such as pak choi or spinach, or on thinly cut vegetables.

■ Season lightly (salt takes moisture out of the fish).

■ Place the basket over simmering court bouillon (see page 411) or fish stock (see page 409) to give flavour to the fish. Plain water can also be used.

■ Cover and steam for 3–7 minutes for fillets and steaks, 8–10 minutes for whole fish weighing up to 375 g (12 oz), 15–20 minutes for fish weighing up to 1 kg (2 lb).

■ You can steam fish *en papillote* (in a parcel of greaseproof paper or baking parchment, see page 397). Put herbs or thinly cut vegetables inside the parcel with the fish, and allow 5 minutes extra cooking time.

■ Bamboo steamers are good for Asian recipes – over time the bamboo becomes scented with the ingredients used, which adds extra flavour to the fish. Spring onions, lemon grass, fresh ginger, coriander, star anise, soy and sesame are some of the flavours that go well. Add them to the water, and scatter them over the fish in the basket.

Stew

Fish is good in stews, soups and curries because it absorbs other flavours so readily. French *bouillabaisse* and *bourride*, American chowder, Spanish *zarzuela*, Thai and Goan curries, Moroccan tagine, Malaysian *laksa*, and Mongolian hotpot all illustrate this point very well.

■ Choose fish that is thick and firm, so it doesn't fall apart. Monkfish is the most obvious choice, and swordfish, tuna and cod loin also hold their shape well. More delicate fish can be used, but they should be saved until last and dropped in towards the end of cooking so there is less chance of them breaking up.

Stir-fry

This method is healthy for two reasons – quick cooking over a high heat retains nutrients, and very little fat is used. The downside is that the fish tends to break up during stirring and turning. Very firm fish such as monkfish, shark and tuna are best, but you can use softer fish like salmon or cod loin if you are careful.

■ Cut skinless, boneless fish into strips or cubes.

■ Marinate for 1–2 hours (see Marinades for Fish, page 417).

■ Heat 1–2 tbsp vegetable oil in a wok over a moderate to high heat until very hot.

■ Toss the fish in small batches into the pan and stir-fry for 2–4 minutes. Lift out and repeat with more batches. It is essential not to overcrowd the pan or the temperature will drop and the fish will be soggy.

HOW TO SERVE A WHOLE ROUND FISH

Use this technique for any round fish, such as mackerel, salmon or trout, no matter how it is cooked.

■ *Cut off the head and tail.*

■ *Run the point of a knife along the backbone.*

■ *Peel the skin off the top fillet.*

■ *Ease the top fillet from the bones.*

■ *Flip the top fillet over and set aside.*

■ *Pull the bones away from the bottom fillet.*

■ *Replace the top fillet.*

FRESH FISH A–Z

The following fish are commonly available at the fishmonger and super-market, and by mail order and over the web for home delivery. Wild fish is seasonal and more expensive than farmed fish, which is usually available all year round. Allow 125–175 g (4–6 oz) filleted fish or 225–250 g (8–9 oz) fish on the bone per person.

For general preparation, see pages 394–6. For cooking instructions and times, see pages 396–405.

Brill

Oval, flat, white fish, sometimes called 'poor man's turbot' – it looks and tastes similar, but is less expensive.

CHOOSE Steaks (sometimes called cutlets) that have one large bone. Fillets have a few tiny bones, if any.

COOK Fillets are good baked, braised, grilled, microwaved, pan-fried, poached, roasted or steamed. Cutlets are good grilled. Goes well with Mediterranean or Asian vegeta-bles and flavourings.

USE INSTEAD Turbot, sole or hake.

Cod

Round, white, juicy fish that falls into large, moist flakes when cooked. The bones are large, and easily removed.

CHOOSE

■ Small cod weighing about 700 g (1½ lb) are sometimes available, but most cod is large and sold as fillets or steaks, or cut crossways into cutlets with a central bone.
■ You may also see cod loin, which is cut from the thickest part of the fillet.

COOK

■ Small whole cod can be braised, poached or roasted.
■ Fillets and cutlets can be baked, braised, grilled, microwaved, pan-fried, poached, roasted or steamed.
■ The flavour of cod holds its own when cooked with strong herbs and spices, and with pungent Mediterranean-style tomato sauces.
■ It is also good in fish cakes, lasagne and pies, and deep-fried in batter.
■ Cod loin is good cut into chunks for soups, stews and curries.

USE INSTEAD Haddock, hake or coley.

Coley

Round, white fish similar to cod, but blander and cheaper, and not as white.

CHOOSE Best bought as fillets, which may have a few bones. Rub with lemon juice and a pinch of salt to whiten.

COOK

■ As for cod, especially in tomato sauces where the colour of the fish is disguised, although the flesh does get whiter when it is cooked.

■ Coley makes good fish cakes, and mixes well with other fish in soups, stews and pies – if you use it as a base, you will need less of other, more expensive, fish.

USE INSTEAD Cod or haddock.

Conger eel

Very large sea fish, usually sold as steaks on the bone.

CHOOSE Steaks from the tail end are bony, so ask for middle-cut steaks from near the top (head) end. The white flesh is firm, meaty and rich.

COOK

■ Steaks are good for braising and grilling.

FLAT FISH

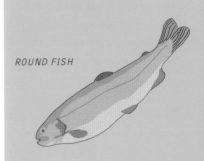

ROUND FISH

■ Cut into cubes, conger eel is also excellent in soups and stews because it retains its shape during cooking.

USE INSTEAD Cod or haddock.

Gurnard

Inexpensive, round, white fish with an extraordinary-looking head and spiky fins. There are several types, all of which are quite bony. Red gurnard is regarded as having the best flavour.

CHOOSE Although you may see whole fish at the fishmonger, there is a lot of waste, so it is best to ask for fillets.

COOK
■ Goes well with Mediterranean ingredients for baking, braising, microwaving, pan-frying, poaching or steaming.
■ Also good in soups and stews when added towards the end of cooking.

USE INSTEAD Red mullet.

Haddock

Round, white fish similar to cod but smaller, thinner and softer, and with a delicate shellfish flavour. The large bones are easy to see and remove.

CHOOSE Whole fish can be bought, but it is mostly available as fillets.

COOK
■ As for cod, preferably with the skin on to prevent the flesh falling apart.
■ Especially good in fish cakes, lasagne and pies, and deep-fried in batter.

USE INSTEAD Cod, hake or coley.

Hake

Round fish with white flesh. An expensive member of the cod family that isn't easy to find, but worth looking for. The texture is soft and flaky, the flavour delicate. Bones are easy to remove.

CHOOSE Can be bought as fillets, but steaks (cutlets) on the bone are better because they are less likely to fall apart during cooking.

COOK Can be baked, braised, grilled, microwaved, pan-fried, poached, roasted or steamed. Good with Mediterranean flavours.

USE INSTEAD Cod or haddock.

Halibut

Flat fish with meaty, white flesh and a distinctive flavour.

CHOOSE

- Large fish are cut into steaks and have a central bone – the best are the thick ones from the middle of the fish.
- Smaller 'Greenland halibut' aren't true halibut – sold filleted, they are less expensive than the real thing.

COOK Can be baked, braised, grilled, microwaved, pan-fried, poached, roasted or steamed. Especially good with wine-based sauces. To help prevent drying out, cooking on the bone is best.

USE INSTEAD Brill or turbot.

Herring

Small, oily fish. Rich-tasting flesh with many fine bones. See also Whitebait, page 418.

CHOOSE Available whole (the plumpest are the best), or can be filleted.

COOK

- Good barbecued, chargrilled, grilled or pan-fried.

FISH STOCK

Makes about 1 litre (1¾ pints), and keeps in the fridge for up to 2 days or in the freezer for up to 2 months.

500 g (1 lb) fish bones and
*   trimmings, chopped and well*
*   rinsed*
1 onion, peeled and quartered
1 carrot, peeled and quartered
1 celery stick, roughly chopped
juice of ½ lemon
splash of dry white
*   wine (optional)*
12 peppercorns

Put all the ingredients into a large pan or stock pot and cover generously with water. Bring to the boil and simmer for 20 minutes. Skim the surface often as the stock simmers, then strain, leave to cool and use as the recipe requires.

*   To freeze, reduce the stock to half its volume by boiling vigorously, then cool. Pour into ice-cube trays and freeze. Put the frozen cubes into a freezer bag, so you can take them out individually – simply drop them into hot liquids or dissolve in boiling water.*

■ Vitamin-packed herring roes are delicious pan-fried and served on toast.

USE INSTEAD Mackerel or sardines.

Hoki

A member of the hake family that comes from Australia and New Zealand. The flavour is bland, but the flesh is white and nicely flaky, with very few bones.

CHOOSE Most often sold as fillets, which are usually frozen.

COOK Best pan-fried with flavoursome sauces, especially tomato-based ones.

USE INSTEAD Cod, haddock or hake

John Dory

A round fish that looks flat because of the way it swims. It has firm-textured white flesh with a good flavour, but is expensive. Also called St Peter's fish (St Pierre in French) because it has marks on either side of its head that are said to be the finger and thumbprints of St Peter.

CHOOSE Available whole but there is a lot of waste, so best filleted. There are hardly any bones in the fillets.

COOK
■ The fillets are good cooked in a variety of ways – baked, braised, grilled, microwaved, pan-fried, poached or steamed, and they go well with wine-based sauces.
■ Also good in soups and stews, when added towards the end of the cooking time.

USE INSTEAD Brill, turbot, halibut or sole.

Mackerel

Oily fish with a rich flavour. The bones are easily removed.

CHOOSE Sold as whole fish and fillets. At its best when very fresh.

COOK Can be baked, barbecued, braised, grilled, microwaved or pan-fried.

USE INSTEAD Herring or sardines.

Monkfish

Only the tail is eaten of this large fish, which has a very ugly head. The flesh is white, dense and meaty, with a mild, sweet flavour. There is only one central bone.

CHOOSE

■ Sold as whole tails or long fillets from either side of the central bone.
■ Check before cooking that the purple-grey membrane has been removed or the fish will be chewy. To remove it, nick it with the tip of a sharp knife and pull it away with your fingers.

COOK

■ Whole tails are good braised or roasted (and especially tasty when wrapped in Parma ham or bacon).
■ When the fillets are cut into cubes or strips, monkfish is excellent for skewering and barbecuing, and for cooking in soups, stews, lasagne and stir-fries, because it holds its shape so well.
■ It is also good sliced into medallions or escalopes and chargrilled, grilled or pan-fried.

USE INSTEAD Lobster, conger eel, cod loin.

COURT BOUILLON
Makes about 1.2 litres (2 pints) and keeps in the fridge for up to 5 days.

1.2 litres (2 pints) water
splash of dry white wine
2 carrots, chopped
2 onions, chopped
1 large bouquet garni
1½ tsp rock or sea salt
2 tsp black peppercorns
125 ml (4 fl oz) white wine vinegar

Combine all the ingredients, except the vinegar, in a large pan. Bring to the boil, then simmer, uncovered, for 15–20 minutes, adding the vinegar for the last 5 minutes. Cool before use.

Mullet

There are two main types – red and grey. Red is the smaller of the two, with delicately flavoured, firm, white flesh and skin that crisps up well. Grey mullet is coarser and cheaper, and can taste muddy.

CHOOSE
■ Buy red mullet for preference, either as small whole fish or fillets.

COOK Whole fish and fillets can be baked, barbecued, braised, grilled, pan-fried or roasted. Goes well with Mediterranean flavours.

USE INSTEAD Sea bass, sea bream or red snapper.

Plaice

Flat fish with very soft, moist, white flesh and a delicate flavour. Virtually bone-free.

CHOOSE Sold as a whole fish (which you can fillet yourself or ask to be filleted) and as fillets.

COOK
■ Fillets can be baked, grilled, microwaved, pan-fried, poached or steamed.

■ Also good deep-fried in breadcrumbs or batter.

USE INSTEAD Sole or brill.

Salmon

Oily fish with orange-pink, meaty flesh and a good flavour. The bones are few and can be easily removed.

CHOOSE
■ Available whole, as joints and fillets, and as steaks with a central bone.

COOK
■ Can be barbecued, baked, braised, chargrilled, grilled, microwaved, pan-fried, poached, roasted or steamed.
■ Can also be made into gravad lax, and used in fish cakes, kedgeree, lasagne and pies.
■ Also good with Asian flavours, especially ginger, lime and soy.

USE INSTEAD Trout.

Sardine

Small, oily fish with a good flavour, but many bones. Pilchards are the same fish, only larger.

CHOOSE Available whole, and can be filleted. Best with the head and backbone removed, so it can be opened out flat (butterflied) for cooking.

COOK Great barbecued in summer, but also good chargrilled, grilled or pan-fried.

USE INSTEAD Herring or mackerel.

Sea bass

Round fish with fine, white flesh that is moist, delicate and sweet-tasting. It holds its shape during cooking, and the shiny, silver skin crisps up well. The bones are few and easily removed.

CHOOSE

■ Whole fish vary in size from 375–500 g (12 oz–1 lb) for 1 serving, up to 3 kg (7 lb) that will feed 6–8 people. Large sea bass are expensive.
■ You can also buy fillets, which are sold with the skin on.

COOK

■ Whole fish are best baked, braised, poached, roasted or steamed.
■ Fillets are good grilled, pan-fried, microwaved, steamed or stir-fried.
■ Goes well with Mediterranean and Asian vegetables and flavourings.

USE INSTEAD Sea bream, red mullet or red snapper.

WHAT'S IN A NAME?
Plaice and sole are the best-known flat fish, but there are other, smaller, family members that you may see at the fishmonger or freshly caught by the sea. In season these are well worth buying, and are excellent grilled or pan-fried whole, on the bone. These are the names to look out for:
■ *DAB*
■ *DOVERS*
■ *FLOUNDER*
■ *MEGRIM*
■ *SAND SOLE*
■ *WITCH SOLE*

Sea bream

There are many types of this white fish, but the gilt-head bream (called *daurade* in French) is the one to look for. It has juicy, white and tender flesh, and the best flavour of all the bream. Check that the fish has been properly scaled when buying.

CHOOSE Buy whole fish, or ask for it to be filleted.

COOK

■ Whole fish are good roasted, or braised with Mediterranean vegetables and flavourings. Fillets can be baked, grilled, pan-fried, poached, steamed or microwaved. They are also good in fish stews, when added towards the end of cooking.

USE INSTEAD Sea bass, red mullet or red snapper.

Shark

There are many members of the shark family, but they are unlikely to be named. They are all boneless, meaty and thick, with a dense texture.

CHOOSE Available as steaks, loin and fillets.

COOK

■ Can be barbecued, braised, char-grilled, grilled or pan-fried, preferably marinated beforehand to make the flesh juicier.

■ Shark is also good barbecued in chunks on skewers, or used in curries, stir-fries, soups and stews.

USE INSTEAD Swordfish, tuna or monkfish.

Skate

The kite-shaped wings are the only parts of this fish that are eaten. They yield tender, sweet, white flesh between the cartilage (there are no bones).

CHOOSE

■ Wings or parts of wings are sold ready-skinned — for each person allow 1 small wing or a third of a large wing. The thick piece cut from the centre of a large wing is best and is called the 'middle cut' — this is the meatiest part and is up to 5 cm (2 in) thick.

■ Skate knobs are chunks of solid white fish that look similar to scallops. You will need about four of these per person.

COOK

■ Best poached, pan-fried or roasted.

■ Skate knobs can be used in stir-fries and stews.

USE INSTEAD Ray (very similar to skate and from the same family), brill, turbot or sole fillets.

Snapper

There are many kinds, but red snapper is the most common. The flesh is white, with a sweet, slightly nutty, flavour. The bones are easy to see and remove.

CHOOSE Available as whole fish, fillets and steaks.

COOK
■ Whole fish can be baked, barbecued, braised, poached, roasted or steamed.
■ Fillets are good baked, barbecued, grilled, microwaved or pan-fried. Always cook with the skin on to help keep the flesh together.
■ Especially good with herbs and chillies, and in Cajun, Caribbean, Mexican and Asian recipes.

USE INSTEAD Red mullet or sea bass.

WHAT'S IN A NAME?
Rock salmon, rock eel, huss and dogfish are all one and the same fish – a small member of the shark family – given different names depending on where you buy it. You are most likely to see it in a fish and chip shop – often referred to simply as 'rock'. Its white, moist flesh is excellent coated in batter and deep-fried. Conger eel (see page 407) is a different fish altogether.

Sole

A flat, white fish of which the two main types are Dover and lemon. Both have a delicate flavour and a firm, juicy texture, but Dover sole is the better fish, and the most expensive.

CHOOSE Available whole and as fillets.

COOK

■ Whole fish can be baked, barbecued, chargrilled, grilled or pan-fried.
■ Fillets can be grilled, microwaved, pan-fried, poached or steamed.
■ Strips (goujons) can be deep-fried or pan-fried.

USE INSTEAD Plaice.

Swordfish

Firm and compact, meaty, white flesh with a pinkish tinge. Low in fat, so can be dry if not cooked carefully. There are no bones.

CHOOSE Available as loins or steaks, or buy a piece of loin and cut it into steaks yourself. Steaks should be cut thick to prevent overcooking and dryness.

COOK

■ Can be barbecued, braised, chargrilled, grilled, pan-fried or roasted, preferably marinated beforehand to make juicier.
■ Also good cut into chunks and barbecued on skewers.

USE INSTEAD Tuna or shark.

Trout

Oily fish, the most common being the rainbow trout, a freshwater fish farmed on a large scale, and the sea trout, a freshwater fish that sometimes migrates into the sea like salmon, and is often called salmon trout.

CHOOSE Available whole and as fillets.

COOK Can be baked, barbecued, braised, grilled, microwaved, pan-fried, poached or roasted.

USE INSTEAD Salmon.

Tuna

Huge fish with dense, meaty flesh that varies from pink to red. There are many types – bluefin, bonito and yellowfin are three good ones, but most tuna is not sold by name.

sole–turbot

CHOOSE Available as steaks, with no bones.

COOK

■ Can be barbecued, braised, grilled, grilled, pan-fried or roasted. Best when thick, marinated and undercooked, or it can be dry.

■ Good with Mediterranean and Asian flavours.

USE INSTEAD Swordfish.

Turbot

Flat, white fish with thick, tender flesh and a superb flavour. Very expensive, but worth buying for a special treat.

CHOOSE Whole small fish are available, and can serve up to 4 people, but most turbot is sold as thick, boneless fillets or steaks (cutlets) with one large bone.

COOK

■ Whole fish can be baked, braised or roasted.

■ Fillets and steaks can be baked, braised, grilled, microwaved, pan-fried, poached, roasted or steamed.

USE INSTEAD Brill or halibut.

MARINADES FOR FISH

Most fish is lean with little natural fat, so marinating before cooking is a great way to inject moisture and flavour and prevent dryness. It is especially effective for fish that is to be cooked by dry heat such as barbecuing, grilling, chargrilling and roasting.

■ *Marinades for fish are most often based on a mixture of olive or sunflower oil and an acid such as citrus juice, wine vinegar or wine (the usual ratio is 3 parts oil to 1 part acid). Natural yogurt can also be used as part of a marinade base, and it works especially well with lemon juice and tandoori or other Indian spices.*

■ *Fresh herbs and garlic go well with fish – add some for extra flavour.*

■ *Fish absorbs marinades rapidly, and 1–2 hours marinating is enough, especially if you turn the fish over halfway through the marinating time. In any case, don't marinate for longer than 4 hours, especially when citrus juice is included. The acid in citrus juice 'cooks' the fish so that it turns opaque, as in the Mexican ceviche, where lime juice is used for this effect.*

Whitebait

These tiny, silver fish are baby herring or sprats.

CHOOSE Almost always sold frozen.

COOK
- Coat whole fish in spiced or seasoned flour and deep-fry in hot oil for a few minutes until crisp.
- Eaten whole (skin, bones and all), which makes them an excellent source of calcium.

USE INSTEAD There is no substitute.

Whiting

Round, white fish similar to haddock, but with less flavour.

CHOOSE Available whole and as fillets. Must be very fresh or the texture will not be good.

COOK
- Can be baked, braised, grilled, pan-fried, poached or roasted.
- Also good in soups, stews, fish cakes and pies.

USE INSTEAD Haddock.

PRESERVED FISH

Fish is preserved in many different ways – smoked, salted, dried, pickled or canned. All keep well, are on a par nutritionally with fresh fish, and most need no preparation or cooking.

Dried and salted

As you would expect, fish that are preserved by salting and drying have an intense flavour.

Dried salt cod: This is popular in Scandinavia, the Caribbean and Africa, but especially around the Mediterranean – in Italy it is called *baccalà*, in Spain *bacalao*, and in Portugal *bacalhau*. To soften and remove excess salt, traditional salt cod needs soaking for days in cold water before use. Modern light cures are softer and less salty and need only 24 hours soaking. Look in Mediterranean cookbooks for salt cod recipes, or in French cookbooks for *brandade de morue*.

Mojama: Dried salted tuna, this is shaved or sliced wafer-thin and served with olive oil, lemon juice and black pepper, on its own or on bread. For a starter, it makes an unusual alternative to smoked salmon.

Roes: These are often salted and dried (see page 423).

Smoked

There are two types of smoked fish – 'hot smoked' and 'cold smoked'. Hot smoking cooks the fish at the same time as smoking; with cold smoking, the fish doesn't cook.

STORE Wrapped tightly in cling film to exclude air, smoked fish will keep in the fridge for up to 10 days.

CHOOSE
Eel
■ Available as fillets.

■ Rich and dense, and expensive compared to other smoked fish, but a little goes a long way. A 60–90 g (2–3 oz) serving is ample for 1 person.

■ No need for cooking. Use as a first course or in salads and fish pâtés.

Haddock
■ Available as fillets, and as whole split fish on the bone called Finnan haddie, originally from the village of Finnan, near Aberdeen.

■ Buy the pale, naturally cured fish, rather than the artificially dyed, bright yellow kind (which is sometimes cod or coley rather than haddock).

■ Needs cooking – poaching in milk or milk and water, or grilling with a

SOMETHING DIFFERENT
Many unusual and exotic fish are available by mail order and over the web, and occasionally at the fishmonger and supermarket. Supplies vary, as they come from different parts of the world at different times of the year, so you can't count on a particular one being in stock when you want it. Ask your supplier for preparation and cooking instructions – anyone selling these kinds of fish will know what to do with them. The following are some of the best that are most widely available:

■ *BARRACUDA*
■ *BARRAMUNDI*
■ *CARP*
■ *DENTON*
■ *EMPEROR FISH*
■ *ESCOLAR*
■ *GROUPER*
■ *KING GEORGE TREVALLY*
■ *KINGFISH*
■ *LING*
■ *MAHI-MAHI*
■ *MARLIN*
■ *MILKFISH*
■ *ORANGE ROUGHY*
■ *POLLACK*
■ *SCABBARD*
■ *STURGEON*
■ *TILAPIA*

knob of butter. Smoked haddock is also very good in kedgeree, fish cakes and pies.

- Arbroath smokies are small, hot-smoked haddock, on the bone and without heads. They are usually sold in pairs, tied together with string, and they need splitting open. They are ready to eat as they are, and also good warmed under the grill for a few minutes. The flavour is milder than that of other smoked haddock.

Herring

- The most common are kippers, split-open whole fish that have been brined and oak-smoked. They are traditionally sold in pairs. The undyed kind are best, especially the famous Manx and Loch Fyne kippers.
- Strong-flavoured flesh with many tiny bones. If these bother you, buy kipper fillets.
- Needs cooking. Grilling is traditional, although microwaving and poaching are also good (if you add a pinch of sugar to the poaching liquid, the kippers are less likely to repeat on you). Cooked fillets are good in pâtés.
- Bloaters are ungutted, cold-smoked herrings with rich-tasting flesh. They are whole, and need to be gutted before grilling.
- Brisling, buckling, sild and sprats are hot-smoked herrings that are usually eaten cold, but they can also be grilled.

Mackerel

- Available whole and as fillets.
- Plump, juicy flesh that is tasty, and less bony than kippers.
- Needs no cooking, although can be grilled. The flavour is good in pâtés.

Salmon

- Cold-smoked salmon is available both as a whole side (most often sliced and interleaved) and as thin slices. You can also buy trimmings, which are cheaper than slices.
- Lox is a Jewish speciality, a cold-smoked salmon that varies in colour and flavour according to the cure. It is usually cheaper than other types of smoked salmon.
- Hot-smoked salmon looks and tastes like a cross between smoked, poached and roasted fresh salmon. It is available as thick fillets and flaked pieces.
- Both cold- and hot-smoked are ready to eat as they are, and are also good diced or flaked in salads, scrambled eggs, omelettes, quiches, pasta sauces and risotto. Hot-smoked salmon fillets are good grilled and served hot. Cold-smoked salmon is good pan-fried very briefly. Sliced lox can be used like smoked salmon, and is traditionally served with bagels and cream cheese.

Trout

- Hot-smoked trout is available as whole fish and fillets. Cold-smoked trout is sold thinly sliced like smoked salmon.

■ The delicate, moist flesh of hot-smoked trout is plump and pale pink, and less bony than that of smoked herring and mackerel. Cold-smoked trout looks and tastes very like smoked salmon, but is cheaper.

■ Use as for smoked salmon.

Marinated and pickled fish

Oily fish are preserved in either brine or vinegar and flavours vary, from sharp and vinegary to mild and sweet. They can usually be kept unopened in the fridge for up to 10 days, though you should check the 'best before' date on the packaging.

Boquerones: Marinated anchovies with white flesh and silver skin. Sweet and milky, they aren't like canned or bottled anchovies (see pages 74 and 422). Use as a starter or in salads, or fry them.

Gravad lax: Raw salmon cured with dill, salt and peppercorns. Serve thinly sliced as a starter.

Herrings: There are numerous varieties of pickled, soused and marinated herrings. Good ones are the Dutch Maatjes, sweetcure herring fillets, and rollmops. Serve them as a starter, or use in salads.

RING THE CHANGES

Thinly sliced smoked salmon is one of the easiest and most popular starters, but there are other smoked fish that can be served in the same way, and they are sold thinly sliced just like smoked salmon. If you find them a little on the expensive side, cut the cost by mixing them with smoked salmon – the different colours make an interesting presentation and the flavours also complement one another well.

■ *SMOKED HALIBUT – pale, delicate flesh tinged with a golden-orange border.*

■ *SMOKED STURGEON – fine-grained flesh that is very pale pink and delicately flavoured.*

■ *SMOKED TUNA – deep red with an open texture and an intense flavour.*

In the can

Canned fish provides protein, vitamins and minerals just like fresh fish. If you keep a few cans in your cupboard, you can whip up a nutritious meal quickly, without cooking.

CHOOSE

Anchovies: Tiny, slim fish packed in oil or salt in jars or cans, see also page 74.

Salmon: Pink is cheapest, red the most expensive, and it will say on the label whether it is wild or farmed. Eat the bones (which are soft) because they are a good source of calcium.

Sardines: The ones in good-quality olive oil are best for flavour, but those in tomato sauce provide a nutritional double whammy because the tomatoes contain lycopene, a valuable anti-oxidant. Pilchards are large sardines that are usually packed in tomato sauce. Both sardines and pilchards are a good source of calcium when the bones are eaten.

Tuna: The pale-coloured albacore fillets are very good, either in olive oil or spring water (often in jars rather than cans). Look too for *ventresca de bonito*, oil-rich belly fillets in olive oil. See also page 122.

RAW FISH

In Japanese sashimi, sushi and maki, very fresh raw fish is sliced wafer-thin and served uncooked. You can make these easily and safely at home, as long as you are sure of the provenance and freshness of the fish you are using. Buy from a reputable source, letting your supplier know what you are making.

■ Fish that are suitable include halibut, red mullet, salmon, sea bass, sea bream and tuna.

■ Buy the freshest possible fish and use it on the same day, keeping it in the fridge from the moment you get home.

■ When you take the fish out of the fridge to prepare it, work quickly in a cool kitchen with cool hands, then return it to the fridge immediately, until just before serving. Use within 4 hours.

KNOW YOUR ROE

Roes are fish eggs, which are preserved and used in many different ways. The flavour is very strong, so they are used in small quantities.

■ **Bottarga** is the salted, dried and pressed roe of grey mullet or tuna, and is regarded as a great delicacy all around the Mediterranean. In Italy they soften it in olive oil and serve it thinly sliced on bread with lemon juice and black pepper. It is also grated over pasta that has been tossed in olive oil to make the classic pasta dish *spaghetti alla bottarga*.

■ **Caviar** is salted sturgeon's roe. The best and most expensive is the black Beluga. Second best is Oscietra, while Sevruga is the cheapest.

■ **Keta** is salted salmon roe, sometimes called salmon caviar. Larger than real caviar, it is orange-red, soft and moist. It can be used like real caviar, at a fraction of the cost.

■ **Lumpfish roe** is salted and dyed black to look like caviar, so it is also known as mock caviar. Another name for it is Danish caviar, and it is sometimes dyed orange or red.

■ **Smoked cod's roe** is most often used for taramasalata, although traditionally grey mullet roe is used. Before use, soak the roe in boiling water for 1–2 minutes, to take the edge off its strong flavour, then drain and dry and peel off the skin.

SHELLFISH

SUPERMARKETS AND FISHMONGERS HAVE A GOOD CHOICE OF SHELL-
FISH ALL YEAR ROUND, AND SO TOO DO MAIL ORDER COMPANIES
AND WEBSITES, WHERE YOU CAN OFTEN FIND MORE UNUSUAL
VARIETIES. SHELLFISH DIVIDES INTO TWO GROUPS – CRUSTACEANS
AND MOLLUSCS. BOTH HAVE SHELLS, BUT CRUSTACEANS HAVE
LEGS AND MOLLUSCS DON'T.

CHOOSE

Shellfish is highly perishable, so always buy from a reputable source with a quick turnover.

- All shellfish should have a clean, fresh smell.
- The shells should be in perfect condition, not broken or cracked.
- Live clams, mussels and oysters should have their shells closed. If you can see a lot of open ones, don't buy.

Buying frozen shellfish

A lot of shellfish is frozen at sea, and sold either frozen or defrosted – 'fresh' prawns, for example, are usually defrosted frozen prawns. There is nothing wrong with this (in fact, it ensures freshness), but you shouldn't refreeze them when you get home. Check with the fishmonger to be absolutely sure. When buying frozen shellfish, check the following:

- The packaging is unopened and undamaged and the shellfish inside is frozen solid, with no sign of thawing.
- There is no sign of freezer burn (dry, white patches) or dark discoloration.

STORE

Shellfish should be handled quickly and carefully.

- Keep well wrapped in the fridge and eat on the day of purchase, or within 24 hours of buying.
- Frozen shellfish should be well wrapped and stored in the freezer, where it will keep for up to 6 months.
- To thaw, unwrap and place on a plate, then cover loosely with cling film or foil. Put in the bottom of the fridge and leave for at least 4 hours, or overnight, until no ice crystals remain (for more rapid defrosting, use the microwave). Before cooking, pat thoroughly dry with kitchen paper.

crab

CRUSTACEANS

This group of shellfish has shells and legs. It ranges from expensive lobsters for special occasions to value-for-money prawns that are good for everyday meals.

Crab

From seaside stalls to the super-market, crab is on offer all year round, but it is especially good in the summer months. The common or brown crab is the most widely avail-able, but you may also see spider crabs on sale if you are on the coast. Whole and dressed crabs are usually sold fresh; white and brown crab meat and claws are often sold frozen.

CHOOSE

Whole live crab: This is the freshest option, but it is time-consuming and fiddly to boil a crab and remove the edible meat from the shell and claws, so you may prefer to buy a **whole cooked crab**, the next best thing, and ask the fishmonger to do the job for you. Whole crabs should feel heavy for their size – weight indicates there is plenty of meat. A crab that weighs 1 kg (2 lb) will feed 2–3 people; for 4 people you will need one that weighs at least 1.5 kg (3 lb). Small crabs are

GOOD FOR YOU

Nutritionists recommend we eat fish, including shellfish, two or three times a week.

■ Low in fat, shellfish provides protein and valuable vitamins and minerals (especially potassium, iodine, iron and zinc).

difficult to deal with, so the bigger, the better.

Dressed crab: This is a more practical choice than a whole crab because the white and brown meat have already been extracted and piled back into the shell. Dressed crab must look fresh and lively, and have a visible amount of good white meat and decent-sized claws.

Crab meat: If you need lots of **white meat** for a recipe, it is best to buy this on its own – it is unlikely you will get enough from a whole or dressed crab.

■ The best white meat comes from the claws, and you can buy cooked claws separately, but if you don't have the time to extract the meat yourself, buy packets of white meat. Check where it has come from if you can – the best is claw meat only; other types may be a mixture of claw and body meat. Allow 125 g (4 oz) per person.

If **brown meat** is what you want, you can buy this separately, although it often comes packed with white meat. Allow 60–90 g (2–3 oz) per person. Another option is **canned crab**, an all white meat that is excellent quality and handy for fish cakes, salads, soups and pasta sauces.

PREPARE

■ Frozen crab should be defrosted before use – leave it in its packaging in the fridge overnight.

■ Crack open crab claws with a claw cracker or hammer and extract the meat with a skewer (see opposite).

■ Pick over all crab meat and remove any pieces of shell.

■ Canned crab can be watery, so drain it well in a sieve before flaking with a fork.

COOK

■ The meat from a boiled crab can be eaten cold just as it comes, or tossed over the heat for a minute or two and served hot.

■ Dressed crab can be served straight from the shell, or you can take out the white and dark meats and use them in recipes.

SERVE

■ Flaky white crab meat has a mild, sweet flavour that goes equally well with creamy or fiery sauces. It makes an excellent crab cocktail, is good in salads, soups and pasta sauces, or as a filling for stuffed pasta shapes such as ravioli. It marries well with Asian ingredients like lime, ginger, chilli and coriander, and is good in stir-fries, curries and fish cakes.

■ Dark crab meat is rich and filling, and is good mixed with white meat to intensify the crab flavour. It also gives body and flavour to sauces and soups.

Lobster

The ultimate luxury, lobster is expensive but worth every penny – its firm white meat is incomparably succulent and sweet, especially in the summer months. A live lobster has a black shell that turns red when cooked.

CHOOSE

■ A whole live lobster is the freshest choice, but then you will have to kill it, split it in half and remove the inedible parts from the shell – not a job for the faint-hearted. A freshly cooked lobster is a more practical option, which you can buy split in half, cleaned and ready to eat. Allow half a 700 g (1½ lb) lobster per person.
■ Rock lobster tails come from the clawless rock lobster (crawfish). All the meat is in the tail, which is sold on its own and is usually raw. Preparation is easy, with little waste, and the meat is firm and juicy with an excellent flavour. Allow 1 tail per person.

PREPARE

■ If you have bought a ready-to-eat halved lobster, there should be nothing to do, unless the claws are still intact. If they are, crack them open with lobster crackers or a hammer and extract the meat – or leave this to be done at the table if you prefer.

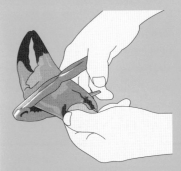

CRACKING CRAB CLAWS

SOFT-SHELL CRABS

These are blue crabs caught after shedding their hard shells and before growing new ones (they shed their shells several times before they reach maturity). Allow 2 per person – the whole thing is eaten, soft shell and all. The flesh is creamy and very tender, with a sweet taste.
■ If they are frozen, they should be defrosted in the fridge before cooking. Allow a minimum of 4 hours, or overnight.
■ For a starter or lunch, lightly coat soft-shell crabs in seasoned flour and pan-fry in hot oil or butter (or both) for 2–3 minutes each side until golden. Remove and deglaze the pan with lemon juice, then add chopped parsley and Worcestershire sauce. Pour over the crabs and serve hot.

■ Some recipes call for tail meat only. Remove and discard the dark intestinal 'vein' from the top of the tail meat, then lift the meat out of each shell. For medallions, slice crossways along the length of the tail (see illustration, opposite).

■ To prepare a whole raw rock lobster tail, put it hard-shell-side down on a board and cut round the flat shell with scissors. Lift this away to reveal the flesh, and snip off any fins.

COOK

■ When you buy a cooked lobster that has been split in half, you can eat it as it comes – the simpler, the better. It is good cold with mayonnaise, as a lobster cocktail, or in a salad. To serve hot, grill flesh-side up in the half shell for 5 minutes, brushing the exposed meat with melted butter before and during cooking.

■ Medallions can be pan-fried in olive oil and/or butter, or used in stir-fries. They are also good in curries. Allow 2–3 minutes' cooking time – just enough to heat the lobster through.

■ Marinate raw rock lobster tails in the fridge in olive oil, citrus juice and herbs or spices for up to 4 hours, then run a skewer through the flesh from the wide end to the narrow end, and cook with the flesh-side facing the heat for 6–7 minutes. Turn the tail over and cook the shell side until it turns red – this will take about 4–5 minutes.

■ Another way to cook the tail meat of rock lobsters is to remove it from the shell in one piece, then slice it crossways into medallions, as for normal lobsters (see illustration, opposite). These can then be pan-fried or stir-fried, or poached in stock. Allow 3–4 minutes, or until the flesh is opaque.

■ Asian ingredients like fresh ginger, coriander, chilli, garlic, spring onions, lime and coriander suit the flavour of lobster well, and so too do rich ingredients like cream, cheese, wine and brandy.

■ Lobster and pasta make a good team – either in a tomato or creamy sauce, or as a filling for stuffed pasta such as ravioli.

Prawns

There is a huge variety of prawns on offer, both raw and cooked, cheap and expensive. All are quick and easy to prepare and cook, and you can use them in many ways.

CHOOSE Depending on size, buy 3–4 tiger or king prawns per person for a starter, 5–6 for a main course. Allow 90–125 g (3–4 oz) peeled North Atlantic prawns per person for a

lobster–prawns

starter, 175 g (6 oz) as a main course. If the prawns are in their shells, buy double this weight.

Raw prawns: These are blue-grey in colour, although they are sometimes referred to as green prawns. Tiger prawns, sometimes labelled king prawns, are the big and juicy expensive ones that are most often sold raw. You can buy them whole in their shells, or with their heads off. When the heads are off, they are called prawn tails and are also sold peeled. Banana prawns from Australia are even larger than tiger prawns. They are grey-white, juicy and flavoursome, and are usually sold headless, with their shells on or off. North Atlantic prawns are the smallest of the raw prawns, usually sold whole.

Cooked prawns: These are pink. The largest are the tiger or king prawns, which you can buy whole, or with their heads off. When their heads are off, they often have their shells off too (but not their tails). North Atlantic prawns are smaller. They are sold whole or headless. When their heads are off, they are often sold peeled, but they may still have their tails on.

PREPARE

Peel: This means to remove the shells, which you can do before or after cooking, but the prawns will be

CUTTING A LOBSTER TAIL

TIPS & TRICKS: PRAWNS

Raw prawns are good dipped in tempura batter (buy an instant mix from a Japanese store or the supermarket), then deep-fried in hot sunflower oil for 3 minutes. Serve them with a soy or chilli dip for a quick and easy canapé – the tails make perfect handles. They can be butterflied or straight.

■ *For butterflied prawns – peel and devein, leaving the tail on (see page 431). Cut a deep slit along the belly of the prawn and open it out, then press it flat.*

■ *For straight prawns – peel and devein, leaving the tail on. Insert a wooden satay stick along the length of the prawn.*

juicier and tastier if they are peeled after. Pinch and twist off the head, then split the shell open along the belly with your fingertips, and prise apart until you can pull the prawn free of its shell, working downwards from the head end. You may remove the tail shell or leave it intact, whichever you prefer (see illustration, opposite top)

Devein: After removing the shell, check to see if there is a black line (the intestinal tract) running along the back of the prawn. This can be eaten, but it looks unsightly and may be gritty, so is best removed. With the tip of a small, sharp knife, make a shallow cut along the length of the black vein (see illustration, opposite centre), then lift out the vein with the tip of the knife (see illustration, opposite below).

COOK

- Prawns should be cooked as briefly as possible or they will be tough and chewy. Keeping the shells on helps guard against this.
- Raw prawns take 3–4 minutes max, and are cooked when they turn pink all over.
- Cooked prawns can be eaten cold as they are. If you want them hot, heat for 1–2 minutes at the most.
- Prawns are good in stir-fries, and dropped into soups, sauces, curries and stews towards the end of cooking.

- To barbecue or grill, toss in olive oil with herbs or spices and seasonings, and thread on skewers.
- To chargrill or pan-fry, toss them in olive oil with herbs or spices and seasonings and cook over a moderate to high heat, tossing and turning them often.

MOLLUSCS

This group of shellfish has shells but no legs. Mussels are the best-known and most often eaten; clams come a close second. Scallops and oysters are more expensive, and usually reserved for special occasions. Squid and octopus are special kinds of molluscs called cephalopods.

Clams

The craze for clams has spread from America, and there is an increasingly large choice available at different times of year. They are sold live in their shells like mussels, and the two can be used interchangeably in recipes.

CHOOSE

- Size varies from very large and meaty quahogs to large verni and small *amandes de mer*, Venus and carpet shells (also called *palourdes*).

prawns–clams

Cherrystones and littlenecks are small clams – in fact they are small quahogs. Then there is the long and narrow razor shell, which looks totally different from the others. All are sold in their shells.

■ Canned or bottled clams in brine are cooked and ready to use. They are sweet and tender, and worth buying when you can't get fresh ones.

PREPARE

■ Clams can be sandy and gritty. Soaking them before cooking helps get them clean. Put them in a large bowl of cold water with a handful of salt and leave for an hour, then drain and scrub the shells clean with a stiff brush under the cold tap. Discard any with cracked shells, or with shells that are open or don't close when tapped hard on the work surface.

COOK

■ Small clams and razor shells can be eaten raw like oysters, but they are most often served cooked like mussels.
■ To serve them raw, prise open their shells with a small, sturdy knife or an oyster shucker, sever the hinge muscle and discard the top shell, then loosen the clam from the bottom shell by digging underneath with a sharp-edged teaspoon. Serve on the half shell like oysters (see page 435).

PEELING AND DEVEINING PRAWNS

1 *Peel off the shell.*

2 *Cut down the length of the black vein with a small, sharp knife.*

3 *Lift out the vein with the tip of the knife.*

■ The easiest way to get the shells open is to steam them like mussels (see opposite) for about 5 minutes. Discard any that remain closed. After steaming, you can eat them as they are, like mussels, or remove them from the shells and drop them into soups (especially chowders), sauces and stews just before serving.

■ Another way to cook them is to drop them raw into soups, sauces and stews in their shells, or put them on top of a paella or risotto. To avoid overcooking (when they become rubbery), do this at the last minute, cover tightly with a lid or foil and serve as soon as the shells open.

■ Large clams need to be cooked. They can be steamed and served like small clams (see above), but they are also good if they are steamed, taken out of their shells and then baked or grilled. Put them back in the half shell and top with a spoonful of pesto or a knob of herb butter (see page 133), then bake in the oven at 190°C/375°F/Gas Mark 5 (170°C/340°F in fan ovens) for 5–7 minutes, or put under a hot grill for 3–4 minutes.

■ Large steamed and shelled clams can also be dropped into soups, sauces and stews. Cut them into smaller pieces first if you prefer, and cook only briefly until just heated through. They are also good deep-fried. Coat in seasoned flour, egg and breadcrumbs and drop into hot sunflower oil for 2–3 minutes until golden and crisp.

Mussels

Although they are available all year round, mussels are best eaten from September to April.

CHOOSE Mussels are usually sold live in their shells. You can buy them loose by weight, or in nets or bags. Allow 225 g (8 oz) per person for a starter, 500 g (1 lb) per person for a main course.

European mussels: These are the familiar-looking mussels with blue-black shells. Their size varies, and the smallest take the most time to prepare, but they are usually the sweetest-tasting because they are the youngest, and so are well worth the extra effort.

New Zealand green-lip mussels: These are larger and meatier than European mussels, but their flavour isn't quite as good. They take their name from the green edging on their shells.

Shelled mussels are available frozen. They are cooked and ready to eat, and useful for dropping into sauces, soups and stews.

clams–mussels

PREPARE

■ Scrape any barnacles off the shells with a small, sharp knife.

■ Scrub the shells clean with a stiff brush under the cold tap and yank out the hairy beards from between the shell hinges, grasping them between your finger and thumb with the help of a small, sharp knife (see illustration, right).

■ Discard any mussels that have broken, cracked or open shells, or that do not close when tapped sharply on the work surface.

■ If you aren't cooking the mussels at once, keep them in a bowl of salted cold water in the fridge for up to 2 hours. If you want to leave them longer than this, leave the debearding until just before cooking. They should be cooked and eaten the same day.

COOK

■ Steam mussels in a covered pan with just enough liquid to cover the bottom – they should take 5–8 minutes. Drain and discard any that are still closed. You can use plain water, but for the best flavour use wine, cider or fish stock (or mix these half and half with water), to which you can add fresh herbs, sliced onion, chopped garlic and seasoning as in the classic French *moules marinière*. A modern Asian alternative is to use fish stock flavoured with soy and/or sesame, chillies and garlic, or coconut

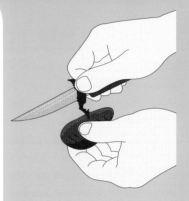

DEBEARDING MUSSELS

TIPS & TRICKS: MOLLUSCS

■ *Clams and mussels on their half shells wobble when you are grilling or baking them. To keep them stable, wedge them in a bed of rock or sea salt.*

■ *When removing steamed mussels from their shells, check any large ones for a rubbery ring surrounding the central part of the flesh. This can be chewy, so pull it off and discard it.*

■ *Always keep the juice from clams and mussels, tipping it into soups and stews for extra flavour.*

milk flavoured with lemon grass and coriander.

■ Once the mussels are open you can either serve them as they are, or remove the top shells and detach the mussels from the bottom shells, then drop them into soups, sauces and stews for a few minutes just to heat through (take care not to overcook or they will be chewy). Or you can put them back in their bottom shells and coat them in a stuffing, herb butter, breadcrumbs or a sauce and grill them until hot for 2–3 minutes, or bake them in the oven at 190°C/375°F/Gas Mark 5 (170°C/340°F in fan ovens) for 5–7 minutes.

■ Another way to cook them is to drop them straight into soups and stews with their shells on, cover the pan and cook them for a few minutes until the shells open. They can also be cooked this way in rice dishes like risotto and paella, and in sauces for pasta.

Oysters

The ultimate in style and luxury, oysters are an acquired taste – not everyone likes their slippery texture and salty flavour.

CHOOSE

■ Oysters are available all year round, but are at their best when there is an 'r' in the month, especially in winter.

There are two main types – native oysters and Pacific oysters. Both are sold live and graded according to size – the bigger the better. Native oysters are regarded as the finest, and they are the most expensive.

■ The best way to buy oysters is in their closed shells, so they will be as fresh as possible when you open them, but you can ask the fishmonger to do the job for you. Once they are open, keep them covered in the fridge until just before serving, and eat on the day of purchase.

■ Shelled oysters are available frozen, and smoked oysters are sold in cans. Both are good for cooked dishes.

PREPARE

■ If you have bought live oysters, check the shells are closed with no cracks. Discard any damaged ones. Scrub the shells with a stiff brush under the cold tap, then open them with a shucker or sturdy knife (see opposite).

■ Frozen shelled oysters should be defrosted in the fridge before use. Leave them for at least 4 hours or overnight.

COOK

■ Fresh oysters are very delicate and best eaten raw because they can quickly overcook and become rubbery, but they can be grilled in their half shells,

mussels–oysters

seasoned and protected by breadcrumbs and herbs, a light stuffing
mix, or a splash of cream and/or some
grated Parmesan cheese. They can also
be tipped out of their shells and pan-
fried in butter, poached or steamed.
For any of these cooking methods,
allow 2–4 minutes at the most.

■ Shelled and smoked oysters are
most often used in pies and stews, and
are traditional in steak and kidney
pudding. They are also good in
canapé-size tartlets and baby quiches.

■ To make angels on horseback to serve
as a canapé, wrap raw shelled oysters
in small pieces of streaky bacon, Parma
ham or pancetta and thread on skewers, packing them close, so they don't
unravel and overcook. Roast in the oven
at 200°C/400°F/Gas Mark 6 (180°C/
350°F in fan ovens) for 6 minutes.

SERVING OYSTERS RAW

The usual serving is 6 per person,
although oyster lovers think nothing of
eating 9 or even 12. Opening the
shells is safer and easier if you use an
oyster shucker with a guard to protect
your hands should the blade slip (see
right), but you can use a short, sturdy
knife with a sharp tip instead.

■ Serve on a bed of crushed ice with
some seaweed if you can get it, lemon
halves and sea salt, black pepper and
Tabasco for seasoning.

SHUCKING AN OYSTER
Insert the tip of the shucker or
knife next to the hinge of the oys-
ter's shell, holding the rounded end
of the shell firmly in a cloth with
your other hand.

■ *Work the shucker slowly between*
the two shells, twisting it from side
to side until they are prised apart.
■ *Scrape the oyster carefully from*
the top shell, then discard the top
shell.
■ *Detach the oyster from the*
muscle in the bottom shell, leaving
the oyster sitting in the shell with
its juice around it. Take care not
to spill the juice – it is drunk
from the shell after the oyster
has been eaten.

Scallops

Also known by their French name of *coquilles St Jâcques*, scallops are quick and easy to prepare, cook at lightning speed, and taste exquisitely sweet and tender.

CHOOSE

■ There are two main types of scallop. King scallops are the largest, and you can buy them in or out of their shells. The freshest are in their shells, which your fishmonger will open to release the scallop within. Allow 2–3 per person for a starter, 4–5 as a main course. The shells make attractive serving dishes, and the fishmonger should give them to you free of charge if you ask. Queen scallops are much smaller than king scallops, and cheaper, although their flavour is just as good. They are most often sold out of their shells. You should allow 5–6 per person for a starter, 10–12 for a main course.

■ The roe or 'coral' of a scallop is bright orange, and a great delicacy. King scallops have large, crescent-shaped corals; queen scallop corals are small and pointed. If the scallops you buy have their corals attached, this is a bonus, but not guaranteed. Scallops sold loose out of their shells are less likely to have them.

■ Frozen or defrosted scallops aren't worth buying. They are watery and tasteless compared to fresh, and some may have been soaked in water to plump up their flesh.

PREPARE

■ If the orange coral is attached, pull it away gently and set aside. Also pull away the little white muscle that is attached to the side of the scallop – it is tough and will spoil any dish you are making. If it is stubborn, cut it off. Gently pat the scallops and corals dry with kitchen paper.

■ Small and medium scallops are best left whole. Large, thick scallops can be difficult to cook – the outsides may overcook while the centres remain raw. The way to avoid this is to cut them in half through their thickness. For stir-fries, cut each scallop into four chunks.

■ If you are using the shells, scrub them with hot, soapy water and rinse well, or put them in the dishwasher.

COOK

Only the briefest of cooking is needed, or the scallops will be tough and chewy. Pan-frying is the easiest method, and the one most chefs prefer – often described on menus as 'seared' or 'pan-roasted'. Scallops can also be poached, stir-fried or grilled.

scallops

Pan-fry/sear/pan-roast: Season the scallops on both sides, and brush with runny honey if you like (this helps give them a good golden colour). Heat a splash of olive oil and a knob of butter in a heavy frying pan over a moderate to high heat. When it's foaming, put in the scallops and cook for 2 minutes on each side for whole scallops, 1 minute on each side for halves and chunks. Press them flat with a fish slice or spatula so that they get nicely coloured. Add any corals for the last minute. Lift out the scallops and corals, deglaze the pan with a splash of wine or balsamic vinegar and drizzle over the scallops to serve. Or deglaze with white wine and make an instant sauce with infused saffron and cream.

Poach: Bring fish or chicken stock to a gentle simmer, lower in the scallops and poach for 4 minutes. Drain and serve warm or cold in salads (they taste very good with a balsamic or lime vinaigrette), or slice and add to pasta sauces at the last minute.

Stir-fry: Heat sunflower oil in a wok until very hot, add quartered scallops and stir-fry for 2–3 minutes max.

Grill: Wrap scallops in small pieces of streaky bacon, pancetta or Parma ham, thread on skewers and cook under a hot grill for 6 minutes, turning halfway through the cooking time.

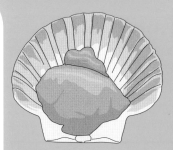

SCALLOPS

Squid

Cheap and available all year round, squid deserves to be eaten more often. It is quick and easy to cook, and has a pronounced shellfish taste. The smallest squid are the sweetest and most succulent.

CHOOSE

■ You can buy whole squid complete with its ink sac, but it is messy to clean, so ask your fishmonger to do the job for you. Cleaned squid tubes (the pouch or body of the squid) are readily available in any case, so too are squid rings, which save you doing anything. Allow 2 small tubes or 125 g (4 oz) rings per person.

PREPARE

■ Rinse tubes and rings, drain well and pat dry with kitchen paper.
■ For chargrilling or stir-frying, cut tubes open along one of their sides and open out flat, then score in a criss-cross pattern on the inside of the flesh. If you like, marinate before cooking in olive oil and lime juice with finely chopped chillies and garlic.

COOK

■ Tubes can be stuffed and braised in a sauce (a tomato sauce spiked with chillies goes especially well). They are good filled with a breadcrumb or couscous stuffing, to which you can add chopped onion, peppers, herbs, ham or cooked bacon, or crumbled cooked sausagemeat. Fill only two-thirds full to allow for expansion during cooking, and fasten the open ends with wooden cocktail sticks. Pan-fry in olive oil and butter for a few minutes until nicely coloured on all sides, then cover with your chosen sauce and braise on top of the stove or in the oven at 170°C/ 340°F/Gas Mark 3 (150°C/300°F in fan ovens) for 30–45 minutes until tender when pierced with a skewer.
■ Rings can be deep-fried in batter, but they are healthier when pan-fried. Use them as they are or cut into strips, and pan-fry in hot olive oil – they take only a few minutes. Good flavourings for squid are chilli, garlic, fresh ginger and lime, and they are especially tasty served with a dipping sauce. They can also be used in paella, pasta sauces and seafood salads.
■ To chargrill scored squid, brush it lightly with olive oil (or its marinade) and cook on a preheated griddle pan for 3–4 minutes, pressing down hard with a fish slice or spatula. Cut into strips to serve – they look and taste good in salads. Or cut it into strips and add to stir-fries (Chinese black bean sauce is a favourite with squid).

squid–octopus

Octopus

For novelty value, this is hard to beat – and it tastes good too.

CHOOSE

- Available fresh and frozen.
- The smaller, the better – large octopus can be tough. A whole 1 kg (2 lb) octopus will feed 4 people.

PREPARE

- Frozen octopus usually comes ready-prepared. If buying a fresh octopus, ask the fishmonger to prepare it for you so that it is ready for cooking, without its innards, beak and eyes.
- Blanch in boiling water for 4 minutes, drain and peel off the skin (with a very young octopus this may not be necessary).
- To help tenderize the flesh, pound with a rolling pin or the base of a saucepan.
- Cut into strips.

COOK

- Braising in a thick, flavoursome sauce is the best option, after browning in hot oil over a high heat. Onions, garlic, tomatoes, wine and herbs all suit octopus well, and the cooking time should be about 1½–2 hours in the oven at 170°C/340°F/Gas Mark 3 (150°C/300°F in fan ovens).

SQUID INK

If you buy fresh squid from the fishmonger he may ask whether you want the ink sac (it is inside the squid and is very black). In Spain they cook squid in its own ink, and in Catalonia they use it to colour and flavour paella. Italians colour their pasta with it, and use it to make a sauce to serve with pasta. As well as buying it fresh, you can also get it in sachets at fishmongers, delis and supermarkets.

SHELLFISH

WHAT'S IN A NAME?

- **Crawfish** are often confused with crayfish (see below). They are not the same — crawfish is another name for a rock lobster (see page 427).
- **Crayfish** are miniature fresh-water lobsters, about the size of a large prawn, that are sold live or frozen. Poach them in fish stock (see page 409) or court bouillon (see page 411) for 5 minutes if fresh, 7 minutes if frozen and serve hot or cold as a starter, allowing 8–10 per person. Only the succulent and flavoursome tail meat is eaten. The heads and shells are good for making stock.
- **Crevettes** are whole Mediterranean prawns in their shells. They look good as a garnish and taste good too.
- **Langoustines** belong to the lobster family and are also known as Dublin bay prawns. The tail meat is sold as scampi. They are usually sold frozen, either raw or cooked, and are pale pink in colour even when raw. Poach or chargrill for 1–2 minutes (don't overcook) and serve hot or cold as a starter. Allow 6 per person.
- **Shrimp** are small prawns, sold cooked. There are pink and brown ones. They are very fiddly to peel, so buy ready-peeled ones if you can get them.

CHAPTER

Milk, Cheese and Eggs

MILK

INVALUABLE AS A FRESH AND NATURAL INGREDIENT IN COOKING, MILK IS ONE OF OUR MOST NUTRITIONALLY COMPLETE FOODS. IT CONTAINS PROTEIN AND FAT, CARBOHDRATE IN THE FORM OF THE MILK SUGAR (LACTOSE), AND MINERALS AND VITAMINS IN ABUNDANCE – ESPECIALLY CALCIUM, ZINC, MAGNESIUM, VITAMINS A AND E, THIAMINE (B1), RIBOFLAVIN (B2) AND B12 – ALL ESSENTIAL FOR GOOD HEALTH.

CHOOSE
Cow's milk

There are three main types, each containing a different amount of fat. All are pasteurized, which means they have been heat-treated to kill any harmful bacteria and extend shelf life.

Whole milk is sometimes described as 'full-fat' milk because none of its natural fat has been taken away. It has more vitamin A than other milks. Fat content is about 4%.

Semi-skimmed milk has had about half of its fat taken away, which makes it less rich in vitamins A and D, but it has slightly more protein and calcium than whole milk. Fat content is about 1.7%.

Skimmed milk has had virtually all of the fat taken away, together with fat-soluble vitamins A and D, but on the plus side it contains slightly more calcium than whole milk. Fat content is 0.1–0.3%.

Speciality milks

Not all milk comes from cows, and most can be drunk and used in cooking in the same way. Check the label for exact usage.

Goat's and sheep's milk are both available fresh, either whole or semi-skimmed, and have similar fat contents to their cow's milk equivalents.

Oats and rice are used to make long-life, lactose-free 'milks' that are low in fat and cholesterol. They are good for the lactose-intolerant, or if you need to restrict your intake of animal fats for health reasons.

Soya milk is made from soya beans, and is available in fresh and long-life, plain, sweetened and flavoured varieties. Lactose-free and low in fat, soya milk is often calcium-enriched.

STORE

Fresh milk must be stored in the fridge to keep it fresh and out of

choose–store

direct light, which can cause valuable vitamins to be lost. For storage times, check the 'use-by' date on the bottle or carton – it is usually about 5–7 days from the day you buy it.

Freeze

Semi-skimmed milk and skimmed milk can be frozen for up to 1 month, though they may separate when thawed. For best results use homo-genized milk (less likely to separate) and defrost overnight in the fridge.

Long-life milks

Fresh milk keeps for several days, but there are alternatives with long shelf lives that are useful for times when you run out of fresh. They are especial-ly good in cooking.

Coconut milk comes in many differ-ent forms. See page 80, for how to choose and use.

Condensed milk is cow's milk that has been concentrated by being heated and homogenized, then sweetened and evaporated. Sold in cans, it is very sweet and sticky, with a thick, spoon-able texture that is velvety smooth. Use for making caramel (as in millionaire's shortbread), fudge and desserts.

Dried milk is produced by evaporat-ing the water from cow's milk. It

LABELS ON MILK – WHAT THEY MEAN

■ *CHANNEL ISLAND comes from Jersey or Guernsey cows. Sometimes labelled breakfast milk, it is a whole milk that is available homogenized (see below) or with a visible layer of cream on top. Both types are very rich and creamy, with a fat content of about 5%.*

■ *HOMOGENIZED is whole or semi-skimmed cow's milk with its fat distributed evenly throughout so the cream doesn't rise to the top.*

■ *ORGANIC comes from cows that have grazed on pastures that have had no chemical fertilizers, pesti-cides or agrochemicals used on them. Producers must be registered with an approved organic body. Research indicates that organic milk has more vitamins A and E than non-organic milk, and is richer in antioxidants and essential fatty acids.*

■ *RAW MILK hasn't been pasteur-ized. Also described as 'untreated' or 'green', this is the one type of cow's milk that can't be bought in the shops or from the milkman – it can only be bought direct from licensed farm distributors. You may see it at some farmers' markets.*

comes in powder and granules, and can be made from whole or skimmed milk. Virtually fat-free, skimmed dried milk is not as vitamin-rich as whole dried milk, but it reconstitutes more easily when mixed with water. Dried milk keeps for a year, but once reconstituted it must be treated as fresh. It can be used as a substitute in any recipe calling for fresh milk.

Evaporated milk is cow's milk that has been evaporated at a high heat, then homogenized. It is twice as concentrated as fresh milk, and can be used as a substitute in cooking for extra richness, as long as you like its flavour. It can be whipped.

Oasts, rice and soya beans are used to make long-life milks – see page 442.

Sterilized milk is available whole, semi-skimmed and skimmed, in bottles and cartons. Heated to a very high temperature that destroys virtually all bacteria, it has a very distinctive taste that you either love or hate. It keeps for several months without refrigeration if unopened, but once opened it should be used within 5 days.
Sterilized milk can be used for drinking and in cooking as a substitute for fresh milk, but it has slightly less of the B group vitamins and vitamin C.

UHT stands for ultra-heat-treated milk. Available in cartons as whole, semi-skimmed and skimmed, it is similar to sterilized milk in that it has the same keeping qualities (see left), but it has a milder flavour and more nutrients. It can be used instead of fresh milk for drinking and in cooking.

COOK

■ When heating milk, don't get it too hot or it may boil over and/or scorch on the bottom of the pan. Scorched milk tastes unpleasant, and will spoil the flavour of any sauce. The same is true of milk that has boiled over, which may also have lost many of its nutrients. To scald milk, heat it gently to just below boiling point, when bubbles start to appear around the edge, then remove the pan from the heat.

■ To flavour milk, scald it with aromatics such as vanilla pods or citrus zest, then remove from the heat and leave to infuse for about 20 minutes. Remove the flavourings before use.

■ Don't use skimmed milk in a recipe unless it says so, especially if it is to be heated with acidic ingredients like citrus juice or raw onions. Acid can cause milk to curdle or separate, and the chances are higher with low-fat, skimmed milk. To prevent milk curdling when using these ingredients, keep the heat very low, and cook any onions first.

■ For a quick all-in-one white sauce, see page 461 and omit the cheese.

CREAM

Whether cream is used in cooking or for serving at the table, it will always add a luxurious touch. There are many types to choose from, and many different ways to use them in recipes.

CHOOSE

The fat content of cream determines its uses, so it helps to know this when choosing.

Clotted cream is more yellow in colour than other creams, and nearly as thick as butter. Made by heating the cream of full-fat milk, which gives it a rich flavour and a slightly grainy texture, it has the highest fat content of all the creams, at around 65%. Traditional for topping scones and jam, it is also good spooned over puddings, especially hot ones, and for making rich ice cream. It doesn't whip, and isn't recommended for cooking.
USE INSTEAD Double or whipping cream.

Crème frâiche originated in France, and some of the best brands are imported from there. It is a thickish cream with a smooth texture that comes in full-fat, low-fat and half-fat versions – the full-fat has 40–50% fat

WHICH CREAM FOR WHICH JOB?

- *COOKING – crème fraîche, double, half cream, single, soured, whipping*
- *POURING – double, half cream, single, whipping*
- *SPOONING – clotted, crème fraîche, double, soured, whipping*
- *WHIPPING – crème fraîche, double, whipping*

content. The flavour is tangy, similar to that of soured cream but not quite as sharp. It becomes thinner when stirred or added to hot liquids, but thickens up well when whipped. Use as a spooning cream for puddings (it goes especially well with fruit and chocolate), and in cooking to enrich mixtures and sauces – the full-fat version doesn't curdle when heated to a high temperature.
USE INSTEAD Soured cream or natural yogurt, or a half-and-half mix of one of these with double or whipping cream. Take care when heating, as soured cream and yogurt curdle if they get too hot.

Double cream is luxuriously thick, with a full-on rich flavour and a fat content of 54%. This is the most versatile cream because it can be boiled without curdling, is good as a pouring or spooning cream, and it will whip to one and a half times its volume. It is ideal for floating on top of hot liquids such as soup or coffee, or folding into mousses, fools and soufflés. Extra-thick double cream is homogenized, and best used for spooning over desserts, not for whipping.
USE INSTEAD Whipping cream, crème fraîche.

Half cream is a cross between cream and milk, like top of the milk. It has a 12% fat content, and is good for pouring over puddings and breakfast cereals (especially porridge), and for making drinks and sauces when you want a richer taste than that of ordinary milk. It can be heated without curdling, but it can't be whipped.
USE INSTEAD Single cream or Channel Island milk.

Single cream is a smooth pouring cream with an 18–24% fat content. It is a good table cream to serve with puddings, and it can be used in cooking for enriching sauces, soups, custards, omelettes and quiche fillings, but it shouldn't be boiled or heated to high temperatures as this will cause it to curdle. It can't be whipped. Extra-thick single cream is homogenized. This makes it thicker than ordinary single cream, but it can't be heated to a higher temperature, nor can it be whipped.
USE INSTEAD Half cream or Channel island milk.

Soured cream is single cream that has been soured with bacteria to make it thicker and tangier. It has an 18–21% fat content. It is mainly used as a topping for things like baked potatoes, blini, bortsch, goulash,

choose

stroganoff and chilli, and it is also good in dips and dressings, and dolloped on puddings when ordinary cream is too rich. It separates when overheated, so take care when stirring it into hot liquids – do this off the heat when the liquid has cooled down a little. It can't be whipped.
USE INSTEAD Natural yogurt or smetana (see right). Or make your own soured cream by stirring 1 tbsp lemon juice into 250 ml (8 fl oz) double cream and leaving it to thicken at room temperature for 10–15 minutes.

Whipping cream is thick, but not as thick and rich as double cream as its fat content is lower, around 35–40%. It makes a good alternative to double cream whenever you want a lighter feel and taste with less fat and calories, but it will curdle if boiled. It is best heated very gently, or used for pouring or spooning over puddings, or for whipping and decorating desserts and cakes. When it is very cold, it will whip to double its volume and become light and fluffy. It holds its shape very well, so it is good for piping, dolloping, or floating on top of soup or coffee. It makes good ice cream.
USE INSTEAD Double cream mixed with single cream in the ratio of 2:1.

UHT CREAM

Ultra-heated-treated (UHT) cream is a useful standby because it keeps for up to 3 months without refrigeration if unopened. (Once opened it should be treated like fresh cream.) It tastes slightly different from fresh cream, but it has the same enriching qualities, and the flavour can easily be disguised by combining it with other ingredients. It is useful for adding richness to custards, soups, sauces, quiche fillings and omelettes, and it makes good Chantilly cream when whipped with vanilla extract or sugar.

SMETANA

Smetana, also spelled smatana, originates from Russia and Eastern Europe. A soured cream with a tangy flavour, runny texture and fairly low fat content (around 10%), it can be used as a low-fat alternative to soured cream, or in place of natural yogurt. Use it as a spooning or pouring cream, or for adding to sauces and stews at the end of cooking. It will curdle if overheated, and will not whip thick. If a recipe calls for smetana and you can't get hold of any, use whipping or single cream mixed half and half with soured cream or yogurt.

STORE

All cream must be kept in the fridge and used by the 'best before' or 'use by' date. Once opened it should keep for up to 3 days. Creams with a fat content of at least 35% can be frozen, but they should be used within a month. For best results, whip double or whipping cream lightly before freezing and thaw overnight in the fridge. Thawed frozen cream doesn't whip as well as fresh, but can be used for spooning on to dishes and in cooking. To make it smoother, whip gently before use.

USE

There are a few tips and tricks for using cream that will help you get the best results, but choosing the correct type of cream for the job (see page 445), is the best guarantee of success.

ADDING CREAM TO
HOT MIXTURES

Double cream is best because its high fat content will not allow it to curdle even when boiled, but you may prefer a lower fat alternative. Full-fat crème fraîche is the next best thing, as it can be boiled without risk of curdling, but if you use any of the other creams, you need to take precautions.

■ Remove a few spoonfuls of the hot liquid to a bowl and stir in the cream, then return this mix to the bulk of the liquid a little at a time, stirring well to combine before adding more. Keep over a low heat until just warmed through, and do not allow to boil.

■ As an extra precaution, stabilize the cream with cornflour, allowing ½ tsp for each 4 tbsp cream. Mix the corn-flour to a paste with a few drops of water before adding to the cream, then cook for 1–2 minutes over a low heat, stirring all the time, to get rid of any raw flour taste.

WHIPPING CREAM UNTIL THICK

For speed you can use an electric whisk (see page 60) but you will have more control and get greater volume if you use a balloon whisk (see page 68). If you haven't got either of these, you can use a table fork, but it will be hard work. Both whipping and double cream can be whipped until thick, and they will then hold their shape for several hours in the fridge. Whipping cream will double its volume, double cream will increase by one and a half times. Crème fraîche can be whipped until it is thick, but it will not increase in volume.

■ Chilled cream whips better than warm or room-temperature cream, so take the cream from the fridge just before you are ready to whip, and

store–use

don't use a warm bowl or whisk. The colder everything is, the better.

■ Pour the cream into a deep bowl and start whipping slowly, moving the whisk in a circular motion from the bottom of the bowl to the top so the blades cut through all of the cream and incorporate as much air as possible.

■ As the cream starts to thicken there will be less likelihood of splashing, so you can increase your whipping speed slightly. Don't go too fast – cream has a nasty habit of separating and becoming grainy very quickly. If this happens, the cream is described as 'turned' or 'split'.

■ When a recipe calls for cream to be lightly whipped to a soft peak stop whipping as soon as the cream will hold a floppy peak shape when the whisk is lifted – the top of the peak should fold over on itself and not stand upright.

■ If a recipe specifies that the cream should be stiffly whipped or whipped to a stiff peak, continue whipping a little longer until the peak stands tall when the whisk is lifted. Don't go beyond this stage or the cream will start to turn grainy and buttery look-ing. If this happens the cream will still be edible but it will not look good as a decoration and it will not fold in prop-erly. Use it in a warm sauce where it will melt.

FOLDING CREAM INTO ANOTHER MIXTURE

For some cake mixtures, or when making mousses, fools and soufflés, recipes often tell you to 'fold in' the cream. Folding is a technique that ensures two or more mixtures are evenly blended together without losing air and volume (see also page 26).

■ With a rubber spatula or a large metal spoon (whichever you feel most comfortable using), stir a couple of spoonfuls of whipped cream into the main mixture until it is completely mixed in.

■ Now tip the rest of the cream on top and fold it in using the edge of the spatula or spoon. Cut down into the mixture until you reach the bottom of the bowl, then scoop and roll the mix- ture over. Cut down again and repeat in a figure-of-eight action, turning the bowl round with your other hand until all of the cream is evenly incorporated and there are no streaks.

YOGURT

Made from milk, yogurt is a staple food in many places such as India, Asia, Eastern Europe, Turkey, Greece and the Middle East. Yogurt is made commercially by adding a harmless bacteria culture to milk after it has been pasteurized (heat-treated) then cooled. This creates the characteristic refreshing tangy taste and, under the right conditions of temperature and moisture, causes the milk proteins to set and become yogurt. The milk can be from cows, goats, ewes and buffalos, the most common being cows, and can be skimmed, semi-skimmed or whole.

CHOOSE

There are many varieties and flavours of yogurt to choose from, including ones with sugar, fruit, cream – even with gelatine added. Plain, natural yogurts that have no added flavour- ings, sweeteners or colourings are the most versatile, healthy and the most useful for cooking with. These are some of the types available:

Bio: Uses a particular type of bacteria thought to help digestion. It is the mildest-tasting yogurt, less acidic in taste and creamier than others. Bio is short for probiotic (from the Greek word meaning 'in favour of life').

use–choose

Whole milk: Made with whole milk, this yogurt combines the benefits of this milk (which is a rich source of vitamin A, vitamin E, niacin and biotin) with the benefits of harmless bacteria.

Greek: Made from whole cow's milk and cream, this is a thick, especially creamy yogurt, with a fat content of about 10.2%. There is also a 0% fat variety made with skimmed milk and milk proteins.

Live: Most of the yogurt that we buy is live, which just means that the harmless bacteria added to the milk are still alive. The only yogurt that isn't live has been heat-treated after making. This kills the bacteria, which gives it a longer shelf life but a different taste and fewer health benefits.

Low-fat: Made with skimmed milk, this has less than 2% fat.

Natural: Also called plain, this has no added flavourings or colourings.

Organic: This is made from organic milk, and producers must be registered with an approved organic body.

Set: Made using traditional bacteria cultures, this is allowed to set in the pot it is sold in. This gives the yogurt a texture that keeps its shape.

GOOD FOR YOU
Since yogurt is made from milk, it has the same nutrients – protein, vitamins and minerals – and is a rich source of calcium.

STORE

In its original container in the fridge and eat by the 'best before' date on the packaging. After this date, the taste will start to become much more acidic.

COOK

Yogurt is used a lot in many cuisines, especially in Indian cooking when it is often added to a savoury dish towards the end to make a creamy, tangy sauce. Yogurt can, however, separate when heated, which spoils the look and texture of a dish rather than its flavour. To help prevent this, use the yogurt at room temperature and, if adding at the last minute, beat it until smooth, and stir in just a spoonful at a time so it isn't such a shock when it hits the hot mixture. If the yogurt is going to cook in the dish for longer, stabilize it before adding, by making a paste of cornflour and water and stirring this into the yogurt. (To 4 tbsp yogurt, stir in a blend of ½ tsp cornflour and 1 tsp water.) Gradually stir this into your hot mixture, cooking gently for a few minutes to get rid of the raw taste of the cornflour – but don't let it boil. Alternatively, you can add the yogurt gradually, straight into the pan, at the beginning of cooking. If you wish to add it to frying onions, for example, stir in 1 tbsp of the required amount of yogurt at a time, and let it get absorbed before adding the next.

USE FOR

- Adding a spoonful or two to a spicy curry to make it creamy and tone down the heat.
- Making a drink or sauce (such as Indian lassi or raita or Greek tzatziki).
- Marinating meat and poultry (it helps tenderize at the same time).
- A low-fat substitute for cream or ice cream: use with fresh fruit in a pavlova – you'll never guess that it's not cream.
- Making scones – it will lighten the dough.

store–choose

BUTTER

If you churn cream until it goes solid, you get butter. It is a totally natural product, unlike margarine, which is a processed food that contains additives. Butter contains a minimum of 80% fat with no more than 16% water.

CHOOSE

Most butter is made from cow's milk, but you may also see it made with other milks such as sheep's or goat's. France, particularly Normandy, produces some very fine butters such as *beurre d'Isigny*. This is made with crème fraîche, so has a different taste and texture – very light and creamy. Unsalted Italian butter is delicately flavoured, pale and slightly sweet, similar to American butter.

Buy the best-quality butter that you can afford, as cheaper, often blended butters, tend to have a stronger, more overpowering, taste. Use butters interchangeably for spreading, depending on your taste. Unsalted is often favoured for cooking.

Lactic (cultured): Made by adding a culture of harmless bacteria to the cream, this has a very slight tartness and removes the need to add salt, although it is sometimes added for flavour. A lot of Danish butter is lactic.

TIPS & TRICKS: BUTTER

If you have hot hands and find it difficult rubbing butter into flour when making shortcrust pastry, here's a solution. Firm up the butter by putting it (wrapped in foil or greaseproof paper) in the freezer for about 30–45 minutes to get it really hard. Then, holding it in its peeled back wrapping, coarsely grate it into the flour before mixing in the water. Wrap and chill the pastry for 20 minutes or so before rolling out. This gives a slightly flakier pastry – with no rubbing in to do and no messy hands.

BUTTER v. MARGARINE

Some recipes call for using butter or margarine. The choice is yours, but if it is flavour you are after, butter has more. A low calorie margarine isn't suitable for cooking, as it contains a high proportion of water.

Slightly/lightly salted: This has less salt than salted butter, usually about 1%. Because of this it doesn't keep as long as salted, but is good to use if you like the taste of salt yet are concerned about the amount you eat.

Salted: Butter which has salt added – the amount varies from 1–2.5%. Years ago salt was added as a preservative; today it is added for flavour. Salted butter is fine to cook with and great for baking, but burns more easily than unsalted when used for frying.

Spreadable/easy spread: This isn't pure butter but a blend of dairy fats and vegetable oil. Low-fat versions aren't suitable for cooking.

Unsalted: Butter without added salt, this has a sweet, delicate taste and is good for cooking (especially frying) as it can survive higher temperatures without burning as much as salted butter. Also good for baking. Many continental butters are unsalted.

STORE

Keep, well wrapped, in the fridge, away from any strong-smelling food as butter absorbs flavours easily. Use by the 'best before' date on the packaging. Or store in the freezer for up to 6 months.

PREPARE

If using for baking or anything where the butter has to be very soft, leave it at room temperature for 1–2 hours before using, so it is easier to work with.

COOK

Butter can add creamy texture (in baking and sauces) plus flavour and richness to all cooking.

FRY To keep butter from burning, don't have the heat too high, though unsalted butter can be heated to a higher temperature than salted. Or use half butter and half olive or vegetable oil. That way you still get the flavour but there's less chance of the butter burning. This all changes when you make 'brown butter' as you heat it until it actually turns a golden brown to give a nutty taste. Good for pouring over fish or vegetables. Don't let it get too brown, though, or the butter will end up with a burnt taste.

BAKE When making cakes, the butter may need to be creamed (see page 17) with the sugar to give a light texture, so the butter should be very soft (see Prepare, above) – check for softness by pressing your finger on to the wrapping.

choose–cook

OTHER BUTTER PRODUCTS

▪ Ghee

This is a form of clarified butter that is used a lot in Indian cooking. Clarifying is a process that makes the butter clear by removing the milk solids. Clarified butter and ghee have higher burning points (ghee has the highest), so are particularly good for frying. Both can be used interchangeably, but ghee has a stronger, nuttier flavour. This is because, after the milk solids have been separated out, the liquid is simmered to drive off more moisture which turns the milk solids slightly brown. You can find ghee in Indian shops as well as some supermarkets, or make your own clarified butter (see below).

▪ How to clarify butter

Melt some butter in a pan until completely liquid. Let it stand so the white milk solids settle on the bottom. Skim off any foam with a slotted spoon, then strain off the yellow liquid, keeping the white solids behind. The clear yellow part is the clarified butter. Let it cool, then chill. Use for cooking only, as it has a grainy texture.

▪ Buttermilk

This used to be a by-product of butter-making, but is now made by adding to skimmed milk the same cultures that ripen cream for butter. This gives it a silky thickness and a tangy taste. It is sold as cultured buttermilk. Buttermilk is ultra low-fat (just 0.1%) and, because its slight acidity reacts with raising agents, is good for giving a light texture to scones, teabreads, pancakes and muffins. Or try it instead of milk in a smoothie or milkshake.

CHEESE

CHEESE IS AN INCREDIBLY VERSATILE INGREDIENT FOR COOKING, AND BECAUSE OF THE RANGE OF STYLES, SOME ARE SUITED TO GRATING AND MELTING, OTHERS TO CRUMBLING AND BAKING. THIS SECTION LOOKS AT SOME OF THE MOST SUITABLE CHEESES FOR COOKING AND HOW THEY CAN BE USED.

CHEESE IS MADE FROM MILK (mainly from cows, goats and sheep) which is usually first heated (pasteurized) to kill off any harmful bacteria. Specialist artisan cheese makers tend to use unpasteurized milk which can give cheese loads of character and flavour. Starter cultures (special friendly bacterial cultures) are added to sour the milk, thicken and develop the flavour, then an ingredient called rennet is added which curdles and coagulates the milk, separating it out into solid curds and liquid whey. Most cheeses are made from the curds, but some, such as ricotta, are made from the whey. Salt is added, and the cheese is then stored and left to ripen and mature and to let the flavour develop. There are, however, certain fresh unripened cheeses that don't go through the maturing process at all. Instead, these are ready to eat as soon as they have been made, such as mozzarella and fresh young goat's cheeses.

CHOOSE

There are many cheeses available, from soft, mild and creamy to strong, hard and pungent. The differences are due to the sort of milk used to make the cheese, the animal it comes from and how it is made. Cheese made from cow's milk tends to be richer and fattier, goat's milk is sharper in taste and sheep's milk is nuttier. Your choice is down to personal preference and how you are going to use it. So be aware of the texture of the cheese, how strong its flavour is and how it will behave when heated. There are many ways to classify the styles of cheeses – and the following categories are listed to help you choose the right one for your cooking needs.

Blue

The blue veins running through this style of cheese are created by harmless moulds being introduced into it while still young. As the cheese ages, the blue veins grow, creating a complex labyrinth of tunnels and trails.

CHOOSE For their unique taste and richness which can transform many dishes, including sauces and salads.

TYPES
- Mild and creamy such as Cambozola and mild (*dolce*) Gorgonzola.
- Powerfully assertive such as Roquefort and Danish Blue.
- Mature and rich like Stilton, Irish Cashel blue and mature (*piccante*) Dolcelatte.

USE FOR Melting and crumbling.

GOES WITH Steak, bacon, chicory, leeks, apples and pears, nuts, pasta.

USE INSTEAD Interchangeably within each type.

Hard

These have been pressed so they are firm with a thick rind. The older they get, the harder and more powerfully flavoured they become.

CHOOSE For being good all-rounders.

TYPES
Cheddar: Produced in England as

GOOD FOR YOU
Cheese has a concentrated form of all the nutrients in milk, so is rich in calcium and has protein and vitamins A and B. Full-fat cheese is, however, high in saturated fat.

STYLISH CHEESEBOARD
Rather than offering a board loaded with lots of different cheeses, a different approach is to offer just one or two, with pieces of fresh fruit such as figs with a creamy blue cheese, or slices of apples or pears with a ripe wedge of brie or camembert. Drizzle the figs with some honey and walnuts, or tuck a few crisp lettuce leaves under the apple or pear slices, scatter with toasted pine nuts and squeeze with some lemon juice. Give each person their own individual platter and it makes a very easy dessert – or lunch, served with some interesting bread.

VEGETARIAN CHEESE
Traditionally animal rennet was used in the cheese-making process. However, virtually all cheese sold or produced in the UK is now made using non-animal rennet, so it is suitable for vegetarians. Check the label to make sure.

well as Canada, Australia and New Zealand. Can be mild and sweet or sharp and nutty, depending on its age.
Traditional English such as Double Gloucester, Lancashire, Red Leicester.
White crumbly cheeses like Caerphilly, Cheshire, Wensleydale, feta (authentically made in Greece from 85% goat's milk, 15% ewe's milk. Gets its salty taste from being kept in salted brine).
Hard cheeses for grating such as Italian Parmesan (for the real thing look for *Parmigiano Reggiano*) and Grana Padano.
Tangy sheep's cheese such as Spanish Manchego (good for nibbling), Ossau Iraty from the Basque country and Italian Pecorino.
Swiss-style melters like Emmental, Gruyère, Appenzeller, Fontina (made in Italy). All are stringy and stretchy when melted, perfect for sauces and fondues or dropping in cubes into soups.

USE FOR Grating, shaving, slicing and melting.

GOES WITH Classic English cheeses: Bread, bacon, apples, lettuce, tomatoes, potatoes. **Parmesan and Grana Padano:** Parma ham, salad leaves, pine nuts, basil, peppers, pasta, spring vegetables. **Swiss-style:** Ham, chicken, potatoes, mushrooms, bread.

USE INSTEAD Substitute other English regional cheeses for Cheddar. Use interchangeably within each type.

Semi-soft

These are mostly cheeses that haven't been pressed, so are supple and more pliable. Aged gouda can get very hard.

CHOOSE For their elasticity when melted.

TYPES
■ **Dutch** for grating and slicing such as Gouda and Edam (lower in fat).
■ **Soft sliceables** such as Italian taleggio (fruity flavour), Danish havarti.

USE FOR Grating, melting, slicing.

GOES WITH Pork, peppers, tomatoes, asparagus, potatoes, squash, mushrooms.

USE INSTEAD Within each type, cheeses can be used interchangeably.

Soft

Tend to be milder in flavour when youthful, though cheeses like Brie and Camembert can become pungent with age. May be easy to spread (ricotta), tear (mozzarella), or slice (Brie).

hard–soft

CHOOSE For tossing into pasta, melting into sauces, crumbling or slicing over salads, tarts and pizzas.

TYPES

Young, fresh cheeses such as goat's, also called *chèvre* (there are so many varieties that flavours vary, but they are generally sweet and tangy with a natural rind); mozzarella (mostly made from cow's milk, but the original version made with buffalo's is still considered the best – very elastic when cooked); ricotta (mild and slightly sweet) – use instead of mascarpone (see right) for a lower-fat alternative; halloumi (salty taste) – mostly eaten cooked, it doesn't lose its shape when fried, grilled or barbecued (cut in chunks for making kebabs).

Soft, creamy cheese like Brie and Camembert. Best sliced or chopped for melting, both go runny when ripe. Use them interchangeably.

USE FOR Melting, baking and crumbling.

GOES WITH Goat's: beetroot, asparagus, tomato, salad leaves, herbs. Try other young, fresh ones, such as **mozzarella and halloumi**, with Mediterranean vegetables. **Brie and Camembert** are good with red berries such as cranberries and raspberries.

ONE-OFFS FROM AROUND THE WORLD

- *GJETOST: This cheese from Norway, with its caramel-sweet taste and colour (made with cow's or goat's milk), tastes like no other – rather like a fudgy cheese. Its smooth texture means it can be shaved off beautifully. Traditionally served at breakfast.*

- *MASCARPONE: Considered a cheese, this is really a thickened cream with a high fat content, about 46%, so less than double cream which has 54%. Originally from southern Italy, it has a texture similar to that of clotted cream. It can be used instead of cream and is most famous for being a main ingredient of tiramisu. It melts easily too, to give rich, creamy sauces.*

- *PANEER: An Indian low-fat cheese with a texture similar to that of tofu. Like tofu, it has a bland taste, but absorbs other flavours well. Usually diced into curries, and used a lot with spinach and peas.*

More fresh soft cheeses

Fresh cheeses tend to be the mildest and softest as they are sold when young, often only a few days old. Because of this, they also have no rind.

Boursin: A fresh cream French cheese, often flavoured with chives and garlic or coated in crushed pepper. Melts easily, so use to create a quick creamy sauce for pasta – stir into hot, drained pasta, slackened off with a few spoonfuls of the cooking water and toss in a handful of basil to serve. Or spoon Boursin on to baked potatoes instead of butter.

Cottage: Creamy in taste, lumpy in texture and, as it is made from skimmed milk (so very low-fat), is popular with dieters. Usually eaten raw.

Curd: Like cream cheese but lower in fat. Ideal for blending into mixtures such as cheesecakes to make them lighter.

Full-fat soft (cream cheese): A very smooth, mild cheese with a silky texture. Adds a richness to desserts like cheesecakes. A low-fat version is also available.

Fromage frais: A spoonable curd cheese made from skimmed milk. Tastes a bit like set yogurt, with a similar texture too. Use instead of cream for a low-fat sweet or savoury topping to go with fruit or vegetables.

Quark: The German version of curd cheese (it means 'curd' in German). Made from skimmed milk, so very low-fat, light and tangy. Use for sweet or savoury dishes – if counting calories, put a dollop into your mashed potatoes instead of butter, or on a bowl of strawberries instead of cream.

STORE AND SERVE

Cheese is best bought little and often, so you can enjoy it at its absolute best. Look at the 'best before' date on the pack. If you buy cheese loose, try to use it within a couple of days or it will dry out. Rewrap carefully with fresh wrapping when you put it back in the fridge. For pre-wrapped cheese, keep it in its original wrapping and store in the lower part of the fridge. After opening it is best loosely wrapped in wax or greaseproof paper then put in a polythene bag so it can breathe without drying out. Or wrap in foil, but not cling film as it makes the cheese sweat and go mouldy more quickly. It's best not to put a mix of cheeses in a plastic box as their flavours may taint each other. An important thing to remember with cheese is that if it is served cold,

store–cook

much of the flavour and aroma will be lost. So to allow the flavour to develop, bring the cheese out of the fridge 1–2 hours before serving.

FREEZE Not an ideal way to store cheese as the flavour can be affected. But if you have too much hard cheese, it's best to freeze it grated.

COOK

A few dos and don'ts:
DO
■ Use good-quality cheese – it won't necessarily be more expensive, as the stronger the taste, the less you will need to use.
■ Experiment with different flavours – don't just stick to the ones you know.
■ Substitute if you need to, but only with a similar style and type of cheese.
■ Use cheese straight from the fridge when grating for cooking as it's easier.

DON'T
■ Overcook cheese as the taste and texture will spoil. So if making a sauce, add the cheese at the end, off the heat, stirring until it has melted.
■ Grill cheese on too low a heat. Have the heat high and position the grill rack not too far away from the heat. The cheese will then melt quickly before it has the chance to ooze lots of oil.

EASY CHEESE SAUCE

This is a simple all-in-one sauce that you will find handy for all sorts of dishes – mixing into pasta, pouring over leeks and ham, or serving with grilled fish.

Makes about 300 ml (½ pint); takes 5–10 minutes

30 g (1 oz) butter (cut in pieces)
30 g (1 oz) plain flour
300 ml (½ pint) milk
75–100 g (2½–3½ oz) grated firm cheese, such as Cheddar or Gruyère

Tip all the ingredients except the cheese into a medium saucepan. Stir constantly over a medium heat with a wooden spoon or balloon whisk. If little lumps start to form, the balloon whisk is great for whisking them away. As the sauce comes to the boil it will start to thicken and become smooth and glossy. Once it has, let it simmer for a minute or two to cook off the flour. Take the pan off the heat and stir in the cheese until it has melted.

OPTIONAL EXTRAS: Add any of these with the cheese – 1 tsp Dijon mustard, a handful snipped of chives or chopped parsley, or a splash of Worcestershire or Tabasco sauce.

EGGS

QUICK AND EASY TO COOK, EGGS ARE THE ULTIMATE CONVENIENCE FOOD – KEEP A BOX IN THE FRIDGE AND YOU WILL NEVER BE STUCK FOR AN INEXPENSIVE AND NUTRITIOUS MEAL. EGGS ARE ALSO ONE OF THE MOST USEFUL INGREDIENTS IN COOKING – WITHOUT THEM DOING THEIR QUIET JOB OF THICKENING, EMULSIFYING AND AERATING, MANY RECIPES WOULD JUST NOT BE POSSIBLE.

CHOOSE

'Grade A' or 'Class A' on the box or tray tells you the eggs are of the highest quality. Other things you need to know before buying are as follows.

Age: The 'best before' date is 28 days after the eggs have been laid. Check the date before you buy, and make sure you eat the eggs by then.

Colour: Shells come in a variety of colours, from white through pale to dark brown, speckled and blue. The colour of the shell depends on the breed of the bird, not the quality of the egg, nor what the bird has been fed on.

Condition: Check that no shells have been broken or cracked, and don't buy them if they have.

Size: Eggs are graded according to weight, and there are 4 sizes – see opposite. If a recipe doesn't specify a size, it is best to use medium or large. Most recipes are tested with one of these sizes.

Type: The breed of the bird may be specified, but it is more important to know how the birds were reared. Organic eggs are the most costly, followed by free-range and barn eggs. Cage eggs are the cheapest. Organic eggs are expensive as they are produced according to strict criteria: they are free-range, fed on a diet of organic produce, and ranged on organic land.

Some different eggs

Hen's eggs are the most popular, but eggs from other birds are worth trying too, and an increasing number of different types are becoming available. Farmers' markets and farm shops are often the best source.

Bantam: Weighing no more than 42.5 g (1½ oz), these small eggs are ideal for children. If serving to adults, allow 2 per person. They look and taste similar to hen's eggs, and can be used and cooked in the same way.

choose–store

Duck: Large in size with pale blue shells and a strong flavour, these eggs are good mixed with hen's eggs in omelettes, scrambled egg and fresh pasta. Use 1 whole duck egg or 1 duck egg yolk to 2 or 3 hen's eggs for the right balance of flavour.

Goose: Very large, rich-tasting eggs that have a very short season from mid February to the end of May. One goose egg is equivalent to 3 hen's eggs, so it is the perfect size to make scrambled egg or an omelette for one person. The deep buttery yellow yolk gives a good colour, which is also the reason why bakers love using goose eggs in sponge cakes. If you are making a 3-egg Victoria sandwich, 1 goose egg is all you need.

Quail: Tiny, speckled eggs that are good softly boiled, hard-boiled or fried. Children love them for their size, which is also perfect for canapés, starters and salads.

STORE

Eggs must be stored in the fridge, and should be eaten by their 'best before' date. The shells are quite porous and easily absorb flavours from other foods, so keep them in their box if you can.

■ Store eggs pointed end down, so the air pocket in the rounded end is at the top.

SIZES OF HEN'S EGGS

SMALL	*under 53 g (1⅞ oz)*
MEDIUM	*53–63 g (1⅞–2¼ oz)*
LARGE	*63–73g (2¼–2½ oz)*
VERY LARGE	*73g (2½ oz) and over*

SALMONELLA

If you buy good-quality eggs from a reputable source, the risk of salmonella contamination is minimal because the hens will have been vaccinated against it. In the unlikely event of an egg having bacteria, the risk of food poisoning is greater if the egg is eaten raw or very lightly cooked. For this reason it is inadvisable to serve raw or lightly cooked eggs to babies and very young children, pregnant women, the sick and the elderly.

■ Salmonella bacteria are destroyed at 64.4ºC (148ºF). Recipes that are likely to use raw eggs or eggs cooked below this temperature are mayonnaise, hollandaise sauce, egg custard, meringues, mousses, soufflés, icing, marzipan and ice cream.

■ Timings are given on pages 466–7 for boiling, frying, poaching, and scrambling eggs so that both the yolk and white are set and any bacteria destroyed.

If the date was on the box and you have thrown it out, you can test an egg's freshness by cracking it on to a plate and checking the yolk and white. A fresh egg will have a domed yolk and the white will have two distinct parts – thick near the yolk, thinner at the edges. A stale egg will have a flat yolk and the white will not have two distinct parts.

Eggs are always best used at room temperature, so remove them from the fridge 30 minutes before using.

FREEZE Eggs can't be frozen in their shells, but if you crack them into a rigid container and beat them lightly they can be frozen for up to 6 months. You can also freeze the whites or yolks separately (again you need to beat them lightly first).

PREPARE

Eggs are the ultimate convenience food and there is very little to do in the way of preparation.

CRACKING AN EGG

There is no guarantee that you will not break the yolk, but the following method is the most successful. Always crack each egg into an empty bowl, just in case one has gone bad and contaminates the others.

Sharply tap the middle of the egg at its widest point against the rim of a bowl.

Hold the egg over the middle of the bowl and insert your thumb tips into the crack.

Prise the two halves of the shell apart and let the egg drop into the bowl (see opposite, above).

If any pieces of shell have dropped into the egg, scoop them out with the tip of a teaspoon.

SEPARATING AN EGG

Whites are needed for meringues, and for folding into mousses and soufflés. Yolks are used for mayonnaise, and for enriching and thickening mixtures like batters, sauces and soups.

Crack the shell and prise the two halves apart as above, keeping the egg in one half of the shell.

Tilt the shell so that the white runs out into the bowl, then tip the yolk into the empty shell and tilt again, using the edge of the empty shell to cut off any white that clings (see opposite, below).

When all the white has gone, tip the yolk into a separate bowl.

If you are separating more than one egg, use a clean bowl to catch each white, just in case the yolk breaks. Whites will not whisk stiff if they have even the tiniest trace of yolk in them.

store–prepare

WHISKING EGG WHITES

For meringues, and to give volume and lightness to cakes, mousses and soufflés, egg whites must be whisked to a stiff peak (see page 449).

■ Start with a clean, dry bowl and whisk, and egg whites at room temperature that have no trace of yolk in them. For the greatest volume, chefs traditionally use a large copper bowl and a balloon whisk, but you can also get good results with a stainless-steel or glass bowl and electric beaters.

■ Tip the whites into the bowl and start whisking slowly, working the whisk against the bottom of the bowl to break up the whites and get a foam going.

■ As the foam increases, lift the whisk up to the top of the bowl in a circular motion and sweep it around the sides so the whole of the bowl is covered – this will incorporate air and increase the volume.

■ Keep whisking in this way until the whites turn into a pure-white snow, then keep the whisk low in the bowl and move it vigorously from side to side until you feel the whites tighten. When ready, they will stand in stiff peaks when the whisk is lifted.

■ Use immediately to make meringues or to fold into mousses and cake or soufflé mixtures. The folding technique for whisked egg whites is the same as for whipped cream (see page 450).

CRACKING AN EGG

SEPARATING AN EGG

FIX IT: EGGS

If you overwhisk egg whites they will turn grainy or watery. To put them right, tip in a fresh egg white and whisk for 30 seconds.

COOK

Eggs cook best at room temperature, so take them out of the fridge about 30 minutes before you start.

BOIL

■ One at a time, lower the eggs on a spoon into a small pan filled two-thirds full with simmering water. Don't boil more then 4 eggs at a time or the timing will not be accurate.

■ Bring the water up to a simmer again, then start timing. Allow 4 minutes for a softly boiled egg with a runny yolk, 7 minutes for a set yolk and white, 10 minutes for a hard-boiled egg.

■ When the time is up, remove the eggs from the water with a slotted spoon.

■ To cool hard-boiled eggs, plunge them straight into cold water and leave for 5 minutes, then drain and peel. Leave in fresh cold water until ready to serve.

FRY

■ Heat 2 tbsp groundnut or sunflower oil in a frying pan until hot (you should feel the heat rising when you hold your hand over the pan).

■ Crack the eggs one at a time into a cup or small bowl, and slide each one into the hot oil.

■ Fry over a moderate heat, spooning the hot oil over the yolk until it is cov-ered in a white film. For a soft yolk and set white to serve sunny side up, allow 3–4 minutes. For an 'over easy' set yolk and white, turn the egg over and fry for another 2–3 minutes.

POACH

■ If you have an egg poacher (see page 54), bring water to a gentle simmer in the bottom of the pan, drop a small knob of butter into each cup, then crack in the eggs. Cover and poach for 3 minutes for a runny yolk, 5 minutes for a set yolk.

■ If you don't have an egg poacher, fill a wide, shallow pan two-thirds full with water, add 1 tbsp vinegar and bring to a simmer. Crack the eggs one at a time into a cup or small bowl and slide each one into the water. Turn the heat down to low and cook the eggs gently for 3 minutes for a runny yolk. For a firm set, cook for 4 or 5 minutes. Remove the eggs with a slotted spoon and drain well.

■ If you are making poached eggs on toast or eggs Benedict, rest each egg on a crust or slice of bread after removing it from the water. The bread will soak up excess water from under the egg and your toast or muffin will not be soggy.

SCRAMBLE

■ Whisk the eggs in a bowl (using a

cook

fork or coiled whisk) with cream or
milk and some salt and pepper. Allow 2
eggs and 1 tbsp cream/milk per person.
■ Melt a knob of butter in a pan (a
non-stick sauté pan is ideal, but you
can use a saucepan). When the butter
is foaming, tip in the egg mixture and
cook over a low heat for 1–2 minutes,
scraping the bottom of the pan and
stirring all the time, until the eggs
come together as a soft creamy mass.
■ Remove from the heat and continue
stirring for another 30 seconds until
the eggs are softly set.
■ For a firm set, cook for 3–4 minutes
before removing from the heat.

USING EGG YOLK TO THICKEN

For enriching and thickening a hot
mixture, such as a sauce, soup or stew,
at the end of cooking, mix egg yolks
and cream to make a liaison.
■ Mix 1–2 egg yolks with up to 4 tbsp
double cream or crème fraîche.
■ Whisk in a few spoonfuls of the hot
liquid.
■ Off the heat, pour the egg mixture
slowly back into the hot liquid, whisking constantly until thickened.
■ Return to a low heat and cook, whisking constantly, until the liquid thickens.
■ Take care not to overheat or boil or
the egg yolk may curdle.

MAYONNAISE
*Makes 300 ml (½ pint); ready in
30 minutes*

INGREDIENTS
2 medium egg yolks
1 tsp mustard, such as Dijon
2 tbsp white vinegar
salt and ground black pepper
*225 ml (8 fl oz) sunflower oil (or
    half sunflower and half olive oil)*

*Whisk the egg yolks, mustard,
1 tbsp of the vinegar and a little
salt and pepper until slightly thick.
Whisking constantly, beat in the oil
drop by drop. After about 2 tbsp of
oil have been added and the mixture has started to thicken, slowly
trickle in the rest of the oil, beating
steadily. Season with more vinegar,
salt and pepper to taste.*

*Mayonnaise can also be made in
an electric mixer, food processor
or blender. Combine the egg yolks,
mustard, 1 tbsp vinegar and salt
and pepper in the machine. Turn
on the machine and slowly drizzle
in the oil. Adjust the seasoning to
taste.*

*If the finished mayonnaise is too
thick, thin it by beating in a little
warm water.*

EGGS

Cooking in the microwave

You will get good, quick results in the microwave when poaching or scrambling eggs. Never cook them in their shells in a microwave because pressure will build up inside the shell and the egg may burst inside the oven, or when you take it out.

POACH

- Crack an egg into a microwave-safe cup or ramekin containing ½ tbsp water.
- Pierce the yolk and white in a couple of places with a cocktail stick.
- Microwave on High for 40 seconds in a 750-watt oven, or for 60 seconds in a 650-watt oven. Leave to stand for 1 minute before serving.

SCRAMBLE

- Beat the eggs as for conventional scrambled eggs (see page 467) in a microwave-safe jug or bowl.
- Cover with cling film.
- Microwave on High for 1½ minutes in a 750-watt oven, or for 2 minutes in a 650-watt oven.
- Uncover and stir the eggs.
- Microwave for a further 30 seconds.
- Leave to stand for 30 seconds before serving.

WHAT'S IN A NAME?

- *ALBUMEN is the white of the egg, and there are two types. The thick white stands up around the yolk and the thin white runs towards the edge.*
- *CHALAZAE are the strands that connect the yolk to the thick white. If they stand out prominently, this is an indication that the egg is fresh. You can eat the chalazae, but if you don't like the look of them, strain them out.*

GOOD FOR YOU

Eggs are extremely nutritious and easy to digest.
- *They are an excellent source of protein.*
- *One egg contains as many as 18 vitamins and minerals, including calcium, iodine, iron, phosphorus, zinc and vitamins A, B, D and E.*
- *They are a good source of folic acid and the antioxidant selenium.*
- *Relatively low in saturated fat, one medium egg provides around 76 calories.*

Conversion Tables and Index

CONVERSION TABLES

PLEASE NOTE THAT ALL CONVERSIONS GIVEN HERE ARE APPROXIMATE. YOU SHOULD FOLLOW EITHER THE METRIC OR IMPERIAL SYSTEMS THROUGHOUT A RECIPE, NOT A MIXTURE OF THE TWO.

WEIGHTS

Grams	Ounces
15	½
20	¾
30	1
40	1½
60	2
75	2½
90	3
100	3½
125	4
150	5
175	6
200	7
225	8
300	10
375	12
500	16/1 lb
625	1¼ lb
700	1½ lb
1000/1 kg	2 lb
1500/1.5 kg	3 lb

SPOON SIZES

Spoon	Fluid ounces	Millilitres
1 teaspoon	⅛	5
1 dessertspoon	⅓	10
1 tablespoon	½	15

°C	°F	Gas Mark	TEMPERATURES
140	275	1	
150	300	2	
160	325	3	
180	350	4	
190	375	5	
200	400	6	
220	425	7	
230	450	8	
240	475	9	
250	480	–	

Millilitres	Fluid ounces (UK)	Cups (US)	VOLUME
30	1	⅛	*Please note that*
50	2	¼	*there are 20 fluid*
100	3½	–	*ounces to a pint*
125	4	½	*in the UK, but*
150	¼ pint	–	*16 fluid ounces*
200	7	–	*in the US.*
250	8	1	
300	½ pint	–	
400	14	1½	
450	¾ pint	–	
500	16	2	
600	1 pint	2½	
900	1½ pints	3½	
1000/1 litre	1¾ pints	4	
1.2 litres	2 pints	–	
1.5 litres	2½ pints	–	
1.8 litres	3 pints	–	

INDEX

ENTRIES FOR INDIVIDUAL FOODS INCLUDE FULL DETAILS OF PREPARATION AND COOKING TECHNIQUES. THESE ARE NOT NORMALLY INDEXED AT THE SPECIFIC TECHNIQUES. PAGE NUMBERS IN BOLD INDICATE RECIPES.

AUTHOR BIOGRAPHIES

Angela Nilsen's career has always involved food,
either teaching or writing about it for books, magazines, newspapers, both in England and North America (where she was a food writer with the *Vancouver Sun* newspaper, Canada for 7 years). From May 1994 to July 2004, she was Food Editor of BBC *Good Food* magazine, and is now a freelance writer and editor. In 2003 she was short-listed for the Glenfiddich Cookery Writer Award, and is the 2004 winner of both the Glenfiddich Cookery Writer Award and The Guild of Food Writers' Cookery Journalist of the Year Award.

Jeni Wright has been writing about food and cookery for
over thirty years, and has published as many cookbooks in that time – her first book was the best-selling *All Colour Cookery Book* for Marks & Spencer in 1976. Cooking techniques are her speciality, and she is the author of three cookbooks for Le Cordon Bleu School, most notably the acclaimed *Le Cordon Bleu Complete Cooking Techniques*. For four years she was a colleague of Angela Nilsen's at BBC *Good Food* magazine, where she worked closely with many of Britain's top chefs.

ACKNOWLEDGEMENTS

The authors would like to thank the following for their expertise and valuable advice given during the research for this book:

Fiona Beckett; Alistair Blair at The Fish Society (www.thefishsociety.co.uk); The Dairy Council (www.milk.co.uk); Roz Denny; British Egg Information Service (www.britegg.co.uk); English Beef and Lamb Executive (EBLEX); Sarah Jane Evans; Nichola Fletcher (www.fletcherscotland.co.uk); Flour Advisory Bureau; Game-to-eat (www.gametoeat.co.uk); Lee & Phyllis Harper at The Highgate Butchers, London N6; Steve Hatt Fishmongers, London N1; Dr Beckie Lang, Public Health Nutritionist; Dan Lepard; Norma MacMillan; Meat Livestock Commission; Mushroom Bureau (www.mushroom-uk.com); Douglas Pattie at the Fresh Produce Consortium; British Potato Council (www.britishpotatocouncil.co.uk); Alan Porter, Managing Director of the Chocolate Society; British Poultry Council (www.poultry.uk.com); Judy Ridgway; The Seafish Industry Authority (www.seafish.org); Emma Sharp, Jamaican chef and cooking teacher; Claire Symington, Seldom Seen Farm (Geese), Billesdon, Leicester; British Turkey Information Service (www.britishturkey.co.uk); Kate Williams; Carol Wilson, Cookery Consultant to Billingtons Unrefined Sugars.